Buddhism in World Cultures

ABC-CLIO Religion in Contemporary Cultures Series

Islam in World Cultures: Comparative Perspectives,
R. Michael Feener, Editor

Modern Paganism in World Cultures: Comparative Perspectives,
Michael F. Strmiska, Editor

Buddhism in World Cultures

Comparative Perspectives

Edited by

STEPHEN C. BERKWITZ

A B C ⬤ C L I O

Santa Barbara, California   Denver, Colorado   Oxford, England

Library of Congress Cataloging-in-Publication Data

Buddhism in world cultures : comparative perspectives / edited by
Stephen C. Berkwitz
    p. cm. — (Religion in contemporary cultures series)
    Includes bibliographical references and index.
    ISBN 1-85109-782-1 (hardback : alk. paper) — ISBN 1-85109-787-2
(e-Book) 1. Buddhism—History—21st century. 2. Buddhism and culture.
I. Berkwitz, Stephen C., 1969– . II. Series: Religion in contemporary
cultures.
BQ316.B85 2006
294.309—dc22

2006001760

10 09 08 07 06   10 9 8 7 6 5 4 3 2 1

This book is also available on the World Wide Web as an e-book.
Visit abc-clio.com for details.

ABC-CLIO, Inc.
130 Cremona Drive, P.O. Box 1911
Santa Barbara, California 93116-1911

This book is printed on acid-free paper.
Manufactured in the United States of America

Contents

Buddhism in World Cultures
Comparative Perspectives

Contributors

Stephen C. Berkwitz (PhD, University of California at Santa Barbara), Department of Religious Studies, Missouri State University, Springfield, Missouri

Stuart Chandler (PhD, Harvard University), Department of Religious Studies, Indiana University of Pennsylvania, Indiana, Pennsylvania

Stephen G. Covell (PhD, Princeton University), Department of Comparative Religion, Western Michigan University, Kalamazoo, Michigan

Ellen Goldberg (PhD, University of Toronto), Department of Religious Studies, Queen's University, Kingston, Ontario, Canada

Justin McDaniel, (PhD, Harvard University), Department of Religious Studies, University of California at Riverside, Riverside, California

Pori Park (PhD, University of California at Los Angeles), Department of Religious Studies, Arizona State University, Tempe, Arizona

Juliane Schober (PhD, University of Illinois at Urbana-Champaign), Department of Religious Studies, Arizona State University, Tempe, Arizona

Nicolas Sihlé (PhD, Université de Paris X-Nanterre), Department of Anthropology, University of Virginia, Charlottesville, Virginia

Ashley Thompson (PhD, Université de Paris 8-Saint Denis), Department of Fine Art, History of Art and Cultural Studies, University of Leeds, Leeds, United Kingdom

Preface

When Frank Korom, editor for the Religion in Contemporary Cultures series published by ABC-CLIO, invited me to edit a volume on contemporary Buddhist cultures, I accepted his flattering offer soon after. I realized then that a work that reexamines the state of Buddhism around the world is long overdue. Heinrich Dumoulin edited a similar volume called *Buddhism in the Modern World* (New York: Macmillan, 1976) several decades ago based on research largely conducted in the 1960s. This earlier work is impressive in its scope, covering sixteen countries and regions. However, much has changed in the world since the 1960s and early 1970s, and thus the present volume seeks to bring the analysis of contemporary forms of Buddhism up to the present.

It seems appropriate here to explain some of the editorial choices that were made concerning the scope, organization, and approach of this volume. I was given considerable freedom to determine the contents of this work. I decided to include chapters that present comprehensive pictures of the contemporary forms and practices of Buddhism in key geographical areas. Nevertheless, constraints in length, although admittedly reasonable, made it necessary to leave some countries out. As a result, this volume regretfully does not include chapters on India, Vietnam, the Malay Peninsula, Laos, Bhutan, or Mongolia. But on the positive side, the limited number of chapters has allowed for longer and more substantial examinations of contemporary Buddhist traditions than other survey texts normally provide.

The volume is organized in a manner consistent with the format used in the series. It opens with a survey of the history of Buddhism that focuses mainly on the major ideas and practices that have been influential across cultures. Chapters two through ten are detailed studies of Buddhism in particular countries or regions. These are followed by an annotated bibliography of additional sources the reader might wish to consult and then a glossary of key terms.

The order of the chapters on specific countries and regions is patterned after the general convention used by many textbooks on the Buddhist religion. Most of these other works are organized around both the historical diffusion of Buddhism and the distinction between Theravada and Mahayana traditions. This organizational method is problematic, given the complex history behind the spread of Buddhism into different countries and the division of the tradition into different schools and lineages. However, it seems preferable to adhere to this convention, if for no other reason than to make this volume more easily used in conjunction with existing textbooks and other sources on Buddhism.

Most diacritical marks for Asian-language terms and proper names have been omitted for the sake of simplicity and convenience. In most cases, these marks are only comprehensible to persons who already know the language and who will recognize the words and know their correct pronunciation regardless. And given the many languages referenced in this volume, the effort to insert, edit, and explain all the diacritical marks would have been unwieldy. In addition, names of authors are usually referenced according to the Western convention (surname followed by comma and first name), although some languages such as Japanese and Khmer do not employ a comma between names. Readers should thus be aware that the names of authors in the reference lists and annotated bibliography may not follow native conventions.

The approach taken in this volume consists of incorporating the most recent scholarship and the scholars' own fieldwork along with critical reflections on Buddhism in the contemporary world. I asked the contributors to offer new ways to conceive of contemporary or modern Buddhism beyond the overused dichotomy of Little Tradition/Great Tradition and the typical bias that results, whereupon ancient, textual constructions of Buddhism are privileged over modern, supposedly less "authentic" forms of the religion. Moreover, the chapters in this volume highlight the most visible features and pressing issues related to the practice of Buddhism in the modern world, including issues such as globalization, cultural change, political conflict, and economic development. This approach reflects the shared conviction of the contributors that Buddhism today is a diverse tradition that is inextricably bound up with particular cultural contexts and global influences like other aspects of contemporary human existence.

I would also like to acknowledge the generous assistance and guidance I received from the editorial and production staffs at ABC-CLIO. Steven Danver, Peter Westwick, Sharon Daugherty, and others played critical roles in shaping this volume and making it better than I could have done by myself. The editorial skills of Deborah Lynes and her staff are also much appreciated. I am grateful to Frank Korom for his vision for the series and his confidence in my abilities to edit this work. I also wish to acknowledge the dedication and fine work of the contributors of this volume. They took editorial comments and suggestions in good faith and my prodding with good grace, submitting excellent chapters that greatly enhance the value and significance of this work. Lastly, I wish to thank Imali and Rashmi Berkwitz, my wife and daughter, whose support and inspiration were invaluable during this project.

Stephen C. Berkwitz
Springfield, Missouri

Chapter One

The History of Buddhism in Retrospect

Stephen C. Berkwitz

Historical surveys of Buddhism often depict the religion beginning in India with the birth of Siddhartha Gautama sometime between the sixth and fourth centuries BCE; slowly spreading to other lands to the south, southeast, and west; moving into China, where it became "sinicized" by the influences of Chinese culture; making its way into Japan and the Tibetan region; and then becoming modernized through contact with the West before being imported into Europe and North America. The convention of constructing a singular linear narrative for Buddhist history, smoothing out the diverse and complex features of events that took place at different times in Buddhist communities throughout the world, is commonplace but not unproblematic. Such narratives may appear historically sound and accurate, but they often mask the author's imaginative act of discovering a clear, coherent structure to events in the world and constituting their collective meaning (White 1987, 36). However, the complex histories of diverse Buddhist cultures frequently do not lend themselves to being organized into one all-encompassing historical narrative.

Conventional histories of Buddhism have also traditionally employed various evolutionary or devolutionary models to depict the sequential rise of the Hinayana, Mahayana, and Vajrayana schools of Buddhism (Lopez 1995a, 6–7). According to the Buddhist studies scholar Donald S. Lopez Jr., some scholars have viewed the Hinayana traditions—often but erroneously equated with Theravada—as the pure, original form of Buddhism that is closest to the religion established by the Buddha himself. In this view, the later Mahayana and Vajrayana traditions are corruptions wherein, in the former case, the Buddha became deified and multiplied into countless heavenly beings who grant salvation to their devotees and, in the latter case, the ritual use of sexuality and

intoxicants absorbed from Hindu influences were improperly promoted as vehicles for enlightenment. Another view presupposes that Mahayana represents
the culmination of the Buddhist tradition. In this view, Hinayana monks became obsessively concerned with pointless philosophizing and their institutional authority until a lay movement from below restored the Buddha's original emphasis on wisdom and compassion and spurred development of the
Great Vehicle that promises liberation, even Buddhahood, to all beings
through the dedicated efforts of bodhisattvas. A third view holds that Vajrayana
was the latest and highest development of the tradition, improving on the simplistic creeds and practices of the Hinayana and Mahayana schools and replacing them with a more rapid and efficient path to enlightenment through the
discovery of the ultimate reality in everyday practices and artistic creations. All
of these views fail at a certain level since they presuppose a clear historical progression or regression from one Buddhist school to another. They also tend to
deemphasize modern forms of Buddhism since they cannot be neatly placed
within a simple chronological development based on schools of thought and
practice.

Rather than reproduce a conventional narrative of the history of Buddhism
here, this essay will present a survey that moves backward in time from the present to the past. Such a move is justified by several factors. First, since this book
is primarily concerned with contemporary Buddhist cultures worldwide, it
makes sense to highlight the period broadly and variously described as modern, late modern, or postmodern. Starting this survey in the present ensures
that the contemporary period will not be treated as an afterthought at the end
of a more detailed discussion of earlier periods. In addition, writing a history
of Buddhism backward exposes the artificially constructed nature of historical
narratives in general. A growing number of critical historians argue that historical narratives are made, not found; that they reflect discrete events pieced together into a plot that the historian crafts and then interprets for its overall significance as a story (e.g., White 1987; Jenkins 1991).

In this sense, historical surveys of Buddhism or any other subject can never
be transparent accounts of the way things "really happened" because, in part,
the events written about are selectively chosen and arranged into a linear narrative that deviates from the often haphazard, unconnected manner in which
they occurred as discrete events in the past. Indeed, the writing of history is
contingent on present views of the past, as well on as contemporary usages of
language and explanatory theories (Jenkins 1991, 12). Thus, though history is
typically written chronologically beginning in the past, it always constitutes a
practice whereby one recollects events retrospectively from the present. History, at root, comprises stories people tell about the past. But unlike with most
fictional narratives, we already have a clear idea about the ending, since histories are typically crafted to explain how certain events happened. Histories

often presuppose both a notion of historical causation, according to which later events are cast as the consequences of earlier ones, and a notion that one can identify a specific beginning or foundational event responsible for setting in motion a whole series of subsequent events. Such ruptures in the fabric of time are not self-evident but only exist because a historian decides that a particular birth, war, or text, for example, was significant enough to affect everything that happened afterward.

Yet another reason for writing a history of Buddhism in reverse is that the very notion of Buddhism itself was constituted long after Gautama lived and spread his teaching (the Dharma), monks were ordained and monasteries built, texts were written and transmitted, rituals were codified, and physical objects of veneration—now known as art—were produced. The very idea of a religious tradition called "Buddhism"—a concept that unites the diversity of ideas and practices of communities throughout much of Asia and the West that affirm that the Buddha (or Buddhas) discovered and shared a path leading toward greater comfort and liberation—is a relatively recent development. Although there is a long tradition of monks who traveled great distances and visited monasteries to acquire religious texts or to become reordained in other monastic lineages, it was largely emissaries and Orientalist scholars from Europe who decided that geographically and culturally diverse communities of people who worshipped the Buddha were all members of a single religious tradition called Buddhism, *bouddhisme,* or *Buddhismus.* In the nineteenth century, Buddhism was first rendered into a discrete entity that exists, albeit in a variety of forms, in Oriental cultures open to the gaze of Western travelers, scholars, and missionaries, before later being reinvented as an object of knowledge to be found in the texts and manuscripts housed in Oriental libraries and institutes in Europe (Almond 1988, 10–13). When scholars began to locate Buddhism in texts and artifacts, they eagerly started to make increasingly systematic investigations into its history as a single tradition.

Moreover, Buddhists themselves have consistently taken a retrospective view of their own traditions, making sense of and legitimating the present with selective references to the past. The future orientations of millenarian movements and acts of merit notwithstanding, one can fairly state that the practice of remembering the Buddha (buddhanusmirti) and his acts and achievements is one of the most basic and universal practices among his adherents. Indeed, the life story of the Buddha is paradigmatic for most communities and a popular resource for all sorts of textual and iconic constructions. Furthermore, Buddhist monastic lineages are predicated retrospectively on a history of ordinations and the transmission of teachings from master to student. The validity of such lineages throughout Asia is evidenced by the renown and respect given to their original founders and earlier teachers. And while there has always been room for textual innovation in Buddhist communities, adherents have stressed the historical origins of their teachings and monastic lineages while drawing on the past to compose new texts and authorize new monastic communities. Looking backward in time to construct religious traditions and acquire a sense of identity is, of course, not unique to Buddhism. However, the value and attention that most Buddhists have characteristically given to the past shows that the historical development of the religion has always been accompanied by visions of the past and selective appeals to its authority, even in the midst of innovation and change.

This introductory survey of Buddhism will therefore begin in the modern period and move backward in time, highlighting earlier eras identified nominally as the colonial period (ca. seventeenth through nineteenth centuries), the late medieval period (ca. tenth through fifteenth centuries), the classical period (ca. first through eighth centuries CE), and the formative period (ca. fifth through first centuries BCE). This periodization is admittedly arbitrary and imprecise, but it is heuristically useful to group distinct ideas and developments that were important for the discourse and practice of what we now call Buddhism at different points of history. And instead of implying causal links from one period to the next in the development of Buddhism, we will suggest by moving backward that this development is largely characterized by improvised acts of remembering and representing a past that was retrospectively formed and imagined in various Buddhist communities. The development of Buddhist doctrines, ethics, and practices in different eras thereby reflects repeated—but always contemporary—efforts to construct a tradition that invested current forms of thought and practice with the significance and authority of antiquity. In other words, any sense of coherence and continuity in Buddhist traditions was the result of purposeful efforts to pattern the present after a particular (and contemporary) vision of the past. Thus, rather than evaluating whether or not certain innovations of thought and practice were authentically Buddhist compared with their historical antecedents, we will discuss examples of Buddhist thought, values, and practice that gained importance or influence in each period and note how people related these things to what they thought of the past.

Each of the following sections in this introductory essay will therefore highlight activities and events that are important for understanding how people in those eras practiced and represented Buddhism. Different cultures will be treated in each section, but there will be no attempt to present comprehensive historical surveys for any particular country or school of Buddhism in this essay. Instead, Buddhism will be treated here as multiple and dynamic fields of discourse and practice that people have connected with the Buddha yet defined in various ways across time and space. The hope is that this attempt to destabilize conventional views of the historical development of Buddhism will permit us to avoid the all-too-common habit of drawing unflattering contrasts between contemporary forms of the religion and the allegedly pristine form of original or early Buddhism from the distant past. The subsequent essays in this book that examine the contours of contemporary Buddhism in specific geographical locations may thus be put in a context that recognizes the shifting and contested grounds from which people have traditionally practiced and talked about the Buddhist religion.

Buddhism in the Modern Period

The encounter between Buddhists and modernity has produced several significant developments with respect to how the Buddhist religion is represented and practiced. Whether one chooses to describe the current age in terms of modernity, late modernity, or even postmodernity, it is clear that what counts as Buddhism has been subject to tremendous revision and reinterpretation. However, scholars of Buddhism often treat modernity as a chronological fact and nothing more than the period in which we now live. This matter-of-fact approach fails to consider modernity as an intellectual construction and a sociopolitical project to redescribe and reshape the world in ways that liberate individuals from community-based identities and customs for the sake of adopting broader national identities and universal standards of law and truth administered by translocal institutions. To be modern, then, involves something more than simply living in the present age. It implies a certain complicity in attempts to reorder the world in line with European Enlightenment values of progress and rationality, believing that science and technology can be used to assist people in their search for greater knowledge and power over their environments and, at times, each other.

Nevertheless, as the subsequent essays will show, the tremendous changes in the economic, political, and social spheres of modern life are not uniformly experienced and do not always evoke similar responses. In fact, it may be necessary to distinguish modern Buddhism, with its more intensive dialectical engagement with the various projects of modernity, from contemporary Buddhism, which may refer both to modernizing forms of the religion and to other forms that resist the transformations of modern and postmodern influences as best they can. However, scholars of Buddhism who turn their attention to the modern period have, in general, done little to theorize the current contours of the Buddhist tradition, save from making overly simplistic contrasts between the alleged purity of ancient traditions and the supposedly corrupt forms of modern Buddhist thought and practice that deviate from the early texts.

In all likelihood, scholars of Buddhism have been slow to theorize modernity because their training has been largely in the translation of centuries-old texts in Sanskrit, Pali, Chinese, Japanese, and Tibetan. Reflections on the conditions of modern life require scholars to step out from their own or adopted cultural locations and consider large-scale processes of social, political, and economic change. To those who are trained to think of Buddhism as possessing a timeless, essential core that can be discovered and deciphered from textual sources, such investigations must surely seem beside the point. But recent scholarship has begun to consider the characteristics and ramifications of modern Buddhism, a phenomenon that is generally described as rejecting ritual, stressing principles of universality and equality, and extolling the beginnings of the tradition (Lopez 2002, ix). This form of Buddhism is said to be distinctive for its embrace of modern rational and ethical philosophy that stands apart from much of everyday practice among most Buddhists (Lopez 2002, xvii). And although we are making headway in charting significant changes in a tradition in which local concerns and identities are purposely subverted in favor of universal ones, much is left for scholars to consider when they attempt to explain contemporary forms of Buddhist traditions.

If one agrees that the practice and representations of Buddhism in the modern period are somehow distinctive and reflect broader social realities, it makes sense to identify what contextual influences are brought to bear on contemporary expressions of Buddhism. Globalization, secularism, and humanism are particularly powerful factors affecting how Buddhism is practiced and conceived in the contemporary age. Several theorists of modern society and cultures have advanced compelling ideas to describe how such factors exert influence over people and institutions in the present. Globalization is defined in part as the stretching of relations between local and distant social forms and events across heretofore unimaginably vast areas of land, so that local happenings are shaped to an increasingly large degree by events occurring many miles away (Giddens 1990, 64). As a result, local practices and ideas are disembedded from their traditional contexts as seemingly natural or invariable modes of life, and they instead become options that compete with other practices and ideas introduced from distant areas. What this suggests is that an individual's self-construction is not clearly determined, not given in advance, and profoundly susceptible to changes over time (Bauman 2000, 7). As a result of the globalization of economic markets and cultural forms, a person's livelihood and identity become unfixed and uncertain. The resulting need for individualization transforms a person's identity from something that is given to a task for which a person is responsible (Bauman 2000, 31–32). This condition has been described in terms of an increased reflexivity, wherein all forms of knowledge about oneself and the world are constantly subject to revision in the face of new ideas and opportunities to act (Giddens 1991, 20–21; Beck 1992, 135).

Such conditions, whereby the authority of local knowledge and customs is regularly challenged by competing forms of thought and practice introduced from afar, make innovation and reform in Buddhism more commonplace. Insofar as modernity is seen as a disruptive influence that disembeds traditional customs and patterns of life from their formerly privileged positions in local societies, observers of modern Buddhism are faced with an ever-expanding repertoire of discourse and practice wielded strategically by Buddhist actors in complex and changing cultural contexts. In this sense (contrary to the view of Weber and some other earlier theorists, who thought of modernity as an "iron cage" that increasingly restricts the freedom of individuals to pursue their ambitions and exercise their autonomy), the modernity of the late twentieth and early twenty-first centuries is characterized by the radical emancipation of individuals from traditional social networks that once exerted considerable control over people's lives. This disruptive effect of globalization has contributed to distinctively modern reworkings of what it means to be Buddhist and how one can model and develop this identity in practice. And consequently, it becomes ever more important for scholars to recognize that totalizing and essentializing claims made on what constitutes Buddhist identity and tradition are, at root, historically contingent and differently authorized within the shifting grounds of contemporary debates over issues such as politics and religion (Abeysekara 2002, 15–16). In other words, it has become increasingly easy for people to contest and revise notions of authenticity and legitimacy in Buddhism—to differentiate between that which is Buddhist and that which is not—because there are a plurality of authorities and interpretations on which to advance and sustain such claims.

A key factor contributing to what some may describe as the marginalization of religious discourses and practice in the modern world has been the development and expansion of a doctrine of secularism. The invention of the secular as a principle around which to govern human society has usurped some of the power and influence of religion in decisions taken to order social life. Asad (2003, 16) identifies the secular as the critical feature in steps made to advance the project of modernity. For him, the secular refers to a variety of concepts, practices, and sensibilities that together work to uphold the freedom and responsibility of the sovereign self against religious discourses that seek to constrain it in various ways. The privatization of religion, its exile from the public to the private realms of people's lives, has allowed other powers such as the modern nation-state, capitalist economies, and military institutions to exert more control over the public aspects of human societies. Secular powers, including those advanced by globalization, obtain a greater ability to effect the ordering of societies when a generalizable system of ethics is disjoined from religion and justified in terms of its pragmatic benefits for the public as a whole. Serving as the counterpart of religion, the secular works to confine religion to the private sphere and offers alternative rationales for managing social interactions between people.

Buddhist monk using cell phone, Jokhang monastery, Lhasa, Tibet. (Angelo Cavalli/zefa/Corbis)

It is important to remember, however, that the project of modernity, which employs the secular to attain some of its rationalistic goals, is universal in scope but frequently varied in its application. The engines of modernity, including global capitalism, nation-states, military power, communications media, and modern industry, do not transform all people's working conditions and social relationships in the same manner or at the same rate (Giddens 1990, 56–62, 76–77). The significance of this for scholars of contemporary Buddhism lies in the fact that different Buddhist communities will be linked to modernizing projects to different degrees. Some Buddhists might appear to embrace characteristically modern values and practices, whereas others may not. Consequently, while it is commonplace to speak of modernity as a universal condition, the effect of modernity on Buddhist (and other) communities has been unevenly felt.

Indeed, the allegedly emancipatory nature of modernity contains within itself a tendency to exclude and distinguish different degrees of reason and progress among different groups of people. The institutions of modernization that have given rise to modernity tend to celebrate human freedom while positing a united but internally hierarchized world where some peoples are described as measurably more advanced and more fit to serve as the models for the rest of the world to follow (Chakrabarty 2002, 90). Thus, because some Buddhist groups may embrace such modernizing values as reason and human equality more than others, one can expect to find some debate and jockeying among people to assert that their understanding and practice of Buddhism is the most progressive and appropriate for the modern age.

Since the modern period developed in the wake of the European Enlightenment and its validation of human reason and capacity to remake the world into a more orderly and beneficial place, it is not surprising to find that modern forms of Buddhism are also colored by a humanistic orientation. In this sense, modern Buddhism typically envisions the Dharma as a body of wisdom discovered by a human Buddha and taught for the benefit of other human beings, each of whom is thought to possess an equal share in the ability to comprehend and follow what the Buddha taught. This relatively optimistic, human-centered message stands apart from Buddhist discourse found in the texts of previous centuries, wherein the Buddha frequently appears as a more supramundane figure with miraculous powers, a figure whom people are encouraged to venerate and sometimes petition for help in achieving a range of goals below that of Awakening (bodhi) and nirvana. The writings of Daisaku Ikeda, the leader of the lay Buddhist group Soka Gakkai International, may exemplify the modern tendency to humanize the Buddha and Buddhism. Ikeda notes to this end that before attaining Buddhahood, Shakyamuni was a "humanist" and a "seeker after truth" who was moved to discover that suffering is an inevitable part of all human life (Ikeda 1976, 12–14). A Buddha who in previous centuries was often

Painting depicting Shaka, the Japanese name for Shakyamuni, the historical manifestation of the Buddha as Siddhartha Gautama. (Corel)

depicted as feeling compassion for all sentient beings is now seen as particularly focused on the problems of humans. Moreover, Ikeda's account of the Buddha's life story, presenting him primarily as a role model for others to follow rather than a semidivine being whose magnificent qualities and attainments make him seem far removed from the capacities of ordinary humans, resembles many other modern works (Gómez 1996, 32).

Thus, the Buddha of the modern period appears more like us than ever before. It is commonly presumed that his Awakening is something feasible for contemporary practitioners if they simply follow his example and dedicate themselves to the goal. Of course, more traditional views of the Buddha continue to exist, and we continue to find contemporary Buddhists chanting the name of Amitabha Buddha to enlist his help in obtaining a heavenly rebirth and liberation and, elsewhere, performing meritorious deeds and making aspirations to be reborn during the time of Maitreya Buddha, who can help them attain nirvana. Nevertheless, with a wider range of religious options and goals now available to Buddhist practitioners, people may feel emboldened to apply their powers of reason and initiative to the goal of seeking liberation in this very life. Not bound to more localized and traditional conceptions of the Buddha and the means to attain nirvana, people may and often do set higher goals to become like the Buddha in the context of a modernized Buddhism that frequently transcends the concerns and imagination of one's local community or sect (Lopez, 2002, xi). The humanistic ideology in modernized forms of Buddhism stresses notions of individual autonomy and agency, opening up a broader range of possibilities in terms of practice, thought, and attainment.

At the same time that Buddhists are pushed to develop their own sense of religious identity and a more or less individualized repertoire of religious practices and conceptions, Buddhism in the contemporary period has on numerous occasions become intimately linked with various political projects. While the connection between Buddhism and politics is far from new, the manners in which people have employed the discourse, the symbols, and the institutional power of Buddhism for modern political ends reflect significant developments. The rise of nationalism as an effective strategy to supplant colonial powers and later to challenge the indigenous elites who often inherited power from European rulers in Asian states was sometimes accompanied by the explicit politicization of Buddhism as a force to mobilize opposition to political authorities or to marginalize non-Buddhist populations. Some countries, including Myanmar (Burma) and Sri Lanka, moved officially to recognize Buddhism as the state religion in the latter part of the twentieth century. In this way, Buddhism has continued to serve as a major focal point for efforts among Buddhists to reassert the significance of their national identities and cultural heritage, both of which may be threatened by the postcolonial forces of globalization.

Furthermore, the concern for material well-being, social justice, and economic influence has led many modern Buddhists to combine their religious values with political goals. Development projects initiated throughout Asia have periodically been supported or challenged by Buddhist organizations. The intervention of highly visible and respected monks into political disputes can affect the resolutions eventually obtained, and thus in several countries it is not uncommon to see politicians paying respectful calls to leading monks to gain either an explicit or implied show of support. Public talks and protests carried out by Tibetan monks in support of efforts to liberate their country from Chinese rule are only some of the many examples of Buddhists deciding to intervene in contemporary political affairs. The apparent problems and contradictions that may arise when monks and nuns exhibit such active concerns for worldly life are frequently rationalized in terms of one's duty to promote peace and welfare on behalf of one's neighbors and nation.

Conversely, the modern period of Buddhist history has also witnessed episodes of considerable persecution and bloodshed among Buddhists who have fallen afoul of hostile foes. Buddhist monastics and laypersons have been the victims of political violence in many lands during the twentieth century—including Tibet at the hands of the Chinese army, Cambodia from the Maoist revolutionaries called the Khmer Rouge, Sri Lanka from Tamil rebels as well as government-sponsored police and paramilitary organizations, and Myanmar from the governing military regime. The growth of communism in Asia has had particularly deleterious effects on Buddhist communities, leading in some cases to the seizure of wealth from monasteries and their patrons, as well as to initiatives to suppress the practice and promotion of Buddhism in society. The deportation and imprisonment of monks in places such as Mongolia has coincided with deliberate efforts to destroy Buddhist texts and monuments in China, Vietnam, and other lands. Even when communists were not openly hostile to Buddhist interests, the cold war that played out between global superpowers could attract unwanted military campaigns to lands where communism was embraced, leading to devastating economic and social effects.

In Western nations, as the trickle of Buddhist immigrants and texts gave way to a steady flow in the latter half of the twentieth century, people's interest and knowledge regarding Buddhism grew steadily. On the basis on earlier scholarship that posited the widespread existence of Buddhist practitioners and schools in many parts of Asia, Buddhism was transformed into a world religion open to general scholarly and public inquiry. The move to make Buddhism into a world religion has been accomplished by abstracting a historically and culturally embedded tradition out of history and culture, treating it synchronically as a tradition that is characterized by certain universal characteristics common to all religions (Flood 1999, 3, 234). Once separated out from a particular time and place, Buddhism becomes imagined as a transhistorical entity

Buddhist monks participate in a demonstration against the Tamil Tigers organized by Sri Lanka's Marxist People's Liberation Front in Colombo, Sri Lanka, August 23, 2005. More than 2,500 leftist activists marched in the Sri Lankan capital, calling on the government to abandon planned peace talks with Tamil Tigers rebels and instead to punish them for a rash of killings blamed on them. (Anuruddha Lokuhapuarachchi/Reuters/Corbis)

for which change affects only the externals of the tradition and does not touch its allegedly essential principles and features. The essentialist fallacy of world religions in general and, in this case, of Buddhism posits that at the core of this tradition lies an essential Buddhist soteriology that appears in and unites Buddhist traditions from all regions of the world (Fitzgerald 2000, 6).

The transformation of Buddhism into a world religion in the modern period has also made it possible for observers to disregard historical change and downplay cultural variation in favor of locating the authentic basis of Buddhism. This focus on universals rather than particulars was born out of European Enlightenment thought, leading people to search for the notions of pure doctrine and unadulterated practice or a form of Buddhism that can exist apart from the communities of people who practice and discursively represent it. As such, Buddhism is represented as just another religious faith that shares, among other things, a religious conviction of the importance of the holy (an ultimate reality that is in a category of its own), a belief in the spiritual nature of humankind and its capacity to relate to a higher power, and a common core of ethical principles such as reverence for life and respect for human dignity (Macquarrie 1997, 168–169). Presumed to be motivated by spiritual impulses found in persons of all religious backgrounds, Buddhism is thus sometimes thought to contain similar myths, rituals, and symbols that can be compared cross-culturally with other traditions to promote interreligious dialogue and insights into the allegedly religious nature of humanity. This transformation of Buddhism has also allowed some people to embrace it as part of their own spiritual practice while retaining their former religious identities as, for example, Christians, Hindus, or Jews.

The varied impact of diverse cultural and political influences in the modern world has shaped the ways that people discursively represent Buddhism as a religion. Although the proliferation of learned voices authorized to speak about Buddhism results in various portrayals of this religion, certain key features in these representations exemplify how Buddhism has been imaginatively reconstructed in the past 100 years. Scholarly activities centered on uncovering the original forms of Buddhism have spurred research and writing on the historical, human Buddha and his allegedly rationalistic teachings. Accordingly, surveys of Buddhism and world religion textbooks regularly include a fairly standard list of Buddhist doctrines. Heading the list are the Four Noble Truths, a set of Buddhist teachings extracted from the Buddha's first sermon and thought to summarize the Dharma. The Four Noble Truths comprise assertions that (1) life in the cycle of birth and death (or samsara) is characterized by suffering (dukkha) or dissatisfaction, (2) dukkha is caused by ignorance and desire for sense pleasures that cannot be maintained without end, (3) one can put an end to the pain and dissatisfaction normally experienced in life, and (4) the way to put an end to dukkha is to follow the Noble Eightfold Path. While these assertions do offer a concise summary of some important Buddhist insights, the importance of the Four Noble Truths in the modern period is founded equally on the conviction that they reflect the Buddha's original message and on their rationalistic assessment of the human condition.

Modern discussions of the Four Noble Truths often link this concept with the notion of the Buddhist path as the Middle Way between sensual indulgence and self-mortification. While this same connection is made in the Samyutta Nikaya of the Pali Canon (Bodhi 2000, 1843–1844), the ascetic moderation preached by the Buddha has been greatly expanded in recent decades to include a wider range of ordinary lay behavior. Strenuous religious practice and prohibitions can be relaxed if one's intentions are generally good and one maintains whatever standards for religious practice are recognized within one's own cultural environment. Modern practitioners are likely to emphasize the importance of intention in determining the moral quality of one's actions, as some Buddhist texts assert. Thus, if karma is determined by the relative wholesomeness or unwholesomeness of the intention behind one's deeds, Buddhist practitioners can be expected to focus at least some of their efforts on trying to purify their minds and motivations. Barring complete success in this endeavor, however, people may also try to earn merit, or the unripened fruits of morally beneficial deeds, in the hope of canceling out the potential negative fruits of deeds they performed out of selfish or malicious intentions. The flexibility built into the notion of the Middle Way in Buddhism may be adjusted to speak to both monastic and lay communities, permitting new interpretations of what comprises Buddhist practice in the modern period.

Another important doctrinal concept frequently recounted in modern treatments of Buddhist thought is pratitya-samutpada, or Dependent Arising, which reflects the teaching that all life in samsara is conditioned by a set of constantly changing factors and both arises and ceases in conjunction with these factors. The twelve links in the chain seen to cause the prolonging of life and suffering in samsara are presented as interdependent, so that none of them can exist independently of all the others. The twelve links that condition an ultimately unsatisfactory existence are said to include (1) ignorance, (2) mental formations, (3) consciousness, (4) name and form, (5) six sense fields, (6) contact, (7) feeling, (8) desire or craving, (9) attachment or clinging, (10) becoming, (11) conception and birth, and (12) old age and death. Each factor is conditioned by the previous one and, in turn, conditions what follows it, so that this twelvefold chain is commonly depicted as a wheel of recurring life and death. Such a description is traditionally used to explain why rebirth occurs and to explain the absence of any permanent, self-existent core of one's personality that could be said to transmigrate from one lifetime to the next.

The full existential ramifications of the related Buddhist notions of anatta (no-self) and shunyata (emptiness), however, are not always recognized in everyday thought and practice. People frequently retain conventional notions of their continuing identity and personhood, instead directing their efforts at weakening feelings of selfishness and egotism. This ambiguity is also reflected in Buddhist writings. Many Buddhist narratives, including the Jataka stories, promote the notion of an enduring personality that either enjoys or suffers the effects of karmic deeds done in previous lives. At the same time, however, Buddhist teachings clearly state that there is no equivalent to a permanent soul that transmigrates from one lifetime to the next. Not only do many texts argue that there is nothing permanent about one's individuality, many philosophical works also claim that conventional notions of one's individuality are mistaken and empty in the sense that there is no existence that is not conditioned by other equally empty factors. Dependent Arising is a significant Buddhist idea because it reinforces the notions that life is impermanent, subject to change and dissolution, and radically interdependent with other factors. While some Buddhists in the modern world are willing to accept and embrace these ideas, others may simply maintain the continual change and interconnectedness of all life.

Modern forms of Buddhist practice are liable to incorporate at least some of the ideas related to the Four Noble Truths, the Middle Way, karma, Dependent

Arising, and emptiness. And though there is ample evidence in traditional texts of a stress on performing good deeds and individual self-cultivation, there are additional reasons to emphasize the need to put the Buddha's teachings into action in the modern period. Among them is the perception that to fall short in living the life extolled by the Buddha constitutes laxity and failure, leaving one open to charges first lodged by colonial-era missionaries and scholars that contemporary Buddhists are corrupt and lack commitment to their religion. In many Buddhist societies in more recent times, there still exists the notion that real or authentic Buddhists model the behavior set forth in the canonical writings. People who are judged to be Buddhist in name only may thus find themselves open to criticism and contempt within their communities for falling short of textual ideals.

Similarly, the modern need to embody textual norms also stems from comparisons made with other religious groups. Christian and other religious organizations that undertake ambitious and conspicuous projects in social welfare and poverty reduction put pressure on Buddhists to do similar kinds of work that exhibits their compassion and selflessness. Of course, Buddhists have long been involved in acts to help alleviate the suffering of other people and animals, even before the arrival of well-organized and well-funded missionary groups from other religions. But the development of Engaged Buddhism in the modern era speaks to the desire among many Buddhists to make concerted efforts to "leave the meditation halls in order to help the people" who are in need (Hanh 1991, 91). The implication behind the name of this growing movement is that more traditional forms of the religion have been reclusive and inactive when it comes to people's suffering. While this conclusion is surely not intended, it does reveal some uneasiness and defensiveness among Buddhists who have grown tired of other people characterizing their religion in terms of quietude and self-absorption. As a result, there are now Buddhist-inspired peace activists, development workers, and environmental campaigners who feel compelled to practice their religion in visible and tangible ways for the benefit of society.

More generally, modern representations of Buddhism often stress the pragmatic nature of the religion. In keeping with humanistic and utilitarian values, modern practitioners frequently emphasize the practical steps that may be taken to bring people closer to Awakening. In these instances, the Buddha is represented as a role model whom modern practitioners can fully imitate, particularly when it comes to following the Noble Eightfold Path. The eight steps of this path ought to be practiced concurrently to put an end to suffering and attain the transcendent, indescribable, and unconditioned state of nirvana. This path (marga) that the Buddha is said to have taught comprises (1) right view, (2) right intention, (3) right speech, (4) right action, (5) right livelihood, (6) right effort, (7) right mindfulness, and (8) right concentration. When practiced together, the Noble Eightfold Path works to purify one's bodily, verbal, and mental acts, weakening the negative factors that promote suffering in oneself and others and strengthening one's ability to make progress toward nirvana. These steps are held to develop morality, meditation, and wisdom, leading to clear vision and blameless conduct. Once again, since this notion was formulated in early Pali texts, modern practitioners seeking to emulate the original model of the Buddha are often inclined to embrace this teaching as a guide for their own religious practice.

One final, prominent feature in modern representations of the Buddhist religion is the emphasis given to meditative experiences. Although there is little evidence in earlier eras to indicate that meditation was common among anyone but the most disciplined monks and nuns, modern Buddhist monastics and laypersons are more likely than ever before to recognize the centrality of meditation to the path and to undertake its practice. Laypersons are routinely encouraged to meditate at temples and in lay meditation societies, many of which are of relatively recent origin. In many societies, mindfulness training of either the Insight Meditation variety or systems derived from Zen practices appeal to significant numbers of people. The chanting of particular Buddhist treatises (sutras) remains a popular practice in many Buddhist communities and may also qualify as a kind of meditation insofar as it is thought to purify and calm the mind. Furthermore, by depicting the experience of meditation as the alleged core of the tradition, it has become possible for lay-oriented reform movements to wrest some authority away from the clergy, who traditionally preside over ritual and scholastic activities, while establishing a less rigorous form of urbanized meditative practice (Sharf 1995, 258, 267). Therefore, contrasts between the unquestionable validity of inner experience and routinized forms of monastic conduct and hierarchy are usually drawn to privilege the former and break down traditional boundaries subordinating laypersons to monastics.

In sum, modern representations of Buddhism tend to use a vision of the tradition abstracted from early texts that is consistent with the values of humanism, pragmatism, and universalism. Buddhism therefore is held to offer a singular path for all people in search of a variety of ethical and soteriological ends. Cultural differences are frequently devalued and deemed inessential to the allegedly generalizable truths discovered and taught by the Buddha more than 2,000 years ago—and selectively recalled by scholars and teachers of Buddhism in more recent times.

Buddhism in the Colonial Period

In the seventeenth through nineteenth centuries, the practice and conception of Buddhism were profoundly affected by the experiences of colonialism.

Most Asian countries with sizable Buddhist populations fell under the control of one or more European states. Even Thailand and Japan, which retained nominal independence, were obliged to respond to the presence of Europeans and the radical technological and epistemological changes they introduced throughout Asia in this period. While the effects of colonialism on societies beyond Europe and North America remain hotly debated and subject to revision as scholars discover increasing evidence of resistance and agency among colonized populations, the intervention of Western political, economic, and cultural forms in Buddhist communities gave rise to significant disjunctures and innovations with regard to how people embodied and recalled their traditions.

The European colonization of other lands was already under way in some parts of the world by the sixteenth century. The processes whereby Great Britain, France, Portugal, the Netherlands, and other colonial powers conquered and controlled the people and goods of other lands also entailed the complete restructuring of native economies and systems of knowledge from the seventeenth century onward (Loomba 1998, 2–3, 57). Although the colonial domination of Buddhist communities varied in form and experience, the activities of Oriental scholars and Christian missionaries contributed to local revisions in Buddhist thought and practice in many cultures. Again, it is in this period that European scholars inferred the existence of a cross-cultural religious tradition called Buddhism and publicized their discovery in academic and political circles. Interest in collecting and reading Buddhist texts preserved in multiple Asian languages helped to generate a flood of new information about what was then imagined as a single religion with many cultural variants.

Like colonialism, Orientalism appeared in many varieties in the seventeenth century and onward. The study of what were then called "Oriental" religions, languages, and cultures grew out of the encounters that took place when Europeans assumed control of the markets, natural resources, and peoples in Asian lands. In these historical circumstances, the pursuit of knowledge was intricately tied up with colonial pursuits of power, so that the more a colonial administration knew about the people and land it governed, presumably the more effective it could be in governing and using them. Such practical objectives notwithstanding, the seventeenth through nineteenth centuries witnessed a rapid growth of knowledge and interest in Asia among Europeans both at home and abroad. While many European Christians were dismayed, if not horrified, by what they witnessed or read about the religions of the East, others were fascinated by Oriental cultures, seeing in them resources to reappraise and reform the institutions and thought systems in the West (Clarke 1997, 27). Sympathetic Westerners felt they could adopt certain aspects from Oriental civilizations to enrich their own. Western interests in the Orient and, by extension, Oriental religions were not only grounded in Romantic escapist fantasies, but they were also based in the desires of some Westerners to criticize and correct problems in their own societies (Clarke 1997, 19–20).

It is in this context that Buddhism became a subject of colonial-era investigation and knowledge. The apparent antiquity of its traditions and its presence throughout many different Asian cultures fed the appetites of European scholars, civil servants, and missionaries, who studied and produced numerous writings about the religion of the Buddha in the colonial period. This Buddhism, however, was largely a historical projection abstracted out of the vast world of Asian texts that were being discovered, cataloged, and translated at the time. The Westerners who controlled or commanded these works also gained control and command over Buddhism, and they used this idealized construction of the pure and original Buddhist tradition as a mirror against which contemporary expressions of the faith were measured and found sorely lacking (Lopez 1995b, 7). Native informants, usually monks, were often consulted, but greater trust and confidence were placed in ancient texts. Medieval and contemporary forms, in contrast, were typically seen as derivative and corrupted reflections of a more pristine tradition from antiquity. This gap in authenticity also proved useful to Orientalist scholars, as it allowed them to become the authoritative voices who could speak for Buddhists about their own tradition, which had allegedly been lost and forgotten.

The nineteenth century witnessed a marked increase in knowledge about Buddhism among both scholars and the public at large. Eugène Burnouf published the scholarly work *Introduction to the History of Indian Buddhism* in 1844, helping to spark further investigations into Buddhism. In 1853, the Reverend R. Spence Hardy, an avowed opponent of the Buddhist religion, published *A Manual of Buddhism*—a work that reconstructed the legendary life of the Buddha for a broad reading audience in Europe. The British civil servant T. W. Rhys Davids used his posting in Ceylon to acquire proficiency in Pali, leading him to found the Pali Text Society and to embark on an ambitious publishing program resulting in numerous editions of Pali works that are still in use today. In 1874, Max Müller established his *Sacred Books of the East* series, contributing numerous translations of Buddhist and Hindu works, among others, and making such works accessible to Western audiences.

Although the Orientalist production of knowledge about Buddhism at times resulted in a fairly positive view of the tradition as rational and humanistic, not all of the Western representations of Buddhism were so kind. The nineteenth century also witnessed a surge in negative portrayals that characterized Buddhism as a font of nihilism and pessimism, although it is likely that many philosophers of this age, including Hegel, Schopenhauer, and Nietzsche, were reacting to the growth of atheism and materialism in Europe and transferred their fears and desires to the Buddhist tradition. Buddhism became popularly caricatured as a religion of nothingness that denies the existence of God and the immortal soul (Droit 2003, 20–21). Christian apologists in Europe, seeking to defend the church and Christian dogma, used these negative portrayals in their critiques of Buddhism. The move to equate Buddhism with pessimism and nihilism has proved to be a lasting legacy in Western representations of the religion, as the ineffability of nirvana continues to invite astonishment and incredulity among Westerners.

One of the most successful books on Buddhism published in this century was Edwin Arnold's *The Light of Asia,* a poetic and positive treatment of the Buddha's life story published in 1879. This best-selling work did much to popularize Buddhist ideas in the late nineteenth century and appealed particularly to the growing numbers of liberal thinkers who believed divine truth could be found in many different religions (Clarke 1997, 88). Yet Arnold, too, subscribed to the view that ancient Buddhism was much more legitimate than later forms, as he wrote:

> The extravagances which disfigure the record and practice of Buddhism are to be referred to that inevitable degradation which priesthoods always inflict upon great ideas committed to their charge. The power and sublimity of Gautama's original doctrines should be estimated by their influence, not by their interpreters; nor by that innocent but lazy and ceremonious church which has arisen on the foundations of the Buddhistic Brotherhood or "Sangha." (Arnold 1989, 4)

Such words speak volumes about the historicist and occasionally anti-Catholic bias that colored much Protestant scholarship on Buddhism. For such scholars, the original and pure form of Buddhism represented a rejection of Brahmanical ritualism in favor of a sober religion based on reason and restraint, demonstrating the capacity of individuals to flourish without the excesses of institutional religion (Lopez 1995b, 28–31).

In the face of such critiques and representations of their religion, many Buddhists responded to Western observers by appropriating rather than rejecting outright such characterizations. Modern Buddhist reformers advocated returning to the historical roots of their traditions, privileging the textual accounts of canonical works in a way that mirrored Protestant Christian calls for relying on scripture as the sole source for religious knowledge and conduct. Diverse Buddhist leaders such as Shaku Soen, Anagarika Dharmapala, and T'ai Hsu became vocal proponents of more modernized forms of Buddhism that embraced values of reason, scientific thought, and increased lay participation in religious activities traditionally confined to monks. That such modern values could be seen as a return to the religion established by the Buddha illustrates how people in the nineteenth century had transformed him into a human embodying the traits that were most esteemed by Victorians in Britain and other modernists elsewhere. The Buddha appeared in many nineteenth-century accounts as the heroic exemplar of the movement he founded, a movement whose agnostic, rationalistic, and ethical outlook inspired those Europeans who sought to find alternatives to revealed religion that could serve as a basis for morality in everyday life (Hallisey 1995, 45).

Buddhist works from the colonial period are understandably diverse in content and form. Some Buddhist societies were thoroughly colonized, and their literary works reflect the intensive contact people had with Western technologies and ideas. The use of printing presses gave rise to new forms of writing, including short pamphlets and tracts meant for general consumption and sometimes addressing criticisms that Europeans made about Buddhism. The attention given to canonical works, not entirely attributable to Orientalist biases, was seen in the production of vernacular commentaries on canonical material, such as sannayas in Sinhala and samrays in Khmer, in the eighteenth and nineteenth centuries. Such works made canonical and commentarial texts more accessible to a broader audience, yet reinforced the centrality of the classical texts at the same time. There is also evidence of authors writing texts surveying the historical development of Buddhism in their native lands. Systematic accounts of the history and teachings of Buddhist schools were written in early modern Japan and, in Burma, the Sasanavamsa that details the history of the Buddha's Dispensation (sasana) as it moved from India to Burma was composed in 1861. Such historicist enterprises speak to colonial-era interests in mapping out the national landscape for the development of Buddhism. In these and other ways, new forms of Buddhist identity with explicit ties to language and the state were constructed and promoted.

Developments in Buddhist thought and practice in this era often revolved around larger cultural trends that were shaped by colonial encounters with the West. Many practitioners of Buddhism embraced the rationalistic description developed by Western Orientalists and stressed the compatibility of Buddhism and modern science. By emphasizing the supposedly empirical bent of Buddhist methods for gaining knowledge, Buddhists of the nineteenth century and early twentieth century redefined their traditions in a modernist manner. In Thailand, King Mongkut drew on his own monastic background and education to found a new monastic order called the Thammayut based on a romantic desire to return to the Pali Canon and recreate the idealized image of textual Buddhism that was, as the name suggested, in accordance with the Dharma. His encounters with Christian missionaries led Mongkut to seek to defend Buddhism from the pressures of the West by revitalizing the original Buddhist tradition and purifying it from later cultural accretions.

Mongkut's move signifies an important development in several colonial-era representations of Buddhism throughout Asia. With the intrusion of Christianity and the introduction of Western-style discourse about religion in terms of individual experience and the rejection of superstition, the religion called

Buddhism came to be imagined and defined as a discrete religious tradition in opposition to the Christianity of the colonizers and imperialists. Much like Christianity, this Buddhism was portrayed as a singular faith with its own set of scriptures, an ethical code of conduct, and an institutional order of religious specialists. While the specific characteristics may have differed, the overall structure was thought to be the same.

A defining moment in this era, when a coherent Buddhism was depicted in opposition to Christianity, was the public debates between Buddhist monks and Christian evangelical preachers in the 1860s and 1870s in Sri Lanka. The monk Mohottivatte Gunananda led a group of monks from different fraternities in a spirited defense of Buddhist principles and practices, answering the criticisms of Buddhism lodged by missionaries and founding the Society for the Propagation of Buddhism to answer the evangelists' tracts with polemical works of their own (Malalgoda 1976, 220–226). Such a response helped mobilize the supporters of Buddhism in Sri Lanka, and they were led to define their religion more clearly and exclusively, specifying what doctrines were central to Buddhism. A similar sort of Buddhist backlash against the influence of Christianity took place in Korea in the nineteenth century, witnessed by the founding of new Buddhist organizations that could counteract the growth of Christian ones. And more broadly, the colonial presence in Cambodia, Taiwan, and elsewhere tended to generate greater levels of self-consciousness about issues of religious and ethnic identity, leading to the formation of new texts and new ideas of Buddhist orthodoxy.

While it would be an overstatement to say that all colonial-era reformist movements were directly sparked by contact with Western Orientalists or missionaries, many reinterpretations of the Buddha and Buddhism did occur in environments that were dramatically changed by the introduction of Western systems of knowledge and power into Asian lands. Since Buddhist monks and monasteries depended on lay donors for material support, any changes in a country's economic situation would have a direct impact on the conditions of the Sangha and the laity's ability to sustain it. Even though more laypersons began to obtain a Western education in schools established by colonialists, Buddhist monks were usually the leading voices expressing definitions and support of Buddhism. Monastic renunciation and ordination remained important practices in this period, although innovations could be made in ordination lineages. Giving the monastic requisites to monks and nuns and showing respect to the Buddha or Buddhas were important features of everyday Buddhist practice. There is little evidence that could point to the widespread practice of meditation by the laity, but instead they could be expected to have performed various rituals associated with protection and death despite the devaluing of such practices by Orientalist scholars and Buddhist modernists.

Nevertheless, the propensity of Western scholars and missionaries to inquire into what Buddhist texts actually said in order to learn about Buddhism probably encouraged Buddhists to rely more on textual representations of their religion. The search for origins and purity in religion had the effect of privileging texts over native practitioners and supplied the lasting dichotomy between precept and practice, the ideal and the real, that survives in much contemporary discourse about Buddhism. But the attention given to texts, particularly ancient ones, encouraged the revitalization of scholarship among Buddhists themselves. Some monks and lay scholars produced new works explaining the teachings of Buddhism and presented new editions of older literature through the technology of the modern printing press. Theravada monks were encouraged to engage in Pali scholarship in the lands where the Pali Canon remained authoritative. Under the Ch'ing dynasty, editions of the Tibetan and Chinese Tripitakas were completed in the eighteenth century in China. These facts suggest that the imagination and representation of Buddhism during the colonial era often revolved around the production and dissemination of authoritative texts.

Elsewhere, in Tibet, which some would say lacked a colonial presence until the twentieth century, steps were taken to reorganize the monastic system and attitudes toward Buddhist literature as well. In the seventeenth century, the Fifth Dalai Lama inaugurated the temporal reigns of the Dalai Lama, and Tibetan authors popularized the discovery of Treasure Texts (terma) as well as the autobiographical genre. These Treasures Texts comprised texts allegedly taught by the legendary figure of Padmasambhava in the eighth century and hidden away to be discovered by the future incarnations of his disciples when his teachings were needed. One such discoverer was Jigme Lingpa (1730–1798), whose revelatory works in the eighteenth century revived and reshaped Nyingma meditation traditions in Tibet thereafter (Gyatso 1998). The eighteenth century also witnessed the first woodblock printing of the entire Kanjur and Tenjur Tibetan Buddhist canon. This event illustrates that concerns with preparing new versions of canonical texts in this period were not limited to countries subject to intensive colonization at the time.

Buddhism in the Late Medieval Period

Between the tenth and fifteenth centuries, Buddhist communities and religious expressions became ever more refined and variegated as the distinctive features of local traditions were developed with little thought given to constructing a uniform, overarching Buddhism out of diverse and far-flung cultural forms. The ideas and institutions of the religion had by this time existed in several Asian lands for 1,000 years or more, and there had been ample time for people to study texts, institute new or revised rites, found new schools, and spread doctrinal ideas that spoke more clearly to people in their particular circumstances. At the same time, traditional activities for earning merit such as almsgiving, venerating images and relics, chanting and listening to sermons, and pilgrimage continued to be popular. In most cases, late medieval forms of what would later be termed Buddhism emerged out of changes in the relationships the Sangha maintained with ruling powers and lay supporters, giving rise to new literary works and distinctive ideas about how to attain Awakening and other Buddhist goals in the process.

Many developments during this period reflected attempts to consolidate the position of Buddhist institutions and reinforce the ties that Buddhist laypersons had developed with the religion. A brief survey of some of these late medieval trends reveals a willingness among Buddhist communities to embrace innovative practices and ideas while producing new forms of Buddhist texts to satisfy then-current interests and objectives. One distinctive characteristic of Buddhist traditions in this period is the founding of indigenous schools and lineages reflecting a more sectarian impulse in communities across Asia. The development of new Buddhist identities in this period was frequently accomplished by producing Buddhist texts and through the negotiation of power and recognition by state authorities. Such activities have been commonplace throughout all periods in the history of Buddhism, but the emergence of temporal authorities with ambitions to achieve a more centralized form of power in some largely Buddhist lands effectively involved kings and emperors more intimately in the affairs of the local Sangha.

In China, the emperors of the Sung dynasty (970–1279) pledged their support to Buddhist institutions, arranging for the building of new monastic estates and facilitating the ordination of huge numbers of monks and nuns. At the same time, the Sung rulers imposed strict government control over Buddhist monastic life. Monasteries were arranged into a tripartite system: Many were designated as meditation monasteries and were headed by Ch'an (Zen) monastics; others were designated as teaching monasteries, where the study of texts was emphasized; and a smaller number were designated as ordination monasteries, where novice monks could learn the monastic code or Vinaya, through which the government could regulate who was ordained and how. As a result, monks would normally have been trained in three different lineages, depending on the monasteries in which they received their training. All facets of Buddhist monasticism in late medieval China under the Sung dynasty were devised and regulated by the government.

Elsewhere in East Asia, the Koryo dynasty (918–1392) in Korea embraced Buddhism and likewise supported a strong connection between Sangha and state through royal patronage and regulation of some monastic affairs. The Koryo rulers instituted an examination system for Buddhist monks, at once ensuring a better-educated Sangha and incorporating its members into the state bureaucracy by conferring titles on those who passed the examination. They also encouraged talented monks to become advisers to the royal court. The increased government support of Buddhism had the effect of turning some monasteries into large landowners with serfs and, at times, explicit commercial interests in noodle and tea production. The Koryo rulers strived to support and control Buddhist institutions, since it was thought such patronage afforded them and their country with some measure of protection.

The historical processes of state formation during the late medieval period also encouraged closer ties between governments and monasteries in some South and Southeast Asian countries. In Burma, the promotion of Theravada Buddhism coincided with efforts to centralize the power of the state. King Anawrahta (reigned 1044–1077) created a regional Burmese kingdom by conquering the Mon territory in southern Burma and adopting the Theravada Buddhism of the Mons as the official religion of his rule. Anawrahta based his capital in the city of Pagan and embarked on an ambitious program of temple building. And although his commitment to Theravada was strong enough to lead him to facilitate the reintroduction of Pali texts and an ordination line into Sri Lanka in the eleventh century, there is also evidence that he supported some non-Theravada forms of Buddhism as well.

The coexistence of various forms of Buddhism and Hinduism in Cambodia during the Angkorian period from the ninth through thirteenth centuries was marked by numerous monumental building projects, including a project to build the renowned Angkor Wat temple. The support of the earlier Angkorian kings for Hindu deities gradually gave way to greater Mahayana influences in the tenth and eleventh centuries. King Jayavarman VII (reigned 1181–1218) built several Buddhist temples, including the Bayon in Angkor, and solidified the relationship between Buddhism and the state in late medieval Cambodia. But it was not until the post-Angkorian period of the thirteenth and fourteenth centuries that Theravada Buddhism was widely embraced and assimilated into all levels of Khmer society from the royal courts down to the villages, although older brahmanical Hindu and spirit practices remained on the periphery.

In late medieval Sri Lanka, the periodic rise of strong kings who could fight off foreign invaders permitted some rulers to exercise their authority over Buddhist institutions as well. Emulating the model of the righteous Buddhist King Ashoka from ancient India, King Parakramabahu I (reigned 1153–1186) moved to unify the Sangha by adopting the views and practice of the Mahavihara fraternity as orthodox and forcing monks from other schools either to be reordained in this lineage or to disrobe. A revised code of monastic conduct was created and used to standardize the discipline of all monks. As a devoted patron of Buddhist institutions, Parakramabahu not only established Theravada as the normative form of Buddhism in Sri Lanka, he also continued the practice of giving royal support for the construction of monasteries and relic shrines. In the following centuries, Buddhist institutions were sometimes threatened and even destroyed by invaders, but the model for Sri Lankan kingship as intimately tied to efforts to promote Theravada endured, with some modifications, through the late medieval period and beyond.

In spite of the numerous instances of state patronage and control of Buddhism in the late medieval period, often resulting in government-sponsored attempts to unify and centralize power in the Sangha, there were several successful efforts in this era to establish new sectarian groups of Buddhist practitioners. In many of these cases, sectarian developments in late medieval Buddhism reflected moves to create indigenous schools and lineages that were responsive to local interests and circumstances. At the same time, however, the degree to which sectarian movements could flourish in a particular region was usually dependent on the relative absence of a strong central government with designs to regulate monastic affairs. Examples of this situation were found in Japan and Tibet during this period.

The Kamakura period (1185–1333) in Japan was notable for the development of Buddhist schools that were oriented more toward the interests and needs of a wider population than the imperial court. Earlier Buddhist groups tended to be inclusive and syncretic, combining a variety of practices and ideas into complex ritual systems that were attractive to those in the Japanese court. However, beginning in the latter part of the twelfth century, newer forms of Buddhism became established that emphasized a primary teaching or practice designed to lead even ordinary people to heavenly comforts and Awakening. The Pure Land, Zen, and Nichiren schools attempted to incorporate more indigenous concerns and values into the practice of the Buddha's teaching. These schools were founded by charismatic figures who were dissatisfied with the dominant monastic forms of the religion and instead developed simplified techniques to help practitioners obtain good fortune, heavenly rebirths, and Supreme Awakening. And the efforts to relax government restrictions on religious communities enabled the growth of the new schools in late medieval Japan.

The monk Honen (1133–1212) founded the Pure Land school in Japan, emphasizing a reliance on the power of Amida (Amitabha), the heavenly Buddha presiding over the Western paradise, to enable beings to become purified from the negative impressions of wicked deeds and to obtain a heavenly rebirth in his presence. By chanting the nembutsu, or reverence to the figure of Amida, one would (1) develop sincere faith in Amida's ability to assist his devotees in attaining soteriological goals and (2) cultivate an aspiration to be reborn in the Pure Land. Shinran (1173–1263), a disciple of Honen, extended his teacher's ideas, stressing that beings are completely dependent on Amida for any and all progress along the Buddhist path. By founding the Jodo Shinshu, or True Pure Land School, Shinran argued that a single recitation of the nembutsu was all that is necessary to secure one's future blessings in the Pure Land. In fact, this Buddha's compassionate intervention to aid devotees made celibate monasticism unnecessary, and Shinran took the extraordinary step of getting married, thus initiating the tradition of married priests in Jodo Shinshu. By articulating a doctrine of reliance on the gift of grace from Amida Buddha, these Pure Land schools addressed the needs of everyday persons who sought help from more powerful beings to attain a better existence in the future. The simplicity of following a single, powerful practice—reciting the name of Amida—had great appeal to the wider Japanese population.

In the same period in Japan, Zen temples and traditions were established, having been brought over from monks trained in China. Zen Buddhism in Japan tended to combine strict monastic discipline with simplified forms of practice directed at generating Awakening (satori) in one's present lifetime. Eisai (1141–1215) developed the Rinzai Zen sect, which combined meditation with the use of koans, or paradoxical questions or riddles designed to dissolve the dualistic basis for rational thought and produce the sudden experiential insight of Enlightenment. Later, the monk Dogen (1200–1253) founded the less eclectic Soto Zen sect, emphasizing the quiet practice of "just sitting" (zazen), which was held to be an effective means of realizing one's Buddha-nature, or the inherent condition of possessing an enlightened mind.

Additionally, the controversial and charismatic monk Nichiren (1222–1282) founded a new form of Japanese Buddhism that was later named after him. Having grown dissatisfied with the Tendai school in which he was ordained, Nichiren came to espouse a view whereby only the Lotus Sutra is seen as a perfect and complete expression of the Buddha's Dharma. Nichiren's inflammatory statements criticizing the doctrines of other Buddhist schools and the emperor for patronizing those groups landed him in trouble several times with the authorities. Asserting that the problems befalling Japan were due to the fact that the emperor embraced false Buddhist doctrines, Nichiren maintained that chanting the title of the Lotus Sutra was the means of bringing people to liberation and promoting peace and stability in the country. And although Nichiren condemned the Pure Land and Zen schools harshly, his teachings resembled those of his contemporaries in the sense that he advocated a fairly simple and direct means to accomplish higher Buddhist attainments.

The sectarian trends in Japanese Buddhism are in some ways mirrored by events in Tibet that occurred during roughly the same period. In the Second Propagation of Buddhism to Tibet, which began around the end of the tenth century, several new monastic orders were founded, testifying to the increased complexity of Buddhist institutions in the region. The efforts of the great Indian scholar Atisha (982–1054) to promote the Dharma in Tibet led to the founding of the Kadam school by one of his disciples. Incorporating Atisha's emphasis on the relationship of master and disciple, the Kadam school gained the support of many aristocratic families. The disciplinary code of the Kadam school was adopted by the new Sakya school in the twelfth century. Gampopa (1079–1153), a student of Milarepa in the lineage of Marpa, founded another distinctive Tibetan order in the twelfth century. Combining the Kadam discipline with the meditative practices of Tantra developed by his lineage of masters, Gampopa established the Kagyu school. This school came to emphasize Great Seal meditation, which revolves around the realization of the luminous mind and emptiness of existence. The disciples of Gampopa, in turn, split into five subsects.

The Nyingma school rejected many of the monastic reforms of the Second Propagation and instead claimed to preserve the older, purer teachings of legendary Buddhist masters such as Padmasambhava. Nyingma teachers claimed that their apparently apocryphal texts were in fact Treasure Texts that had been stored away in hidden locations or in the memories of teachers who had been the disciples of Padmasambhava in their former lives. Once rediscovered, these Treasure Texts came to represent the authoritative instructions of respected figures from history, legitimating the practices and positions of Nyingma teachers. Among the more prominent forms of Nyingma practice is a kind of meditation called dzogchen, or Great Perfection. In this practice, a pupil is guided by a teacher to discover the innate purity of his or her awakened mind, concentrating on the essence of consciousness. The ties that the Nyingma cultivated with the past, based on their claims to be reviving an older form of Buddhism imported into Tibet by Padmasambhava, contributed to the success and survival of this school in the midst of the reforms undertaken by others.

Later, in the fourteenth century, the revered scholar Tsong Khapa (1357–1419) devised a synthesis of Buddhist study and practice, combining Indian philosophy, tantric literature, and the Kadam monastic discipline. He maintained that the important Mahayana doctrine of emptiness did not invalidate the ethical rules of the Vinaya but instead pointed the way to a clear vision that sees the various formulations of Buddhist doctrine as unified and coherent. His teachings became famous and widely accepted in certain monasteries, giving rise to a new monastic order, the New Kadam school. The later Geluk school, or Order of Virtue, replaced the Kadam school altogether. Tsong Khapa's curriculum stressed the need for training in logic and debate before advancing in the practice of meditation. The Geluk school became politically influential in later centuries by fostering ties with the Mongols, who recognized their spiritual leaders with the title *Dalai Lama*. The Geluks adopted the practice of searching for and discovering the reincarnated heads of the order, thus helping to resolve the potentially divisive question of monastic succession.

If the growth of sectarianism in some lands reflects another significant development in the late medieval period—a period of mature formation in many Buddhist traditions—it coincided with notable efforts to broaden the appeal and practice of the Buddha's teaching to wider segments of lay societies. One

Statue of the "lotus-born" Padmasambhava, the Guru Rinpoche who carried the teachings of tantric Buddhism from India to Tibet in the eighth century. Towering above the foothills of Sikkim, this statue was built from a design by the fourth Dodrupchen Rinpoche, a master of the Nyingma school who traces his lineage directly back to Padmasambhava. (David Leskowitz)

trend seen in several late medieval Buddhist communities was vernaculariza-tion, or efforts to employ local languages in composing Buddhist literature. This move toward the vernacular signified a growing interest for producing and transmitting texts that would be more accessible to the wider public. Be-yond the conspicuous issue of accessibility, however, the decisive switch from writing and using texts in cosmopolitan languages such as Sanskrit, Pali, and classical Chinese to more localized forms of vernacular languages in the late medieval period marked a transformation in cultural communication and self-understanding, contributing to the formation of new cultural identities that were regional in nature and scope (Pollock 1998, 45–46). As late medieval Bud-dhists began employing vernacular forms of Asian languages to compose liter-ary works, they reimagined and reconstituted the notions of Buddhist commu-nities in their midst. New visions of audiences arose and, it stands to reason, new Buddhist texts were created for them.

At the outset of the late medieval period, authors in China and Japan began to create new forms of writing patterned more closely on their respective vernaculars. Evidence from the Dunhuang cave library in China suggests that the appearance of narratives composed in a more vernacular form of Chinese can be dated to around the tenth century CE. This move was a departure from the artificial style of classical Chinese, a language that very few but the most educated could use. In eleventh-century Japan, the development of Japanese terms and phrasings began to supersede a style of writing that bore a strong Chinese influence. Such shifts, although sometimes subtle, indicate concrete efforts to invoke a more localized vision of texts and audiences. Buddhist texts bearing the traces of vernacularization in East Asia appear directed to broader audiences close to home rather than to educated elites who were schooled in cosmopolitan languages abroad.

In Sri Lanka, a varied and matured Sinhala literary culture developed in the late medieval period. Despite evidence of earlier Sinhala writing, the period between the tenth and fifteenth centuries marks a high point in the vernacularization of Buddhist literature in Sri Lanka. The lay Buddhist author Gurulugomi composed the devotional tract Amavatura (The Flood of Ambrosia) and a more formal commentary, the Dharmapradipika (The Lamp of the Teaching), in the twelfth century, spurring an upsurge of Buddhist writings in Sinhala. Such works were often creative renderings of Pali or Sanskrit texts in Sinhala prose and poetry. These renderings mediated the world of these classical texts and gave them an increased sense of immediacy in a local context through the use of vernacular forms and more familiar cultural symbols (Hallisey 2003, 733). Efforts in the thirteenth and fourteenth centuries to produce Sinhala versions of Pali chronicles recounting the history of particular relics associated with the Buddha and enshrined in Sri Lanka illustrate once again a clear interest in producing local-language texts that deal with a more immediate and familiar terrain (Berkwitz 2004).

The blossoming of Korean vernacular literature occurs later in this same period. Specifically, the fifteenth century marks a significant break in literary production in Korea. Up to this point, Korean Buddhists relied chiefly on texts written in classical Chinese, positioning the peninsula and its inhabitants within the larger sphere of Chinese cultural influence. But developments in the fifteenth century included inaugurating a Korean script that could be used to compose written works in a literary form of the vernacular Korean language. The production of works such as Worin Ch'on'gangjigok (The Songs of the Moon's Reflection on a Thousand Rivers) in 1449 made Buddhist narratives more widespread among the Korean-speaking populace. These works also contributed to the development of more localized forms of Buddhism reflecting Korean interests and tastes.

Another significant development in late medieval forms of Buddhism is the increased pessimism concerning one's ability to span the spatial and/or temporal distance from the Buddha in India and to realize Buddhist goals. In late medieval Buddhist cultures, the view that the Dharma had gone into decline was common, and many people acknowledged that their ability to follow the Buddha's path was severely hampered by circumstances of time and place. The ideas that people were living in a degenerate age and that the Dharma would gradually become corrupted and then disappear were not new to this period. Various timetables of decline, beginning from about 500 years after the Buddha's death and increasing in periodic intervals, had been forecasted much earlier in a variety of Buddhist texts from India, China, and elsewhere (Nattier 1991). At the same time, the growth in cults devoted to the Bodhisattva Maitreya suggests that substantial numbers of people felt that Awakening and liberation were feasible goals only after the appearance of the next Buddha.

A series of disasters that fell on the Japanese city of Kyoto in the tenth century led to the belief that the mappo, or age of a degenerated Dharma, was at hand. Consequently, many Japanese Buddhists in the late medieval period affirmed that they were no longer able to attain higher Buddhist goals by their own efforts. Buddhist schools that emphasized scholastic learning and complex ritual practices fell out of favor next to newer schools that affirmed that a few simple practices were all that was necessary for the masses to progress along the path to Awakening. Although Zen schools and the Tendai doctrine of original enlightenment (hongaku) affirmed the inherent potential for individuals to realize Awakening, the Pure Land and Nichiren schools insisted on relying on an external power such as Amitabha Buddha or the Lotus Sutra for assistance in the attainment of higher Buddhist goals.

Meanwhile in India, Buddhist institutions and communities, which had been on the wane for several centuries, were practically extinguished in most parts of the land of its origin. The rise in the influence of sectarian Hindu movements supported by regional kings did much to marginalize Buddhist monastic institutions. Lacking a widespread base of support from among the laity, Buddhist monasteries and temples were destroyed by invading Muslims in the thirteenth century. This destruction effectively ended the last traces of a substantial Buddhist presence in India, reinforcing the notion that the Dharma was in the midst of a cycle of degeneration. In such contexts, people in the late medieval period could have been expected to look back at the past with nostalgia and a sense of loss but also with a feeling of freedom to establish new monastic sects, texts, and rituals to fit their local circumstances.

Buddhism in the Classical Period

Between roughly the first and eighth centuries of the common era, the religion associated with the Buddha underwent a period of dynamic growth and expansion. The institutional and intellectual developments during this period proved to be foundational for later efforts to establish the Buddha's Dharma in other lands. In contrast to late medieval efforts to consolidate the tradition in localized spheres of influence, Buddhists in the classical period consistently looked to wider horizons to develop and disseminate the Dharma that they had received from earlier generations. Also in this period, Buddhists had to confront rival religious scholars and specialists, such as Hindus and Jains in South and Southeast Asia and Confucianists and Daoists in East Asia. Debates held with the representatives of other religious traditions, who competed for official recognition and support from area rulers, helped to sharpen notions of Buddhist identity. At the same time, disputes among various Buddhist sects also contributed to new discursive representations of what the Dharma actually is and whose account of what the Buddha taught is the most accurate or comprehensive. These claims to authority, moreover, were frequently made with respect to the possession and interpretation of written texts.

Although many in this period maintained that the Buddha had left the world, the physical traces of his person—preserved in the forms of relics, images, and texts—were sought after and venerated with enthusiasm. Although stupas enshrining the bodily relics of the Buddha had been in existence for several centuries, the fashioning of Buddha images and the writing of texts on the Dharma arose mainly during the classical period, spurring new types of Buddhist practice and conceptions of the Three Jewels (Buddha, Dharma, and Sangha). The exact location and reasons for crafting iconic images of the Buddha beginning around the first century CE remain obscure. Two sites where such images were made early on—Mathura and Gandhara—were geographically and stylistically far apart, and the identity of the earliest site to create images of the Buddha is in dispute. Nevertheless, the making of images was doubtlessly conducive to practices of veneration and the giving of honorary offerings (puja) to the Buddha. Images of the Buddha in his early period could be viewed either as relics that reminded people of the Buddha or as objects within which the living presence of the Buddha continued to dwell (Schopen 1997, 262–265). Regardless of these divergent interpretations, such images were evidently quite popular, as the practice of representing the Buddha in iconic forms became firmly established during this period and has continued ever since.

The first concerted efforts to put the Buddha's Dharma into writing also took place around the beginning of the classical period. The earliest attempt at producing a written canon of Buddhist texts probably dates to between 29 and 17 BCE at the Aluvihara monastery in central Sri Lanka, where an assembly of monks recited the Dharma and wrote down the first version of what would later become the Pali Tipitaka. Although Theravada tradition holds that the entire Tipitaka (or Three Baskets) of the Buddha's word (buddhavacana) was formed at this time, scholars maintain that the texts remained susceptible to revision and addition for the next several centuries, up to around the fifth century CE, when monks such as Buddhaghosa began to write commentaries on individual texts in the Pali Canon.

The work of Buddhaghosa, who is the reputed author of as many as fourteen commentaries (Atthakatha) in Pali, exemplifies the outward-looking orientation of Buddhism in the classical period, as he took older commentaries written in the local language of Sinhala and revised them into more coherent and polished accounts in the cosmopolitan language of Pali. The result of this activity was that learned monks across South and Southeast Asia gained access to older Theravada commentarial traditions. Also, Buddhaghosa wrote the influential compendium the Visuddhimagga (The Path of Purification), a lengthy volume that purports to summarize the material found in the Pali Tipitaka and Atthakatha and that would eventually set the standard for Theravada thought. Other Theravada scholar-monks such as Dhammapala carried on Buddhaghosa's work, effectively expanding the collection of Buddhist literature in Pali that would help this school to become established in Sri Lanka and Southeast Asia.

Written Buddhist texts also began to appear in the Indian subcontinent in the first few centuries of the common era. The British Library's recent acquisition of birch bark manuscripts written in the Gandhari language from an area in modern-day Afghanistan or Pakistan yields important evidence of other canons of Buddhist literature that existed alongside the Pali Canon in antiquity. The survival of these invaluable manuscripts, which have been dated to the first century CE, supports the idea that a Gandharan Buddhist canon comprising both written and oral texts was established as early as the first century in a region far away from Sri Lanka (Saloman 1999, 165). Initial research indicates that such works were frequently used in concert with the oral transmission of the Dharma and that Gandhara was an important center for Buddhist scholarly activity. The appearance of ancient manuscripts detailing both known and unprecedented Buddhist texts composed in Gandhari from the first century reinforces the idea that Gandharan traditions played a major role in the establishment of Buddhism throughout Asia, serving as the conduit through which Chinese Buddhists first received texts on the Dharma (Saloman 1999, 6).

In addition to the Buddhist works that were produced in Pali and Gandhari from around the first century CE, the classical period witnessed the inauguration of efforts to compose and transmit Buddhist texts in a host of different dialects. Various communities undertook the writing of authoritative Buddhist texts, although it is unlikely that most of these efforts resulted in an exclusive notion of canon with a finite, clearly defined list of works. Literary activity in a hybrid form of Sanskrit was initiated by a variety of Buddhist groups in the Indian subcontinent. The so-called Abhidharma schools, comprising monastic sects that tended to trace their lineages back to the disciples of the Buddha and the early monastic councils, began to compose original works as well as redactions of texts they shared with other groups. Examples include the Mahavibhasa (The Great Exegesis) by the Sarvastivada Buddhist community and Vasubandhu's Abhidharmakosa (The Treasury of the Higher Teachings), which conveys Sarvastivada teachings in verse and contains a critical commentary on those teachings. Sanskrit Abhidharma texts were transported to China during this period, and they eventually became incorporated into the Chinese Buddhist canon.

Among the most noteworthy literary achievements in the classical period were the compositions of Sanskrit works that served as the foundation for new Mahayana (Great Vehicle) communities of Buddhist monks. Contrary to the belief that Mahayana began as a popular, devotional backlash to the scholastic orientation of the Abhidharma schools, it now appears that Mahayana Buddhism was established by multiple communities of learned monks who organized themselves around particular sutras while remaining more or less institutionally affiliated with the ordination traditions of older Indian sects (Silk 2002, 369–371). In other words, Mahayana Buddhism began in the first centuries of the common era as an idea and a polemic before developing an institutional apparatus that could sustain the existence of a distinctive Buddhist school in the centuries that followed.

Among the texts composed in the first few centuries of the common era that contributed to the gradual formation of a Mahayana identity were the various Prajnaparamita Sutras (The Perfection of Wisdom Scriptures) that worked to explicate the concepts of emptiness and the bodhisattva path, the Vimalakirti-nirdesa Sutra (The Scripture Expounded by Vimalakirti) that extolled the virtues of a discriminating mind even among laypersons, and the Saddharma-pundarika Sutra (The Scripture of the Lotus of the Excellent Dharma) that affirms the infinite glory and life span of the Buddha. These works, introduced centuries after the Buddha passed away, according to many, were legitimated by the Mahayana doctrine of skillful means (upaya), which asserted that the Buddha transmitted more advanced formulations of the Dharma only gradually in concert with the growth of his audience's intellectual abilities or that some of his teachings had been hidden away until the right moment came for people to receive them. These arguments, contained in later Sanskrit works, illustrate the need felt by Buddhists in the classical period to connect their works to the authoritative figure of a Buddha. Whether this Buddha was Gautama (sometimes called Shakyamuni) or a cosmic Buddha like Amitabha, who was said to reside in a heavenly paradise, there is practically no limit to the number of Buddhist texts with claims to authority and authenticity produced during this period.

The tremendous literary output in the classical period among the older Abhidharma sects and the evolving Mahayana school was largely responsible

The world's earliest surviving book is a Chinese wood-block print of the Diamond Sutra that dates from 868 CE in the Tang dynasty. This sutra (literally, "thread") is a concise version of the Prajna-paramita (Perfection of Wisdom) scriptures that are the basis of Zen philosophy. (Werner Forman/Art Resource, New York)

for new developments in Buddhist thought and for the spread of Buddhism into new lands. The renowned scholar Nagarjuna, a monk thought to have lived in South India around the second century CE, authored the influential treatise Mulamadhyamika-karika (The Fundamental Verses on the Middle Way). This dense work elaborated the notion of emptiness (shunyata) in a systematic fashion, arguing for the necessity of eliminating false views and gaining insight into the dependently arisen character of all reality. By maintaining that all views and entities are without inherent existence but instead conditioned on other equally conditioned phenomena, Nagarjuna advanced a forceful argument that the conditioned world of bondage in samsara is no different from the ineffable, liberated condition of nirvana. Under analysis, conventional truth—those descriptions of reality that are expressed positively with language—underscores the inevitability of seeing all of reality as dependently arisen or conditioned by other phenomena. At the same time, the ultimate truth, to which Nagarjuna refers, states that all such dependently arisen phenomena are empty and lacking in any self-existent nature. As such, these Two Truths are used to remind one of the limits of language to express true statements about existence and to realize one's capacity to attain nirvana in samsara presently (Garfield 1995, 332).

The intellectual heirs of Nagarjuna fleshed out the contours of Mahayana Buddhism in the later centuries of the classical period. A Madhyamika school of philosophy arose and developed different branches, applying Nagarjuna's lessons on emptiness to Buddhist thought and practice. Another group of scholarly Buddhists developed a second philosophical school called Yogacara. Founded by Asanga and Vasubandhu in the fourth century, this school examined the deluding effects that an afflicted, unawakened mind has over one's conceptions and experiences. Emphasizing the primary role of consciousness in the subjective awareness of oneself and objective awareness of one's world, the Yogacara thinkers deemphasized the intellectual orientation behind emptiness as a method for exposing the incoherence of false views and instead used their critical examination of mental processes as support for the primacy of meditation in the Buddhist path. In other words, ordinary human consciousness perceives the world falsely. The practice of yogic concentration is used to purify the mind and prevent it from generating false impressions of the dependently arisen world. Yogacara's emphasis on the innate luminosity of the mind that is discovered when one stops the ordinary workings of consciousness contributed to ideas of original Awakening and Buddha-nature that would become important for East Asian thought.

As noted, written accounts of the Buddha's teaching and exegetical works by monastic followers comprised material objects held in great esteem and used for spreading Buddhist traditions to other lands. Buddhist monks traveled out of the Indian subcontinent to East and Southeast Asia during these centuries, often with texts in tow, to preach the Dharma and lead others to accept Buddhist practice. In this way, the Buddha's Dharma was transmitted to China along the Silk Route and to the ancient regional capitals of peninsular Southeast Asia. The presence of charismatic monks and allegedly powerful relics contributed to successful efforts to have new communities take refuge in the Buddha's teachings, but the material presence of physical texts was an invaluable aid.

In western China, traveling monks from central Asia persuaded local authorities to set up translation centers where Buddhist texts in central Asian and Indian languages could be rendered into Chinese. The first Chinese translations were less than accurate, but the production and use of texts permitted Buddhist ideas to be conveyed in accessible ways to a Chinese population that was unfamiliar with Indic languages and thought. The use of native terms from Daoist thought (e.g., *wu-wei* or "nonaction" for *nirvana*) led to many misconceptions that were only gradually corrected by more knowledgeable and skilled translators such as the fourth-century monk Kumarajiva. As such, the importation of Buddhism into China during this period was effected chiefly through the translation and study of texts, activities that formed the basis for the rise of a native Chinese Sangha in the early centuries of the common era.

The method and context for the establishment of Buddhism in Southeast Asia are less well known. However, there is evidence of a Buddhist presence among the Mon in southern Burma from about the fourth century of the common era. There appears to have been an eclectic mix of Buddhist traditions in the south and especially farther north among the Pyu people. Archaeological evidence at the ancient regional kingdoms of Thaton (located in modern Myanmar), Dvaravati (in modern Thailand), and Champa (in modern Vietnam) suggest that monks from India and, to a lesser extent, China were involved in transmitting the Dharma to these lands. Texts and images of the Buddha were no doubt instrumental in establishing a lasting presence of Buddhism in the region, though the Theravada monks who brought such devotional objects were by no means in ascendancy here until much later.

Near the end of the classical period, efforts continued to spread and develop Buddhism by authoring texts and instituting rituals. Although the growth of Buddhism in this period was not without its setbacks—including, most notably, the rise of sectarian Hindu kingdoms in India and the periodic persecutions of Buddhist monks by hostile rulers in China—these centuries continued to witness dynamic developments that contributed to the establishment of Buddhist institutions and communities in more lands, as well as the diversification of Buddhist forms of thought and practice. An example of this diversification is the composition of a class of texts known as tantras in India from the sixth century onward.

Sharing in the esoteric practices of certain Hindu groups, Buddhist tantras typically outlined methods to achieve a ritualized identification with divine forces to accomplish both worldly and world-transcending goals. Buddhist tantras contained directions for becoming empowered by the forces of Buddhas and bodhisattvas through ritual consecrations (abhisheka) and the use of powerful incantations (mantras), gestures (mudras), and diagrams depicting other worlds on which to meditate (mandalas). Initiation into a tantric community and the guidance of a guru were required to instruct the initiate in the secretive, powerful practices outlined in written tantras. The inclusion of techniques for visualizing a subtle, physical body filled with powerful but latent forces, as well as antinomian practices such as sexual yoga, were marked departures from earlier practices. However, the promise that Buddhist tantras offered a more rapid and effective way toward obtaining Supreme Awakening, along with the judicious use of older traditions connected with meditation and the ritual chanting of texts, enabled the establishment of a new Vajrayana (Diamond/Thunderbolt Vehicle) Buddhist school in conjunction with certain

Mahayana traditions. Vajrayana traditions would grow in popularity in India and spread into the Himalayan region and beyond before the decline of Buddhist institutions in India by the late medieval period.

Buddhism in the Formative Period

The era spanning roughly the fifth to the first centuries BCE marks what could be called the formative period of Buddhism. Beginning with the birth of Siddhartha Gautama, variously estimated between the sixth and fifth centuries BCE, and extending to the era wherein Buddhist texts were first put into writing, this period has generated intense interest among scholars seeking to reconstruct the so-called original form of the Buddha's religion. However, the meager archaeological and epigraphical evidence cannot provide a clear and definitive picture of the Buddhism practiced by the Buddha, or even of how he was remembered by his earliest disciples. Instead, we must rely on written accounts produced around the beginning of the common era or later for information on the early development of Buddhism. But with this qualification in mind, we may proceed to recount as the key events that took place in the formative period the Buddha's life, the formation of the Sangha, the first councils of monks, the subsequent schisms within the monastic order, and the career of King Ashoka.

The life story of the Buddha is the central narrative in the Buddhist tradition, a story that has been variously recalled in texts and depicted in art ever since his time. Tradition holds that Siddhartha Gautama's life was only the culmination of an almost incalculable number of life spans wherein he cultivated the Perfections (paramitas), or moral virtues, as a bodhisattva who had made a vow to become a Buddha and help all beings escape the cycle of repeated births and deaths. Later biographies of the Buddha such as the Mahavastu (The Great Story), Buddhacarita (The Life Story of the Buddha), and Jataka-nidanakatha (The Account of the Origin for the Jataka Tales) provide the basic outlines of the Buddha's life, as well as some entertaining elaborations on it. In brief, Siddhartha Gautama is said to have been born into a royal family in northern India. His youth was marked by great comfort and a comprehensive education in all the arts and sciences to be learned by future kings. An arranged marriage to a woman named Yashodara resulted in the birth of a son named Rahula. But the pleasures of family life and royal wealth could not dissuade Siddhartha from renouncing the world at twenty-nine and living as a homeless ascetic in search of the wisdom that could lead to the cessation of suffering and rebirth in samsara, the continual cycle of birth and death.

After spending six years practicing yoga and austerities, Siddhartha realized that the Middle Way between sensual indulgence and severe self-mortification,

Pilgrims and students gathered at the historic Shri Maha Bodhi Tree enshrined in Anuradhapura, Sri Lanka. (Courtesy of Stephen C. Berkwitz)

or between the pleasures of his palace life and the rigid course of fasting and ascetic purification of the body, held the key to attaining the liberating experience of Awakening that he sought. And so, having accepted food again, he sat beneath a bodhi tree and entered into a deep meditative trance leading to the complete cessation of all desire, ill will, and delusion, as well as the extinction of all karmic factors that could lead to another rebirth. At this point, he obtained nirvana and became a Buddha at the age of thirty-five. After some apparent hesitation, he resolved to teach others the path that leads to the cessation of suffering and rebirth. This teaching, or Dharma, became the basis for all of his subsequent instructions to those who came to listen to or dispute with him.

Later texts portray the Buddha as quickly gaining several followers. Some volunteered to become ordained as celibate monks and nuns who were required to submit to an evolving code of monastic discipline called the Vinaya. These monastic regulations mandated a lifestyle of moral self-control and detachment from sensual pleasures and comforts. From an early date, female monastics were required to submit to an even longer list of disciplinary regulations, effectively subordinating them to their male counterparts. In some accounts, the Buddha only reluctantly agrees to ordain his stepmother Mahaprajapati Gautami and a large band of noblewomen as female Buddhist renunciates. Many who are sympathetic to the Buddhist tradition defend his al-leged hesitation as based more on social norms than on doubts about the ca-pacity of women to practice the path, since the Buddha is thought to have af-firmed that women may attain nirvana in the same way as men.

Many of the original monks and nuns who followed the Buddha and his teaching were said to have attained a similar state of Awakening and release from samsara. Meanwhile, the lay supporters of the Buddha and his monastic disciples were expected to take the Three Refuges, articulating their confi-dence in the Buddha, the Dharma, and the Sangha as the means to attaining nirvana and other Buddhist goals. The laity would make offerings to the Bud-dha and the Sangha while receiving sermons on the Dharma. And although it is far from clear that many lay devotees pledged their support exclusively to the Buddha instead of other Hindu or Jain teachers in ancient India, there was enough support to sustain a growing population of Buddhist renunciates.

Near the end of his life, the Buddha is depicted as having successfully estab-lished the institutional basis for transmitting the Dharma for the sake of pro-moting wisdom, happiness, and liberation among his followers. A community of monks and nuns had been founded, and its members had received the Dharma and were able to transmit it orally in the forms of sermons to the laity and texts that were memorized and preserved by lineages of teachers and pupils in the Sangha. The Buddha had traveled around the Gangetic plain of northern India, and a substantial number of followers had taken refuge in him. Literary accounts portray the Buddha as having some degree of control over his death, or at least a foreknowledge of when it would occur. Having knowingly accepted and eaten some bad food that was offered by a well-meaning devotee, the Buddha became stricken with a mortal illness. The tradition holds that he subsequently reclined between two trees in the village of Kusinara and invited his disciples to pose some last questions to him. When they failed to do so, he entered into a meditative trance and passed away in nirvana without any phys-ical remainder (parinirvana) at the age of eighty. Great weeping and lamenta-tion took place among those who had not yet become fully awakened into the true nature of existence, and his followers resolved to give him the funerary rites of a king. Wrapped in fine cloth, the Buddha's body was set ablaze on a fu-neral pyre, and his physical remains were allegedly collected and distributed to some of his lay devotees, who enshrined these relics in stupas.

While the Buddha's life inspired the formation of a religion with a monastic community dedicated to imitating his moral discipline and preserving his teachings, his death spurred several other recurring events in the formative pe-riod of Buddhist history. Since the Buddha refused to name a formal successor but instead declared that the Dharma and the Vinaya would be the guides for people in the future, his teachings occupied a critically important role from the beginning. It is said that some close disciples of the Buddha arranged for a council of leading monks to be held shortly after the Buddha's death for the sake of rehearsing and standardizing what they had learned from him. The monks arrived at an apparent consensus over the specific teachings of the Buddha, and the resulting oral texts were identified by later Buddhists with the Sutta Pitaka (Basket) and Vinaya Pitaka, or discourses and monastic rules, respectively. A third collection of canonical texts called the Abhidharma Pitaka, although attributed to the first council, was likely a later elaboration on older lists of mental and physical constituents and their activities.

Unity among the monastic disciples over the teachings of the Buddha was short-lived. Disagreements over Vinaya rules and doctrinal positions sparked disputes within the Sangha. The Second Council, which was held about 100 years after the Buddha's death in the city of Vaisali, was apparently called to settle a dispute over monastic regulations. While the exact nature of the dispute is unclear, tradition holds that one result of this council was the first schism in the Sangha. One group, which dissented from the decisions over the rules of discipline, came to be known as the Mahasanghikas (those of the great community), and later northern Buddhist schools portrayed them as the larger of the two groups (Cox 2004, 502). The other group was known as the Sthaviravadins (those of the way of the elders). The Third Council, held at Pataliputra under the royal auspices of the powerful Indian king named Ashoka, appears to have functioned as a response to growing concerns about disunity in the Sangha. Sanghabheda (formal divisions within the monastic community) was clearly disapproved of in the formative period. Tradition holds that the king enforced the council's rulings on monastic conduct and heretical views by disrobing large numbers of monks who refused to submit to the teachings and the discipline of the favored monastic community.

Efforts to prevent divisions in the Sangha would ultimately fail, as numerous monastic sects and schools called *nikayas* were formed in the centuries before the common era. These nikayas, named in ancient Buddhist texts, comprised monastic communities with distinctive identities and interpretations of the Buddha's teaching. Many of these groups comprise what later critics called "Hinayana Buddhism," representing the Lesser Vehicle of the tradition that was thought to be incapable of leading many people to the ultimate goals of Awakening and nirvana. But as this pejorative designation would only come later in the form of some Mahayana polemics, it is enough to remark that the nikayas consisted of various monastic communities that disagreed with each other on disciplinary and sometimes doctrinal grounds. Nevertheless, there is reason to believe that monks from different nikaya lineages could still reside together and maintain cordial relations. Groups such as the Sarvastivadins, Dharmaguptakas, and Theravadins exerted considerable influence in particular areas, although only the latter group managed to survive into the second millennium of the common era.

Another direct result of the Buddha's death was the birth of the Buddhist relic cult. Although they were viewed skeptically by scholars for years, it now appears that activities to enshrine and venerate the corporeal remains of the Buddha originated in the formative period of Buddhist history. The construction of stupas at locations such as Sanci and Bharhut in India and the accompanying epigraphical evidence point to the existence of a relic cult by the second century BCE with extensive participation by monks and nuns (Schopen 1997, 92). Further, there is also some archaeological evidence to support dating the construction of Buddhist stupas to the fifth or fourth centuries BCE, which clearly suggests that the earliest material evidence of the presence of Buddhism in India is connected to the cult of relic veneration (Trainor 1997, 43–45). The remains surrounding Buddhist relic veneration indicate that both monastics and laypersons were regularly involved in making ritualized offerings to the Buddha's relics in the hope of earning personal merit or transferring merit to others, living or deceased, to facilitate their well-being in present and future lives. Such efforts speak both to the ritualistic character of what is otherwise known as "early Buddhism" and the tremendous interest that devotees had concerning the physical body of the Buddha, even after his death.

One historical figure who played a large role in supporting the growth of Buddhism in the formative period was King Ashoka (ca. 300–232 BCE), a powerful leader from the ancient Mauryan dynasty who extended his rule throughout the subcontinent. Ashoka erected several stone pillars on which his royal edicts were inscribed. In these edicts, he speaks of propagating the Dharma throughout his realm, and he displays an ethical concern for humans and animals. An edict erected at the reputed site of the Buddha's birth confirms that this king made a pilgrimage to the site and evidently held the Buddha in high regard. Later textual sources credit Ashoka with purging the heretical influences from the Sangha in the Third Council, constructing 84,000 stupas throughout his realm to enshrine the Buddha's relics and make them available for his subjects to venerate, and sending monks (including his son Mahinda) out to propagate the Dharma to the far reaches of his empire and beyond. Despite Ashoka's patronage of a variety of religious communities in ancient India, he has gone down in history as a pious and just Buddhist king who served as a role model for the leaders who came after him.

Thus, to the extent that formative Buddhism can be reconstructed through textual and archaeological glimpses of the period, it would seem that the first few centuries in the existence of Buddhism were marked by early institutional development and the oral dissemination of the Dharma. Practices of meditation, monastic discipline, almsgiving, and transferring merit were prominent features in early Buddhist communities. Doctrinal notions related to the experience of suffering, the origins and effects of karma, the reality of impermanence, and the cultivation of wisdom as a means to become liberated from samsara are prominent in the earliest surviving texts. And although the historical Buddha was not long gone, at least comparatively speaking, there are indications that early Buddhist communities were already engaged in recalling his life and teachings in ways that encouraged looking back to a not-so-distant past for guidance and authority.

References

Abeysekara, Ananda. 2002. *Colors of the Robe: Religion, Identity, Difference.* Columbia: University of South Carolina Press.

Almond, Philip C. 1988. *The British Discovery of Buddhism.* Cambridge, UK: Cambridge University Press.

Arnold, Sir Edwin. 1989. *The Light of Asia: Or the Great Renunciation (Mahabhinishkramana).* Reprint. Madras, India: Theosophical Publishing House.

Asad, Talal. 2003. *Formations of the Secular: Christianity, Islam, Modernity.* Stanford, CA: Stanford University Press.

Bauman, Zygmunt. 2000. *Liquid Modernity.* London: Polity Press.

Beck, Ulrich. 1992. *Risk Society: Towards a New Modernity.* London: Sage Publications.

Berkwitz, Stephen C. 2004. *Buddhist History in the Vernacular: The Power of the Past in Late Medieval Sri Lanka.* Leiden, Germany: Brill.

Bodhi, Bhikkhu, ed. 2000. *The Connected Discourses of the Buddha: A New Translation of the Samyutta Nikaya.* 2 volumes. Boston: Wisdom Publications.

Burnouf, Eugène. 1844. *Introduction à l'histoire du buddhisme indien.* Paris: Imprimerie Royale.

Chakrabarty, Dipesh. 2002. *Habitations of Modernity: Essays in the Wake of Subaltern Studies.* Chicago: University of Chicago Press.

Clarke, J. J. 1997. *Oriental Enlightenment: The Encounter between Asian and Western Thought.* London: Routledge Press.

Cox, Collett. 2004. Mainstream Buddhist Schools. In *Encyclopedia of Buddhism,* vol. 2, ed. Robert E. Buswell Jr., 501–507. New York: Macmillan Reference.

Droit, Roger-Pol. 2003. *The Cult of Nothingness: The Philosophers and the Buddha.* Trans. David Streight and Pamela Vohnson. Chapel Hill: University of North Carolina Press.

Fitzgerald, Timothy. 2000. *The Ideology of Religious Studies.* New York: Oxford University Press.

Flood, Gavin. 1999. *Beyond Phenomenology: Rethinking the Study of Religion.* London: Cassell.

Garfield, Jay L., trans. 1995. *The Fundamental Wisdom of the Middle Way.* New York: Oxford University Press.

Giddens, Anthony. 1990. *The Consequences of Modernity.* Stanford, CA: Stanford University Press.

———. 1991. *Modernity and Self-Identity: Self and Society in the Late Modern Age.* Stanford, CA: Stanford University Press.

Gómez, Luis O. 1996. *The Land of Bliss: The Paradise of the Buddha of Measureless Light.* Honolulu: University of Hawai'i Press.

Gyatso, Janet. 1998. *Apparitions of the Self: The Secret Autobiographies of a Tibetan Visionary*. Princeton, NJ: Princeton University Press.

Hanh, Thich Nhat. 1991. *Peace Is Every Step: The Path of Mindfulness in Everyday Life*. New York: Bantam Books.

Hallisey, Charles. 1995. Roads Taken and Not Taken in the Study of Theravada Buddhism. In *Curators of the Buddha: The Study of Buddhism under Colonialism*, ed. Donald S. Lopez Jr., 31–61. Chicago: University of Chicago Press.

———. 2003. Works and Persons in Sinhala Literary Culture. In *Literary Cultures in History: Reconstructions from South Asia*, ed. Sheldon Pollock, 689–746. Berkeley and Los Angeles: University of California Press.

Hardy, R. Spence. 1853. *A Manual of Buddhism, in Its Modern Development*. London: Partridge and Oakey.

Ikeda, Daisaku. 1976. *The Living Buddha: An Interpretive Biography*. New York: Weatherhill.

Jenkins, Keith. 1991. *Re-thinking History*. London: Routledge Press.

Loomba, Ania. 1998. *Colonialism/Postcolonialism*. London: Routledge Press.

Lopez, Donald S. Jr., ed. 1995a. *Buddhism in Practice*. Princeton, NJ: Princeton University Press.

———. 1995b. *Curators of the Buddha: The Study of Buddhism under Colonialism*. Chicago: University of Chicago Press.

———. 2002. *A Modern Buddhist Bible: Essential Readings from East and West*. Boston: Beacon Press.

Macquarrie, John. 1997. Dialogue among the World Religions. *Expository Times* 108(6):167–172.

Malalgoda, Kitsiri. 1976. *Buddhism in Sinhalese Society, 1750–1900: A Study of Religious Revival and Change*. Berkeley: University of California Press.

Nattier, Jan. 1991. *Once upon a Future Time: Studies in a Buddhist Prophecy of Decline*. Berkeley: Asian Humanities Press.

Pollock, Sheldon. 1998. India in the Vernacular Millennium: Literary Culture and Polity, 1000–1500. *Daedalus* 127(3):41–74.

Saloman, Richard. 1999. *Ancient Buddhist Scrolls from Gandhara: The British Library Kharosthi Fragments*. Seattle: University of Washington Press.

Schopen, Gregory. 1997. *Bones, Stones, and Buddhist Monks: Collected Papers on the Archaeology, Epigraphy, and Texts of Monastic Buddhism in India*. Honolulu: University of Hawai'i Press.

Sharf, Robert H. 1995. Buddhist Modernism and the Rhetoric of Meditative Experience. *Numen* 42(3):228–283.

Silk, Jonathan A. 2002. What, If Anything, Is Mahayana Buddhism? Problems of Definitions and Classifications. *Numen* 49(4):355–405.

Trainor, Kevin. 1997. *Relics, Ritual, and Representation in Buddhism: Rematerializing the Sri Lankan Theravada Tradition*. Cambridge, UK: Cambridge University Press.

White, Hayden. 1987. *The Content of the Form: Narrative Discourse and Historical Representation*. Baltimore: Johns Hopkins University Press.

Chapter 2

Buddhism in Sri Lanka
Practice, Protest, and Preservation

STEPHEN C. BERKWITZ

The island of Sri Lanka (formerly Ceylon) lies off the southeast tip of India and is widely recognized as one of the world's important centers of Buddhist history and practice. Approximately two-thirds of the country's people are Buddhist and overwhelmingly, though not exclusively, Sinhala in ethnicity. Despite the presence of significant numbers of Hindus, Muslims, and Christians on the island, there are recurring efforts to label Sri Lanka as first and foremost a Buddhist country, evidenced by the long recorded history of Theravada Buddhist practice and numerous archaeological remains—some dating back to around the third century BCE—that attest to the ancient and widespread practice of Buddhism throughout much of the island. Ever since King Parakramabahu I accomplished the task of unifying the Sri Lankan Buddhist Sangha during the twelfth century CE, the Theravada school of Buddhism as developed by the Mahavihara sect in ancient Sri Lanka has remained authoritative. Moreover, the form of Theravada Buddhism found in Sri Lanka is distinctly conservative in character, maintaining that close adherence to the Vinaya and other canonical texts that make up the Pali Tipitaka are essential for correct practice and understanding.

Indeed, Sri Lankan Buddhists typically see themselves as the preservers of the authentic form of Buddhism established by the Buddha some 2,500 years ago in India. The early introduction of Buddhism around the third century BCE by Ven. Mahinda and the religion's continued presence in the island as documented by numerous ancient and medieval chronicles (vamsas) support the popular notion that the purest form of Buddhism is found in Sri Lanka. Consequently, one of the defining features of contemporary Sri Lankan

Buddhism is the preoccupation with discerning and preserving "true Buddhism." Fidelity to the word of the Buddha and the Theravada tradition, which many Sri Lankans believe is closest to the original form of Buddhist thought and practice, is an important standard for evaluating the authenticity of Buddhism in today's world. And because Sri Lankan Buddhists generally believe that their tradition is the most authentic one—the occasional deviation or corruption notwithstanding—there is a widespread impetus to preserve their form of Buddhism in the face of modern challenges to its continued existence. This notion of preserving true Buddhism in Sri Lanka was reinforced by much Western scholarship in the nineteenth century, wherein the Pali Canon was extolled as the oldest and most authentic version of the historical Buddha's teachings, and the Theravada tradition—at least in its idealized, textual form—was widely acknowledged to be more authentic than its Mahayana and Vajrayana counterparts elsewhere (Lopez 1995, 6–7).

The strong sense among Sri Lankans that they serve as the custodians for true Buddhism is tempered by the existence of internal divisions and debates over what constitutes authentic Buddhist conceptions and practice. Despite the tendency for Sri Lankans to speak about Buddhism as a singular entity that they practice and possess, there are numerous differences of opinion over the details of monastic discipline and devotional practice. At times, these differences become magnified into public debates over what actually constitutes Buddhism versus what is a digression or deviation from the norm. Ananda Abeysekara rightly observes that whatever counts for tradition in Sri Lankan Buddhism is actually a rhetorical marker through which opposing moral claims are authoritatively and visibly positioned and fought out about what represents religion, orthodoxy, and truth (Abeysekara 2002, 174–175). Such debates, in which various Sri Lankans regularly engage, become the venues for defining and contesting the notion of true Buddhism. These debates can evolve into large-scale public controversies that are argued out in newspapers and public speeches, or they may occur in more circumscribed surroundings among family members and neighbors. In all cases, one finds that contemporary Sri Lankan Buddhists are adept at asserting the orthodoxy of their own singularly conceived tradition while disputing some of the particular characteristics that their fellow practitioners may attribute to it. In other words, many people believe that there is one essential form of Buddhism in Sri Lanka, even if not everyone understands or follows it correctly.

As a result, the idea of an orthodox Sri Lankan Buddhist tradition may exist more in rhetoric than in reality. Influential scholarly theories of modern Sri Lankan Buddhism have a propensity to speak of either a revival or a transformation of the tradition (e.g., Bond 1988; Gombrich and Obeyesekere 1988). One problem with such theories is that they presume the existence of a single, relatively fixed Buddhist tradition located in the past that can either be revived or used as a measure for evaluating modern changes in the religion. While some generalities in terms of Buddhist thought and practice may hold for most Sri Lankan Buddhists, one soon finds that individuals often hold different opinions and conceptions about what this true form of Buddhism really is. In other words, the largely conservative ethos of contemporary Sri Lankan Buddhism is unable to prevent a diversity of ideas and practices from being expressed by those who count themselves among the adherents of this tradition. Nevertheless, the idea of true Buddhism and the intent to both preserve and practice it hold widespread currency among Buddhists in Sri Lanka, and these factors give some coherence to the diversity of religious forms one finds in today's society.

The ongoing efforts made to reform and reimagine Buddhism in the context of a rapidly changing world are another source of consistency in Sri Lankan Buddhism. Consequently, many contemporary Buddhists in Sri Lanka are engaged in a kind of balancing act, wherein they strive to preserve an ancient tradition—however they conceive it today—while making slight adjustments and innovations where necessary to respond to internal pressures and external forces.

Colonial and Postcolonial Contexts

Buddhism in contemporary Sri Lanka is expressed, to some degree, in response to a set of historical events and developments from around the nineteenth century onward. Earlier, periodic invasions from foreign armies in the late medieval period weakened the vitality of the Buddhist Sangha in Sri Lanka. By the beginning of the sixteenth century, when the Portuguese made their first attempts to gain access to the island's cinnamon supply, Buddhist monastics and institutions in the maritime regions were unable to protect themselves from periodic looting and destruction at the hands of Portuguese troops. As Portuguese power expanded in successive decades, agents of the Catholic Church made strong efforts to convert Buddhists and Hindus to the faith. The Portuguese were replaced in the seventeenth century by the Dutch, who helped the Sri Lankan king to expel the Portuguese at the cost of submitting to Dutch rule. While the Dutch displayed less hostility to Buddhism than the Portuguese, their efforts to bring much of the coastal area of the island under their political control contributed little to the material support and development of the Sri Lankan Sangha.

Nevertheless, until the early nineteenth century, the island's interior hill country, where the royal capital of Kandy was located, remained largely independent of foreign rule. Yet even Kandy eventually succumbed to foreign domination when the British, who were looking to secure and expand their colonial holdings in the Indian subcontinent, wrested control of the island from the

Dutch in 1796. A military campaign to capture Kandy met little resistance, as many Sinhala chieftains in the kingdom were alienated by the king's previous efforts to reduce their power. In 1815, the largely Buddhist kingdom was formally ceded to British control under the terms of the Kandyan Convention, which among other things stated that the British would protect and maintain "the Religion of Buddhoo, its rites, ministers and places of worship" (K. M. De Silva 1981, 231). This clause was included to win the loyalty of the Sinhala subjects, but it appears that while the Sinhalas understood the convention to be a solemn agreement, the British interpreted the document as an ordinary treaty that could be amended at their pleasure. Sinhala Buddhists soon discovered that their British rulers would not maintain and protect their religion with all the vigor they expected. On the contrary, the British colonialists displayed a desire to gain increased political and economic control over the entire island. Efforts to establish new, Western-style systems of justice and education, along with the appearance of well-organized Christian missionary groups, began to marginalize the position and status of Buddhist monks in the island.

Without the traditional support of the state and facing new competition, several Buddhist monks began to campaign against Christian missionary efforts and for the promotion of Buddhism in Sri Lankan society. In the 1860s, responding to repeated challenges from Christian missionaries to public debates, nearly fifty monks from the different nikayas led by Ven. Mohottivatte Gunananda and Ven. Hikkaduwe Sumangala engaged a group of Sinhala converts to Christianity in a series of debates held at various locations. Moved by Ven. Gunananda's stirring speaking style and vigorous refutation of charges lodged against Buddhism, crowds of five to ten thousand people in the town of Panadura hailed the monks and left the Christians to question their success in converting Buddhists (Malalgoda 1976, 225–227). At the same time, some Buddhists began to publish pamphlets defending their tradition against the criticism of missionaries. Yet the Buddhist response was hindered by the lack of state support for its institutions, including monastic education. Lay Buddhist organizations were called on to assist in promoting the religion, and the efforts to combat the challenges to Buddhism were greatly helped by the timely arrival of Colonel Henry Steele Olcott (1832–1907), an American Civil War veteran and leader of the Theosophical Society. Olcott's work in Ceylon during the 1880s did much to boost the confidence of Sri Lankan Buddhists and helped spur the founding of Buddhist schools to educate children in their native faith.

Around the turn of the twentieth century, aspirations to promote Buddhism in the island were fused with aspirations for independence. The lay Buddhist leader Anagarika Dharmapala (1864–1933), while influenced by Olcott, went further in campaigning to restore Buddhism to what he considered was its rightful place as the official religion of the state. Educated in Christian schools, Dharmapala was exposed to puritan values of discipline, hard work, and thrift, and he embraced such values when he began promoting a reformed version of true Buddhism that celebrated the ethical and psychological roots of the religion as found in its Pali scriptures (Seneviratne 1999, 35–38). Dharmapala's efforts to establish and use true Buddhism as a resource to reform Sinhala society and ready the people for independence from British rule were made chiefly through writings and public speeches. His impact on modern Sri Lankan Buddhism was substantial, as he led the efforts to rid Buddhism of folk superstitions and excessive ritualism, so that its allegedly pure and rationalistic core would be left to discipline and motivate Sinhalas to become morally pure and politically independent as they strived to infuse their daily lives with Buddhist values and precepts. Moreover, his calls for Buddhist monks to lead this spiritual and political revival set the stage for later generations of monks to embrace a mission of political activism (Seneviratne 1999).

By the time Great Britain granted Ceylon its independence in 1948, its inhabitants were left with the unfortunate legacy of a sharply defined ethnic consciousness that drew clear distinctions among Sinhalas, Tamils, and Muslims. Administrative policies reinforced ethnic and religious identities, at times generating resentment that spilled over into riots. The people to whom the departing British handed over political control were a group of Western-educated elites who wished to maintain good relations with Great Britain and continue many of its policies. At the same time, after the British left, the majority Sinhala community felt free to realize its claims and assert its privileges over against the aspirations of the minority Tamil and Muslim communities. These interests reached a peak in the 1956 general election, in which S. W. R. D. Banadaranaike defeated the United National Party, which had inherited power from the British, by winning the support of a broad coalition of village elites, ayurvedic physicians, vernacular teachers, young people with bleak prospects, and monks, all of whom resonated with his more egalitarian message pitched especially to traditional elements in Sinhala society (Manor 1989, 247–252). In the aftermath of this political upheaval, Bandaranaike was pushed to forward the now infamous "Sinhala-only" bill that was designed to privilege the Sinhala language over both English and Tamil in government correspondence. These efforts provoked strong protests from Sri Lankan Tamils. Thereafter, a move to place the Sinhala characters for the word *Sri* on license plates led some militant Tamils to deface the plates and attack cars that bore them (Manor 1989, 266). Ill feelings between extremist groups in both communities increased despite Bandaranaike's attempts to promote social harmony, leading up to a series of communal riots between Sinhalas and Tamils in late May of 1958.

This upsurge of Sinhala nationalism was accompanied by efforts among its proponents to restore Buddhism to what they considered to be its proper place as the favored religion of the majority. Inspired by the recommendations of a 1956 government-sponsored report titled *The Betrayal of Buddhism*, many

Sinhala nationalists campaigned to restore the official state support and protection of Buddhism that had been withdrawn during British rule. Years later, in 1972, a clause was inserted into the country's constitution affirming that Buddhism would have the "foremost place" as the religion of the majority, largely fulfilling the aspirations and objectives that had been expressed by both lay and monastic Sinhala Buddhist nationalists since the 1956 elections (Tambiah 1992, 63). The collective result of the various campaigns to promote Sinhala language, culture, and religion was to alienate the Tamils, the second-largest ethnic group, who were mostly Hindu and had enjoyed certain privileges in the system of communal representation devised under British rule. The onset of a Sinhala-dominated government after independence shifted the equation of power and helped to spark Tamil nationalist groups, some of which agitated for a separate Tamil state in the island.

The Tamil nationalist movement became increasingly militant after 1983, when, in response to the killings of eighteen Sinhala soldiers by Tamil insurgents belonging to the Liberation Tigers of Tamil Eelam (LTTE), riots in Colombo and other towns left as many as two thousand Tamils dead and hundreds of thousands homeless. The riots themselves appear to have been well-organized attacks rather than spontaneous spasms of violence, but they served to polarize the two communities and draw the condemnation of foreign governments. In the meantime, the LTTE moved to consolidate its position as the primary representative of Sri Lankan Tamils by intimidating and sometimes assassinating Tamils who belonged to other political parties. Ever since 1983, the Sinhala-dominated Sri Lankan government has fought a civil war with the guerrilla army organized by the LTTE, a conflict that has been marred by extralegal killings and serious human rights violations on both sides. The impact of the war on the country's economy has been substantial, but it also has colored contemporary expressions of Buddhist nationalism, most notably by causing some monks to advocate war in an effort to preserve the territorial integrity of the state. A fragile cease-fire signed in 2002 has brought some semblance of normalcy to the northern Tamil-dominated areas and southern Sinhala-dominated areas, allowing for the freedom of movement and more money in the forms of investment, foreign aid, and tourism dollars to flow into the island. However, Buddhism in Sri Lanka faces newer challenges from the increased globalization of economic markets and cultural forms, offering more choices but also rendering some familiar customs and traditions obsolete.

Buddhist Nationalism in Sri Lanka

The avowed link between the religion of the Buddha and the nation of Sri Lanka permeates the ways that contemporary Sri Lankan Buddhists think and speak about religious identity. To be sure, the phrase "Buddhist nationalism" is something of a oxymoron to those who feel that the religion as taught by the Buddha stresses the renunciation of worldly attachments and desires. And to those Sri Lankans, any attempt to relate the Buddhist religion to nationalistic interests and ethnic exclusivism is misguided. However, many broad-minded Sri Lankan Buddhists continue to believe that their country has a specifically Buddhist heritage and that their culture has been fundamentally shaped by Buddhist traditions. For all of its problems, the notion of Buddhist nationalism is a useful one to designate the diverse and complex ways that Sri Lankans associate Buddhism with the nation of Sri Lanka and the Sinhala people.

It is preferable, moreover, to view Buddhist nationalism in Sri Lanka as a form of discourse that is polemical in nature. Rather than presuming its existence as a static entity or movement with enduring organizational structures, people more often see Buddhist nationalism as a kind of rhetoric used by those who wish to assert or emphasize the integral relation between Sri Lanka and Buddhism while advancing various political or religious interests. In other words, Buddhist nationalism exists primarily in the language some people use to posit which kinds of persons and practices belong to the nation and which are characterized as different or other (Abeysekara 2002, 172). If we refrain from identifying Buddhist nationalism as a real thing that objectively exists over a long period of time—like government bureaucracy or the armed forces, for example—we can recognize and better understand its primarily discursive and fluid character.

At the broadest level, the association drawn between Buddhism and the Sri Lankan nation is articulated in terms of a heritage (urumaya) that is held to be pervasive and ancient. Significantly, the Sinhala word *urumaya* also has the connotation of ownership, suggesting quite literally that the island belongs first and foremost to Sinhala Buddhists. The idea that the modern nation of Sri Lanka enjoys a specially Buddhist heritage is supported by the existence of countless archaeological sites and an ancient tradition of history writing that chronicles how early kings promoted and defended the Buddha's Dispensation (sasana), or the historical manifestation of the Buddha's teaching in its institutional and ideological forms. Many of these sacred sites are believed to house relics of the Buddha's body or objects he used when he lived in India. An even larger number of sites are ancient monastic dwellings that exist today in various stages of renovation or disrepair. Some relic shrines (dagabas), such as the Ruvanveliseya (Mahathupa) in Anuradhapura, have histories of more than two thousand years and persist today as popular pilgrimage sites. The Sacred Mahabodhi Tree, enshrined in the same city, is another important location where thousands of Buddhists flock to venerate a tree that began as a sapling taken from the Bodhi Tree under which the Buddha obtained his Awakening in India. At numerous other sacred sites in Polonnaruwa, Mahiyangana,

Buddhist pilgrims visiting the ancient Thuparama stupa in Anuradhapura, Sri Lanka. (Courtesy of Stephen C. Berkwitz)

Dambulla, and Kandy, to name just a few, Buddhist monuments with storied pasts are found and visited by pilgrims on a regular basis.

Sri Lanka's Buddhist heritage is a topic frequently explicated in newspaper features and television programs, not to mention the sermons of monks and speeches of Sinhala politicians. As such, the identity of the nation is often defined in terms of a national history that is marked by a huge number of archaeological remains and the narration of significant events in the development of the Buddhist tradition. The latter includes the arrival of Ven. Mahinda to Sri Lanka in the third century BCE, the reunification of the island under King Dutugemunu in the second century BCE, the writing down of the Pali Tipitaka for the first time decades before the start of the common era, and the arrival of the Buddha's Tooth Relic in around the fourth century CE. Sacred sites (pujyabhumis), many of which are attested to in Sri Lanka's Buddhist histories (vamsas), are often the destinations for religious tourists, as many Sri Lankan Buddhists regularly make pilgrimages and family outings to such locations.

These sites also become hosts to large-scale ritual spectacles where television cameras film thousands and sometimes hundreds of thousands of devotees flocking to venerate at a particular temple or relic shrine and participating in

*Buddhist tourists visiting the monumental reclining Buddha image at the Tantirimale
monastery northeast of Anuradhapura, Sri Lanka. (Courtesy of Stephen C. Berkwitz)*

practices believed to earn merit (Berkwitz 2003, 63–64). Usually held on Full
Moon Days (poya) such as Vesak or Poson—which respectively commemorate
in May the birth, Awakening, and death of the Buddha and in June the arrival
of Ven. Mahinda and establishment of Buddhism in Sri Lanka—these ritual
spectacles receive considerable media coverage on television and in newspapers. A recent Poson Full Moon Day was publicly celebrated at religious sites located in Mihintale, Tantirimale, and Somawathie, with different businesses
sponsoring each event and media outlets covering them. Although such events
are rarely intended to be political, they are moments when Sri Lanka's Buddhist heritage is visibly reaffirmed and broadcast throughout the island. Moreover, it is typical for leading Buddhist politicians to appear at these events and
be photographed making offerings (puja) to the relics of the Buddha in public displays of piety.

For Sinhala Buddhists who maintain that Sri Lanka is fundamentally a Buddhist country, pilgrimages and ritual spectacles simply confirm what to them is
an inseparable bond between Buddhism and the nation. Since independence
in 1948, this belief has motivated numerous Buddhist monks to become actively involved in the political affairs of the country. The idea of the "political

monk" has long been controversial, because many lay Buddhists expect their world-renouncing monks to remain detached from the mundane affairs of society. However, spurred by Dharmapala's calls in the early twentieth century for monks to revive the fortunes of Buddhism and the nation, significant numbers of monks—though never a majority—have inserted themselves into political debates and sought out roles as advisers to the country's leaders. The late Ven. Walpola Rahula also played a role in advancing a redefinition of the monk's role away from ritual performance toward social service, which he understood as basically advising the laity on politics and other secular subjects (Seneviratne 1999, 196–200). Ven. Rahula's work Bhikshuvage Urumaya (Heritage of the Bhikkhu), originally published in Sinhala in 1946, attempted to justify monastic political activism by arguing that Buddhist monks had always served as advisers to Sri Lanka's kings and as guardians of Buddhist culture. This important role, he maintained, was interrupted only by the British when they disestablished Buddhism in 1815, severing the state's support of the religion as well as the monk's position of moral leadership in society.

The voices of Dharmapala and Rahula, among others, have inspired several generations of Buddhist monks to participate actively in Sri Lankan politics. Although many more monks continue to remain aloof from the turbulent affairs of nationalist politics, the twentieth century witnessed the rise of monastic participation in political demonstrations, rallies, and special-interest associations (Tambiah 1992, 82). In most cases, these so-called political monks have campaigned for promoting Buddhism, protecting the territorial integrity of the Sri Lankan state, and advancing the welfare of the Sinhala community.

In the 1980s, the Marxist-inspired revolutionary group called the People's Liberation Front (Janatha Vimukthi Peramuna, or JVP) adopted a specifically Buddhist rhetoric calling on young patriots and especially monks to join their cause and overthrow the successive governments of Prime Ministers J. R. Jayawardene and Ranasinghe Premadasa. Thousands of young monks, particularly those studying in the country's universities, were attracted to the cause of liberating the "motherland from all enemies"—including Tamil separatist rebels and the then-current Sri Lankan government (Abeysekara 2002, 220–221). A majority of young JVP monks came to support the JVP in various ways, including drawing posters, writing flyers, organizing rallies, and sometimes even hiding weapons in temples (Abeysekara 2002, 225). The presence of monks in JVP activities was an attempt to give moral legitimacy to the JVP's revolutionary agenda, which included intimidating and assassinating their Sinhala opponents in political, intellectual, and security circles, as well as some senior monks. The response of the Premadasa government in 1989 was equally violent; it mobilized several paramilitary death squads to arrest, detain, torture, and sometimes kill suspected JVP members, including monks. At the same time, the government tried to challenge the group's Buddhist identity, representing JVP members as terrorists who were estranged from authentic Buddhist values and acts (Abeysekara 2002, 231–232).

Generally speaking, Sri Lankan monks who have chosen to get involved in politics renounce violent insurrection, yet they continue to be outspoken critics of any attempt to settle the nation's ethnic crisis by making concessions to the Tamils in the north and east of the island. Monks were among the loudest opponents of the Indo–Sri Lanka Peace Accord in 1987 that brought the Indian army to occupy parts of northern and eastern Sri Lanka in what was a short-lived and ultimately futile attempt to enforce the accord and disarm the LTTE in those regions. Subsequent efforts at brokering a lasting peace agreement between the government and the LTTE have also usually met with resistance from the more nationalist-minded Buddhist monks. Such vocal opposition to peace settlements that involve granting autonomy to the LTTE in the north and east helps to sustain debates over whether monks should be involved in politics. These debates inevitably revolve around the issue of the authentic role of the monk.

Critics of political monks charge them with being the chief obstacles to peace and good governance, inflaming anti-Tamil chauvinism among the populace and tying the hands of Sri Lanka's democratically elected leaders (Tambiah 1992; Seneviratne 1999). At the same time, politically active monks justify their actions by citing past examples of when bhikkhus allegedly participated in the political affairs of the state and by asserting that they, as the custodians of Buddhism, have a duty to ensure that the state continues to protect the religion (Rahula 1974, 20–22). From time to time, laypeople even implore monks to use their powerful voices and condemn perceived political injustices and corruption. Arguments from both sides of the controversy occasionally spill over into newspaper columns and public speeches, reinvigorating the debate over the proper role of a monk in society. Furthermore, the Sangha itself is often divided on this question. Some monks quietly condemn the political activity of their coreligionists, while others strive to organize the monks into political associations and collectively denounce efforts to reach a political settlement with the LTTE (C. R. De Silva and Bartholomeusz 2001, 8–10, 18–19).

At the beginning of the twenty-first century, the voice of one politically concerned monk has become particularly influential in contemporary Sri Lanka. Ven. Gangodawila Soma (1948–2003), a skilled preacher who belonged to a suburban Colombo temple that is renowned for its monastic discipline, employed a variety of means such as public sermons, newspaper articles, pamphlets, and television programs to broadcast his call for religious and political reform in Sri Lanka (Berkwitz 2003, 67). His persistent and often pointed critiques of immoral conduct among Sinhala Buddhists and Sri Lankan politicians, as well as his condemnations of evangelical Christian missionaries and nongovernmental organizations (NGOs), were thus carried to the general

A large statue set up in suburban Colombo, Sri Lanka, to honor the well-known monk Ven. Gangodawila Soma after his death in December 2003. (Courtesy of Stephen C. Berkwitz)

public through a variety of media, and he has had an influence shaping the views and opinions of many Sinhala Buddhists.

After returning from several years in Australia, where he established a Buddhist temple in Victoria, Ven. Soma began efforts to educate Sinhala Buddhists about true Buddhism and to criticize the Sri Lankan government's failure to promote Buddhist morality and institutions in the country. His untimely death—rumored by some to have been an assassination rather a heart attack as officially reported—has made him into something of a hero and a martyr for Sinhala-Buddhist nationalist causes. He received a state funeral that was televised live and, according to newspaper reports, brought out unprecedented crowds in the hundreds of thousands who lined the twelve-mile route of his funeral cortege from the Sri Vajiraramaya Dharmayatanaya Temple in Maharagama all the way to Independence Square in the heart of Colombo. His followers and sympathizers continue to buy his books and watch rebroadcasts of his television program Nena Pahana (The Lamp of Knowledge), and many have displayed pictures of Ven. Soma in their homes, shops, and vehicles.

Ven. Soma's version of Buddhist nationalism advances calls for religious, political, and cultural reform grounded in traditional Buddhist values. While the influences of earlier figures like Dharmapala and Rahula are clearly evident in his writings and sermons, the particular rhetoric he used was more distinctive for reflecting contemporary unease about Tamil separatism, population growth rates, and globalization. According to him, the current condition and future outlook for Sri Lanka are bleak, and immoral politicians, not political monks, are to blame for the widespread lack of security and economic misfortune that Sri Lankans experience today. Ven. Soma frequently warned that greedy leaders attempt only to expand their power and incomes, sacrificing the welfare of Sinhala Buddhists as a result. Claiming that it was the British colonialists who first tried to promote bad conduct such as drinking alcohol among Sinhala Buddhists, he went on to argue that the country's leaders are continuing this trend by promoting liquor shops and smoking for the sake of lining their pockets and increasing tax revenues (Soma 2004, 5). According to Ven. Soma, moreover, these aims complement the goal of the growing numbers of evangelical Christian missionary organizations, which, he claimed, encourage immoral conduct such as drinking to make people poor, and then offer them bribes of money and jobs to make them convert to Christianity (Munasinghe 2004, 28–29).

The highly cynical view Ven. Soma took of his country's politicians and foreign missionaries formed the backdrop of his strong call to demolish the "false views" that he claimed many Sinhala Buddhists hold. Drawing on an impressive knowledge of Buddhist literature, Ven. Soma argued that Buddhism is not a religion of blind faith, and that the belief in the efficacy of praying to Hindu deities for assistance is wholly contrary to the Buddha's teachings (Soma 2002, 64–67). He blamed "crafty businessmen" and some monks for promoting the worship of Hindu deities at Buddhist temples in Sri Lanka, as this could be highly profitable, but at the cost of causing simple Buddhists to spend considerable sums of money on offerings to the gods. His later sermons at times reflected the biting sarcasm of cultural critique, while at other times they contained dire warnings about the impending disappearance of Buddhism and the Sinhala race from Sri Lanka. According to him, Sinhala families were not having enough children compared with Muslims and Tamils, and this was because the rampant immorality of many Sinhala Buddhists make them crave alcohol and cigarettes more than children (Munasinghe 2004, 41). Ven. Soma lamented the current state of Buddhism, the country of Sri Lanka, and the Sinhala nation. To him, their fortunes are intimately linked and are therefore threatened by the moves to grant a Tamil autonomous region in the north and east, the worship of Hindu deities, the conversions of Buddhists to evangelical Protestantism, and the spiraling cost of financing a national debt to foreign donors.

Like Dharmapala before him, Ven. Soma looked to virtuous monks to help lead the country out of its current problems. The country's leaders, he claimed, were corrupted by greed and a lust for power. Only monks who care nothing for themselves can care enough for the country to guide it toward future development and prosperity. Thus, near the end of his life, Ven. Soma began advocating for monks to enter politics in order to purify what he described as a political "mudhole" (Munasinghe 2004, 48). Although he made some initial steps toward forming a new political party and even openly entertained the idea of running for president, his sudden death prevented him from following up on his activist program.

The reasons for Ven. Soma's great popularity among Sinhala Buddhists can perhaps be traced to his uncompromising critique of corrupt political and business elites, his learned and entertaining oratory on true Buddhism, his advocacy on behalf of ordinary Sinhala Buddhists, and the identity he cultivated as a virtuous monk who spent time meditating in forests and wandering across the country receiving alms and delivering sermons to poor villagers (Sumanasekara 2003, 15–20). While Ven. Soma drew on a broad base of Buddhist nationalist influences, including Dharmapala, earlier generations of political monks, the Jathika Chinthaya (National Thought) movement of Sinhala nationalist authors, and other extreme Sinhala nationalist groups, he expanded and updated his message to appeal to a wider group of people. Not all of his admirers and supporters condone everything he said, as his exclusivist stance against Tamils and Muslims and his incipient campaign to have monks enter politics were controversial. But the many roles he embraced—learned and virtuous Buddhist monk, ardent defender of Sinhala nationalism, fearless cultural critic, and so on—have enabled, in turn, huge numbers of Sri Lankans to embrace Ven. Soma as a heroic voice who roused the country out of its slumber and motivated Buddhists to practice and protect their religion.

One of the legacies of Ven. Soma has been the formation of a new political party called the Jathika Hela Urumaya (JHU), or the National Sinhala Heritage Party, which is led by Buddhist monks. Initially sponsored by members of a moribund Sinhala nationalist party called Sihala Urumaya and supported by significant numbers of female lay devotees (upasikas) and university lecturers in and around Colombo, the JHU was established in the wake of Ven. Soma's funeral and just three months before scheduled parliamentary elections in April 2004 (Deegalle 2004, 88–89). Ven. Soma's unrelenting critiques of Sri Lankan politics and his suggestion that only monks can fix the country's problems helped pave the way for the genesis of the JHU. Although a monk had earlier been elected as a member of parliament representing the socialist Sama Samaja Party in 2001, the JHU campaign of 2004 put a list of 280 monks forward as possible candidates for parliamentary elections on a platform to protect the majority Sinhala community, oppose a federal solution to the civil war, and rid the country of corruption (Beck 2004). This virtually unprecedented entry of monks into national elections caught observers by surprise when the monks managed to win nine seats, instantly becoming a critical power bloc in a divided parliament. The JHU monks have also quickly become a lightning rod for renewed debates over the proper roles and conduct for Buddhist monks.

The leading monks who formed the JHU, namely Ven. Ellawala Medhananda, Ven. Aturaliye Ratana, Ven. Omalpe Sobhita, and Ven. Uduwe Dhammaloka, are all skilled speakers who come from different ordination lineages. Their speeches and statements are widely covered by the media, giving them a more powerful platform from which to advance their party's interests. Among the priority issues for the JHU is an anticonversion bill that threatens punishments for people who use unethical means to convert Sri Lankans to other religions. Vigorously opposed by numerous Christian organizations, the JHU bill and a similar bill forwarded by the ruling party are supposedly designed to prevent evangelical groups from using bribes and intimidation to convert Buddhists, Hindus, Muslims, and mainstream Christians to nonindigenous faiths. The JHU is also publicly rejecting plans to grant an Interim Self-Governing Administration over the northern and eastern provinces to the LTTE in the name of obtaining a peaceful settlement to the civil war. JHU monks have also called for ending the slaughter of cattle and have denounced the privileges and luxuries awarded to cabinet officials and ministers of the government.

In the early period of its existence, the JHU has struggled to maintain its independent image of not being beholden to one or another political party. While the two chief parties engage themselves in attempts to win over a majority in parliament, the JHU monks have come under intense pressure either to support President Chandrika Kumaratunga's government or to work against it as part of the opposition. The defection of two JHU parliamentarians to the government precipitated a political crisis in early June 2004, when attempts to replace them with members of parliament (MPs) loyal to the party sparked fisticuffs on the floor of parliament and an ugly shoving match between rival MPs, with some monks caught in the middle (Abeywardena and Wijewardena 2004). In the immediate aftermath of this crisis, a flood of newspaper editorials, opinion columns, and television commentaries debated whether the ruling-coalition MPs mistreated the clergy or whether monks belong in political office. The failure in party discipline that provoked this crisis reflects a serious problem for the JHU, and the party may eventually implode if various monks pursue conflicting aims while in office. Another indication of the threat that internal dissension poses for the JHU came in late 2005 after Ven. Dhammaloka broke from the party to proclaim his support publicly for the opposition presidential candidate. This event led the remaining JHU monks to expel Dhammaloka from the party and accuse him of accepting bribes.

Ven. Medhananda, a party leader and a scholar of archaeology, has claimed that he will happily leave the parliament once the party has achieved its goals and developed lay politicians to take the place of the monks (personal interview, July 18, 2004). According to him, the heritage of Sinhala Buddhists—which he interprets broadly to include all aspects of the religion, culture, language, and land that have come down through the generations to the Sinhalas—is under threat of destruction by negligent politicians, evangelical missionaries, and Tamil separatists. As a consequence, he decided to enter the parliament to address these problems on behalf of Sinhala Buddhists and for the sake of preserving the ancient archaeological sites in the north and east of the island. However, it is entirely possible that not all of the JHU monks will be so willing to leave office. Were this to occur, the JHU may not survive as a viable political party if voters begin to view its members as selfishly seeking power and political spoils.

In the wake of the devastating tsunami disaster of December 26, 2004, the JHU was reenergized by the focus given to its signature issues. Reports of Christian relief organizations proselytizing while distributing disaster aid in the island renewed calls from the JHU monks and others to get the Sri Lankan government to legally prohibit conversion efforts by evangelical Christian groups. In addition, efforts in 2005 to resolve the dispute between the government and the LTTE over the distribution of aid in the Tiger-controlled northeast also enabled the JHU to take a prominent and fairly popular stand against the government's plan to entrust the Tiger rebels with the relief aid for the region. The JHU monks, along with other nationalists, feared that this action would form the first step to establishing an independent Tamil state. Ven. Sobhita, a JHU MP, went on a six-day fast to the death without food or liquids before President Kumaratunga agreed to consult the monks before deciding on plans to distribute aid to the Tigers. In the intervening period, scores of monks, many of them affiliated with the JHU, held protests in Colombo and Kandy, blockading roads and calling on businesses to close in support of Ven. Sobhita's hunger strike. As these incidents show, external events can sometimes lead to opportunities for the JHU monks to unite and rally around causes that evoke sympathy from among large numbers of Sinhalas.

Women's Roles in Sri Lankan Buddhism

Another area of public debate over Buddhism in Sri Lanka is found in discourses and practices related to the position of women in Theravada Buddhism. Competing representations and expressions of women's roles in Buddhism often hinge on ideas about the authentic Theravada tradition, democratic notions of female participation in society, and enduring gender

stereotypes in Sinhala culture. While Sri Lankan women like to think of themselves as comparatively better off than their Hindu counterparts due to the
Buddha's universalist message of human morality and the individual potential
for Awakening, few women enjoy complete equality with men in terms of authority and leadership roles in either the Sangha or the lay community. However, generally speaking, female Buddhists in Sri Lanka enjoy the reputation of
being more frequent visitors than men to Buddhist temples and more eager
donors to the Buddha and the Sangha. These female lay devotees (upasikas)
are instantly recognizable by their white sarees or skirts and blouses, and they
contribute an immense amount in the material support and volunteerism that
enable temples to function. One also finds large numbers of female meditators,
Buddhist "Sunday school" teachers, and authors of scholarly and popular
books on Buddhism.

Scholarship on women in Sri Lankan Buddhism has tended to focus on the
ambiguous position of female renunciants in modern Sri Lanka. Sri Lankan
Buddhist women in ancient times could opt to renounce the world and become a bhikkhuni, which is the Pali term for a female monastic. These
bhikkhunis, or nuns, adopted code of monastic conduct similar to that for
monks, shaving their heads and wearing orange robes. However, they had to
follow even more rules that made them institutionally subordinate and required to honor monks, no matter their age or experience (Harris 1999, 57).
According to the Theravada Buddhist tradition as codified in the Vinaya, an aspiring bhikkhuni must be ordained in the presence of higher-ordained
bhikkhunis. This was established after the Buddha himself ordained his stepmother, Mahaprajapati, and numerous other women who sought to renounce
the world and attain nirvana in ancient India. The bhikkhuni order was
brought to Sri Lanka and established there by Ven. Sanghamitta, an accomplished female renunciant and daughter of the renowned King Asoka in the
third century BCE. For several centuries, the bhikkhuni order grew and flourished in ancient Sri Lanka. However, due to historical circumstances not completely understood, the lineage of Theravada bhikkhunis died out in Sri Lanka
around the eleventh century and in other Theravada countries in Southeast
Asia shortly thereafter. Although the Theravada monastic lineage has been periodically revived through the assistance of monks from other countries, the
lineage of nuns was not resuscitated in Sri Lanka.

As a result of the extinction of the Theravada bhikkhuni order, Buddhist
women in Sri Lanka could not legitimately pursue a monastic path. This was
the case until the late nineteenth century, when a growing movement of anticolonial Buddhist revivalism supported the reestablishment of female renunciants to help teach Sinhala youth about Buddhism (Bartholomeusz 1994,
45–52). Although these local and foreign women were trained in Buddhist
thought and practice, they were unable to be fully ordained as bhikkhunis due

Newly ordained Buddhist nuns leaving the Dambulla Golden Temple in Sri Lanka. A sacred pilgrimage site for 22 centuries, this cave monastery, with its 5 sanctuaries, is the largest, best-preserved cave-temple complex in Sri Lanka. The Buddhist mural paintings (covering an area of 2,100 square meters) are of particular importance, as are the 157 statues. (Courtesy of Stephen C. Berkwitz)

to the absence of any existing bhikkhunis in the Theravada tradition. Instead, they became known as Ten-Precept Mothers (dasa sil mata) who renounce marriage and observe the traditional Ten Precepts on a permanent basis. This newer, marginal status exists between the more established identities of upasika and bhikkhuni; and thus, such women embrace the somewhat paradoxical identity of "lay nun" in Sri Lankan society. Buddhist devotees tend to recognize and respect them for their austere, religious lifestyles, but the fact that they have not been fully ordained also serves to make them less attractive recipients for alms given by lay devotees seeking merit. Furthermore, limits on the religious educations made available to Buddhist nuns in recent decades have meant that the majority of female renunciants in Sri Lanka have not received a thorough training in Buddhist thought and literature; instead, they have gravitated to more meditative and social activities (Salgado 1996, 67–68).

Recently, however, there have been several attempts to reinstitute the higher ordination ceremony for bhikkhunis in the Theravada tradition. In 1988, several women were ordained in an upasampada (higher ordination) ceremony in Los Angeles before some Sri Lankan monks and bhikkhunis from Taiwan. Since the nuns belonged to a Mahayana tradition, however, these ordinees were generally not recognized as bhikkhunis in Sri Lanka (Bhadra 2001, 25). The refusal to recognize the validity of the 1988 upasampada occurred despite the fact that Chinese historical records testify to establishment of a bhikkhuni order in China by Sri Lankan nuns in 434 CE. Then, in 1996, several Sri Lankan Ten-Precept Mothers were ordained in another bhikkhuni upasampada ceremony conducted by Korean monks and nuns in Sarnath, India. Again, since this ceremony was led by monastics in the Mahayana tradition, there was considerable protest and opposition to this event in Sri Lanka. Nevertheless, the debate that sprang up as a result of that ceremony led a number of female renunciants and senior monks to begin plans to reintroduce a Theravada bhikkhuni upasampada in Sri Lanka.

Ven. Inamaluwe Sumangala, abbot of the Dambulla Golden Temple, was selected to lead the organization formed to support the bhikkhuni ordination, and he donated a building to serve as a training institute for aspiring Buddhist nuns (Bhadra 2001, 26). Ven. Sumangala, who in the 1980s broke away from the Siyam Nikaya order to form a new ordination lineage that explicitly rejects caste as a criterion for ordination, has been active in public debates over what constitutes the authentic Theravada tradition of Sri Lanka (Abeysekara 2002, 182–184, 196–197). His leadership in the restoration of a Theravada bhikkhuni order and its recognition by at least some members of the Sri Lankan Sangha may be part of a broader agenda to reform the local Theravada tradition. In 1998, he welcomed Sri Lankan nuns ordained in a ceremony at Bodh Gaya, India, in the presence of monastics from Taiwan and monks from Sri Lanka. These bhikkhunis, in turn, conferred the upasampada on several female novices on March 12, 1998, thereby reestablishing the Theravada bhikkhuni order in Sri Lanka (Bhadra 2001, 27).

Since that event, the Dambulla Temple has held several higher ordination ceremonies, as well as ceremonies to ordain women as novices (samaneri). Although many Sri Lankan monks still oppose this effort and denounce it as illegitimate, the bhikkhunis of Sri Lanka have numerous lay and monastic supporters. Their numbers are still relatively small, as the avenues for training as a bhikkhuni are extremely limited. Some recent scholarship has found that many Ten-Precept Mothers were not interested in being ordained as bhikkhunis, since this process would subordinate them to the monks of the Sangha and impose constraints on the autonomy and power they enjoy as renunciants who are not bound either to husbands or parents (Bartholomeusz 1994, 136–137). However, now that an indigenous Theravada upasampada tradition exists for women in Sri Lanka, it is likely that a steady stream of female novices will continue to join the bhikkhuni order and become full-fledged Theravada nuns.

And although these ceremonies are not accepted as valid by all Buddhists, they do serve to raise the status of female renunciants in the eyes of many Sri Lankans.

Social Activism in Sri Lankan Buddhism

Spurred in part by the critiques of earlier Christian missionaries, who denounced the Buddhist ideals of withdrawing from society to pursue individual liberation, increasing numbers of Sri Lankan Buddhists have made efforts to link social welfare projects with religious practice. Moreover, the realities of civil war, rural poverty, environmental destruction and pollution, drug addiction, and constraints on government assistance in contemporary Sri Lanka have presented people with ample opportunities to apply Buddhist values of compassion, generosity, and loving-kindness to alleviate poverty and other forms of suffering. Buddhist temples were once the traditional centers offering education and medicine to nearby villagers. But many of the social roles once ascribed to Sri Lankan monks were stripped away after the disestablishment of Buddhism at the hands of the British colonialists and the subsequent creation of missionary schools and a Western-style government that gradually brought the various social, economic, and health-related needs of society under the control of the secular state (cf. Asad 2003, 190–191). The social and political changes ushered in by colonialism effectively weakened the position of Buddhist monks in Sri Lanka, as the laity became accustomed to turning to government agencies for assistance and the governors did not have to seek the advice of the Sangha to devise and implement state policies.

In response, Dharmapala and other nationalists who opposed colonial rule sought to reclaim some of the influence of the monks in everyday life. Although Dharmapala likely exaggerated the social role of the monk in traditional Sri Lankan society, he advocated giving monks the role of instructing people in moral virtues, good habits, and skills in agriculture, crafts, and commerce to uplift Sinhala society (Seneviratne 1999, 27–32). Such efforts to expand the influence of monks appealed both to those seeking to revive the influence of Buddhism in the island and those seeking to provide social welfare to people in need. In the 1930s, rural development movements spearheaded by monks such as Kalukondayave Pannasekhara aimed to improve the living conditions in Sri Lankan villages by founding societies that would promote rural education, health centers, crime eradication, and temperance, among other societal benefits (Seneviratne 1999, 73–75, 124–127). Such efforts to direct Buddhist values and resources toward social welfare have continued up to the present day.

One of the oldest and best-known examples of social activism inspired by Buddhism in Sri Lanka is the Sarvodaya Movement, which has worked in the areas of rural and spiritual development since 1958. Founded by a Buddhist lay-man named A. T. Ariyaratne, Sarvodaya has grown into the largest local NGO working in Sri Lanka today. Maintaining that a social and spiritual infrastruc-ture is needed for launching successful economic development activities, Sar-vodaya combines social, economic, and technological empowerment activities to regenerate village life (Bond 2004, 61). Combining Gandhian ideals of spir-itual and economic development through village-based service with Buddhist notions of spiritual Awakening and the alleviation of suffering through reduc-ing egoistic desire, the Sarvodaya Movement has emphasized the idea of self-realization through voluntary labor for the benefit of others. Thus, in Sri Lanka, the meaning of the Gandhian term *sarvodaya* is changed from "the wel-fare of all" to "the Awakening of all," suggesting that service to society is a vi-able path toward spiritual enlightenment.

Today, Sarvodaya represents a diversified organization with a central head-quarters located in Moratuwa, 34 district centers, and 345 divisional centers es-tablished throughout the island (*Sarvodaya Annual Service Report* 2003, 3). Funded in part by foreign donor organizations, it is involved in a variety of de-velopment programs including teacher training, volunteer training, health clinics, children's camps, shramadana (voluntary labor) camps, relief assis-tance, technology training, village banks, and biodiversity programs, as well as the construction of homes, wells, and latrines. Sarvodaya's development proj-ects have been instituted throughout the island, even in the war-torn northern and eastern provinces, and are made available to all communities irrespective of religious affiliation. The organization has made efforts to incorporate mi-nority Tamils and Muslims into its training and labor activities with modest suc-cess, although the organization has long been dominated by Sinhala Buddhists and continues to be perceived as a Buddhist organization (Kantowsky 1980, 144–146; Bond 2004, 98–101). The recent, albeit fragile, cease-fire between the government and the LTTE has allowed Sarvodaya to expand its development work in the north and east; it has received additional funds to launch new re-lief, rehabilitation, and reconstruction efforts that would allow persons dis-placed by war to rebuild homes and develop a sustainable form of livelihood (*Sarvodaya Annual Service Report* 2003, 38–39). And following the tsunami that battered and swept away miles of coastline on December 26, 2004, Sarvodaya assumed a leading role in disaster relief, partnering with international relief agencies to distribute aid and assisting in managing refugee camps set up after tens of thousands of Sri Lankans lost their homes.

Again, the manifold service activities sponsored by Sarvodaya are designed to have both practical and spiritual benefits. Development work is under-stood as leading to the personal realization of the Four Divine Abidings (brahmaviharas)—namely, loving-kindness, compassion, sympathetic joy, and equanimity (Bond 2004, 18). The selfless donation of voluntary service to provide others with material needs and comforts affords Sarvodaya volunteers with the opportunity to develop and reflect on ethical virtues. And the spiritual growth that is rooted in service and labor offered freely to others is held to inaugurate the Awakening of whole villages and societies as well. Sarvodaya activities are designed to be carried out together by volunteers and resident villagers in a spirit of mutual generosity, kindness, usefulness, and equality, offering all participants the chance to cooperate in the building of a community founded on Buddhist ideals (Bond 2004, 19). Local development projects undertaken largely by residents under the guidance of Sarvodaya officials are supposed to be a means by which people can begin to extricate themselves from the harmful influences of capitalist economics and its concordant emphasis on greed, competition, and inequality. Instead, the focus given to selfless service and ethical development in Sarvodaya projects should ideally result in a more harmonious community that values cooperation and mutual concern.

The spiritual framework for Sarvodaya is guided largely by Buddhist thought, despite the organization's ecumenical ethos and inclusive attitudes toward other religions. Sarvodaya maintains that the values of compassion and loving-kindness can be found in all religions, and it welcomes the participation of Hindus, Christians, and Muslims, even incorporating rites from these traditions on occasion (Bond 2004, 13–14). Nevertheless, Sarvodaya's debt to Buddhist thought and attention to Buddhist institutions are clearly evident. Buddhist ideas of interdependence and freedom from suffering are among the cornerstones for the movement's work. It has been said, moreover, that Sarvodaya's programs are instruments through which participants develop an insight into the nature of reality and reduce the craving and suffering in themselves while working to reduce the suffering of others (Kantowsky 1980, 43–44). More concretely, Sarvodaya recently supplied a temple with a Buddha image and built a monastery and a shrine room for a village in the southern Matara district (*Sarvodaya Annual Service Report* 2003, 19). Sarvodaya also instituted a bhikkhu training center in 1974 to train monks to become facilitators in village development efforts. According to observers, this effort has had only limited success (Bond 2004, 25). Recently, however, Sarvodaya reactivated its Bhikkhu Services Program and held meetings to discuss challenges and encourage monks to lead development projects (*Sarvodaya Annual Service Report* 2003, 72–73).

In addition, Sarvodaya has drawn on Buddhist values and practices for the inauguration of its Peace Action Plan. Responding to the many years of civil war and ethnic disharmony in Sri Lanka, Sarvodaya has resolved to promote peace among the island's communities. This peace plan has been instituted independently by Sarvodaya, and the movement hopes to employ peace meditation programs to foster reconciliation and national unity, as well as to create a culture where violence is unacceptable and unthinkable (Bond 2004, 41).

One of the main techniques to realize peace is the movement's sponsorship of large-scale peace meditations (sama samadhi), where people gather at a public site and meditate for peace. Often accompanied by protest marches, these peace demonstrations have attracted hundreds, thousands, and sometimes hundreds of thousands of participants who wish to see an end to the violence and conflict in their country. The first peace meditation was held in Colombo in August 1999 and was followed up by other sama samadhi in other regions (Bond 2004, 40–41). In August 2002, a peace meditation held near the Temple of the Tooth in Kandy was disrupted by right-wing nationalists who objected to the group's calls for a peaceful settlement between the government and the LTTE (Bond 2004, 97–98). In the same month, however, Sarvodaya staged a peace meditation in front of a Hindu temple in Jaffna accompanied by religious leaders from all faiths (*Sarvodaya Annual Service Report* 2003, 65–66). Sarvodaya plans to continue these peace demonstrations and work to realize peace through other methods such as workshops on conflict resolution, language instruction, and exchange programs between members of Sinhala and Tamil villages.

Critics of Sarvodaya point out that the movement's origins are in the Buddhist revival of the 1950s and that it draws liberally from the nostalgic vision of traditional Buddhist village life that has been promoted as an alternative to Westernization. Efforts to launch a village-based social revolution of values and economic empowerment strikes some as utopian and reflecting a bourgeois fantasy of village life that is supposedly free from strife and exploitation (Gombrich and Obeyesekere 1988, 250–251). Indeed, at a time when Sri Lankans find themselves ever more dependent on global markets, tourism, and trade, it may be unrealistic to imagine that a revival of self-sufficient villages holds the key to national economic development. Furthermore, with respect to the Bhikkhu Services Program, there are real tensions found in efforts to train monks to be community development leaders. In the Theravada tradition, the monk who is most detached from the world is generally seen as the most virtuous, but monks who engage in social and economic activity may be seen as compromising the ideals of the tradition (Gombrich and Obeyesekere 1988, 254–255). On a practical level, the many divisional centers and the huge number of local projects cannot all be equally efficient and successful, and the movement employs a complex bureaucratic system and terminology to run its islandwide programs. Nevertheless, with such great ambitions, it is noteworthy that Sarvodaya still achieves significant accomplishments despite the tremendous challenges and obstacles it faces while undertaking development and empowerment projects.

If the Sarvodaya movement is the best-known example of Buddhist social activism in Sri Lanka, it is probably because other efforts are dwarfed by Sarvodaya's size and because of the foreign interest Sarvodaya receives. There are other, less visible examples of engaged Buddhism in Sri Lanka, wherein monastics and laypersons engage in social and animal welfare projects out of their commitments to Buddhist virtues of generosity and loving-kindness. One example is Ven. Kalyanatissa, the chief resident of the Etambagaskada Temple, who looks after eighty-two orphans aged one to seventeen in his rural temple located north of Vavuniya in a war-torn area (Hettiarachchi 2004). Twenty children are Tamils, and most of the children have been orphaned by the war. Ven. Kalyanatissa keeps the children with him in his monastery, arranges for them to be fed, and bathes each of the younger children by hand. A nearby army camp supplies him with rice, clothes, and books for the children, and the monk's mother does the cooking. The monk sends the children to local schools each day and checks their work to make sure they are learning. In addition, he teaches the older children job skills such as brick making so that they can earn a living for themselves as adults. Ven. Kalyanatissa carries out this work without foreign assistance and without much public recognition, but he is one example of the small-scale Buddhist social activism found in Sri Lanka today.

It is also true that many ordinary Sri Lankan Buddhists involve themselves in small-scale efforts to alleviate the poverty and hunger of their neighbors and take steps to promote animal welfare and environmental health. On major poya days such as Vesak and Poson, it is common for Buddhist laypersons to go house to house collecting donations of food for the malnourished. Groups of people often band together to make donations of food, clothing, and money to orphanages, government hospitals, and homes for the elderly. Some Buddhists choose to perform an abhayadana, whereby they collect money and buy animals otherwise destined for slaughter. Translated literally as "gift of the freedom from fear," abhayadanas are widely understood to be humane acts of merit to bestow the gift of life on cows who would otherwise be killed and eaten. While such acts do not directly work to close slaughterhouses or improve conditions for animals, they do promote an awareness of and respect for the First Buddhist Precept against taking life. Such acts, moreover, can support other forms of animal welfare activity and encourage vegetarianism among Buddhists who are otherwise not required to adopt this diet.

Conclusion

Many Sri Lankan Buddhists have neither the time nor the inclination to become involved in special Buddhist societies or movements, to join protest marches in support of protecting Buddhism or promoting peace, to become ordained as a monk or a nun, and to donate their labor for rural development. Instead, most Buddhists are more likely to devote themselves to regular or occasional practices associated with earning merit and moral development. Contemporary Sri Lankan Buddhism is marked largely by people giving danas (almsgiving) to monks and people in need; listening to sermons and pirit (protective verses); chanting; and offering puja (offerings) to relic shrines, bodhi trees, and images of the Buddha. These activities can often be done with a minimum of advance planning and expense, and they are fairly accessible methods for doing meritorious deeds in the hope of receiving good fortune in this life as well as good rebirths and nirvana in the future. Buddhists who elect to observe the monthly poya day—or at least the major Full Moon Days—often give dana, listen to sermons, and offer puja on those occasions. A smaller but growing number of Buddhists may also practice vipassana (insight) meditation, either at temples under the instruction of monks or at meditation centers under lay teachers (Bond 1988, 196–198). To develop insight into the impermanent, conditioned factors of one's body is seen to be conducive to spiritual growth and progress toward nirvana, and such practice is universally esteemed if still not widely practiced.

Alongside these forms of everyday Buddhist practice are debates and discussions over what constitutes true Buddhism in Sri Lanka and over what people should do to preserve it. Many Sri Lankan Buddhists combine concerns for their own religious practice and the well-being of themselves and their loved ones with concerns for promoting the vitality of their tradition. Many Sri Lankans accept the statement presented in the sixth-century Mahavamsa (The Great Chronicle) that Sri Lanka is the land that illuminates the Dharma as originally taught by the Buddha (Buddhadatta 1959, ch. I, v. 20). Thus, there is considerable sentiment behind efforts to protect Buddhism from its perceived threats, whether internal threats such as Tamil separatists or external ones such as Western cultural influences. While the LTTE continues to be frequently condemned by Buddhist nationalists as a threat to both the integrity of Sri Lanka and the survival of Buddhism, other factors are deemed hostile to Buddhist interests, factors that represent a perceived conflict between external forces of modernity and local traditions.

Recently, Sri Lankan Buddhist leaders have led public protests against Western attempts to make commercial profits off of images of the Buddha. Sensitive to unflattering and insulting uses of the Buddha's image in Western culture, Sri Lankans have shown an ability to mobilize and vocally express their outrage over what they consider to be the degradation of the founder of their religion. When photos of Victoria's Secret Ltd. bikinis with the face of a Buddha over the crotch area were published in local newspapers, the Buddhist community and monastic organizations pressured Sri Lankan politicians to lodge formal protests against the manufacturer. The manufacturer issued a formal apology and pulled the bikini from its catalog and Web site as a result. In a similar case, after promotional posters for the U.S. film *Hollywood Buddha* were published showing the director sitting on the head of a Buddha image, Buddhists in Sri

Lanka (and Thailand) lodged formal protests against the film. Hundreds of monks protested outside the U.S. Embassy in Colombo, demanding that the release of the film be canceled (BBC News 2004). Although this effort to have the film banned did not succeed, Buddhist activists and politicians did win an apology from the director and the withdrawal of the offensive advertisement. Such incidents occur regularly due to the ease with which images and advertisements are transmitted electronically from the West to Sri Lanka, and they serve as flashpoints that trigger the anger and resolve of Sri Lankan Buddhists to protect the dignity of their religion.

These isolated cases of Western disrespect for Buddhism often serve to unite the Sri Lankan Buddhist community in protest, but they also mask—at least temporarily—substantial differences and disagreements among Sri Lankans over the correct form of Buddhist thought and practice. Where there is unity in the resolve to practice and protect Theravada Buddhism, there are also debates over issues such as the worship of Hindu deities by Buddhists, monks serving as members of parliament, the ordination of bhikkhunis, the restoration of ancient Buddhist sites, and appropriate forms of almsgiving to monks. Despite claims to the contrary, contemporary Sri Lankan Buddhism is a varied phenomenon characterized by a diversity of ritual practices and lively debates over what constitutes true Buddhism. The close relationship posited between Buddhism and the historical and cultural heritage of the Sinhala people results in frequent references to Sri Lanka as a Buddhist country and a strong desire to preserve the religion alongside the Sinhala community's vision of its traditional customs and ancient heritage. An individual's practice of Buddhism, however imagined and carried out, takes place in this context where Sri Lankans accept the responsibility for preserving the correct form of the Buddha's religion in the face of the island's political instability, the globalization of Western cultural and economic forms, and internal disputes over what Buddhism truly is and how it is correctly practiced.

References

Abeysekara, Ananda. 2002. *Colors of the Robe: Religion, Identity, and Difference.* Columbia: University of South Carolina Press.

Abeywardena, Kesara, and Sajeewan Wijewardena. 2004. MPs in Maul and Mayhem. *Daily Mirror,* June 9.

Asad, Talal. 2003. *Formations of the Secular: Christianity, Islam, Modernity.* Stanford, CA: Stanford University Press.

Bartholomeusz, Tessa J. 1994. *Women under the Bo Tree: Buddhist Nuns in Sri Lanka.* Cambridge, UK: Cambridge University Press.

BBC News. 2004. "Degrading" Film Angers Buddhists. http://news.bbc.co.uk/go/pr/fr/-/2/hi/south_asia/3651684.stm, September 13.

Beck, Lindsay. 2004. Monks Set to Steal Protest Vote in Sri Lanka Poll. *Reuters,* March 29.

Berkwitz, Stephen C. 2003. Recent Trends in Sri Lankan Buddhism. *Religion* 33(1):57–71.

Bhadra, Ven. Bhikkhuni. 2001. *Higher Ordination and Bhikkhuni Order in Sri Lanka.* Dehiwala, Sri Lanka: Sridevi Printers.

Bond, George D. 1988. *The Buddhist Revival in Sri Lanka: Religious Tradition, Reinterpretation and Response.* Columbia: University of South Carolina Press.

———. 2004. *Buddhism at Work: Community Development, Social Empowerment and the Sarvodaya Movement.* Bloomfield, CT: Kumarian Press.

Buddhadatta, Ven. A. P., ed. 1959. *The Mahavansa: Pali Text Together with Some Later Additions.* Colombo, Sri Lanka: M. D. Gunasena.

Buddhist Committee of Inquiry. 1956. *The Betrayal of Buddhism: An Abridged Version of the Buddhist Committee of Inquiry.* Balangoda, Sri Lanka: Dharmavijaya Press.

Deegalle, Mahinda. 2004. Politics of the Jathika Hela Urumaya Monks: Buddhism and Ethnicity in Contemporary Sri Lanka. *Contemporary Buddhism* 5(2):83–103.

De Silva, C. R., and T. Bartholomeusz. 2001. *The Role of the Sangha in the Reconciliation Process.* Monograph no. 16. Colombo, Sri Lanka: Marga Institute.

De Silva, K. M. 1981. *A History of Sri Lanka.* Berkeley and Los Angeles: University of California Press.

Gombrich, Richard, and Gananath Obeyesekere. 1988. *Buddhism Transformed: Religious Change in Sri Lanka.* Princeton, NJ: Princeton University Press.

Harris, Elizabeth J. 1999. The Female in Buddhism. In *Buddhist Women across Cultures: Realizations,* ed. Karma Lekshe Tsomo, 49–65. Albany: State University of New York Press.

Hettiarachchi, Gunasinghe. 2004. Sopakala Asudedenakuta vena Etambagaskada Buddha Putrayano. *Silumina* June 6, Sunday edition.

Kantowsky, Detlef. 1980. *Sarvodaya: The Other Development.* New Delhi: Vikas Publishing House.

Lopez, Donald S., Jr., ed. 1995. *Buddhism in Practice.* Princeton, NJ: Princeton University Press.

Malalgoda, Kitsiri. 1976. *Buddhism in Sinhalese Society 1750–1900: A Study of Religious Revival and Change.* Berkeley: University of California Press.

Manor, James. 1989. *The Expedient Utopian: Bandaranaike and Ceylon.* Cambridge, UK: Cambridge University Press.

Munasinghe, Chamika, ed. 2004. *Ape Dharma Kathikavatha.* Imbulgoda, Sri Lanka: Senarath Publishing.

Rahula, Walpola. 1974. *The Heritage of the Bhikkhu: A Short History of the Bhikkhu in Educational, Cultural, Social, and Political Life.* New York: Grove Press.

Salgado, Nirmala S. 1996. Ways of Knowing and Transmitting Religious Knowledge: Case Studies of Theravada Buddhist Nuns. *Journal of the International Association of Buddhist Studies* 19(1):61–79.

Sarvodaya Annual Service Report (01/04/2002–31/03/2003). 2003. Moratuwa, Sri Lanka: Lanka Jathika Sarvodaya Shramadana Sangamaya.

Seneviratne, H. L. 1999. *The Work of Kings: The New Buddhism in Sri Lanka*. Chicago: University of Chicago Press.

Soma, Gangodawila. 2002. *Deshaya Surakina Ran Asipatha*. Colombo, Sri Lanka: Dayawansa Jayakody.

———. 2004. Sudda Langa Konda Nemu Upasaka Candalayo. *Janavijaya* 3(4):5.

Sumanasekara, Gamini. 2003. *Janathavage Hamuduruvo: Pujya Gangodawila Soma Svamindra Caritapadanaya*. Olombo, Sri Lanka: Buddha Sasana Ministry and Department of Cultural Affairs.

Tambiah, Stanley Jeyaraja. 1992. *Buddhism Betrayed? Religion, Politics, and Violence in Sri Lanka*. Chicago: University of Chicago Press.

Chapter Three

Buddhism in Burma
Engagement with Modernity

JULIANE SCHOBER

Modern Buddhist practices and beliefs generally do not presume that religion will provide an encompassing cosmology in which all of life's experiences cohere, be they social or economic, secular or scientific. The practices and beliefs often instead recognize the fragmented nature of modern bodies of knowledge. Some modern Buddhist thinkers and communities create new interpretations that integrate social and conceptual disparities. This tradition has been exceptionally adaptive to local cultures and contexts throughout its history. Other forms of modern Buddhism seek new ways to reinterpret the meaning of the past. Still others either challenge or seek to revive received beliefs and practices. In this essay, modern Buddhism will be defined as those practices and beliefs that no longer presume a worldview in which political and economic power is seen as a direct reflection of religious action or is based on an internally coherent, totalizing cosmological system. Although this discussion illustrates thematic changes within a broader cultural landscape and focuses on selected examples that articulate themes of modern Buddhism, it cannot claim to be a comprehensive catalog. Among the omissions are the ways in which Buddhists have interacted with other religious communities, be they Christian, Muslim, Hindu, or animist. Nor will those cultural expressions of modern Buddhism that intersect with the popular worship of Burmese nats (Spirit Lords) be discussed here.

Scholars have noted some general trends that characterize Buddhist transformations from traditional cosmologies to modern ones. In his seminal work entitled *World Conqueror and World Renouncer* (1976), Stanley J. Tambiah developed this categorical distinction common to classic Buddhist civilizations of

South and Southeast Asia. Although the biography of the Buddha encompasses both ideals—renouncer and conqueror—Tambiah shows that the institutionalization of Buddhism after the Buddha's departure from the world rested on the reciprocal functions between the two. World conquerors were represented by political leadership and other laypeople who were making a living and engaged in perpetuating involvement in the world. They represented the ideal actions of a world conqueror, the cakkavatti. In contrast, Buddhist monks emulated the ideal of renouncing worldly concerns in favor of religious practice that lessened the potential for future suffering and nurtured eventual moral perfection. Traditionally, world renouncers were mostly members of the ordained Buddhist Sangha. In modern times, however, Theravadins and other Buddhists have experimented with new ways to renounce the world beyond traditional monasticism.

The separation of world renouncers, who traditionally were Buddhist monks, from laypeople, who are engaged with the world, defines the practice of traditional Theravada monastic lineages. For example, the Shwegyin Nikaya, a reformist monastic lineage founded in nineteenth-century Upper Burma, exemplifies what its monks consider a strict and literal interpretation of the Vinaya, or the Monastic Code of Ethics. However, the requirements of modern contexts have frequently brought about reinterpretations of monastic practice and its textual models. Such reinterpretations concerned the daily practices of monks, their ability to purchase needed items, and their use of modern communication technologies. As cultural definitions of monastic roles undergo innovation—a development some characterize as a decline in monastic authority—the religious authority of lay Buddhists has been steadily on the rise. New forms of renouncing the world, and hence new social roles for spiritual leadership, have been promoted through meditation and religious movements like Socially Engaged Buddhism. Particularly noteworthy is the rise in the status of women renouncers—be they sila shin (female novices) or even, as some advocated in recent years, fully ordained nuns—who have reestablished lineages of women renouncers in the Theravada tradition. Some modern Buddhist movements have also sought a new synthesis with modern political ideologies like nationalism, militarism, democracy, and socialism. Others have developed Buddhist strategies to accommodate the political powers of the modern state within a Buddhist worldview. Especially, the popularization of meditation among laypeople has opened new venues for spiritual achievement among the laity.

The practices and beliefs of modern Buddhism in Burma have many faces and defy ready classification into neat categories, as one finds much diversity among them. Modern Buddhists consider their religious communities authentic, and most are tolerant of other religious interpretations as well. Some Buddhist communities focus on ritual, others on meditation, and still others venerate a particular individual they believe to embody Moral Perfection (nibbana).

Some take on familiar neotraditional traits, and others advocate a more radical break with the religious authorities of the past. Some of them have religious organizations that are local or regional in scope, whereas others focus on national communities and even appeal to a global diaspora of Burmese living abroad. To traverse the territory charted by modern Buddhism in Burma, this essay focuses on the ways modern history has transformed traditional links between politics and religion. Beginning with a sketch of traditional cosmological features, the discussion turns to the influence British colonialism had on Burmese Buddhism and the kinds of religious reforms colonialism invited or necessitated. Next, the essay considers the role of state Buddhism in the nation-building process and then turns to Buddhist ways of resisting the power of the state. The essay concludes with a discussion of the role of Buddhism in shaping Burmese transnational communities.

Additionally, it should be noted that, in 1989, the State Law and Order Restoration Council (SLORC) changed the country's official name to Myanmar, a term that is linguistically related to its previous designation, Burma. Although this change was intended to express a postcolonial national identity, many academics and those opposed to the regime continue to refer to this Southeast Asian nation as Burma. Without wishing to engage the politics of terminology, this essay will continue to use the terms "Burma" and "Burmese" throughout, reserving the term "Myanmar" to discussion of social and cultural realities specific to the identities constructed by the military regimes in the aftermath of the prodemocracy uprising in 1988.

The Conceptual Orders of Cosmological Buddhism

Scholars have convincingly argued that the nexus between religion and politics is rooted in the biography of the Buddha and his close relationships with royal supporters like King Bimbisara, who donated the Deer Park near Benares to the early Buddhist community. The king's gift provided these early Buddhist mendicants with an opportunity to lead a sedentary life. The domestication of the Sangha was thus brought about by a transition from a mendicant community to one that was settled, accessible to lay supporters, and endowed with land and buildings.

The later Theravada tradition continued to cultivate a close and reciprocal relationship with political leaders. Central to the tradition's institutionalization and subsequent rise in Sri Lanka was King Asoka's (270–232 BCE) sponsorship of the Third Buddhist Council. Several lineages of the Buddhist tradition spread to Southeast Asia by land and sea routes. Asoka's royal patronage of Theravada monastic lineages continued to inform the reigns of Mon kings, who emulated Asoka's example in ways in which they governed their polities as early as the sixth century CE. Burmese history credits King Anawrahta (1044–1077) with establishing, by the middle of the eleventh century, Theravada as the religion of the Pagan dynasty and its empire. In his book on Pagan, the desert capital city of Burma's classical dynasty of Pagoda Builders where hundred of stupas were built between the eighth and thirteenth centuries, Michael Aung Thwin (1985) shows how royal obligation toward the Buddhist's Dispensation (sasana) created such spiraling pressures on the state's economy that it precipitated the economic involution and eventual collapse of the Pagan dynasty.

In the politics of a classical Southeast Asian kingdom, the court's hegemony radiated from a cosmic center to the periphery. Buddhism legitimated a social hierarchy in which the king's political fortune depended largely on mobilizing communities through rituals and other religious works (Schober 2001). A dhammaraja—a king whose office comprised simultaneously religious and political responsibilities—ruled a Theravada Buddhist polity such as the Pagan empire and later Burmese kingdoms. As a righteous Buddhist ruler, the dhammaraja was expected to govern in accordance with the Buddhist Law (dhamma) or Universal Truth.

The responsibilities of his office also required a king to act in ways that caused suffering, such as by imposing punishment on criminals or conducting war against neighboring polities. A Buddhist king was therefore likely to acquire negative merit in this life. Good governance included maintaining a civic context in which the Buddha's Dispensation (sasana) could prosper.

An important part of the king's duty was to ensure the prosperity of his people by keeping war and famine at bay. Future prosperity is also assured through the material support (dana) the laypeople give to the community of monastic world renouncers, the Sangha. The king served as the primary patron of religious causes that ranged from donations to the Sangha to sponsoring the construction and consecration of pagodas, monasteries, and sacred icons, including Buddha images and stupas, which are reliquaries that contain the Buddha's remains or similar sacred items. From a Burmese cultural perspective, the religious and ritual obligations of the king were basic to his political leadership. Royal power was culturally understood as the contemporary expression of religious merit. In the absence of rules for dynastic succession in Burma, royal patronage of Buddhist lay and monastic communities was essential to legitimating a dhammaraja's power.

In response to European encroachment on Burma's coastal regions and the British colonization of Lower Burma, King Thalon of the restored Toungoo dynasty (1597–1752) moved his capital north to Ava in 1635. Following an intermittent Mon conquest, King Alaungpaya (1752–1760), founder of the Konbaun dynasty (1752–1885), reconsolidated a Burmese empire. This dynasty ruled from several capitals in Upper Burma, namely Amarapura, Ava, and Mandalay. The traditional rule of the dhammaraja collapsed when the British conquered the last capital of Mandalay in 1885. Until then, the rule of the Konbaung dynasty embodied the very kind of encompassing social system Tambiah (1985) described as "galactic"—polities that expanded and contracted through time, cycling from periods of ascendancy to eventual decline, only to be encompassed within the spheres of influence of competing Theravada polities. Traditional Theravada histories, polities, and economics cohered in these ways to affirm an encompassing cosmologic reality, constituting a "total social fact" (Tambiah 1985).

The British conquest of the Mandalay court in 1885 marked the collapse of traditional Buddhist kingship and the decline of cultural values and lifeways in Burma. The colonizers transformed Mandalay Palace into Fort Dufferin, exiled King Thibaw (1878–1886), and moved the polity's cosmic center, the Lion Throne, from Mandalay to Rangoon and eventually to Calcutta (Mendelson 1975). As the Buddhist court's cultural influence on the southern delta region waned after 1825, the modern crisis of authority in Burmese Buddhist culture escalated. The British conquest was devastating to Burmese intellectual, social, and religious elites in many ways. Its greatest cultural impact was rooted, however, in the radical conceptual shifts colonial rule required. Nonetheless, Buddhist conceptions of power as rooted in past ethical action continued then, as they do in contemporary Burmese society, to inform religious and political practices. Although traditional Buddhist cosmological conceptions underwent modern transformations in many cultural contexts, they still inform contemporary religious communities in a variety of ways. For these reasons, the following passages briefly outline Theravada Buddhist cosmological conceptions.

The Buddha's legacy and Dispensation comprise two bodies, his physical remains (rupakaya) and his spiritual body (dhammakaya). Strictly speaking, rupakaya are the Buddha's relics, but Burmese also include in this category other sacred objects like sets of canonical texts (Tipitaka), consecrated Buddha images, and stupas (Schober 2001). Sites that contain the Buddha's rupakaya constitute cosmic centers of power around which Buddhist communities form. The presence of such sacred objects plays an important role in defining Buddhist communities. The Buddha's physical presence in a locality constitutes a cosmic center of power (Schober 1997b, 2001). Buddhist communities at such sacred sites are defined socially and ritually through merit making and veneration of the Buddha's rupakaya. For Burmese Buddhists, sacred places such as the famous Shwedagon Pagoda in Rangoon or the Mahamuni Buddha image in Mandalay have national significance. By the same token, local groups often identify their communities by worshiping at and offering donations to a pagoda in the vicinity (Schober 2004). The Buddha's rupakaya may also be represented by the canon of the Theravada traditions, the Three Baskets of the Tipitaka, which is believed to comprise the complete word and teachings of the Buddha.

Worshippers at the Buddhist Shwedagon Pagoda in Burma (present-day Myanmar). (Corel)

A complete set of Buddhist scriptures may therefore stand in place of his physical presence, or rupakaya, in certain ritual contexts.

The cosmological link between Buddhism and political power was affirmed through cultural expectations about kingship, and it was sustained through merit-making rituals among communities. A Buddhist lay community constitutes a ritual community within which individuals are hierarchically differentiated according to status, power, and a perceived store of past merit, namely their kamma. Most lay Buddhist rituals focus on the economy of merit, and the tradition offers much social opportunity and doctrinal motivation for the laity to demonstrate generosity. It is the primary religious obligation of Buddhist laypeople to maintain and uphold the Buddha's rupakaya, the material presence of his Dispensation, by giving generously and participating in merit-making rituals. Occasions to do so abound, as one commonly hears invitations to join others in merit-making activities. Merit determines the material and ethical quality of one's rebirth, and laypeople acquire merit by giving material support (dana) to religious causes that sustain the Buddha's Dispensation. Lay donors acquire merit by giving generously to Buddhist causes that perpetuate the physical legacy of the Buddha's sasana and bring spiritual rewards to donors in future lives.

Giving to Buddhist causes, demonstrating generosity, and making merit are religious actions that also create differences in the social and political status of laypeople. Sponsorship of merit-making rituals can also be interpreted as a claim to a position of power. The religiosity and political aspirations of an individual may combine to create lavish sponsorship of religious causes. As Burmese believe that religious merit will manifest itself in status, power, and prestige, making merit is an integral part of achieving political goals. By this cultural logic, political status and prestige are indications of past merit making. Participating in merit-making rituals obligates an invited guest to reciprocate socially to the Owner of Merit (kutho shin) who organized the occasion.

The Buddhist monastic community, in turn, is ideally dedicated to perpetuating the Buddha's teaching or spiritual body (dhammakaya) through practice and study of the path to nibbana. Monks may attain enlightenment through a variety of practices, all of which, in the Theravada traditions of Burma, are premised on renouncing the social world of the laity and all claims to power, status, and wealth in society. By becoming a monk, a young man not only forgoes his worldly possessions and familial ties. With ordination, he assumes a new identity and status within the Sangha. Cultivating detachment from the kind of karmic action that prolongs one's involvement with the world, monks in Burma are expected to live apart from lay society. Monks who are ordained within monastic lineages and practice the Buddha's dhamma become sources of merit for their lay donors. Traditionally, young men joined the Sangha at least temporarily as novices to honor their parents and make merit for them.

Full ordination into the Sangha is a ritual that confers membership within the community of monks, and its performance has karmic significance for both laypeople and monks.

The Sangha's role was to preserve and practice the Buddha's dhammakaya, and monks were expected to embody his spiritual message (dhamma) through practice, knowledge, and insight. Hence, the Sangha occupied a place of authority and veneration within Burmese society. Monks were regarded as repositories of knowledge about the dhamma and the history of the sasana. The traditional role of monasteries in teaching basic skills of literacy to young Burmese boys was equally significant. Because of the Sangha's role as an educational institution, home for the intellectual elite, and social location for the production of cultural knowledge, monks in general and select individuals in monastic groups (in Burmese, *gain*) within the Sangha have had profound influence on Burmese culture and history. Monastic world renouncers have played powerful roles in Burmese politics and society, not only because they are believed to embody the teachings of the Buddha, but also because some monks have counseled kings on the affairs of the state.

The conduct of the monastic community is bound by the Vinaya, which is interpreted with some variation among the particular ordination lineages or nikaya (gain). The Burmese Sangha's internal structure is hierarchical, and monks acquire seniority with each full year they remain in the Sangha. Regardless of their chronological age, junior monks are deferential to monks with greater seniority as disciples pay homage to their teachers, resident monks show obedience to their abbot, and novices show respect to their preceptors. Besides this principle of internal hierarchy, the Sangha in Burma embodies other distinctions and differences as well. Practice in some monasteries is exclusively dedicated to one of the many methods of meditation for which Burma is well known. Other monasteries excel in the study of the Theravada textual traditions, the Theravada's commentaries, and other secondary literatures. Three institutions, in Rangoon, Mandalay, and Pakokku, offer university-level curricula. Some monks live in forest monasteries with consecrated ordination halls (sima), and a small minority reside in solitary hermitages. The majority of monasteries are designated as town dwellers where monks minister to the lay community and perform merit-making rituals. The thathanabain was the Supreme Patriarch of the Burmese Sangha. He was appointed by the king, who generally looked toward monastic teachers and lineages with close relations to the court. The thathanabain counseled the king on matters of governance. While his authority was strengthened by its proximity to the court, centralization of the Sangha under the authority of the thathanabain was not always enforced in traditional Burma.

It would be misleading to view the Sangha in Burma as monolithic or uniform. Despite efforts to unify the Sangha and rationalize its teachings through

A young monk makes contact with a gong inside the Mahamuni Pagoda, Mandalay, Myanmar. (Richard Bickel/Corbis)

reforms commenced under King Mindon in 1871, under U Nu in 1954, and by the Ne Win government since 1980, the Burmese Sangha comprises considerable variation in the practices of local monasteries. Although nearly 90 percent of the country's citizens are Buddhist and the majority among them are ethnically Burman, Theravada Buddhism is also practiced among some ethnic minorities, including the Shan, Mon, Arakanese, Karen, and others. In conjunction with each reform, the state published new editions of the Tipitaka to uphold Theravada orthodoxy and to implement standardized texts with approved ideals of normative practice. However, efforts to centralize monastic authority in the hands of the state have usually encountered some resistance within an ethnically diverse Sangha and were only partially successful in constructing a unified body of world renouncers. A great deal of collaborative work among scholars of Buddhism in Burma awaits doing to document the diversity of local, regional, and ethnic Buddhist traditions through time.

British Colonialism and Other Forms of Modernity

The Burmese experience of modernity was largely synonymous with the beginning of colonialism that rapidly eclipsed traditional cultural values, institutions, and lifeways (Myint-U 2001). The collapse of traditional institutions, initially in

Lower Burma and after 1886 in Upper Burma, accelerated a restructuring of Burmese society that reflected Western secular values. Colonial rule became in large measure a vehicle for introducing modernity to the region. In this process, facets of power considered secular in the West were effectively dislodged from the Buddhist cosmological worldview in which Burmese cultural notions had been traditionally embedded. In addition to establishing an administration in which pragmatic issues of military, economic, and political power were transacted separately from the Buddhist foundations of the earlier political administration, the British also implemented a deliberate policy of noninvolvement in the religious affairs of the colony. For instance, the British refused to confirm the authority of the Taungdaw Sayadaw, who had been installed in office by King Thibaw as the Sangha's Supreme Patriarch (thathanabain) in Upper Burma. When this monk passed away in 1895, the colonial administration did not exercise the traditional responsibilities of a dhammaraja to appoint a successor, leaving this important office vacant for nearly a decade. This vacuum in monastic leadership hastened the political and organizational decline of the Sangha, the sole institution of traditional culture to survive the British annexation of Upper Burma in 1886. In the eyes of traditional Burmese Buddhists, who expected the British Crown to act like a righteous Buddhist ruler, the British refusal further diminished respect for colonial authority.

Colonial rule introduced alternate configurations of power that had not been a part of Burmese cultural knowledge. It created administrative structures that rationalized and centralized state powers and furthered the economic and political goals of the empire (Furnivall 1956). To protect their mercantile interests, the British reorganized society and promoted administrative rationalization, modern values, and Western education (Cohn 1996). These changes helped establish the colonial state and simultaneously paved the way for other forms of modernity. In their totality, they had a profound impact on Burmese cultural institutions, religious authority, and the everyday lives of Buddhists. Various modern Buddhist practices and organizations emerged in reaction to the cultural and religious discontinuities that colonial rule created (Schober 1997a, 2005). Despite its stated goal not to become involved in religious matters, the colonial government nevertheless was confronted with various forms of resistance motivated by Buddhist beliefs and practices, forcing it to address Buddhist concerns in various ways. Meanwhile, the ways in which the Burmese Buddhist laity and Sangha engaged the challenges of modernity and secular power varied by region and social class.

The colonial divide between secular politics and a Buddhist worldview on the one hand and between Buddhist lay and monastic authority on the other further intensified in 1919, when the British government determined to subordinate the administration of colonial Burma to the government of India. In the

absence of a centralized or unified Sangha, internal fragmentation characterized the monastic engagement with colonization and modernity. Monastic lineages largely relied on the internal organization of their respective nikaya, which
operated independently from other monastic groups. Reformist lineages like
the Shwegyin order sought to assert their monastic status through strict obser-
vance of the Vinaya. Other groups of laypeople and monks fostered millennial
and traditionalist expectations. In response to the disarray of the Sangha, a
Western-educated Burmese lay elite felt increasingly motivated to define what it
meant to be Burmese and Buddhist within a rapidly changing, cosmopolitan,
and colonial society of Lower Burma. One such movement was the Young Men's
Buddhist Association (YMBA), founded in 1906 in Rangoon. Like other groups
oriented toward meditation, it claimed greater religious authority for laypeople.
Its pursuit to define a modern national and religious identity developed out of
a need to accommodate increased ethnic and religious diversity and political,
economic, and cultural challenges colonization had brought. In the final analysis, colonial rule and the advent of cultural modernity in Burma dislodged traditional worldviews characteristic of the traditional cosmological Buddhist polities that Tambiah (1976) described and created social disjunctures within it.
Although colonial policy did not succeed in separating Burmese politics from
Buddhist worldviews, it greatly weakened traditional Buddhist institutions.

Such changes often create contradictions that Charles Keyes (1993) and
Keyes, Kendall, and Hardacre (1994) described as a Buddhist crisis of authority. One of the hallmarks of modernity rests in the fact that moderns often affirm simultaneously distinct and even contradictory bodies of knowledge, such
as science and religion. In those contexts, and particularly in the absence of
long-established political institutions, religion tends to reassert its role in shaping public discourse in new ways. To appeal to popular support for broader political objectives and authority, the political strategies of modern states, including colonial empires, often seek to harness religious expressions among civil
organizations or gain their neutrality toward the state's agenda. Regardless of
stated aspirations, modern Buddhist organizations are therefore by definition
both religious and political entities, for they function in contexts in which social power is constituted and transacted. Buddhism and politics thus continue
to shape the modern history of Burma, and their modern transformations have
brought about innovative cultural practices.

One of the most far-reaching developments the colonial project promoted
concerned the acquisition of knowledge, and through that, shaped conceptions of national identity in Burma. Traditionally, knowledge was based on Buddhist principles, and the Sangha facilitated its acquisition. Both basic literacy
and higher education were firmly established within the domain of the Sangha,
which acted as the source of and authority over knowledge. In a decision that
proved to be pivotal in the history of education in Burma, the Sangha firmly

rejected British attempts to introduce new educational subjects into the monastic curriculum. On substantive grounds and likely due to the inherent disjuncture with Buddhist cosmology, the Sangha took a particularly negative view of the teaching of mathematics, geography, and drawing. Still more objectionable to the monks was the manner in which the colonial government sought to insert its curriculum and lay teachers into the preexisting monastic educational structures.

Concerned about compromising its authority, the Sangha ultimately rejected collaboration with the colonial government in matters of education. The collaboration had envisioned employing monks as teachers and adding lay teachers to the teaching staff at monasteries. The thathanabain argued that compliance would amount to a breach of the Vinaya, which prohibits monks from employment for compensation to safeguard monastic authority and practice. This decision contributed to the further decline of monastic education, which already had been relegated to mostly rural areas and had suffered from attrition of bright students to English-speaking schools. This was but one aspect among several that hastened a general disintegration of the Burmese Sangha from its position of authority during royal times. Internal fragmentation, organizational disarray, and diminishing economic support for the Sangha contributed to marginalizing monastic influence among Burmese colonial elites, especially in Lower Burma.

By contrast, Christian missionary schools and government schools flourished under imperial patronage. The colonial government was in need of a large number of Burmese who were educated in the canons of modern knowledge to help administer its many projects (Cohn 1996). Due to this fact and to the economic boom Lower Burma enjoyed at the start of the twentieth century, obtaining a Western education and joining the Indian civil service offered indisputable social and economic opportunities that could not be duplicated by a traditional monastic education or by basic literacy in Buddhism. By the early twentieth century, Burmese colonial elites in the cosmopolitan port city of Rangoon had been educated largely abroad in India and England. English had become the language of colonial erudition among the upper class, while colloquial Burmese was used mostly in interactions with lower-class Burmese and in rural areas. Among nearly all Burmese, familiarity with Burmese classic literature and cultural and religious knowledge had nearly vanished. Along with new cosmopolitan horizons, modern innovation, and rapid social change, Burmese experienced estrangement from their own cultural traditions and spiritual disenchantment with the unfulfilled promises of the modern age.

Emerging from this collision of Western and Buddhist worldviews was not just a radically changed social and political order. More significantly, the experience of modernity in Burma through British colonization brought about a cultural and religious crisis of authority that had an enduring impact on the country's history. The authority of Buddhist worldviews, values, and knowledge was now no longer undisputed, but was in competition with other bodies of knowledge and power structures that captured radically transformed cultural realities. Concepts rooted in Buddhist cultural truths, such as the rule of a dhammaraja and the righteousness of the Universal Law (dhamma)—as well as Burmese notions of power denoting physical might (ana), influence (oza), one's store of merit (phon), and personal power (tagou) that granted protection over a Buddhist center of power since times immemorial—were among those transformed and challenged by the colonial rule of the British Empire. Many Burmese subjects of the British Crown now found themselves displaced to the periphery of an entirely different, affluent, and irreligious world.

From this cultural and religious crisis of authority developed new forms of Buddhist practice and beliefs that were at once in conflict and in collusion with the profound social changes Burma experienced under colonial rule. The cultural, political, and religious divisions created by the British administration of Burma varied considerably by social and geographic location. Throughout the twentieth century, local differences in the ways Burmese Buddhists engaged colonialism, transnationalism, and modernity reinforced corresponding cultural differences between Upper and Lower Burma and between lay and monastic authority, respectively. The experience of colonial rule in Upper Burma differed vastly from the cosmopolitan interactions that characterized the colonial Rangoon and the region of Lower Burma. By contrast, Upper Burma's population was largely rural and traditional in its educational background, political views, and religious practices. Upper Burma was colonized more than half a century later, when the Konbaun dynasty in Mandalay fell in 1886 at the end of the Third Anglo-Burmese War. Particularly in the royal capital of Mandalay, the Burmese experience of modernity commenced with a colonial eclipse of traditional cultural values, institutions, and lifeways.

The collapse of traditional institutions hastened the restructuring of Burmese society through colonial forms of knowledge and classification. Although diminished in its authority, the Sangha in Upper Burma came to articulate an anticolonial discourse objecting to the presence of a foreign power that refused the responsibility of the traditional state to protect the sasana and hence was seen as anti-Buddhist. This spurred the rise of millennial movements advocating a return to the previous status quo and to the reestablishment of a traditional Buddhist polity to recapture a past now seen as a better, if not ideal, order of things. Reacting against colonial modernity, a series of millenarian Buddhist revolts against the British presence developed in Upper Burma in 1906, 1910, and 1916, fostering expectations of the imminent appearance of a Universal Monarch (setkya min) (Sarkisyanz 1965). These traditionalist reactions to colonial rule culminated with the Saya San Rebellion of the late 1920s (Herbert 1983).

By contrast, other Buddhist movements aimed to forge new Buddhist identities in consonance with modern social and political realities. The YMBA gained widespread popularity in Lower Burma during the 1910s (Maung Maung 1980). The movement was started by a group of young Western-educated Burmese; its educational mission was modeled after that of the Young Men's Christian Association (YMCA). It grew rapidly, promoting the concept of "the modern Burman" among the population of Lower Burma. The YMBA began its activities as a procolonial organization and aimed to popularize a new national identity among the colonial elite and among an emerging middle class that was modern, Burmese, and Buddhist. "To be Burmese is to be Buddhist" was the slogan initially coined by the YMBA and subsequently reinterpreted by later political groups, most prominently Burma's postindependence prime minister, U Nu. The YMBA's agenda emphasized modern public education, particularly literacy in Burmese and mathematics. Its leaders argued strongly with the colonial government for the inclusion of Buddhism in the elementary curriculum. In the view of the YMBA, the modern Burman was an educated colonial subject of the British Crown. At the same time, the cosmopolitan elites expressed their estrangement from traditional cultural roots and sought to mitigate against the disenchantment of their times by constructing a rationalized Buddhism stripped of cosmological mythologies. As the conflict between British and Burmese national interests intensified, public debates about what constituted a national Burmese identity developed in Buddhist and secular directions. The latter included the nationalist movement led by university students, among them the famous Thirty Comrades, who became the country's heroes of the independence struggle. Various anticolonial Buddhist groups, such as the General Council of the Sangha Samgetti, eventually eclipsed the predominantly procolonial Buddhism of the YMBA and superseded its organization, renewing monastic influence over the Buddhist nationalist movement.

The rise of lay authority is a general feature of modern Buddhist practices across the tradition, and the growing popularity of lay meditation in particular contributed to this development in Burma. The internal fragmentation within the Burmese Sangha further opened the way to increased lay authority. Traditionally, along with education (pariyatti), the practice of meditation (patipatti) had been the spiritual prerogative of the Sangha, for meditation was considered fruitful only if practiced within the context of monastic renunciation. Meditation is a necessary step in mastering the path to nibbana. Burmese pride themselves on not only the strict adherence to the Vinaya that Burmese monks are known for, but also for the many monks known for their accomplishments in practicing and teaching vipassana meditation methods. These are advanced meditation methods that presume mastery of preliminary trance states (samatha). By the mid-twentieth century, the popularization of meditation and the role of the laity in it had become significant. Lay meditation also played an important role in the public ethos of U Nu's Buddhist revival in the newly in-dependent country. The Buddha Sasana Council inaugurated the Thathana Yeitha in Rangoon as its premier meditation center under the abbotship of the Mahasi Sayadaw, who was well known for his methods for teaching vipassana meditation. The Mahasi Sayadaw initiated a process for granting financial sup-port and certification to numerous meditation centers throughout the country that agreed to adopt his methods and send delegates to participate in medita-tion training courses. This strategy marked the beginning of tremendous ex-pansion of the Mahasi meditation network in Burma and eventually abroad, which attracted numerous laypersons. Among those who became well-known lay meditation teachers was U Ba Khin, who developed a meditation network with international branches.

Laypeople in general and civil servants in particular were encouraged to meditate, as the spiritual wealth of the nation generated by this practice would also nourish its future material prosperity. This development allowed individ-ual laypeople to aspire to attain insight characteristic of the higher stages of the path to nibbana. In doing so, they implicitly claimed for themselves a role as repositories of Buddhist knowledge and the authority to teach meditation, until then the sole prerogatives of the Sangha.

Buddhist Reforms and Modern Political Ideologies

The crisis of authority in Burmese Buddhism produced new interpretations of Buddhist values and roles, especially those concerning power and renuncia-tion. This brought traditional Buddhism into conflict as well as into collabora-tion with modern political ideologies like nationalism, democracy, socialism, and communism. The tensions and dynamics that developed around issues continued the sort of religious and cultural debates that are epitomized in the history of Burmese Buddhist reforms since the late nineteenth century. The re-forms under each political rule sought to bring about a synthesis of Buddhism with modern political ideologies, and they also demonstrate the historical processes by which modern Buddhist interpretations have engaged political ideologies and the pragmatics of the modern state.

In fact, Theravada reforms have long provided a cultural template for the consolidation of political power. The reforms strengthen political values and authority by defining normative Buddhist beliefs and practices, at least for political elites. Reforms thus also present opportunities to establish new kinds of religious authorities in texts, monastic conduct, normative practice, and management of wealth acquired by the Sangha. Successful reforms, pro-moted as purification and propagation of the sasana, in turn lent legitimacy to traditional kings and modern heads of state, who are credited with their implementation. Reforms also entailed editing the Pali Canon to purge its accretions and restore what was believed to be the original word of the Buddha.

King Mindon's Sangha reforms in 1871 aimed to centralize monastic administration under the offices of the thathanabain and put into place a new kind of monastic orthodoxy that limited the number of officially recognized monastic lineages and imposed monastic registration. Particularly the Shwegyin Nikaya emerged from these reforms as a royally sponsored lineage that emphasized a strict interpretation of monastic discipline. The entire set of Tipitaka texts was carved on 728 marble monoliths and enshrined at Kuthodaw Pagoda in Mandalay to celebrate the accomplishments of the Fifth Council and to preserve Theravada textual purity. Local traditions of practice, including the veneration of spirits (nat), were discouraged, but the population continued to practice them.

In 1952, after decades of internal fragmentation in the Sangha, Burma's democratic prime minister, U Nu, began to promote a Buddhist revival for which he appointed a committee of prominent laypeople, the Buddha Sasana Council. This committee initiated the convocation of the Sixth Buddhist Synod in 1954, the Sanghayana, which lasted for several years. U Nu's revitalization coincided with worldwide celebrations of the 2,500-year anniversary of the Buddha's Dispensation. It was intended to promote not only Buddhist piety among the population, but also to usher in an era of prosperity for the new nation (Smith 1965). U Nu was himself a deeply religious person committed to ascetic practice in his daily life. His government sponsored monastic reforms and large-scale Buddhist rituals and eventually instituted Buddhism as a state religion. In doing so, U Nu gave in to escalating monastic demands and hoped to strengthen his political power. A hallmark of his charismatic leadership was to infuse the new nation with a popular ideology, namely the Burmese-Buddhist Way to Socialism, which presented the country's modernization and development as steps in the gradual attainment of the Eightfold Path toward enlightenment. Although many Burmese had millennial expectations of U Nu as a righteous ruler (dhammaraja) or even Universal Monarch (setya min), he was eventually unable to contain escalating pressures from the Sangha, political factions within his government, and separatist rebellions fought by ethnic minorities. A decidedly modern revitalization of Buddhism and Burmese national identity formed the historical legacy of this era, despite the collapse of U Nu's government through a military coup. The establishment of a Ministry for Religious Affairs undoubtedly had enduring consequences for Burma, as it provided the state with a mechanism for regulating religious practice among the laity, monks, and minority religions.

The U Nu government was followed by the military regime of Ne Win, who came to power in 1962. Initially, Ne Win's reforms focused on the state, and

Prime Minister of Burma U Nu joining in public prayer during a celebration marking the 2,500th anniversary of the Buddha's death. Rangoon, Burma, 1956. (John Dominis/Time Life Pictures/Getty Images)

society was organized into socialist workers' collectives. In the early 1980s, however, Ne Win initiated religious reforms that once again sought to centralize administration of the Sangha in the hands of the state, renew monastic registration, control monastic property, and determine the succession of abbots in monasteries. These reforms expanded government control over internal monastic affairs to a far greater degree than had reforms implemented by the previous government. In tandem with reforms of other state agencies governed by the ideals and realities of Ne Win's military regime, the Ministry of Religious Affairs convened the Sangha Mahanayaka Council to bring Buddhist institutions under the control of the state (Tin Maung Maung Than 1988, 1993). Its official charge was to implement the preservation, purification, and propagation of the Dispensation. The council's policies aimed to forge greater uniformity among monastic lineages and to control the donations that charismatic monks received from their lay supporters. In a huge wave of excommunications over a few years, the council disrobed many popular monks for allegedly transgressing the Vinaya or preaching heretical doctrines (adhamma). For example, the enterprising Poppa Sayadaw, who received generous support from politically powerful donors, was targeted by the purge. At the same time, the government lavishly supported the monastic leadership it had assembled in the Sangha Mahanayaka Council. Most of the members of this council were less distinguished than the monastic dignitaries assembled by U Nu's Sanghayana. The Mingun Sayadaw, for instance, presided over U Nu's reforms but kept his distance from the Sangha Mahanayaka Council in the 1980s.

To enhance the legitimacy of the reforms, the Ne Win government asked U Nu to return from exile in Thailand and lead a project to publish a new edition of canonical texts. Ne Win's government also put in place administrative structures to oversee monastic instruction and examinations. It instituted ecclesiastical courts to adjudicate Vinaya infractions, disputes over monastic property, and the alleged preaching of heretical doctrines. Lastly, the state engaged monks in development and education projects in the territories of tribal minorities who were predominantly animist or Christian. Increasingly, reports of forced conversion emerged from tribal areas. The Ministry of Religious Affairs imposed similar controls on other religious minorities, including several Christian denominations, Muslims, Hindus, and Jews. Burma's Ministry of Religious Affairs became a forceful instrument of state policy, in contrast to similar agencies in countries like Thailand, Laos, Cambodia, and Sri Lanka, where Theravada Buddhism is likewise practiced by a majority of the population. This trend has increased in recent decades as the political guarantees of the modern state, such as governance based on a national constitution, have been suspended. Ruling elites under Ne Win's successor regimes, the State Law and Order Restoration Council (SLORC) and later the State Peace and Development Council (SPDC), turned increasingly to Buddhist sources of legitimation.

In doing so, they reinterpreted a traditional paradigm of power, namely the role of the dhammaraja, to meet the pragmatic requirements of the modern state.

Rituals of the Modern Buddhist State

The most innovative transformation achieved by Ne Win's religious reforms and subsequently continued under SLORC and the SPDC concerned the roles bureaucrats and military generals assumed in the Buddhist rituals of the state. Representing the state and its worker collectives, ministers and military leaders performed merit-making rituals in public contexts. Initially, these large-scale rituals were occasioned by the calendar of Burmese Buddhism, in which major religious holidays are celebrated on full moon days. High-profile politicians officiated at rituals in which lavish donations were given to monks who frequently were also members of the Mahanayaka Council (Schober 1997a). State agencies and worker collectives organized and collected donations within their own communities. The amounts given by each group were then publicly announced in the media, especially the state's daily newspapers. In a manner reminiscent of a precolonial social order, worker collectives not only contributed to the total amount of donations made to the Sangha, they also shared in the merit that the state's leadership made on their behalf. In return, their contributions to state rituals awarded them karmic rewards in the future and access to networks of political power and social indebtedness at local, regional, and national levels. In contrast to reforms during U Nu's era, when similar state support for Buddhism motivated a charismatic personality cult of the prime minister, the religious benefits under later political regimes have been credited to the state and its institutions, not to charismatic individuals. This increased the power of the state and rendered individual leaders replaceable within the ritual economy of merit. The Buddhist validation of state institutions (such as the military) for generating merit also undermined the moral legitimacy of voices critical of state policies and their implementation. Laying claim to symbols of future prosperity, the new Buddhist state ideology also limited the relevance of competing secular, political ideologies. Democracy and socialism were presented and critiqued as offering promises for this world only, not for future lives. The current regime seeks to demonstrate that the Burmese nation prospers from the ways in which its politics are embedded within an overarching Buddhist framework, namely the new cosmology of modern state Buddhism (Schober 2005).

Perhaps the most insightful instance of celebrating the cosmology of modern state Buddhism occurred in the early 1990s, when SLORC promoted the restoration of Burmese national culture and traditional Buddhism along several dimensions. Critical features of this cultural reconstruction included familiar

Buddhist strategies to enact the Buddha's sacred biography: a hearkening back to an idealized and glorified past under powerful Burmese kings, the reaffirmation of sacred places and stupas that locate the Buddha's presence in the Burmese nation and its history, and, lastly, the celebration of a national community that simultaneously constituted a political and social hegemony. SLORC's appeal to this classic Buddhist strategy accomplished a variety of objectives. It insulated the regime and its politics from accountability to citizens and the international community. It further allowed the regime to present itself as heir to the glorious past of powerful kings and thus boost its legitimacy. Finally, the state's emphasis on ritual merit making at a national level and the concurrent silencing of the Sangha shifted public attention away from other crises facing the state. Burmese television and print media frequently report on Buddhist rituals performed in conjunction with the restoration of ancient sites and royal palaces at which military generals and government officials officiate on behalf of Burmese citizens.

Two ritual events stand out in particular. In 1994, SLORC organized a pilgrimage for the Buddha's Tooth Relic as part of its cultural diplomacy with China (Schober 1997a). For six weeks, the sacred relic traveled on pilgrimage from Rangoon to Mandalay and back to the capital. At each stop throughout the journey, various social groups, professional organizations, and other community groups prepared grand celebrations, and the national news media published names of donors and amounts donated. In this manner, the political regime turned a national community into a ritual community structured by a hierarchy of public generosity and merit making. Second, a ritual cycle accompanied the construction, begun under Ne Win's sponsorship in the 1980s, of the Maha Wizaya Pagoda located near Shwedagon Pagoda, the national symbol of Buddhism in Rangoon. Although many Burmese show considerable cynicism toward Ne Win's work of merit, it is the site of ongoing official rituals of merit making, culminating in the hoisting of a diamond umbrella over its spire.

Buddhism of the Resistance

Buddhism in twentieth-century Burma has also periodically been a rallying point for resistance against political governments. While modern forms of Buddhist practice do not necessitate a particular political perspective, they frequently embrace corresponding political views. Modern Buddhist communities—such as political organizations in the Sangha and the Socially Engaged Budhism of the prodemocracy movement, including its reach into meditation centers—have articulated Buddhist critiques of contemporary politics.

The Burmese Sangha has a long history of resisting the forces of the state.

Monks assumed a pivotal role in organizing popular resistance against British colonial rule in the 1920s and 1930s. More recently, the Sangha was an important element in the popular uprising of 1988, an event that has become a watershed in the national history of Burma. Amidst the chaos of the uprising, the Burmese Sangha transformed itself spontaneously into an underground organization aiding the popular uprising (Mathews 1993). Monasteries became sanctuaries for student demonstrators, particularly at night when military police made frequent arrests at the homes of suspected agitators. Monks provided logistical support in organizing demonstrations, relayed information through an internal monastic network, and even stepped up to administer some judicial and civil infrastructures in those towns and areas considered "liberated" by the democratic uprising. As the yellow robes of the Buddha offered anonymity to those fleeing from government persecution, the monastic network became a conduit for safe travel to the border and into exile. Along with numerous other exile and refugee organizations, the All Burma Monks Union was formed to speak for the Sangha from the relative safety of the Thai border. Burma's monks once again had become a political force, acting as facilitators in a widespread antigovernment mobilization.

Still, the Buddhist organizations that oppose the current regime are not monolithic. As the tensions of 1988 and thereafter have persisted, some monks have successfully circumvented the policing efforts of the state by selectively collaborating with political powers and accepting the taxation levied on foreign donations they receive. In the early twenty-first century, most of the antigovernment Sangha organizations are far underground, as the Sangha overall is effectively controlled by the state.

Aung San Suu Kyi, the daughter of Burma's national martyr, Aung San, who founded the armed forces, entered politics in 1988 and subsequently won overwhelmingly popular elections for her party, the National League for Democracy (NLD) two years later. Prevented by the regime from assuming office, she spent years under house arrest. She received the Nobel Peace Prize in 1991 in recognition of her dedication to democratic reform in Burma. Although the NLD proposes a secular form of government, Suu Kyi herself has made frequent statements concerning her practice of meditation, which she views as an integral aspect of Socially Engaged Buddhism and the spiritual strengths she derives from it. Her message has been one of nonviolent resistance, emphasizing spiritual strength through meditation in preparation for political action and social change. Along with right speech and truthfulness, Suu Kyi encourages the practice of mindfulness (sati), faith (saddha), energy (viriya), concentration (samadhi), and wisdom (panna), all of which are considered benefits of meditation. In her *Letters from Burma* (1997), she frames her critique of contemporary Burmese political culture from the perspective of Socially Engaged Buddhism and advocates a grassroots-level engagement with democratic reforms to

An Indonesian activist rallies in support of Buddhist dissident Aung San Suu Kyi and proclaims the situation in her nation of Burma to be the shame of the Association of Southeast Asian Nations. The rally was held in front of the presidential palace in Jakarta, Indonesia, on the occasion of the Myanmar foreign secretary's state visit in 2003. (Dadang Tri Image/Corbis)

bring about material and moral improvement in society. Accordingly, the Buddhist engagement with society begins with providing for basic human needs like adequate livelihood, public health, and education. These are basic responsibilities of good governance that make possible self-empowerment and social action at the local level and, in turn, contribute to the greater common good. Suu Kyi maintains that her political work is enhanced by the practice of meditation, selflessness, and reliance on a Buddhist ethos of nonviolence. Meditation, she says, has given her the spiritual strength to endure house arrest and persevere in seeking democratic reforms in Burma.

Many of her supporters also take refuge in meditation, where silent practice and freedom of thought are protected in a secluded community based on temporary retreat from society, spiritual cultivation, and trust. Like Gandhi's ashram, Burmese meditation centers are separate and perhaps at times utopian communities engaged in a common spiritual and social resistance against an oppressive government. Already popular among Burmese laypeople, the meditation movement has further grown as an alternate setting for Buddhist practice that is often synonymous with political resistance. In part, this has been as response to the government's policy prohibiting NLD supporters from organizing public merit-making rituals or seeking ordination in the Sangha. The retreat to secluded meditation centers therefore shields supporters of the prodemocracy movement to some extent from omnipresent government scrutiny of civil and religious life.

The practice of meditation in Burma continues to enjoy widespread popularity. Meditation, the practice of and reflection on the path to nibbana, is often seen as a silent form of resistance against the regime's politics. As such, it can be a powerful and evocative symbol to counter the state's public displays of merit making. Among the country's intellectual elites for whom public expression of ideas is severely censored, meditation has been a venue for intellectual involvement and the articulation of a prodemocratic stance. According to Gustaaf Houtman (1999), meditators believe that there is an intrinsic affinity between cultivating the Eightfold Noble Path through meditation and the popular desire for democracy in Burma. While meditation is clearly integral to mainstream Buddhist practice in Burma today, many also conceive of the silent retreat into meditation as political action to change society.

The theme of ascetic power renewing society has a long history in Hindu and Buddhist traditions. The appeal to it among Socially Engaged Buddhists and practitioners of meditation is a new interpretation of the traditional Theravada doctrine whereby it is held that society benefits materially and spiritually from the presence of perfected individuals (arahant) within it. Traditionally, however, world renouncers are presumed to be ordained members of the Sangha. Modern interpretations, and particularly the Buddhist commitment to political activism of Aung San Suu Kyi, have paved the way for new perspectives on what it means to renounce the modern world and who can successfully embark on that kind of path. While Socially Engaged Buddhists in Burma still consider merit making a significant part of Buddhist practice, meditation assumes special significance within this modern Buddhist movement.

Buddhism in the Transnational Burmese Diaspora

Modern Burmese Buddhism has substantial extensions in transnational and diasporic communities. This trend amplifies the ways in which Burmese lineages, meditation practices, and Buddhist communities are represented outside the country. Since the 1970s, more than two dozen Burmese monasteries have been able to support resident monks on the east coast of the United States, in California, Indiana, Illinois, Texas, and, most recently, in Phoenix, Arizona. At least two Burmese monasteries exist in England, and others are located in Australia, Singapore, Malaysia, and Thailand. One of the oldest Burmese monasteries abroad is found at Bodhgaya, India—the place of the Buddha's enlightenment. Several factors combine in fostering these institutions. Like many immigrants, Burmese who managed to establish themselves abroad support the development of a resident Sangha because they welcome the opportunity to make merit locally. A resident Sangha also fosters community ties among Burmese living in the region and strengthens networks and connections with monks and laypeople in Burma. In their reinvented roles of peripatetic wandering, monks assume a particularly important role in shaping these relationships as they travel from abroad to visit sacred sites in Burma or carry their mission from Burma to the Burmese diaspora.

Since independence, each government, and particularly the current regime, has been keen to present Myanmar to its Asian neighbors as a devout Buddhist nation and as the land in which the Theravada tradition continues to flourish unspoiled. Consequently, international delegations attending state-sponsored Buddhist rituals have been significant components in the conduct of public diplomacy. In the absence of a national constitution, the regime experienced international pressures to move toward democracy and abandon practices that most other nations see as human rights abuses. In its effort to present a Buddhist national ethos to the international community, the government counters such criticism with expressions of Buddhist piety. This public demonstration also appeals to implicit romanticist and Orientalist ideals still widespread among Westerners, while affirming an explicit appeal to Asian values.

Information technology and other mass media help foster this representation of modern Buddhism. Although the democratization of access to knowledge through the Internet has not reached Burma, where information technologies are heavily censored, Burmese state Buddhism as well as other forms of Buddhist practices are richly represented on the Web. For instance, www.nirvana.com is a comprehensive site that offers a reliable perspective on contemporary Burmese orthodoxy. It contains many recent sermons and commentaries on Theravada teachings. Other more community-oriented Web pages such as "Buddhism in Myanmar" (http://web.ukonline.co.uk/buddhism/binburma.htm) richly document the social and geographic locations of modern Burmese Buddhism. The site www.e-dhamma.com relates primarily teachings and activities of the Burmese community in the San Francisco Bay Area. Finally, Buddhist teachings can also be found at http://web.ukonline.co.uk/buddhism/tipilist.htm, which describes its mission by stating, "The original Teachings of Gotama Buddha are available online in simple English, translated by distinguished Buddhist Scholars from Burma (Myanmar) where Theravada Buddhism prospers in pristine form." In these ways, the World Wide Web facilitates communication among disparate individuals and communities worldwide. It opens the Burmese Buddhist world to many Western Buddhist sympathizers or converts who are otherwise unlikely to be exposed to its practices and beliefs.

Missionizing continues to be an important aspect of modern Burmese Buddhist practice. However, such efforts are now carried out in social contexts that have already been structured by modern forms of social organization, communication, and technology. In other words, the missionary work of Burmese Buddhism abroad is likely to encounter public spheres where knowledge is necessarily fragmented into different spheres and does not exist, as Tambiah (1985) defined it for the classical Theravada world, as a total social fact. The pervasive presence of modern notions of nation, science, and technology means that an increasing number of ideas no longer cohere within an overarching Buddhist worldview. This, in turn, requires Burmese Buddhists to rethink what constitutes ideal practice, tenable doctrine, and appropriate beliefs in the modern world. Debates about science and religion, the rationalization of Buddhist doctrine, Socially Engaged Buddhism, and particularly meditation, as well as ecumenical conversations among interfaith groups, have been important milestones in this development. Converts to Buddhism necessarily also bring to their newly acquired faith some implicit or salient conceptual structures and cultural values of other groups and places. The interest Western converts show in Burmese meditation will bring further transformations to Burmese Buddhism. While such innovations do not replace the parameters of mainstream Burmese Buddhist practice, cross-cultural encounters within the Burmese diaspora nonetheless hold opportunities for further changes in the future.

Looking toward future developments among Buddhist communities, it would be difficult to imagine radical changes in the orientation of the Sangha and its leading monks without a concurrent change in the country's governance. Although several monastic organizations continue the struggle for actual monastic self-governance and accountability, they are not free to participate in the public sphere. In addition, violent attacks allegedly carried out by Buddhist monks against Muslim Burmese have marred the otherworldly status of the monks in Burma. Despite the repeated promise of significant political reforms, not much has been accomplished. Aung San Suu Kyi's house arrest has been renewed following a brutal and bloody attack in May 2003 that was orchestrated by agents of the regime on her and her supporters. Perhaps more than 100 people perished or disappeared in this ambush. Without a doubt, the spirit of change so popular in the 1980s and 1990s has been weakened by increased restrictions on the organization and membership of the NLD. At the same time, the leadership of the military regime is embroiled in internal power struggles that occasion periodic shake-ups among top-ranking generals and their client cliques. Supporters and family members of Ne Win, and recently also of his protégé Khin Nyunt, have been brought to trial on corruption charges of one kind or another, reflecting more broadly a widespread abuse of public trust among those with privileged access to power and perhaps indicating a colonial governing mentality among the elites of the state, whose primary mission appears to be to ensure stability for the extraction of resources. Opportunities for constructive engagements with regional issues or forums, such as the Association of Southeast Asian Nations (ASEAN), are allowed to fade as the ancient regime struggles for its continuity. Access to higher education is severely restricted, forcing the brightest among the younger generation to make their futures in social contexts over which shadows of fear of reprisals do not loom as dark.

Burmese Buddhism, however, has come to its own terms with modernity. The developments discussed previously inform public merit making and the orthodoxy of state Buddhism as much as they shape individual, familial, or communal interactions with local monks and monasteries. Charismatic individuals believed to be near the attainment of nirvana continue to emerge among communities of devotees, and meditation centers retain great popularity in the daily lives of most Buddhists in Burma. And so one is led to wonder when and how this rich plethora of modern Buddhist practices will engage the secular, should Buddhism in Burma ever escape the political repression and turmoil it has experienced in recent decades.

References

Aung San Suu Kyi. 1997. *Letters from Burma*. London: Penguin Group.

Aung Thwin, Michael. 1985. *Pagan: the Origins of Modern Burma*. Honolulu: University of Hawai'i Press.

Cohn, Bernard S. 1996. *Colonialism and Its Forms of Knowledge: The British in India*. Princeton, NJ: Princeton University Press.

Furnivall, John Sydenham. 1956. *Colonial Policy and Practice; a Comparative Study of Burma and Netherlands India*. New York: New York University Press.

Herbert, Patricia. 1983. *The Hsaya San Rebellion*. Brisbane, Australia: Monash University.

Houtman, Gustaaf. 1999. *Mental Culture in the Burmese Political Crisis*. Tokyo: Institute for the Study of Languages and Cultures of Asia and Africa, Tokyo University of Foreign Studies.

Keyes, Charles. 1993. Buddhist Economics and Buddhist Fundamentalism in Burma and Thailand. In *Fundamentalisms and the State: Remaking Polities, Economies, and Militance*, ed. Martin Marty and Scott Appleby, 367–409. Chicago: University of Chicago Press.

Keyes, Charles, Laurel Kendall, and Helen Hardacre, eds. 1994. *Asian Visions of Authority: Religion and the Modern States of East and Southeast Asia*. Honolulu: University of Hawai'i Press.

Mathews, Bruce. 1993. "Myanmar's Agony: The Struggle for Democracy." *Round Table: The Commonwealth Journal of International Affairs* 325(1):37–49.

Maung Maung. 1980. *From Sangha to Laity: Nationalist Movements of Burma 1920–1940*. Columbia, MO: South Asia Books.

Mendelson, E. Michael. 1975. *Sangha and State in Burma, A Study of Monastic Sectarianism and Leadership*. Ed. J. P. Ferguson. Ithaca, NY: Cornell University Press.

Myint-U Than. 2001. *The Making of Modern Burma*. Cambridge, UK: Cambridge University Press.

Sarkisyanz, Emanuel. 1965. *Buddhist Backgrounds of the Burmese Revolution*. The Hague: Martinus Nijhoff.

Schober, Juliane. 1997a. Buddhist Just Rule and Burmese National Culture: State Patronage of the Chinese Tooth Relic in Myanmar. *History of Religions* 36(3):218–243.

———. 1997b. In the Presence of the Buddha: Ritual Veneration of the Burmese Mahamuni Image. In *Sacred Biography in the Buddhist Traditions of South and Southeast Asia*, ed. Juliane Schober, 259–288. Honolulu: University of Hawai'i Press.

———. 2001. Venerating the Buddha's Remains in Burma: From Solitary Practice to the Cultural Hegemony of Communities. *Journal of Burma Studies* 6:111–139.

———. 2004. Mapping the Sacred in Theravada Buddhist Southeast Asia. *Sacred Places and Modern Landscapes: Sacred Geography and Social-Religious Transformations in South and Southeast Asia*, ed. Ronald Bull, 1–29. Tempe, AZ: Program for Southeast Asian Studies Monograph Series, Arizona State University.

———. 2005. Buddhist Visions of Moral Authority and Civil Society: The Search for the Post-Colonial State in Burma. In *Burma at the Turn of the Twenty-First Century*, ed. Monique Skidmore. Honolulu: University of Hawai'i Press.

Smith, Donald E. 1965. *Religion and Politics in Burma*. Princeton, NJ: Princeton University Press.

Tambiah, S. J. 1976. *World Conqueror and World Renouncer*. London: Cambridge University Press.

———. 1985. *Culture, Thought and Social Action: An Anthropological Perspective*. Cambridge, MA: Harvard University Press.

Tin Maung Maung Than. 1988. The Sangha and Sasana in Socialist Burma. *Sojourn* 3(1):26–61.

———. 1993. Sangha Reforms and Renewal of Sasana in Myanmar: Historical Trends and Contemporary Practice. In *Buddhist Trends in Southeast Asia*, ed. Trevor Ling, 6–66. Singapore: Institute for Southeast Asian Studies.

Chapter Four

Buddhism in Thailand
Negotiating the Modern Age

J U S T I N M C D A N I E L

This essay on Buddhism in modern Thailand will not offer a definition of modernity, but it will instead provide an overview of the ways in which Thai Buddhists have negotiated and confronted modernity. It examines two major aspects of Thai Buddhism since the beginning of the twentieth century: movements supportive of the state and movements resistant to the state. Both supportive and resistance movements are similar in the ways they justify themselves and their choice of a common foe. Both justify their reforms by calling for a return to an ideal past, when Buddhist practice was well organized, simple, pure, canonical, and uncorrupted. Both see protective magic and prognostication as corrupt and superstitious. Many Buddhist modernists from both movements believe the true Buddhism of the past will thrive in modern Thailand once these superstitious practices are abandoned.

However, although this dichotomy is a convenient heuristic tool, it is questioned throughout this essay. The dichotomy tends to depict Thai Buddhists as affected by globalization or rampant modernization. It sees the traditional Buddhist worldview challenged by technology and the global market with dramatic consequences. This type of approach, which has been taken by most Buddhist studies scholars over the past century, establishes a dichotomy of victim and victimizer among the Thai Buddhist community. It suggests that Thai Buddhism was a static entity that existed in a pristine state before modernization (i.e., the West) assaulted it. Instead, I view Thai Buddhists as dynamic arbiters and sponsors of ideology and innovation on the global stage. Thai Buddhists are not simply the supine receivers of modernization who choose to profit from it or be overrun. Many figures in modern Thailand neither chastise the deleterious effects of magic nor claim that their practice is original, genuine, or pure. Many have developed unique and new practices outside of negotiations with non-Thai Buddhist groups and non-Buddhists. Many (from both the supportive and resistant camps) negotiate with, rather than blindly embrace or passively ignore, the modern age. These figures dynamically respond and adjust according to the times rather than becoming either the victimizers or victims of modernity. Furthermore, by comfortably incorporating diverse practices, many Thais expand the parameters of what is Buddhist and what is Thai.

Order and the Ideal Past: The State and Its Supporters

In the nineteenth century, the Siamese kings Rama the Fourth (Mongkut) and Rama the Fifth (Chulalongkorn) made great efforts to formalize the Buddhist ecclesiastical system and educational practices in Siam and in their spheres of influence (or vassal states) in the north, northeast, and south. This was part of the nation-building and social control process to suppress regionalism, strengthen the country against foreign missionary influence, formalize the curriculum, and modernize the entire education system. Siamese ecclesiastical ranks, textbooks printed in Siamese script, monastic examinations, the Pali Buddhist Canon, and teachers approved from Bangkok and central Siam were sent to the rural and urban areas in Siam and its holdings. Monks from the recently pacified north, northeast, and south were brought to Bangkok to study in two new monastic universities (Mahachulalongkorn and Mahamakut). Localized forms of expression, language, curricula, and script were considered irrelevant to this formalization and centralization. One of the most significant features of Buddhism in modern Thailand is its apparently well-organized and centralized institutional structure. Since Siam (later Thailand) is the only country in Southeast Asia that was never colonized, the nation-building project in which religious reform played a major part could be considered a success. Although the Buddhist ecclesia has grown in wealth and numbers since 1902, there are still deep fissures in Thai Buddhism that existed before 1902 and persist today.

Royal reform of Buddhism is not particularly modern. Consistently from the earliest thirteenth-century records to 1902, Siamese kings and high-ranking monks saw it as their duty to collect and edit Buddhist texts, rewrite Buddhist history, purge the community of monks (Sangha) of corrupt persons, and rein in renegade independent-minded practitioners. By 1902, these techniques had become more efficient and widespread. In 1902, King Chulalongkorn and Prince Wachirayan, who was an ordained monk and who had become the Supreme Patriarch of the entire Thai Buddhist Sangha, made it the role of the Sangha to educate the Thai people and regulated the organization of monastic education. Those two men, working with another half-brother, Prince Damrong (the minister of the interior), released the Act on the Administration of the Sangha ("Acts of the Administration of the Buddhist Order of Sangha of Thailand: 2445 [1902], 2484 [1941], 2505 [1962]"; see specifically R. S. 121, cited in Ishii 1986, 68). Before this Sangha Act, monastic education and administration in Thailand were neither formal nor centralized (Mulasilpa 1996; Reynolds 1972). They depended largely on the aims of the monks of each monastery. The Sangha Act was designed to make those residing in a monastery a "service to the nation" and to deflect criticism from European missionaries who denounced the poor and idiosyncratic state of Thai Buddhist education and organization.

The Sangha Act comprises largely administrative rules dividing the Buddhist ecclesia into formal ranks and assigning national, provincial, and district heads of the Sangha (Ishii 1986, 69). They are still in effect today. Each of the regions (north, south, central, and northeast) has a formal hierarchy of monks, all of whom report to the Mahathera Samakom (Council of Elder Teachers) headed by the Supreme Patriarch. Individual monasteries are still run by abbots (chao awat) and deputy abbots (rong chao awat), but after 1902 the abbots had to report regularly to their district and regional heads. All monks had to be registered with a particular monastery and were issued identification numbers and cards. Prince Wachirayan commented on the act, "Although monks are already subject to the ancient law contained in the Vinaya [Buddhist Book of Precepts], they must also subject themselves to the authority which derives from the specific and general law of the State" (Ishii 1986, 70).

In 1902, about 80,000 monks became subject to the law of the royal government of Siam, which controlled their admission to monkhood, the right to ordain, the size and status of monastic ground, and the ranking of monks. There was certainly sporadic resistance in the form of renegade monks in the north like Krupa Siwichai and rebellions of holy men in the northeast until 1924. Still, the suppression of the independent-minded outer kingdoms was not cited as the main impetus for the state's monastic reforms. Prince Wachirayan believed that reform was necessary to ensure that Siamese Buddhism could purify itself. He believed, as did the king, that Buddhism was simpler and more pure in the distant past. True Buddhism was that designed by the Buddha himself in India 2,400 years earlier. The only way to return to that purity was to go directly to the Buddha's words—the Pali Canon.

There is little evidence that the Pali Canon was available to and accessible by the majority of Thais in or previous to 1902. The canon was rarely found as a set in one monastery, and the authoritative parts of the canon were not commonly agreed on at any time in Thai history (McDaniel 2002). Still, the prince considered the canonical Pali texts to be the most important source of Buddhist ethics, law, and history. Therefore, he wanted to make the study of the

Pali Canon more prominent. To facilitate this goal, he also wanted to promote the study of Pali grammar. He composed six volumes of Pali grammar, as well as several guidebooks for students (including the still standard Navakowat), outlining what he saw as basic Buddhist ethics; the Buddhasasana Subhasit, a selection of short pithy Buddhist proverbs from the canon; a Buddha biography; and a guide to the Vinaya. These textbooks, all written in simple and straightforward Thai, began to form, ideally, the standard curriculum for monks in Siam. Monks in both monastic universities were encouraged to take examinations in Pali and Thai designed by the prince and based on these and other anthologized Buddhist texts. Interestingly enough, most of the examinations were on commentarial texts, not on canonical texts themselves. It was not until 1913 that Prince Wachirayan's system was standard for all monks in the kingdom. Generally, after 1902, Siamese/Thai Buddhism became reified, formalized, and intertwined with nation building.

The state-centered and state-sponsored reform movements of King Mongkut, Prince Wachirayan, King Chulalongkorn, and Prince Damrong, among others, portrayed Thai Buddhism as overly corrupted by those claiming magical and fortune-telling powers and, thus, in need of renewal. Prince Wachirayan in particular believed that there was an ideal past when Buddhist practice did not involve protective magic, when all monks studied Pali for many years, and when the Buddhist ecclesia and benevolent Buddhist kings worked together to care for the common people. His reform efforts have had mixed results.

The Forest Tradition of Thammayut Monks

These mixed results are represented in many ways by the history of the Thammayut sect. The Thammayut (in Pali, Dhammayuttika) sect (nikaya) of monks was founded in Thailand by King Mongkut and Prince Wachirayan in the mid-nineteenth century. The Thammayut sect was originally initiated to protect the royal ideal of pure Buddhism. However, the Thammayut monks changed over time from being representative of the state Buddhism of Bangkok to being a collective symbol of independent forest practice. The Thammayut monks can be seen as supporting both the state's centralization policies and the ideal of a rational, nonmagical, nonritualistic Buddhist ideal. It is interesting that these Thammayut monks have gained popularity among magical amulet dealers, prognosticators, and spirit mediums, who trade on the names of these forest ascetics and draw on them for protection and power. The state's efforts to eradicate these practices failed, and the Thammayut has grown to be an independent source of charisma and power, offering its members and followers an alternative resource in the modern practice of Buddhism.

The modern lineage of forest monks is seen as beginning with Phra Ajahn Man Bhuridatto and Phra Ajahn Sao Kantasilo. Scholars sometimes portray these and other Thammayut monks as symbols of pure Buddhist simplicity. They are described as straight-talking monks for the people—monks who do not sully themselves with excessive textual scholarship, monastic examinations, the practice of protective magic, or elaborate rituals. They lead the ideal monastic life in the forest, meditating, preaching, and not harming trees. They are not interested in politics or modernization and are not involved in the commercialization of Buddhist practice. However, most descriptions of the Thammayut monks do not mention their connection with state centralization, the suppression of local Lao religious practice and independence, or their participation (perhaps unwilling) in the marketplace of amulets and fortune-telling.

In contrast, Hayashi Yukio asserts that the beginnings of the forest tradition in northeastern Thailand were part of a state-sponsored program to pacify and incorporate the regional Lao populations into the Thai polity. Phra Ajahn Man and Phra Ajahn Sao were agents of Thai nationalism sent by Prince Wachirayan, who believed that pure Buddhism was textual and canonical Buddhism. He believed that the local religious practice of the northeast was defined by superstition and ignorance simply irrational in their most benign forms but dangerous to the state (because many rebellions in the northeast were led by religious leaders) in their most malignant forms. Yukio writes that the wandering forest monks were part of the nationalization of religion,

> the centralization of the Buddhist Sangha, the elimination of indigenous beliefs, and the popularization of meditation practices in the northeast region. All these directly or indirectly resulted from the efforts . . . to purify and reorganize state Buddhism . . . [and the] realization of these objectives required intervention of charismatic monks or "teachers of the masses." . . . The successors and perpetuators of the doctrinal system of Theravada Buddhism were originally the elite. (Yukio 2003, 285)

Yukio continues to show that the first monastery of the forest tradition, Wat Supatthararam, was built by the elite in 1853 with funds granted by King Mongkut. Soon six other royal monasteries were established in this region, which was considered a hot spot for Lao rebels and still was not under centralized Siamese control. Previously, the local leader of the Sangha in this region had been a Lao monk who possessed rank and insignia in the Lao royal government. When he died, King Mongkut had him replaced by a Bangkok-trained monk who spread the centralized, elite Siamese interpretation of Buddhism. This monk promoted the study of the Thai languages, disparaged local religious practice, built monastic Pali libraries, and appointed other Bangkok-trained monks to take over the local ecclesia (Yukio 2003, 285). By 1899, the word *Lao* was removed from administrative documents for the region. Centralization and nationalization were seen as urgently necessary because of the millenarian rebellions of local holy men (phu mi bun or mo wiset) with claims to power because of their protective magic and ability to predict the future. Several rebellions in the north and northeast were started by local monks and a mo wiset from Laos who either claimed that the future Buddha was coming or that they themselves were the future Buddha. They attracted followers by magically curing disease, teaching the Dhamma (Dharma), exhorting followers to follow the precepts, and refraining from meat eating. In 1924, they claimed that the new Buddhist era under the power of Metteya (the future Buddha) would be centered in Vientiane, Laos, a particularly dangerous claim to make to the Siamese authorities. Using their supernatural powers and stolen rifles, they destroyed Siamese governmental regional offices and refused to pay taxes. The Thammayut were part of the Siamese government's efforts to destroy this Lao resistance movement, which sought its strength in the popular beliefs of protective magic and prognostication.

Phra Ajahn Man and Phra Ajahn Sao and were assigned to the "strategic bases for promulgating doctrinal studies and meditation" (Yukio 2003, 286) in the northeast. While pointing out that the head monks of the Thammayut temples in the northeast were all natives of Bangkok, Yukio further notes that Phra Achan Sao Kantasinthera (an alternative spelling for Phra Ajahn Sao) went on to lead an important school of meditation practice in the northeast and established an influential lineage of monks in the region.

Sao had a prominent disciple named Phra Achan Man Phurithat (alternative spelling for Phra Ajahn Man), a charismatic monk from Ubon who was born in 1870 and died in 1949 and who was to promulgate the practice of meditation throughout the country. Man also produced an important disciple. These three monks, beginning with Sao, are spoken of today as venerable monks who devoted themselves to the national dissemination of meditation. Their disciples later worked in the Sangha, and some were given administrative posts as educators (Yukio 2003, 286).

Yukio correctly notes that Phra Ajahn Man and Phra Ajahn Sao are commonly mentioned as the founders of the meditative schools of the northeast (and, by extension, modern meditation practice in Thailand) but that they were also in fact actively trying to replace long-held regional practices of meditation and Buddhist ritual. Therefore, these new meditation teachers were initially rejected by many in the northeast. Only gradually did they come to impress local Buddhists with the severity of their asceticism, especially their practice of meditating in charnel grounds and wearing robes made out of rags from funeral pyres. They also gained popularity by making extensive tours throughout the region. For example, the well-known Thammayut monks Phra Ajahn Thet Thetrangsi, Phra Ajahn Sing, and Phra Ajahn Fan Acaro accompanied seventy other monks to "eliminate spirit beliefs by spreading thamma [Dhamma] and erecting forest temples" (Yukio 2003, 292). Their popularity grew because of they were seen as

> beings feared by the guardian spirits and evil spirits who lurk in forests and caves. They enter natural graveyards, acquire wisdom (pannya law wicha), and have no fear of death; they conquer the forest world. They heal themselves with spiritual unity (thamma) when afflicted with illness during their ascetic practices. They subdue evil spirits and destroy the guardian spirits cults in every village they visit during their wanderings, converting them to Buddha's teachings. They convert mo wisa, wielders of wisa [magical powers] to be pious Buddhists. They hold religious services morning and night and can cure illness by chanting sutras. They preach obedience to the precepts and to the Triple Gems [Buddha, Dhamma, Sangha]. . . . They convert local charismatic monks to the Thammayut Nikai. (Yukio 2003, 292)

These wandering teachers were seen as reformers and purveyors of a rational, canonical Buddhism, and their popularity was due to widespread belief in their superior healing powers. They were social activists and serious ascetics. They lived in rural areas, but their lineage and early training were sponsored by royal temples in Bangkok. Over time, these wandering forest monks became valued in the northeast and throughout Thailand as powerful healers and usurpers of the magical power previously associated with the Lao and Thai lay magicians (mo du or phu feuk saiyasat). These monks gained followings because they were socially active in solving local problems, not just because they were solitary mediators. Their amulets are valuable possessions for collectors and healers. Their statues, pictures, magical yantras, and relics are found in taxicabs, city bazaars, rural monasteries, and magicians' altars throughout the country.

Political Activism among Thai Buddhists

Siam changed its name to Thailand in 1939, having changed from an absolute monarchy to a constitutional monarchy in 1932. After 1932, the state sought to gain more direct control over the Sangha than even the absolute monarchy had. In 1934, an independent government committee was established to examine Sangha finances and, in 1941, the new Sangha Act effectively gave the government control over internal Sangha organization and executive offices. The various military and elected governments over the past sixty years have generally asserted that the Sangha should play a more practical role in modern Thai society and become more socially engaged. This social engagement—

Images of monks, kings, and the Buddha on altar shelves at a Bangkok religious store. Both images and shelves are for sale. They are commonplace on home and monastery altars throughout the country. These images are made of brass, porcelain, and plastic, and some have audio-cassette players in their bases so that one can listen to tapes of Buddhist chanting while looking at the image. (Courtesy of Justin McDaniel)

advocated by many Thammayut monks, the government, Christian missionaries, and Western critics of the Sangha—led the two major monastic universities to institute programs in which urban-educated monks would provide social services for the poor, especially in the north, northeast, and south. The role of the monastery in health and education was seen as part of the original vision of the Buddha, even though there were no monasteries at the time of the Buddha and little textual evidence showing that ancient nuns and monks were encouraged to be socially engaged.

In 1966, Mahachulalongkorn Monastic University stated that its students should provide "voluntary social services, both material and spiritual, for the welfare of the community, such as giving advice and help in the event of family problems and misfortunes" (Ishii 1986, 138). Monks from these universities were assigned to be teachers in rural areas, volunteers in hospitals, and assistants in community economic development. The monks also established numerous new monastic schools designed to prepare rural students for future training at the monastic universities in the city, and they disseminated textbooks printed for urban monastic students. The universities provided training courses to prepare their "volunteer" students. The monks who were sent out also became part of the nation-building process to help incorporate the rural areas in the north, northeast, and south. This became an anticommunist movement when the Department of Religious Affairs sent Thammadut (envoys of the Dhamma) to the northeast to spread Buddhist teachings and help with rural development. Most monks were sent to the northeast, the place of most of the communist activity and of ethnic Lao residents. A report of the monks' progress in 1969 confirmed their role in combating communist activity, which they believed "caused the people great suffering" (Ishii 1986, 139; Reynolds 1972). These monks were working side by side with anticommunist government policies and the U.S. military, which had thousands of troops in the region. Monks were also involved in helping the government pacify and incorporate hill tribes and Muslim populations in the north and south of the country.

One well-known monk who led the anticommunist brigade, Phra Kittivuddho, resided at the famous Wat Paknam in Thonburi across the Chao Phraya River from Bangkok and later moved to teach at the monastic university on the grounds of Wat Mahathat. He argued for greater social engagement of monks and novices. He also called for an aggressive conversion campaign to augment the moral coffers of the country. He believed that communist propaganda was influencing the superstitious practices of protective magic by village mo wiset or mo du (magicians) and the millenarian movements that predicted the coming of the future Buddha. He was also suspicious of the allegiance of the ethnic Lao associated with these practices and their possible connections to the communists in Laos proper.

Increasing student activism in the early 1970s, partly in response to the war in Vietnam and the military dictatorship in Thailand, led Phra Kittivuddho to believe that communism would soon destroy the country and ban true Buddhist practice. Therefore, he believed that the Sangha had to defend Thailand from foreign invaders and the threat of communism. In one oft-quoted sermon, he claimed that killing communists was not demeritorious, because they were "enemies" of Buddhism and the Thai state (Keyes 1999, 153). Furthermore, communists were "bestial" and not fully human. He even called for monastic participation in protests against left-leaning student groups and for the disrobing of monks suspected of harboring communist sympathies. Many monks, including the Supreme Patriarch, believed that Kittivuddho was becoming too involved in politics and social reform, but no disciplinary action was taken against him (Keyes 1999, 152).

Phra Kittivuddho, although radical in his views, was not the only monk who viewed Thailand, capitalism, and Buddhism as related entities. Luang Ta

Mahabua, a well-known student of Phra Ajahn Man, believed that Buddhism could be used to support the national market economy. Although not anti-communist (which of course involves much more than rejecting a particular economic system), Mahabua asserted that after the Asian financial crisis of 1997, the subsequent devaluing of the Thai baht, and the massive recession, Buddhists should donate money to the government. He set up his monastery in Udon Thani Province in the rural northeast as a broker for the donations. The campaign, whose moniker translates as "Thai Help Thai," collected more than $US4.3 million and 1,457 kilograms of gold in donations that were given to the Ministry of Finance. Mahabua believed that the money wasted on protective amulets (phra kreuang) and fortune-tellers could be put to better use helping the nation.

After the money was collected and handed over to the ministry, Mahabua inquired how it was serving the country and was not satisfied by the answers he received. He started referring to the ministry as "ever-hungry ghouls seeking to eat people's guts" and "idiots who think of nothing but cheating on the country" (Prangtip 2000). Minister of Finance Tarrin Nimmanahaeminda was seen as the thief of the money. Mahabua's followers collected more than 50,000 signatures in a drive to impeach Nimmanahaeminda. Many believe that that enemies of the Democratic Party, of which Nimmanahaeminda is a well-known member, fanned the flames of controversy to bolster their own party—the Thai Rak Thai (Thais Love Thailand) Party. Despite the possible trickery and alleged corruption in the Ministry of Finance, Mahabua has been widely criticized for being becoming overinvolved in the world of political corruption. The problem with the money is seen as a problem of his own creation. Monks, many believe, should be above these worldly (lokiya) matters. In general, the criticism of Kittivuddho and Mahabua reflects a common modern reaction of Buddhist laypeople and monks to social engagement. This social engagement is often seen as Western, Bangkok-centric, elitist, and potentially destructive to the supramundane status of monkhood. Mahabua, being a part of a lineage of forest monks, was seen as sullying the purity of the Sangha.

The Dhammakaya Movement

Probably the most politically, economically, educationally, and socially engaged of monks in the modern period has been Phra Dhammajayo. Dhammajayo is the head of the well-known Dhammakaya movement in Thailand. Born as Chaiboon Sutipol in 1944, he was heavily influenced by the teachings of the nun Khun Yai, who herself was the primary student of the founder of the Dhammakaya movement, Luang Po Sod (1906–1959). Luang Po Sod (or

Mongkolthepamuni/Sod Mikaeonoi) was the abbot of Wat Pak Nam, a large and well-stocked Bangkok monastery. He started instructing his students, both lay and ordained, in a new type of meditation that he called *Dhammakaya*. He believed that if meditators concentrated with the proper intention and repeated the mantra *samma arahan* ("right attainment"), they would see in their mind's eye a luminescent Buddha figure growing in their stomach. This figure could grow up to 20 centimeters tall and could be seen by anyone in only 20 to 30 minutes of practice.

Although criticized by some who see Dhammakaya meditation as psychological manipulation or implantation, the movement under Luang Po Sod and Khun Yai grew quickly, especially after Dhammajayo started encouraging college students in Bangkok to attend classes with Khun Yai in 1969. The next year, a wealthy laywoman donated a large tract of land in the suburbs and funds to build a meditation center. Dhammajayo glorified Khun Yai with a large photo above the front door and started to arrange mass ordinations for college graduates. He appealed to college students and young professionals by stating that there was no need for elaborate Buddhist ritual, protective magic, fortune-telling, and the tools, images, and money that went toward them. He also started university Dhammakaya study groups for well-educated nuns, monks, and laypeople all over the country and obtained support from Princess Sirinthorn and the National Sangha Council to build the Dhammakaya Monastery (Heikkilä-Horn 1999, 93–96). By the early 1990s, the monastery had grown significantly. During those years, one encountered colossal billboards for the Dhammakaya movement on the northern tollway coming out of Bangkok advertising its convenient (saduak) weekend retreats for working adults and students and the talks sponsored by the movement held at Chulalongkorn University.

Up until today, these events have grown even larger despite charges that the movement oversimplifies spiritual attainment in Buddhism. At Dhammakaya retreats, which are attended by up to 10,000 people a week, participants are asked to meditate for two 30-minute sessions and develop self-confidence to help them succeed in family and business matters. They are offered a meditation kit for sale that includes a set of white robes, a plastic umbrella, a bottle of water, and a small pamphlet. Dhammakaya adherents emphasize that magic, amulets, and even ordination are arbitrary for the path to personal well-being and financial and spiritual security. Thais are told of their need to return to the original body of the Buddha and to cast off the accoutrements that have polluted his body and message over the centuries. The iridescent Dhammakaya body growing in a person's belly was the true body of the Buddha. This message has attracted the growing well-educated and entrepreneurial Thai middle class who lack the time to ordain, study large tomes of Buddhist scripture, or meditate for several hours a day in the forest. Dhammakaya has also enjoined the sponsorship of influential politicians like General Chaowalit Yongchaiyud and major financial institutions like the Siam Commercial Bank and the Bangkok Bank. By some estimates, Dhammakaya coffers have grown to over $US50 million. By supporting the state and capitalist ideals, the Dhammakaya movement has been very successful thus far.

Modern Malaise: Resisting the State in Thai Buddhism

Some Buddhist intellectuals and reformers in the modern period have resisted the pressure to support the centralizing, capitalistic power structure of the national Thai government. Resistance both to consumerism and centralization has come from both urban and rural monks, as well as from lay intellectuals. However, like those belonging to the movements supportive of the state, those in these resistance movements generally see their movements as returns to the purity of the true Buddhism of the past. Like Kittivuddho, Prince Vajiranan, King Chulalongkorn, and Dhammajayo, they called for reform and for reviving a more innocent and integral Buddhism. Moreover, they also see practices of protective magic and prognostication as reflecting corruptions of Buddhism.

Santi Asok and Development Monks

The Santi Asok movement, founded by Bodhiraksa (or Mongkol Rakpong) in 1973, calls for a return to the original religion of the Buddha. Bodhiraksa holds that the two major sects of Thai Buddhism, the Thammayut and the Mahanikaya, exploit the laity by accepting lavish gifts, encouraging attachment to material goods, condoning or even encouraging the practice of astrology and magic, and ignoring the fundamental ills of society for their own profit. He refers to the National Sangha Council as an illegal and divisive organization and, instead, calls for a return to the "fundamental teachings and practices of ancient times" that extolled monastic simplicity, poverty, dedicated social engagement, and sincere meditation. Because of this highly critical language, because for ten years he ordained monks under his own sect before he himself had been ordained, and because he does not shave his eyebrows (the last two illegal according to Sangha law), he was forcibly disrobed in June 1989. His ordained followers, a group that had grown to include sixty monks and twenty nuns, were also charged with impersonating genuine monks and nuns. Forty-six other Santi Asok monks were allowed to remain in robes since they had been ordained before joining Bodhiraksa's group.

Bodhiraksa's message gained much publicity because of this criminal case and his many sermons, television appearances, and publications. He claimed that his was the authentic Buddhism, in contrast to the three types of religion practiced by the majority of Thai monks. The first type, occult Buddhism, encourages the lottery, gambling, astrological predictions, and the cult of protective amulets. This type "increases people's desires in life, but the ability to respond to these desires decreases" (Heikkilä-Horn 1999, 100). The second, capitalistic Buddhism, "increases both the desires and the ability to satisfy the desires . . . this form of Buddhism encourages the practice of different types of meditation in order to calm the mind for a length of time. Once the mind becomes clear again, they, i.e., the businessmen, executives and bankers . . . will engage themselves in competition with one another and start to exploit society again" (Heikkilä-Horn 1999, 100). The third, hermetic Buddhism, encourages isolation, simplicity, and meditation but also removes a person's ability to serve society. His authentic Buddhism, in contrast, will "decrease their desires and simultaneously increase their productivity and creativity. It helps people reduce their selfishness, to become more industrious and hard-working, to consume less and share the rest of what they have with society" (Heikkilä-Horn 1999, 101; Keyes 1999, 129–134).

This low-impact ideology also is prevalent among so-called development monks in modern Thailand. A small minority of monks in recent years have asserted that Buddhism naturally supports environmental preservation and protection. James Taylor has followed the work of these monks and their resistance to forest degradation, industrial pollution, and habitat destruction. He provides a few case studies. For example, Phra Ajahn Thui Chanthakaro held a tree-planting day at his monastery in northeastern Thailand (although the Vinaya bars monks from digging holes in the ground and from planting in general) and argued against the government-sponsored project of the monocultural planting of eucalyptus trees in place of natural diverse forests (Taylor 1997, 211). Phra Thui argues that the people are "slowly killing themselves" and creating more suffering in the world when they exploit the environment.

Phra Thui's actions came in the 1980s after decades of deforestation had reduced Thai forest cover from 70 percent to less than 30 percent. This deforestation is the result not only of timber consumption, slash-and-burn agricultural practices, and exotic teak furniture needs, but also because of the Thai government's efforts against the anticommunist insurgency. The area around Phra Thui's monastery was deemed

a potential communist stronghold or "pink area" (*khet siichomphuu*). It was assumed that when the trees disappeared, so would any enticements for insurgents [to hide]. . . . Therefore extensification, forest clearing, and settlement were encouraged by the government and the military as a means of domesticating and civilizing the forests. (Taylor 1999, 46)

Other monks also worked to resist the government's development agenda and devise their own program for economic development in the impoverished rural regions of the country. Luang Po Naan and Luang Po Khamkian from the northeast worked closely with villagers in the 1990s to conserve the environment and expose corrupt local officials who illegally sold protected timber and exploited national parks. Like Phra Thui, these two monks stated that the government's ecological programs were largely failures because of local corruption and because planting solely profitable eucalyptus trees actually damaged sustainable healthy forests (Taylor 1999, 46–48). Both monks have received much assistance from mostly foreign-based nongovernmental organizations (NGOs) and environmental groups. Applying Buddhist approaches to ecology, Phra Khamakian and Phra Naan argue that the government and the people must revive "the sacred in everyday relationships with the world" (Taylor 1999, 46–48) and see the preservation of the forest as part of the Buddhist practice of selflessness.

The most controversial of development monks is Phrajak Kuttajitto. After leaving his wife and five children to take up the monastic life in 1977, he began serious meditation practice in the forests of central and northeast Thailand. He began to see the gradual deforestation and decided that if his practice and that of the forest monk tradition were to survive he would need to actively fight to protect his surroundings. Buddhist practice, he believed, had devolved into superstitious self-protection and a means for winning the lottery. Instead, he believed that Buddhism was based on selflessness and the need to help others, including the environment. He developed the unique method of ordaining trees in the Dong Yai forest. He and other local villagers (who were actually living illegally on national park grounds) tied robes around trees to protect them from loggers. He also fought on the side of the villagers who were being forcefully resettled outside the national park. Phrajak saw, like Phra Naan, Phra Thui, and Phra Khamakian, that the government and corrupt businesspeople were actually selling off the trees in the forest and then planting cash crops. After staging many protests and gaining the support of NGOs and the foreign press, he was arrested in April 1991. Phitaktham (Dhammic Conservation), a group of laity and monastics numbering about 225, fought for his release and began nonviolently resisting the work of loggers. Phrajak was arrested again, and his monastery was attacked by a group of off-duty policemen and some uniformed soldiers. His movement largely fell apart and he left the monastic life. He grew increasingly paranoid and was arrested again in 1995 for illegal gambling. Phrajak's personal troubles aside, his movement succeeded in calling a great deal of attention to the deforestation and forced resettlement of the poor under the military regime of General Suchinda Kraprayoon in the early 1990s.

Buddhist Social Activism

Phrajak's efforts also contributed to the socially engaged Buddhist movement of the well-known Sulak Sivaraksa, who not only has fought to protect forests under the inspiration of Buddhism, but has also built a comprehensive Buddhist group of grassroots activists and social critics. Although Sulak is rightly criticized for not grounding his often inflammatory statements in historical fact or textual evidence and for being egotistical and uncompromising, he, more than any other monk or layperson, has called attention to the social and economic problems facing Thailand today (Swearer 1996, 106). Furthermore, he has contributed to a gradually growing lay activist movement that justifies its protests in Buddhist terminology and idealized Buddhist ethics. Sulak (born in 1933) began his work as a clerk in a Western import-export firm and is from the Sino-Thai Bangkok upper-middle class. He studied in Wales, Thailand, and England and became an editor of one of Thailand's most influential social science journals in 1961. This journal and his later work with foreign NGOs, Thai activist intellectuals, progressive members of the Sangha, and numerous organizations promote democracy, women's rights, land reform, freedom of the press, environmental protection, nonviolence, and poverty relief while calling for a return to core Buddhist values.

These Buddhist values, Sulak claims, are those that promote community-building policies, "economic simplicity," and "spiritual cultivation"(Swearer 1996, 113). According to him, many Buddhist monks have become slavishly attached to the profits made from producing and blessing protective amulets and images, and many have grown fat off the profits of lottery number prediction. True Buddhist principles, when put into action, call for national self-reliance, production for use to meet basic needs, grassroots organization, coalitions, the integration of women into the economy and political realms, protection of sustainable resources, and programs to relieve poverty. Sulak certainly delivers mixed messages in his speeches and writings. Although he calls for grassroots democracy, he avidly supports the royal family and glorifies the largely imaginary golden age of the thirteenth-century paternalistic Siamese King Ramkhamhaeng and the Indian Buddhist King Asoka. He heralds both the conservative values of hard work, a "pull-yourself-up-by-the-bootstraps" mentality, economic isolationism, and fervent nationalism and the liberal values of social welfare, complete freedom of expression, and openness towards Thailand's neighbors Laos, Cambodia, Malaysia, and Burma. Donald Swearer (1996)

Thai monasteries are not simply centers of meditation and scholasticism; they are also community and commercial centers. Here a woman selling lottery tickets searches for change in her purse, as she sits below a bodhi tree and next to a sacred shrine on the grounds of Wat Indraviharn in Bangkok, Thailand. (Courtesy of Justin McDaniel)

points out that many of these same values are expressed more coherently in the works of the famous Thai Buddhist monk, Buddhadasa Bhikkhu.

Buddhadasa (1906–1993) was one of the most prolific writers in modern Thai Buddhist history. Many of his writings have been translated into foreign languages, and his meditation center in southern Thailand, Suan Mokh (Garden of Liberation), has attracted thousands of foreign and Thai practitioners alike. After studying Pali and the official Buddhist university curriculum in Bangkok, Buddhadasa left the city to become a rural preacher and advocate for social justice. He believed that Buddhism could be made simple and accessible to the masses. His sermons often were centered on the creative and expansive translation of Buddhist terms, like *idappaccayata* ("conditionality"), *anatta* ("nonself"), *tathata* ("thusness"), and *samma* ("right") (Santikaro 1996, 155). His concept of Dhammic socialism is perhaps the most influential on activists like Sulak. Dhammic socialism holds that the common good should come first and that selfishness is the root of suffering in society. Buddhadasa believed that humans were "naturally" social creatures and needed to work together for "mutual benefit and support" (Santikaro 1996, 167). The law of nature, he argued, was the "law of interdependence" (paticcasamuppada). Dhammic socialism, as interpreted by Santikaro Bhikkhu, states, "We should observe that from birth through our entire lives we are dependent on parents, relatives, friends, the government, and even enemies. Our lives, well-being, and meaningfulness depend on those of others" (Santikaro 1996, 168).

Buddhadasa rejected Marxian calls for the revenge of the worker and the Leninist belief in the need for an elite ruling class that spoke for the rights of the worker, but he did believe that a society based on communal peace and prosperity over individual achievement and capitalistic competition was more in line with Buddhist ethics. Perhaps this is what Sulak has been calling for—not a particular type of government system or a rigid understanding of liberal or conservative values, but a society that makes decisions based on social well-being and prosperity rather than one whose policies promote individual ambition, a greedy use of magic and fortune telling, sanctioned economic exploitation, unfettered technological progress, and unrestricted profit-driven market forces.

Modern Roles for Thai Buddhist Women

Elsewhere, those same market forces, individual ambition, and economic exploitation are also seen as the causes of Thailand's large prostitution industry. Although the degree to which Thailand's prostitution industry is larger than that in other nations is often overstated, its growth since the late 1960s (fueled, but not necessarily caused, by the American military presence in the country) and the subsequent black market institutionalization of human trafficking is a major concern for the Thai government, concerned citizens, and parts of the Sangha. Often, however, this concern is linked more to the HIV/AIDS epidemic and less to views about the inherent immorality of prostitution.

One major Thai voice that has protested the industry is Chatsumarn Kabilsingh, a foreign-educated associate professor of philosophy at Thailand's elite Thammasat University. She believes that the lack of concern about the problem of human trafficking and prostitution is partly due to a generally myopic view in Thailand that prostitution is a free choice, the long history of the industry being sanctioned by the royalty and the lower classes, and the general lack of female voices of authority in the Thai Sangha. Her protest is part of a larger project to open up the opportunity for women in Thailand to be fully ordained nuns (bhikkhuni) and to bring a French/American type of women's rights movement to her country. Kabilsingh is part scholar, part activist, and part Buddhist practitioner. She has founded a branch of the Sakyadhita Foundation for women in Thailand. She also helps promote the ordination of women as nuns and the training of mae chee (women who lead a religious life, take the first

Professors at the elite Abhidhamma Jotika College in Bangkok, Thailand. (Courtesy of Justin McDaniel)

eight to ten precepts, shave their heads, wear white robes, and live monastic lives) at the Dhammajarinee Wittaya, the first Buddhist school especially for women in Thailand, and she calls for an end to the prostitution industry in Thailand. As for prostitution, she acknowledges that there is no textual evidence that prostitution has ever been condemned for the laity by the Buddha or his disciples and that Buddhism "does not hold a condescending view of prostitutes [in terms of their ability to eventually achieve enlightenment]" (Kabilsingh 1991, 71). The Buddha saw prostitutes and those who patronize them as suffering, unenlightened beings, absorbed in their own foolish desires. Those seeking enlightenment should neither be prostitutes nor visit them, and of course, all monks and nuns are barred from sexual relations of any kind. In turn, prostitutes and those who visit them can achieve enlightenment, according to her, if they abandon their exploitive exchange.

Kabilsingh asserts that if poor women had greater opportunities for education and a legitimate place in the Sangha, then prostitution would not be their only option to escape poverty. Furthermore, a greater number of female voices in the Sangha may inspire women to turn from prostitution to religion. Poverty,

as well as sociocultural factors such as Thai notions of "the ideal male as con-
querer" and the great value "placed on beauty" are very difficult to change, but
if women had a religious voice and space then these factors may be less oppressive (Kabilsingh 1991, 80). She is also against the production of love potions by
Buddhist magicians and the perpetuation of poverty by offering women false
hopes of financial success through the lottery, promoting a belief in spirits that
give magical gifts of money, and so on. Since they cannot become nuns, women
are reduced to being slaves to male magicians and false beliefs. The official reason the Thai Sangha has not reinstituted the full ordination of female renunciates from the time of the Buddha is because the lineage of Theravada nuns
literally died out in Sri Lanka around the thirteenth century. Since the Buddha
himself ordained the first nun, Mahapajapati, any new lineage of nuns would
thus not be initiated by the Buddha and, therefore, would be of questionable
validity.

Kabilsingh instead believes that the reason the Thai male Sangha has resisted the full ordination of women is because it would threaten their own financial support. It is clear from a visit to any Thai monastery that women are the
primary lay supporters. Renewing the lineage of nuns could provide counseling for prostitutes, offer an alternative career path, and institutionalize free
women's education at monasteries. This new lineage of nuns would also allow
Thai Buddhism to return to the past, where, she believes, women were treated
soteriologically and institutionally as equals. She justifies this ideal past by drawing on canonical Pali texts in her research. She asserts that the concept of prostitution and the status of women "in the Buddha's time differs radically" from
today (Kabilsingh 1991, 71). While she does acknowledge that there was still
some androcentrism and misogyny during the time of the Buddha, she asserts
that women had more choices then (although archaeological and epigraphical
evidence in India indicate that the opposite seems to be true). Citing the work
of Sulak Sivaraksa, she sees modernity as removing those choices.

Kabilsingh has been successful in helping to establish a school for mae chee
in Thailand and in publishing feminist Buddhist texts in Thai and English. She
was also ordained as a bhikkhuni herself on February 28, 2003, and lives at a
monastery in Nakorn Pathom Province on the edge of Bangkok. She was ordained in Sri Lanka, but her ordination is not officially recognized (nor particularly protested) in Thailand. Her ordained name is Bhikkhuni Dham-
mananda, and she resides at Wat Songdhamma Kalayani, which was founded in
1971 when her mother, Voramai, became the first Thai woman to be ordained
as a nun in the Mahayana tradition of Taiwan. Nevertheless, the argument in
favor of female ordination in Thailand and the condemnation of the prostitution industry have largely fallen on deaf ears, as the Thai Sangha and scholar-
activists (besides Suwanna Satha-anand [1999]) have generally avoided these
subjects.

Beyond Victims and Victimizers

Despite the scholarly attention given to the modern trends of state centraliza-tion and grassroots social activism in Thai Buddhism, there is little to suggest that these trends are new or widespread. In fact, Buddhist scholarship in the Thai language points to a growing, not a declining, interest in protective mag-ical practices, local (i.e., not centralized) religious practice, vernacular versus classical canonical texts, the amulet market, and a general distrust in new re-form movements like the Santi Asok and development monks. Thai universities are rapidly expanding departmental support for the study of regional religious practices and literary expression, especially in the northeast. The movement to institute the ordination of women as bhikkhunis, although actively supported by foreign observers, has little broad public support or active resistance in the country. Meanwhile, the concern over deforestation and rapid urbanization is focused more on a distrust of Thailand's neighbors—the Burmese, Malaysians, Cambodians, Chinese, and Lao—who are often vilified for their perceived as-sociations with Thailand's problems with narcotics, environmental pollution, prostitution, poverty, and Islamic separatism.

It is not the case that serious practitioners of Thai Buddhism are ignorant of Sangha centralization and socially engaged Buddhism, but there is still a dan-ger in presenting modern Thai Buddhism as fluctuating only between central-izing forces and resistance movements. This dichotomy presents Thai Bud-dhists as either the victimizers or victims of modernity, working in concert with the state or against its interests. It also wrongly suggests that these trends only became concerns to Buddhists because of Thailand's confrontation with the modern world.

Contemporary Buddhist Education

Scholars typically overestimate the influence of the central Thai ecclesia and the government's Ministry of Religion and Culture on the practice of Thai Bud-dhism. The central Thai government's sponsorship of ecclesiastical examina-tions, suppression of local religious practice (especially Lao), and training of Thammayut missionaries have had only limited influence over the past century. The new Buddhist education created by the elite has little commerce among the vast majority of monks and novices in Thailand today. According to na-tional statistics, of the 267,000 monks and 97,840 novices in Thailand in 2000, only 9,775 were enrolled in monastic universities. Of the 9,775 enrolled, only 351 are studying beyond the bachelor degree, and only a handful are studying for their doctorates. The northeast, despite being the poorest and least popu-lated of the four major regions of Thailand, has the largest number of monks and novices in the country (more than 40 percent of the total). The north has 20 percent of the total. However, the northern seven provinces and the twenty-six northeastern provinces produce the fewest university students. They sit for monastic examinations much less frequently than Bangkok monks and novices, even though Bangkok and surrounding provinces only supply 16 percent of the total monks and novices in the country. The south has the fewest; only 6 percent of all the monks and novices reside there.

Before monks and novices can enter monastic universities, they study at primary and secondary monastic schools. There are 31,071 monasteries in Thailand, but only a small percentage of these monasteries actually run schools; 3,554 have Rongrien Pathom (elementary schools). Seventy-eight percent of these schools are in the north and northeast. In central Thailand, only 1.66 percent of the monasteries have monastic elementary schools. The north and northeast have 21,629 and 160,991 monastic elementary students, respectively, while Bangkok and surrounding provinces have fewer than 8,000 students enrolled at monastic elementary schools. The largest number of monastic students in modern Thailand study in Pariyatidhamma secondary schools. In these schools there are three major divisions: Paliseuksa study (Pali language, liturgy, and texts), Dhammaseuksa (ethics, general Buddhist history, and teachings) and Samanseuksa ("common," secular). Most schools teach only Buddhist subjects, but some also teach garuhat (householder or lay subjects).

Besides these three divisions of primary and secondary religious education in Thailand, there are also Buddhist "Sunday schools" (Rongrien Kanseuksa Buddhasasana Wan Athit). The name for these schools was influenced by the popularity of Christian Sunday schools run by missionaries in Sri Lanka and, later, Singapore. Buddhists saw the success with which Christians could teach basic Christian history and ethics to students in large, secular government schools. They adapted this model to teach Buddhism. In 1958 the Sunday schools were introduced formally to Thailand at Wat Yuwarajaransristi in Bangkok. They have spread quickly to other monasteries throughout the country and have become very popular in rural areas where monasteries lack the facilities or teachers to run their own schools. They are usually funded by private donors who are dissatisfied with the purely secular education provided by government schools.

These local and independent Sunday schools design their own curricula and schedules, hire their own teachers (usually monks or lay volunteers), and produce or purchase their own materials. For example, the Sunday school at Wat Sung Men in rural Phrae Province has designed a curriculum that promotes the study of northern Thai culture, the old Yuan alphabet, northern Thai manuscripts, and history. The two-hour class is taught in the northern Thai language, and the abbot himself wrote and photocopied the textbook for his students (both lay and monastic). There are 1,239 registered Sunday schools in

Thailand, 82 percent of them in the north and northeast. Less than 6 percent are in central Thailand. Sunday schools continue to grow as government schools become less accessible, less funded, and more overcrowded and as they provide less in the way of an ethics-based education in a country dealing with the harsh effects of drug abuse, prostitution, economic stagnation, and emigration of the youth to Bangkok.

These statistics are striking because they reflect the sparse influence that the Sangha educational reforms—especially the textbooks, curriculum, and examinations of the late nineteenth and early twentieth centuries—have had on the state of Buddhist education in the country. Among the statistics found in a National Ministry of Religion report (Kaeodaeng 1999), less than 30 percent of all the monasteries in the country have schools. Many novices and monks reside at one monastery and travel to attend classes at another nearby. Many novices and monks have never attended school formally and study with their abbots, older novices, and senior monks. If they do attend a neighboring monastic school or government school, it may be only for two or three years. The vast majority of formally or informally trained monastic students never sit for state-sponsored monastic nak dham or parian examinations. Of those who sit, even fewer pass the exams. The rise of Buddhist Sunday schools, as well as meditation centers, mosques, Christian mission schools, and government schools further reflects the sparse influence that the Sangha educational reform has outside the elite monasteries of Bangkok and a few other major urban centers. The reforms of the kings and princes of the nineteenth and early twentieth centuries have little effect on Buddhist education throughout Thailand today.

The vast majority of monks and nuns (mae chee) who are not attending years of formal monastic schooling nor sitting for state-sponsored examinations are not simply retreating to a hermetic forest practice, resisting the state/urban/elite control of Buddhism by founding alternative social protest movements, attending meditation retreats, or ordaining trees. The vast majority of serious practitioners (laity or monastic, in the city or the countryside) are developing and reimagining their place as Buddhists in Thailand through the daily practice of merit making, magical practice, and problem solving. However, a general perusal of works on modern Buddhism, especially in Western languages, finds an image of modern Buddhism in Thailand as state-centered, corrupt, overly ecclesiastical, obsessed with exploiting women, and profit-driven on the one hand, or socially engaged, ecologically concerned, and socialist on the other. The first group is associated with Westernization, urbanization, royalists, and capitalism, while the second group is associated with the oppressed rural possessors of local wisdom, simple-living nature lovers in forests, and socialist activists. The first group is gendered male and the second is gendered female. This arbitrary and stultifying division creates a tension in modern Thai Buddhism that is exaggerated.

These dichotomies reflect convenient ways to discuss modern Buddhism. The establishment of the idea of a modern, capitalist, textual, dogmatic, oppressive, centrist state religion trying to erase local practice, quietly ignoring the needs of the poor and the environment (which are more often than not in conflict), generally fits in with the perennial colonial scholarly agenda, which sees the developing world and Oriental philosophy as corrupt and repressive or as gentle, mystical, natural, and supine and which depicts monks as stoic, dogmatic ritualists or self-immolating subversives, as mystical forest masters or social activists. Furthermore, if we can see beyond simple dichotomies, we can see Thai Buddhists as responding to modernity in a variety of ways, instead of being victims of modernity. Thai Buddhist women, wandering forest monks, and straight-talking nonelite reformers like Sulak Sivaraksa, Buddhadasa Bhikkhu, and Luang Ta Mahabua are commonly portrayed as victims. The royal family and the urban elite are the victimizers. However, the multivocal, dynamic, and constant interpretation and reinterpretation of Thai Buddhism locally is not easily captured by these dichotomies. Many Buddhist scholars and practitioners in modern Thailand are socially engaged while dedicated to the ascetic life. Many are both students of Pali and practitioners of magic. Many study in the city and practice in the forest. Many continually revisit their practice not by searching for a pure Buddhism that exists somewhere in the golden past, but by responding to the changing needs of the time.

Maechee Sansanee Sathirasut, for example, is a wealthy Bangkok woman who recently began her own monastery and meditation center in northern Bangkok. This center hosts its own television program and discusses ways in which meditation, physical exercise, a healthy cuisine, and active study of Buddhist texts can help reduce stress and lead to a productive and altruistic life (personal communication). She does not claim that this is the way ancient Buddhists lived, that she is the practitioner of the true Thai Buddhism, or that she feels victimized by the male Thai Sangha. Women and men practice together at the center, and she maintains a balance between social activist and ascetic/scholarly recluse, as most monks and nuns in Thailand do. In fact, nuns and monks rarely choose to be completely isolated or completely socially active.

Modern scholarship on women and Thai Buddhism often ignores the important role of mae chee in Thai society and instead focuses on the issue of opportunity and equality which reveals assumptions that Franco-American ideals of human rights, social equality, and the arbitrariness of gender differences are somehow universal. Mae chee like Sansanee Sathirasut, Maechee Pairor Thipayathasana, and Maechee Jutipa Tapasut are recognized scholars and teachers working in major Thai monasteries. Thai universities, especially departments of philosophy, literature, and religious studies, generally have a majority of female teachers and students. Meditation centers and lay Pali and textual study classes at urban and rural monasteries are also mostly populated by women. Women often play a dominant role in modern Thai lay Buddhist schol-arship and practice. We also saw the central role that women like Khun Yai have played in changing modern Thai Buddhist practice. Although the bhikkhuni movement is important, concentrating on the fact that Thai women have never been fully ordained bhikkhunis ignores women's contributions and discounts the role of the mae chee.

Many other modern Thai Buddhist thinkers do not fall into the victimizer/victim dichotomy. For example, Luang Po Tien, who passed away in 1988, developed a new meditation practice, sati meditation, that did not claim to be truly Thai or the original or purest form of concentration development. Instead, Luang Po Tien developed this meditation under the tutelage of Luang Po Pan, a Lao monk in Vientiane; a Zen Roshi named Yamada in Singapore; and by reading the teachings of Hui Neng, a seventh century Ch'an Chinese monk. One of his first students and later popularizer of the practice was a lay-woman named Anchalee Thaiyanond. He also counted among his students a rural northeastern police officer and a scholar monk from Bangkok, Phra Kowit Kemmananda. He taught at monasteries in Bangkok, in the far south and rural northeast of Thailand, in Singapore, and Laos. His sati meditation was an idiosyncratic mixture of rapid bodily movements that he believed could help people meditate whether in the forest or on a city bus. He also saw it as a way to incorporate aspects of Mahayana and Theravada Buddhist meditation.

One of the best examples of a figure who blurs the conventional boundaries in modern Thai Buddhism is Somdej Buddhacharn Toh. Toh was a high-ranking Thai monk in nineteenth-century Bangkok. He was lauded for his scholarly skills, ritual expertise, magical power, and royal connections. After his death in 1872, the amulets that he had blessed slowly became the most valuable in the country, with some selling for more than $US2 million apiece in recent years. Today his pictures are commonly seen throughout the city in restaurants, taxicabs, and barber shops, as well as in the rooms of high-ranking scholarly monks and in monastic university offices. He is equally well known among the upper and lower classes, among monks and laypersons alike. Numerous monas-teries in Bangkok claim Toh as their own, claiming that he taught there, slept there, blessed an image or amulet there, and so on. Multiple hagiographies with conflicting information have been produced, and many shrines have been constructed in his honor.

One of the more popular Toh shrines is housed in the middle of one of the busiest sections of Bangkok. The shrine, on the crowded grounds of Wat In-dravihara near a 90-foot Buddha statue named after Toh, is a small windowless room housing a wax image of the famous teacher. The wax image, sitting in a meditation posture, stares perpetually at those who enter the room. The image's hand holds one end of a white string. The other end of the string is im-mersed in a pool of water. Magical incantations designed to heal the sick are in-

Image of Somdet Toh Brahmaransi, an important royal monk, who lived from approximately 1796 to 1882. It is a common Thai practice to place thin leaves of gold on images of the Buddha and on images of famous monks. These leaves of gold often flake off in the breeze and the air surrounding the images become thick with flecks of gold dust. This image is found at Wat Rang Si in Northern Bangkok. (Courtesy of Justin McDaniel)

scribed on the base of the pool. An audiotape on a continuous loop plays recorded mantras (protective prayers) originally composed by Toh in the nineteenth century. The image, the string, and the chanting of the mantras continually bless the water, which can be used to heal the sick and to ensure success in studies and business. This shrine effectively hypostatizes and animates Toh's dead body and allows his power to remain in the room and in the world. Toh is both a symbol of urban, scholarly, royalist Buddhism and an ascetically powerful meditative monk. His picture is often hung next to those of Phra Ajahn Man and Luang Po Mahabua. He crosses the line between urban and forest, socially engaged and ascetic, scholarly and popular. A number of modern monks, nuns, and laypeople admire Toh because of these multiple qualities.

Thai Buddhism has not merely been impacted by modernity. It has creatively engaged with both foreign influences brought by an increasingly interconnected business and intellectual world. Thai Buddhists have embraced advances in communications, health care, printing/publishing, graphic arts, ethical and philosophical theories, and transportation. Most major urban monasteries have Internet access, and many have in-house publishing ventures,

Full service roadside shrines like this make it convenient for a city-dweller to practice before or after work. Here lotus flowers, candles, and incense sticks are offered to images of the Buddha. Monasteries are often bustling centers in which children play, and the laity play cards, chat, and consult with nuns (mae chee) and monks (phra bhikkhu). They can also be the venues for outside concerts, beauty contests, firework displays, and soccer games. (Courtesy of Justin McDaniel)

formal forums to hold discussions with visiting scholars, libraries holding books in several languages, English classes (and occasionally classes in Hindi, Burmese, Khmer, Malay, French, Chinese, and Japanese), and discussions about Western philosophy, Hinduism, Islam, and Christianity as well as other forms of Buddhism. For example, visiting monks from Britain, Australia, Indonesia, Singapore, Cambodia, Laos, Nepal, and Burma all study at Mahamakut Monastic University. Some of them, who have learned Thai, teach classes to ethnic Thai monks, hold examinations, and possess high Thai monastic ranks. New ideas are generated orthogenetically among monastics, students, and scholars and also come from a growing interaction with the outside world.

This interaction with the outside world is nothing new. Thai Buddhists have been active seekers of either new teachings and practices or older and purer ones in Sri Lanka, Japan, China, Burma, India, and Cambodia for more than

1,000 years. Thai thinkers can be conceived broadly as scholars and practitioners constantly looking for Buddhism, rather than possessing it—constantly reinterpreting and recreating their own religion versus merely learning and transferring a packaged form. Thai Buddhists are not waiting for modernity to crush them or developing firewalls to stop foreign influences or new ideas generated locally. They are simply reviewing, innovating, reforming, and negotiating with their religion. The speed at which new ideas are circulated (although not generated) and the level of interaction with non-Thai speakers has increased exponentially over the past century, but the manner in which these ideas are negotiated, incorporated, and taught has changed little. For most Thai Buddhist thinkers, change is neither feared nor overwhelmingly embraced. Thai Buddhists have remained relatively outward looking and willing to combine multiple practices (including protective magic, amulet collection, Hindu and other image worship, martial arts, Zen meditation techniques, and so on) in the modern era. The new is discussed in relation to the old. Although Thai Buddhism is often wrongly associated with stagnancy, orthodoxy, purity, and isolation, it is instead flexibility, openness, and negotiated innovation that form the hallmarks of contemporary Thai Buddhism.

References

Heikkilä-Horn, Marja-Leena. 1999. Two Paths to Revivalism in Thai Buddhism: The Dhammakaya and Santi Asoke Movements. *Temenos* 32:93–11.

Ishii, Yoneo. 1986. *Sangha, State, and Society: Thai Buddhism in History*. Trans. Peter Hawkes. Honolulu: University of Hawai'i Press.

Kabilsingh, Chatsumarn. 1991. *Thai Women in Buddhism*. Berkeley, CA: Parallax Press.

Kaeodaeng, Rung. 2542 [1999]. *Rai ngan sathiti dan sasana khong brathet thai 2542 samnakngan gana kammakan seuksa haeng chat samnak naiyok ratamontri*. Bangkok: Samnakngan gana kammakan seuksa haeng chat samnak naiyok ratamontri [Office of the National Ministry of Education under the Office of the Prime Minister].

Keyes, Charles. 1999. Moral Authority of the Sangha and Modernity in Thailand: Sexual Scandals, Sectarian Dissent, and Political Resistance. In *Socially Engaged Buddhism for the New Millennium: Essays in Honor of the Ven. Phra Dhammapitaka (Bhikkhu P. A. Payutto) on his 60th Birthday Anniversary*, ed. Pipob Udomittipong, 121–147. Bangkok: Sathirakoses-Nagapradipa Foundation; Berkeley, CA: Parallax Press.

McDaniel, Justin. 2002. The Curricular Canon in Northern Thailand and Laos. *Manusya: Journal of Thai Language and Literature Special Issue*: 20–59.

Mulasilpa, Wutichai. 2539 [1996]. *Kan patirup kanseuksa nai sami phrapatsomdet phracjulachomklaochao yu hua*. Bangkok: Thai Wattana Panich.

Prangtip, Daorueng. 2000. Thailand: Temple Politics. Faith and Charity. An Angry Monk Is Drawn into a Political Row That Threatens the Democrat Party's Election Hopes. *Far Eastern Economic Review*, June 29, 68–71.

Reynolds, Craig. 1972. *Buddhist Monkhood in Nineteenth Century Thailand.* PhD dissertation, Cornell University.

Santikaro Bhikkhu. 1996. Buddhadasa Bhikkhu: Life and Society through the Natural Eyes of Voidness. In *Buddhist Liberation Movements,* ed. Sallie King and Christopher Queen, 147–189. Albany: State University Press of New York.

Satha-Anand, Suwanna. 1999. Looking to Buddhism to Turn Back Prostitution in Thailand. In *The East Asian Challenge for Human Rights,* ed. Joanne Bauer and Daniel Bell, 193–211. New York: Cambridge University Press.

Swearer, Donald. 1996. Sulak Sivaraksa's Buddhist Vision for Renewing Society. In *Buddhist Liberation Movements,* ed. Sallie King and Christopher Queen, 195–230. Albany: State University of New York Press.

Taylor, James. 1997. "Thamma-chaat": Activist monks and competing discourses of nature and nation in Northeastern Thailand. In *Seeing Forests for Trees: Environment and Environmentalism in Thailand,* ed. by Philip Hirsch, 37–50. Chiang Mai: Silkworm Books.

———. 1999. *Forest Monks and the Nation-State: An Anthropological and Historical Study in Northeastern Thailand.* Singapore: Institute of Southeast Asian Studies.

Yukio, Hayashi. 2003. *Practical Buddhism among the Thai-Lao: Religion in the Making of a Region.* Kyoto: Kyoto University's Center for Southeast Asian Studies.

Chapter Five

Buddhism in Cambodia
Rupture and Continuity

A SHLEY T HOMPSON

Cambodia—or Kampuchea, as it is called in the native language, Khmer—has existed as a geopolitical entity, in one form or another, since the early centuries of the common era (CE). Over the course of the first millennium CE, smaller principalities or enclaves were progressively united between the ninth and thirteenth centuries to form an empire covering much of mainland Southeast Asia. This period is generally seen as the golden age of Cambodian civilization, with regional political hegemony accompanied by an extraordinary flowering of cultural activity. With time, and notably as its neighbors Siam (Thailand) and Vietnam each consolidated and expanded their power in the region, Cambodia gradually diminished in size and political reach. It was during this time of geopolitical retreat that Theravada Buddhism took hold across the land. Today, Cambodia shares borders with Thailand to the west and north and Laos and Vietnam to the north and east. Southern Cambodia opens onto the Gulf of Thailand. The large majority of the country's more than ten million inhabitants actively practice Theravada Buddhism. It should be noted that the terms "Cambodian" and *Khmer* are often used interchangeably.

A Brief History of Buddhism in Cambodia

Buddhism has been present in Cambodia throughout the country's long history. Early evidence includes Buddhist statuary and Cambodian and Sanskrit inscriptions on stone found in the region, along with Chinese chronicular records of exchanges between Chinese and Cambodian political entities in the

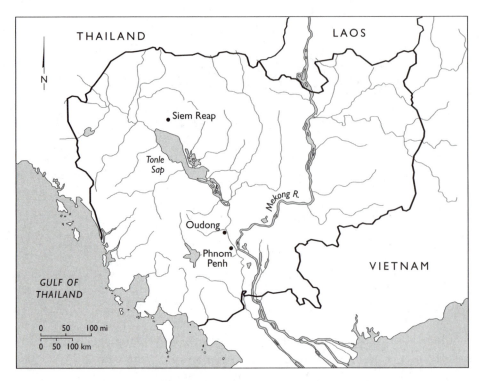

Key geographical locations in Cambodia.

form of Buddhist missions or gifts. However, until the wholesale turn to Theravada that marked the close of the ancient period (around the fourteenth century), successive Cambodian states were by and large formulated and constructed in close association with Brahmanism, most notably Shaivism. The Shiva linga was in fact for hundreds of years the prevalent expression of Cambodian politico-religious unity. It has been argued, however, that the linga replaced indigenous animist religious forms primarily in official contexts. Certain aspects of this animist system, in which a complex relationship between the community and the land is maintained through religious ceremony focused on veneration of a stone-spirit, appear to have been maintained on more local levels in a relatively uninterrupted manner through to the present day.

The Angkorian period of the Khmer empire, from the ninth to thirteenth centuries, represented the apex of Brahmanic religious-political hegemony. The term "Angkor" is the Khmer pronunciation of the Sanskrit *nagara*, meaning "capital city." It is used to designate the capital of the ancient Khmer empire, which was centered in what is now Cambodia's northern Siem Reap province, and, by metonymy, the empire as a whole. During the ancient period, thousands of stone temples (prasat) were built, dedicated primarily to Brahmanic divinities in association with members of the royal family or court. Many were funerary temples, monuments built to honor the gods and commemorate the deceased. They were conceived as replicas of the heavenly palaces in which kings and queens were to reside after death. These prasat can be seen as the foundations of the Angkorian empire's complex structure of governance, in which religion was inseparable from power, a trait that continues in important ways to characterize the Cambodian state.

While Shaivism, and periodically Vaishnavism, thus dominated official religious practice during the ancient period, Cambodian religious practice was remarkably tolerant, even syncretic, and state or local authorities seem to have lent relatively consistent support to Buddhist practice. A single king, for example, sponsored the construction of Brahmanic and Buddhist ashramas (Coedès 1933); a court dignitary served a Shaivite king but erected a Buddhist temple (Coedès 1908, 1952). Notably, both Shaivite and Buddhist tantric ritual were apparently performed in conjunction with the foundation of the Angkorian empire itself. But the precise nature and diversity of most Buddhist practice in the ancient period remain somewhat obscure. The large majority of vestiges attest to the predominance of the Mahayana school, including tantric orientations. As we will see, however, modern practice suggests that the ancient tantric record might in some instances be associated with Theravada rather than Mahayana, as would otherwise be expected. Moreover, Theravada seems to be attested periodically in the ancient archaeological and historical record. Of particular note in this regard is the inscription of a renowned Pali expression from the Vinaya in Cambodian script found on the back of a seventh-century Buddha statue (Skilling 1999), along with an eighth-century Khmer inscription incorporating three Pali stanzas likely to have originated in a Sri Lankan poetical text (Rohanadeera 1988).

Not until the final years of the Angkorian empire was the Buddhist religion clearly and singularly associated with central political organization. This association was in the late twelfth to early thirteenth centuries, when the extraordinary king Jayavarman VII explicitly associated himself with the bodhisattva Avalokiteshvara and the Buddha. Jayavarman VII established a Mahayana Buddhist state and launched a massive architectural campaign across the empire. This involved the construction of innumerable stone temples featuring towers sculpted with four faces, which are thought to represent the king in association with his divine patrons. But Jayavarman VII was the last of the great Angkorian kings; the empire soon collapsed and the capital was moved south. So it was only in the wake of the empire that Theravada Buddhism became a state religion, as it remains today, intimately associated with the monarchy and other governing bodies.

The adoption of Theravada Buddhism was partly an effect of Siamese influence, which grew enormously after the fall of Angkor. Of course, Siamese politico-religious practices and forms, which coalesced in the thirteenth century, had already been greatly influenced by Cambodian models. Sri Lankan influences have also been potent in Cambodia, from at least as early as post-Angkorian times. In fact, Burmese records indicate that one of Jayavarman VII's sons traveled to Sri Lanka with a group of Mon monks for ordination in the Theravada Mahavihara lineage (*Glass Palace Chronicle* 1960). Nonetheless, relatively little is known of the early post-Angkorian spread of Theravada in Cambodia. The rise of Theravada corresponded to the decline of Cambodian power and a radical reduction in nonperishable cultural production, and so today there is very little hard evidence. Theravadin sanctuaries or statues were only rarely made in stone. Stone inscriptions are, likewise, rare for this period. The first full-scale Pali inscription to appear in Cambodia dates to the early fourteenth century (Coedès 1937). Recounting the reigning king's abdication in view of entering Buddhist retreat, along with this same king's foundation of a Buddhist monastery, this is an invaluable document suggesting the official adoption of Theravada. In perpetuation of Angkorian tradition but with a re-markable twist to the Buddhist concept and practice of renunciation, the said king is expressly associated in the inscription with divinity (deva). This hybrid practice will prove to be more than simply a transitional attempt to reconcile the Brahmanic past with newly dominant Buddhism; such association of the king and divinity in the name of Buddhism may have heralded what became a widespread cult of the future Buddha, Maitreya.

However, not until the sixteenth century, with the rehabilitation of royal presence in the Angkor region, did more extensive information became available. More than forty Buddhist inscriptions dating from the sixteenth to the eighteenth centuries are carved onto the walls and pillars of one of ancient Cambodia's most magnificent temples, Angkor Wat. These Theravadin devo-tional texts, called *satyapranidhan* or "vows of truth," recount monastic and lay offerings made at the temple over time. They are largely in Cambodian, with scattered Pali, and are primarily associated with royalty or court figures. We see, for example, a queen mother cutting her hair in offering to the Buddha. The offering is to be burned to produce resin that will then be used as a kind of lac-quer to coat Buddha statues (Lewitz 1970). In other inscriptions, a court digni-tary and his wife record donations of Buddha images and the construction of a vihara at Angkor Wat (Lewitz 1971). Similar inscriptions are found elsewhere, largely in the Angkor region. Of particular note is the repeated appearance of the future Buddha Maitreya in post-Angkorian epigraphy.

Though relatively scarce, archaeological and art historical evidence further contributes to our understanding of this period in which the Brahmanical her-itage was first appropriated and transformed by the Theravadin faith. In fact, as Brahmanic temples were progressively reinvested for Theravadin worship, Cambodia, and most particularly Angkor, seems to have become a site of Ther-avadin pilgrimage during the centuries following the fall of the empire. Devo-tional inscriptions left by Thai and Japanese pilgrims and an Arabic inscription

Aerial view of Angkor Wat temple, Siem Reap province, Cambodia. (Courtesy of the Nata National Cultural Properties Research Institute, Japan, 2001)

at one converted Theravadin site even suggest that Angkor may have been a significant ecumenical spiritual center (Thompson 2004c).

As should be clear from this overview, the historical record provides insight primarily into "official" religious practice. Though it would be incorrect to imagine an absolute gap between elite and popular practice in the Cambodian Buddhist context, one must look beyond traditional historical documentation to develop more substantial understanding of popular religious practice in the past. Ethnographic and textual studies of modern Buddhist practice have proved to be extremely enlightening in this regard. The most intensive and valuable research on Buddhism in Cambodia to date is that of François Bizot, who has explored the historical and doctrinal roots and significations of popular Theravada practice in modern Cambodia by looking at ethnographic and textual evidence (1976, 1980, 1981, 1988a, 1988b, 1989, 1992). This research has illuminated a broad network of esoteric beliefs and practices with intriguing affinities with Tantrism. Quite distinct from official Theravada Buddhism as it is interpreted by modern religious authorities in the Cambodian capital of Phnom Penh, and as it is generally found in neighboring Buddhist states today, these practices clearly predate nineteenth- and twentieth-century reforms, which will later be discussed briefly. Though exact lineage is difficult to trace, this nonreformed tradition may well have inherited from Brahmanic and Buddhist tantric practices established well before the post-Angkorian spread of Theravada. Nonetheless, the terminology and doctrinal background of this modern esoteric tradition is explicitly Theravadin, so it is clearly not a direct descendant of these Angkorian practices, at least as they are typically interpreted in the official record. "Non-Mahaviharavasin," as the tradition has been called, may have connections to the nonorthodox Sri Lankan Abhayagirivihara school. Another theory sees this tradition as the result of Cambodian appropriation of Mon Buddhist practices in the Southeast Asian region during the ancient and/or post-Angkorian periods.

This esoteric tradition is evidenced today in a variety of texts and ritual practices centered on meditation techniques. A recent introductory work on the history and practice of Cambodian Buddhism effectively distills the salient characteristics of this remarkable and complex Buddhist tradition. It typically comprises "initiation by a skilled master who need not be a monk," a "tendency toward the allegorical elucidation of sources," the "nontraditional use of meditation practices," the use of "visualization and sound . . . to hasten the process of spiritual transformation," a "mystic embryology involving the creation of a Buddha within the practitioner's own body," and lastly, "special significance assigned to the Abhidhamma" (Harris 2005, 95).

The decline of the Angkorian empire is undoubtedly associated with a monumental shift in religious practice across the land, but Buddhism underwent its most radical change in Cambodia in the modern era. Two momentous political events can be singled out in this regard: French colonialism and the Khmer Rouge revolution. European colonial expansion in the nineteenth and twentieth centuries triggered Buddhist reform movements across the region. Siamese reforms, formulated in many ways to stave off Western colonial domination (but also in many ways in the image thereof), came to decisively inform if not dominate reform in the Cambodian Sangha. During the post-Angkorian period, the Cambodian crown, along with significant portions of Cambodia's territory, had come under the alternating tutelage of the country's more powerful neighbors, Siam and Vietnam. In the latter half of the nineteenth century, as France was poised to establish a protectorate over Cambodia, the Cambodian king, who had been largely raised, ordained, and later crowned under the auspices of Bangkok authorities, imported into the Cambodian court the recently established Siamese reformed Theravadin order known as the Thommayut. This order sought to establish strict adherence to the words of the Buddha himself and to purify Buddhist practice of what were seen as superstitious, magical, or otherwise nonorthodox accretions of the past burdening the traditional Mahanikay order. Through reforms centered on the establishment of and imposed reference to a singular orthodox Tipitaka Canon (in Pali or Siamese), Buddhism was meant to recover what were conceived as rational, ethical origins and significance. Introjecting in this way Western Enlightenment ideals concerning rationality in association with a textual canon, the Buddhist religion was promoted as a banner of indigenous pride and a barrier against Western encroachment.

The importation into Cambodia of the reformed Siamese order demonstrates the extent of Siamese regional hegemony at the time. Yet this gesture was also taken up in a larger strategy to shed Siamese domination by, likewise, rationalizing Cambodian practice. Shortly after establishing the Thommayut order in Cambodia, the Cambodian king signed the Protectorate Treaty with France. In time, this alliance did in fact allow Cambodia to secure relative autonomy, in both political and religious terms, vis-à-vis Siam. For, in a striking twist of politico-cultural exchange, the French Protectorate attempted in turn to formulate Cambodian Buddhism in view of staving off Siamese domination. The Protectorate shunned the Thommayut order, with its connections to the Bangkok court, while nonetheless mirroring the Siamese project in supporting the development of a Cambodian-based reform movement that became known as the new Mahanikay. Tensions grew during the early twentieth century between the traditionalist old Mahanikay and the reformist new Mahanikay. The Thommayut order, which remained largely confined to court circles, also opposed new Mahanikay reforms.

Perhaps the most crucial impetus for the reformed Mahanikay movement came in the form of the Buddhist Institute. Founded under French auspices in 1930, the Buddhist Institute, a research center producing a series of publications and associated with Pali schools, aimed to foster specifically Cambodian Buddhism. In this, the institute proved crucial to several important twentieth-century developments. These include the flourishing of linguistic and literary movements, during which Buddhist composition in the vernacular achieved relatively widespread distribution through print, Cambodia's first dictionary of Khmer for Cambodians, and the translation and publication of the Tipitaka in Khmer. Surveys conducted during the course of these reforms had shown that Cambodian monasteries generally possessed only the Abhidhamma, the metaphysical portion of the Tipitaka, and this only in fragmentary forms. Introduction of the full Tipitaka Canon was meant thus to refocus Cambodian attention away from metaphysics and on other more mundane issues, such as monastic discipline and ethical conduct in lay life. These developments accompanied others in the educational realm. One important example is the renovation of traditional primary and secondary schools that functioned within pagoda grounds. Curricular reforms brought modern scientific disciplines face to face with Buddhist teaching in the pagoda. Providing a forum for these various vernacular movements grounded in Buddhist morality and seeking to establish Khmer regional autonomy, the Buddhist Institute made a critical contribution to the growth of nationalist independence movements. In this way the French were, at least symbolically, overturned by the logical anticolonial outcome of their own colonial policies. The first full-fledged anticolonial demonstrations in Cambodia, held in 1942, were indeed led by monks protesting colonial policy (Edwards 1999; Harris 2005; Hansen forthcoming).

World War II heralded the end of European colonial domination in Cambodia and elsewhere in the Southeast Asian region. Japanese occupation during the war was short-lived, but so was the French postwar attempt to reassert hegemony in the region. Several Cambodian nationalist movements, all grounded in one way or another in Buddhist rhetoric, led to independence in 1953. King Sihanouk, the actual broker of independence with the international community, soon abdicated in view of presiding over his own political party, the Sangkum Reastr Niyum, which promoted Buddhist Socialism. At the dawn of the cold war, Sihanouk turned to Buddhism to navigate Cambodia's singular course, between rising communism in neighboring Vietnam and increasingly palpable American capitalist hegemony in neighboring Siam. Buddhism, along with the diplomatic policy of nonalignment, was seen as the means for constructing a sociopolitical middle path by which the collective good could be obtained through individual commitment. A key element of this ideology consisted in a trickle-down approach to the redistribution of wealth through merit-making donations to the collective society, thereby allowing for the retention of the principles of private property and accumulation of capital. Sihanouk's Buddhist Socialism dominated Cambodian governance for the next two decades. During this time, the royal court continued its sponsorship of the Thommayut order. Nonetheless, pursuing and expanding Buddhist Institute initiatives in publication and education, Sihanouk's Sangkum Reastr Niyum furthered the agenda of the reformed Mahanikay. In its early years, the Sangkum Reastr Niyum enjoyed widespread support of the monastic and the lay populace. Over time, however, with the war raging in neighboring Vietnam and American bombs killing Cambodian civilians on Cambodian territory, Sihanouk's singular Khmer course became unsustainable. When, for example, monks presided over the inauguration of state casinos, both the "Buddhist" and the "Socialism" of Sihanouk's platform appeared to critics as rhetorical facades for an increasingly desperate and incoherent politico-economic strategy (Harris 2005). Sihanouk was deposed by an American-supported coup d'etat in

1970. Some five years later, the Khmer Rouge overthrew the Republican regime in view of establishing a sort of communist Pure Land.

The genocide perpetrated under the Khmer Rouge regime between April 1975 and January 1979, during which time between one and three million people were killed (up to a third of the Cambodian population), effected unprecedented rupture in Cambodian tradition. Khmer Rouge leaders were largely Buddhist-educated, many having been ordained as monks for more or less lengthy periods in their youth. Indeed, early Khmer Rouge rhetoric made extensive use of Buddhist references. However, gradually conforming to international communist standards, the Khmer Rouge cadre distanced themselves from these religious roots—at least in official discourse. Eventually Buddhism was specifically targeted by the Khmer Rouge for eradication. More details of this tragic period will follow.

Buddhism has again been singled out in the post–Khmer Rouge era, but it is seen now as a primary means of overcoming loss through renewal of tradition along with promotion of democracy. Buddhist practice was gradually allowed to increase by the Vietnamese-controlled regime installed in Phnom Penh after the fall of the Khmer Rouge to the invading Vietnamese army in early 1979. Initial restoration of the Mahanikay order appears to have been aimed at establishing the legitimacy of a government controlled by a historic enemy and at maintaining tight control over activities in the public sector. Monastic authorities were political appointees. Traditional practice was modified in accordance with communist ideals: For example, monks were initially not to collect alms, but were instead to contribute productively (i.e., materially) to the labor force. The official withdrawal of the Vietnamese army in 1989 brought increased freedom in Buddhist practice. Though still supported by the Vietnamese communist government, the subsequent Phnom Penh regime sought to distance itself publicly from its communist heritage. The self-acclaimed ex-communist leaders have in fact at times posited their new free-market orientation as a rehabilitation of Sihanouk's Sangkum Reastr Niyum with, accordingly, a rhetorical basis in Buddhism. With Sihanouk's return to the throne in the early 1990s, the Thommayut order was itself restored.

This period has seen an explosion of Theravadin monastery (wat) construction, ordination, and other commemorative and merit-making acts. The international diaspora has played an important if paradoxical role in this Buddhist renaissance. The diaspora makes essential financial contributions to Buddhist renewal in view of rehabilitating tradition in and ties to the homeland. In doing so, however, it can also contribute to the progressive unraveling of traditional sociocultural village fabric. New forms and scopes of exchange through Buddhist practice are proposed with these transnational movements, yet the equilibrium necessary for sustained development of social order in Cambodia proper is only rarely found therein.

In conjunction with diasporic contribution, modern Buddhist renewal has been significantly affected by the international aid community and local non-governmental organizations, primarily as these agencies promote values and practices perceived to be common to Buddhism and democracy (Hughes 2001; Ledgerwood and Kheang 2003; Poethig 2004). We see here a renewed tension between reformists and traditionalists. The development community took the place of the French Protectorate in orienting Buddhist practice toward dialogue with Western Enlightenment ideals. For the time being, this grouping, constituting an important component of and contributor to the continuing formation of civil society, is predominantly positioned, in political terms, in opposition to the Cambodian government. In perpetuation of the modernist tradition, it seems likely, however, that it might one day turn against its foreign tutors. Traditionalists (i.e., nonreformed Mahanikay, so named only within the context of a self-conscious modernism) are frequently perceived to be politically conservative. They are often associated with ruling government members seeking to harness occult powers for political or personal motives (Harris 2005). It is important, however, to note that this analysis of the situation, and these tensions, are less pertinent the farther one is from the capital, Phnom Penh. What might be labeled "traditional" Buddhist practice in or in reflection of this modernist framework is in much of the rest of the country simply Buddhist practice itself.

Of particular note in this context has been a series of international, regional, and local movements that strive to empower women in and through Buddhism and that have included campaigns for the "revival" of an ancient (and somewhat hypothetical) tradition of female ordination (Löschmann 1995; Poethig 2004; Guthrie 2004b). Several positive aspects of traditional female participation in modern Cambodian Buddhist practice have at times been denigrated or neglected in the campaign for empowerment. It can in fact be argued that the spiritual life of the nonordained female practitioner, or yiey chee—a life that does not, precisely, seek power, even in the form of membership in the Sangha, but in which a certain fulfillment is maintained and transmitted—is indeed of great significance in the realization of Buddhist ideals. The yiey chee is not the equivalent of a monk. Though this is not the interpretation given by the Theravadin institution, which has from its origins established rigid gender hierarchies, the yiey chee embodies another possibility of spiritual progress that, truly powerless, might represent an even higher perfection of Buddhist renunciation than that obtained by a monk. At the same time, it is essential to note that these female empowerment movements have played an important role in calling attention to the unprecedented pervasiveness of misogyny and the oppression of women in contemporary Cambodia. While modern Buddhist authorities, structures, and practices no doubt have some responsibility in this situation, they certainly have the cultural resources to play a decisive role in improving the lot of Cambodian women in the future. This case provides a clear

Chuoy Sarin, more commonly known as "Yiey Pnong." For decades, until her death in 2000, Yiey Pnong, a devout traditionalist Buddhist and herbalist took dozens of distressed girls and women into her care at her residence, pictured here, in Wat Preah Si Ar Metriy, Angkor Thom, Cambodia. (Courtesy of Ashley Thompson)

example of an issue to be taken up at length: The traditional and the modern are not necessarily in an oppositional relation, but they can instead reinforce and even reinvigorate each other on a synchronic level.

The Fusion of "Cambodian" and "Buddhist"

Various aspects of modern Buddhist practice in Cambodia need to be considered against the backdrop of the brief history just provided. This section will be organized around two common and related presuppositions. One emanates from Cambodian popular culture, the other from scholarship on Cambodia. The first is an affirmation one hears frequently in any number of situations when Cambodians come to talk about "Cambodianness": that to be Khmer is to be Buddhist (Hansen 2004, 40). The second, which is implicit in much of the literature on the subject, is that there is something distinctly Cambodian about Buddhism in contemporary Cambodia (Marston and Guthrie 2004, 1). Taken together, these two plausible and perhaps even irrefutable assertions produce a confoundingly circular logic: the essence of Cambodianness is

Buddhism, but Buddhism in contemporary Cambodia is essentially Cambodian. Indeed, as we will see, practitioners of both the indigenous Buddhism and the academic sort of Buddhism—including Cambodian Cambodianists—are hard pressed to disentangle Cambodian and Buddhist.

This situation vividly illustrates a key issue discussed in the introductory essay to this volume regarding Buddhism as a relatively recent scholarly construction. According to this historical reading, Buddhism would exist (authentically) only insofar as it escapes such general definition. That is to say, Buddhism is always contingent on some particular historical, geographical, political, or cultural context; it is always Cambodian or Tibetan Buddhism, of this school or that, in the tenth century or now. Buddhism, in other words, is always already an interpretation of Buddhism. It does not preexist the attempt to define it. Yet, at the same time, this situation points up the theoretical conundrum of writing an essay on Buddhism in contemporary Cambodia. For any essay worthy of the name would be at odds with itself, at once avowing the emptiness of Buddhism as an academic construct and at the same time proposing to address everything in and of Cambodia.

This dilemma suggests that any attempt to master the subject is destined to fail and calls for authorial humility in avowing the fragmentary nature of any singular narrative on Buddhism in Cambodia. Indeed, in highlighting certain aspects of the history given above, the following pages will lead us to glimpse the inadequacy of any apparently coherent linear narrative. This section will include several narratives, none of which stands alone without its own potential deconstruction. To begin with, we will explore the assimilation of being Khmer with being Buddhist and examine what can be seen as the modern matrix of the Cambodian Buddhist. This is the Cambodian landscape, the very element in which Cambodians live today.

Next we will look more directly to the history outlined previously for explanation of the distinctly Cambodian nature of Buddhism in contemporary Cambodia. In identifying contemporary effects of certain historical phenomena, this section explicitly aims to propose a narrative for understanding Buddhism in contemporary Cambodia and to be a meta-narrative that threatens to undermine the historical narrative itself. The historical narrative is one of cause and effect in which we follow the dialectic of temporal, political, cultural progress. The meta-narrative, on the other hand, suggests a more hybrid approach, in which the Benjaminian model of history as constellation (Benjamin 1970) is juxtaposed with cyclical notions of time and in which we read remembrance as modern experience. Importantly (and as will be demonstrated throughout), these methodological strategies are not simply born of postmodern theoretical concerns; they reflect attempts to come to grips with Buddhist experiences of history, and the very Buddhist, very Cambodian case at hand.

As part and parcel of these methodological strategies, this section will maintain the noncontradiction of the modern and the traditional. This is meant as an oblique commentary on the tension between traditionalists and reformists noted previously, particularly as manifest in two seemingly opposed yet related scholarly approaches to defining modern Buddhism. The first approach this essay aims to question dismisses self-consciously modernist Buddhist movements as inauthentic. This characteristically nostalgic approach is committed to uncovering, isolating, documenting, revalorizing, and, in a sense, reinstating a forever disappearing and yet paradoxically always enduring traditional practice and belief system seen as original or unadulterated. Postulating a contemporary existence of the nonmodern, the second scholarly approach proposes to substitute the term "contemporary" (understood to refer to the present moment) for "modern" (which typically implies a narrative of cultural progress). Though rooted in a politically necessary attempt to counteract globalizing definitions of the modern, this linguistic gesture risks inadvertently relegating tradition to a lower order within a singular world. One is reminded of the well-meaning yet retrospectively suspect early twentieth-century defense of the study of "primitive" cultures. Freud gave a classic interpretation of this approach when he posited that primitive man corresponded historically to one of the stages humanity traversed on the way to modern man. But, Freud further argued, primitive man is also our contemporary. On one hand, according to Freud, there are peoples living today who are more closely related to primitive man than to modern Europeans, and so in whom one can recognize an earlier stage of human development. On the other hand, that eminently modern science of psychoanalysis proceeds precisely from the discovery of the unconscious—from the discovery that primitive man is one of the irreducible components, so to speak, of the (modern) human subject (Freud 1918, 3). In this well-intentioned affirmation of the contemporary, the traditional is nonetheless measured against the modern rather than on its own terms, with reference to its own engagements with modernity. It will be argued here that by affirming instead the modernity of tradition, or the tradition-bound nature of modernity, it may be possible to rethink modernity itself. Throughout this essay, use of the terms "traditional" and "modern" is meant, thus, to demonstrate that perceived contradictions between the traditional and the modern are themselves of modernist origin. That is, these are contemporary constructs born of a certain self-referential definition of the term "modern" to begin with, and they are to be understood as a function of a specific time and place.

To Be Khmer Is to Be Buddhist

A small minority of Cambodian nationals today practice religions other than Buddhism. This includes a variety of readily identifiable groups: indigenous ethnic minorities whose religious practices may be somewhat influenced by Buddhism, but who remain animist by and large; the Cham, who traditionally follow the Islamic faith; and some Christians. Technically, therefore, the assimilation of Buddhist and Khmer (or Cambodian) is problematic. However, compared with its Southeast Asian neighbors, Cambodian society is exceptionally homogeneous in ethnic and cultural terms. This is partly due, no doubt, to the centralized hegemonic power exercised by the Khmer court at the time of the empire, and the relative, if not unproblematic, cultural continuity of Cambodian society since then. There is a very strong and very old idea of Cambodia and Cambodianness. This idea, along with this book's project, inspires the focus on the Cambodian mainstream.

The very land called Cambodia, the very landscape of the nation, is defined by Buddhism. The term "Buddhism" is being used here abstractly without reference to a particular school or historical configuration. This is to say that, in some readings of Cambodia, Buddhism does exist as an entity abstracted from space and time—yet only insofar as it is given, each time at each place, particular expression. This important concept will underlie several issues discussed in this essay. In short, in the Buddhist context, what is atemporal and abstract should not be perceived in opposition to the historical and real; each is rather formulated in and through the other. Accordingly, the Buddhist definition of Cambodia that we will examine here is manifest in the lay of the land but is not limited to the physical landscape. It is also, and perhaps most importantly, an inhabitant or a product of the imagination. Buddhism, it may be argued, serves as a (if not *the*) predominant means of conceiving and physically defining Cambodia today as a coherent social, cultural, and political entity. With reference to Thongchai Winichakul's pathbreaking work on the definition of the Thai nation (1994), this essay will argue that this indigenous or Buddhist formulation of the Cambodian nation was never simply supplanted with the imposition of geographical borders under the pressure of nation-building forces during and in the wake of colonialism. Instead, these premodern understandings of space have at times integrated and at other times resisted modern nation-state mapping, and in vital ways they continue to define Cambodia. The path chosen here to elucidate this situation takes us through the Khmer wat.

The Khmer Wat and the Imagining of Reality

The Khmer Buddhist monastery is called a *wat,* an Old Khmer word meaning "to enclose" or "to be enclosed." The most prominent structure of most villages and towns, wat give definition—literally and metaphorically—to rural and urban landscapes across the country. This fact is fundamental to understanding the social design of modern Cambodia, and it will be considered in greater detail shortly. First, however, the formulation of Cambodia may be examined through the figure of the wat on the macrocosmic, national scale. For, just as neighborhoods are organized around the wat, so is the nation at large.

Like many modern Southeast Asian states, Cambodia has two urban poles, corresponding roughly, and above all symbolically, to the modern and the ancient capitals. For Cambodia, these are the cities of Phnom Penh and Siem Reap. These two poles are not necessarily the country's two hubs of economic or political activity. Other urban centers in the country could rival Siem Reap in this respect, while none could truly rival Phnom Penh. They translate, rather, as a fundamental organizational principle by which a balance is established between the two, as between modernity and tradition. And most importantly for our purposes here, this balance is expressed in the figure of the wat. For both capitals, the ancient as the modern, are assimilated with a wat—Angkor Wat in Siem Reap and Wat Phnom in Phnom Penh. These two religious sites function together, playing a crucial role in the symbolic constitution of the Cambodian nation as an enduring entity in time.

Angkor Wat

Angkor Wat is the most famous of the many ancient temples, or prasat, dotting northern Cambodia's Siem Reap Province. By and large, these date to the Angkorian period, when religious life in Cambodia was dominated by Brahmanism. Angkor Wat, like many other Angkorian prasat, was appropriated for Theravadin Buddhist worship in the post-Angkorian period. Unlike others, however, Angkor Wat appears to have been the site of sustained Theravadin practice through to the present day. Archaeological records, including the Buddhist devotional texts inscribed on the temple's walls and pillars mentioned previously, suggest that two modern Buddhist monasteries situated within the temple's outer enclosures date to the early post-Angkorian period. Angkor Wat's central sanctuary seems itself to have been transformed into a great royal stupa during this time. A sixteenth-century inscription records a queen mother's admiration of the acts of her son having recently risen to the throne on his king father's death—having enshrined his deceased father's relics, and renovated the temple's summit, he paid his respects to "four Buddha-ancestors." Originally open to the four cardinal points, the central sanctuary is today closed, its four doorways filled in with sandstone blocks sculpted into four colossal standing Buddhas. These presumably represent the four Buddha-ancestors worshipped by the young sixteenth-century king. This architectural and artistic transformation of Angkor Wat's central sanctuary may well have completed the devotional transformation of the site—originally dedicated to the Brahmanic god Vishnu—for the Theravadin cult. Encasing royal relics, the temple continued thus in its ancient funerary function; yet, as a stupa, it performed this religious perpetuation of power in the name of Buddhism. As discussed later in further detail, the enshrinement of the deceased king's relics in this way served to conflate royal genealogy with that of the Buddha (Thompson 2000 and 2004a). This early Theravadin appropriation of the Angkorian heritage laid the foundations of modern Cambodia. Today, Cambodians continue to reference this inaugural Theravadin moment in the ongoing search for national definition.

The name *Angkor Wat* is itself absent in post-Angkorian epigraphy and seems to be relatively recent. It is curious grammatically and can be rendered as "the capital city which is a monastery" or, perhaps, "the monastery of the capital city." For our purposes, suffice it to note the intimate association of the wat with the ancient capital and, by metonymy, with the empire at large.

Wat Phnom

Wat Phnom ("the mountain monastery") is situated in the northern section of Cambodia's modern capital, Phnom Penh. Set atop a small artificial mountain, the wat is dominated by a large stupa that in turn dominates the city and the adjacent Tonle Sap River. A widely known legend recounts that the stupa was founded in the post-Angkorian period by a woman named Penh who lived in a riverside hut at the future site of Wat Phnom. Penh spotted two statues caught swirling in the river: a four-faced Buddha and a four-armed divinity. She fished the statues out of the river and promptly erected the mountain, and atop the mountain, a vihara, in their honor. The Buddha image, said to have come from Laos, was displayed in the vihara itself, while the four-armed divinity, often identified as the Hindu god Vishnu and said to have come from Angkor, was placed in a shrine on the mountain's northeastern flank. Having abandoned the capital at Angkor following Siamese attacks, the historico-legendary founder of the capital at Phnom Penh, King Ponhea Yat, is said to have erected a stupa directly to the west of Penh's vihara. The king then had the four-faced Buddha enclosed within the stupa and erected a replica in its place in the vihara. Other statues, the legend continues, were subsequently brought from Angkor to be installed in the four-faced Buddha's tall pedestal base within the stupa. Penh's religious foundation gave its name to the city of Phnom Penh—literally "Penh's mountain"—which grew up around the religious site. The stupa of Wat Phnom also enshrined the relics of Ponhea Yat. Though the legendary four-faced Buddha remains inaccessible, a replica can indeed be viewed within the vihara. The statue consists in a column sculpted with a Buddha image on each of its four sides and finished with a rounded crown. It is set just behind an adorned Buddha statue worshipped as the

Central sanctuary of Angkor Wat: one of the four entranceways blocked up with sandstone sculpted into a colossal standing Buddha in the post-Angkorian period. (Courtesy of Ashley Thompson)

future Buddha Maitreya. The vihara was renovated in the 1920s under the patronage of the reigning monarch; these statues seem to date to this renovation, though they are said to be replicas of earlier replicas (Thompson 2004a). Much like Angkor Wat in Siem Reap, Wat Phnom is today a major site of royal ritual and state pageantry, along with more popular religious-cum-tourist practice. And, again like its northern counterpart, Wat Phnom is virtually synonymous with the capital city.

How, then, do the configurations described here bear out the assimilation of Cambodian and Buddhist so often cited in popular discourse? The following discussion will explore ways in which the Angkor Wat/Wat Phnom tandem demonstrates the modern state of Cambodia to be constructed as a singular geobody that endures in time in a distinctly Buddhist framework. In this way, any Cambodian national—Buddhist or not, and regardless of his or her historical knowledge—necessarily conceives of himself or herself as such in looking through a Buddhist lens. When French colonial authorities sought to establish these two wat as emblems of the modern nation—with Angkor Wat figuring on the national flag and coins, for example, while Wat Phnom was landscaped with this explicit aim in view (Edwards 1999, 90–91)—they were drawing on tradition, rather than imposing icons otherwise meaningless to their colonial subjects. The same can be said for contemporary tourist promotion of the country orchestrated by the national government. When promoting a renascent Cambodia around the two poles of Siem Reap and Phnom Penh, tour operators redefine the nation along well-established Theravadin parameters.

Firstly, it should be noted that the modern Cambodian geobody is physically formed and metaphorically conceived around these two poles with explicit reference to the country's historico-legendary conversion to Theravada Buddhism. The official adoption and spread of Theravada marks the very origin of what will become modern Cambodia. One should not conclude, however, that the modern nation is formulated on the basis of a rupture with ancient Cambodia. To the contrary, the ancient is conserved, like a relic, in the Theravadin complex. Angkor Wat and Wat Phnom bear prominent testimony to this conservation in conversion. Angkor Wat is, of course, itself a relic conserved, not unlike the royal relics encased in its body. Wat Phnom, on the other hand, is reputed to have been erected in view of conserving relics that floated downstream—from Angkor, of course, but also from more northerly Theravadin centers. Each of these wat, with their histories and legends, proposes and to a certain extent constitutes a narrative of official conversion to Theravada Buddhism as a new beginning founded on a burial of the past. This burial is not, however, accomplished simply to move on or bring about closure according to a linear progression in time. The stupa burial serves, rather, as the very basis for future regeneration.

The assimilation of wat and capital city is, moreover, conceptually potent.

The two wat in question embody their respective capitals in name, as was pointed out. This embodiment is further realized in physical and metaphysical terms through the architectural body of the stupa. The structural composition of these two wat is in fact exceptional for Cambodia, insofar as the defining architectural element of the wat in these two cases is not the central worship hall (vihara), as is usually the case, but instead the stupa. Standard Buddhist interpretation of the stupa is well known in Cambodia today. The stupa is a microcosmic form of the universe, a replica of Mount Meru, which centers the universe here and now; it is also a representation of the Buddha himself, whose relics are encased within. When drawing a stupa, for example, a traditional Khmer draftsman frequently begins by drawing a seated Buddha; the contours of the Buddha's body are then traced to obtain a correctly proportioned architectural body. With Angkor Wat and Wat Phnom, this serial substitution (stupa, relics, Buddha, Mount Meru, universe), which is so familiar to Buddhist philosophy and which drives Buddhist art, includes a veritably nationalist element. Through the metonymic process, the microcosmic embodiment of the capital city which the stupa is comes to embody the country itself. That is to say, the country of Cambodia, what we might call the Cambodian universe, assumes its body in the body of the Buddha. In the Angkor Wat/Wat Phnom ensemble, the particular relationship between the old and the new borne by the stupa, whereby the relic is reactualized, is given new form as the ancient capital is reactualized in the new.

It is within this historico-religious context that we may best understand certain aspects of annual Khmer New Year festivities focused around Wat Phnom and Angkor Wat today. The New Year, celebrated in April at the end of the hot season just before the onset of the monsoon rains, is a festival of regeneration. It is one of Cambodia's two most important ceremonial events (the other being the Festival of the Dead). For three days, the entire population is involved in elaborate celebrations oriented around Buddhist monasteries but in which normal social order is relaxed in view of subsequent renewal. During the twentieth century and most likely well before this better-documented period, royal or other governmental New Year ritual has been systematically performed at Wat Phnom, the site, as we have seen, of national renewal par excellence. And, not surprisingly, it is during the New Year that Angkor Wat undergoes its annual peak of domestic pilgrimage.

Another aspect common to the Angkor Wat and Wat Phnom cults further emphasizes this principle of reactualization. The central element of both temple complexes is, as was mentioned, a stupa; but each is a specific, rather complex stupa, structurally assimilated with a four-faced Buddha, or more precisely from a plastic arts point of view, with four Buddha images. The legend at Wat Phnom records the discovery of a four-faced Buddha, while the image displayed is that of a stupa sculpted with four Buddhas. The discrepancy points up an important aspect of the cult in question, for the four Buddhas of both sites today represent at once the four historical Buddhas (Kakusandha, Konagamana, Kassapa, and Gotama) and the eternal principle of Buddhahood. Just as the Buddha is one with the stupa, so are the four Buddhas. That is, each historical Buddha is a repeated manifestation of the selfsame. Understanding this conception of the Buddha, in which originality and substitution are irrevocably intertwined, is fundamental to understanding the conception of history in which the Cambodian nation is experienced today. Like the Buddha, the Cambodian geobody is present here and now as a manifestation of an eternal principle. Insofar as history is not strictly perceived in terms of linear progress, the nation is not simply the product of historical evolution. The past is not simply a series of layers for the archaeologist to uncover. The past is rather wholly present now, in new form.

In this context, the four Buddhas appeal to the future as much as to the past, for, together, they evoke Maitreya, the fifth Buddha to come. Buddhist narratives surrounding the coming of Maitreya are also well known in Cambodia today. Maitreya will arrive only when the conditions to receive him are well established. After a period of degeneracy, a morally upright monarch will emerge among a handful of faithful subjects. The monarch will patronize Buddhism under the aegis of Maitreya, who will in turn ensure the prosperity of the renascent kingdom. At Wat Phnom, the appeal to Maitreya is translated graphically in the figure of the crowned Buddha displayed before the four-Buddha-stupa statue in the central worship hall. Though Maitreya is commonly referred to in Cambodian Theravadin practice, rarely is he worshipped as the central image in the vihara. His presence here at the foundation of the modern capital posits Phnom Penh as the site of future Buddhist order. Yet his presence is spectral, like that of any Buddha: he is the promise of return of the past as glorious unprecedented future. Indeed, the four Buddhas of Angkor Wat likewise render Maitreya's promising absence present. While he is not represented directly or anthropomorphically at Angkor Wat, he is nonetheless evoked in the form of the stupa. As noted, the stupa conserves the past in gestation of the future. A common iconic attribute of Maitreya in Buddhist art is, in fact, a small stupa in the future Buddha's headdress. Local caretakers as well as domestic pilgrims, in post-Angkorian times as today, appeal to Maitreya at the summit of Angkor Wat as a figure embodying the future prosperity of Cambodia. We should further note here the close association of the king, the stupa, and Maitreya. The two stupas in question seem to encase the relics of kings who explicitly represented national regeneration—the rehabilitation of Angkor after the empire's fall and the reestablishment of the capital at Angkor.

A wide variety of modern phenomena are best understood in the context of this particular messianic complex, in which Cambodia is identified with Buddhism if not the Buddha himself, whose future coming, along with the prosperity it promises, is prepared for by commemoration of the past. A few paradigmatic examples of this will be found in the concluding section of this essay.

Conceiving Community

The significance of the wat must also be considered on the local or microcosmic scale. Most Cambodian villages have their own wat. Larger rural conglomerations may have numerous wat. In urban settings, the wat typically serves as the primary point of social reference for its associated neighborhood. The most basic element of modern urban planning across the country can in fact be found in the wat (Vann 2003). The town of Siem Reap is a perfect example of this phenomenon. Beneath the facade of tourism-related development, the town is organized in neighborhoods, each associated with a specific wat for which the neighborhood is frequently named. Notably, however, while the wat may be the hub of social interaction, it is not situated at the geographic center of the community. It is somewhat displaced and is frequently found even on the physical margins of the community. This positioning suggests the role the wat plays in the community—what may be termed a matrix for "imagining reality."

A modern Khmer wat generally consists of a vihara, or central worship hall, a secondary multipurpose hall known as a sala, monks' quarters, housing for female practitioners when they are resident, a cremation pavilion, multiple stupas, at least one bodhi tree, and several small shrines dedicated to Buddhist, Hindu, or local divinities, all set in ample shaded grounds enclosed by a fence or sacred border markers. Much has been written about the wat as the hub of social organization and exchange in traditional Khmer society (Ebihara 1966, 1968; Kalab 1968; Ang and Tan 1992). Several festivals are celebrated annually within the wat—most notably the traditional New Year in April and the Festival of the Dead in September-October, neither of which has Buddhist origins—along with specifically Buddhist celebrations such as the commemoration of the Buddha's birth, enlightenment, and death; the end of the monastic rainy-season retreat; or funerals. Communal projects, including local infrastructure construction—roads, bridges, drainage systems, and so on—are frequently organized through the wat; monks can execute these public works. Primary and secondary schools are frequently situated in temple grounds, as are local community support operations such as shelters for battered women. Despite significant transformations in the role of the wat in the social organization of the community over the course of the twentieth century, as was mentioned in the opening of this essay, in large part the wat continues to be one of the centers of life (and death) in Cambodia today.

Much has also been written about the Khmer wat as the locus of traditional artistic expression. Secondary sources allow us to study in relative depth the characteristic architecture of the vihara and sala, evolution in stupa form and decor, or statuary and narrative mural paintings (Giteau 1966, 1975, 1997; Nafilyan and Nafilyan 1997; Marchal 1954; Dalet 1936). The wat provides a forum not only for traditional craftsmanship but also for dramatic performance, such as shadow theater, as part of communal festivities (Phim and Thompson 1999). In the following, the nexus of these two aspects of the wat, the social and the cultural, will be briefly discussed to demonstrate one of the most powerful ways in which the ideas of the Buddhist and the Khmer are inseparable in Cambodia today. Once again, with the wat, Khmer reality is conceived within a Buddhist frame.

It has often been noted that Cambodian culture is founded on an elementary opposition between the srok (the settled, cultured, civilized space) and the prei (the wild forest) (Ang 1986 and 1990b; Chandler 1996; Thompson 2005). This imagined reality—itself a product of the culture it literally represents—finds elaborate and varied expression in the wat. The wat's role in establishing this dichotomy begins outside the wat itself, as the demarcated space of the wat contrasts starkly with the otherwise relatively amorphous physical organization of villages and towns. The one place that is systematically and ritually set off with a fence and boundary markers and a more or less ornate entry gate and is often located, as noted, on the physical margins of the community, the wat constitutes a different world that is nonetheless of this world. In this way the wat can be seen, firstly, as a world of culture within the cultured world.

Even in the poorest of villages with minimal living comfort in bamboo or wooden huts and sparse vegetation, the wat typically harbors a series of buildings in wood or concrete, sculpted or painted in bright colors with scenes from Buddhist or local legend. Statues are displayed across the grounds, amidst trees and flowers. The wat offers shade and relative comfort in an aesthetically pleasing, calm yet animated environment. The wat invariably appears luxurious relative to its village setting; some of the more ornate wat are better described as Buddhist fantasylands and may well be influenced by the modern Western theme park. This luxuriant, dreamlike aspect of the wat points up a paradox fundamental to the wat's role. For if the wat represents the apex of culture within the community, it does so as a representation of the forest. Regardless of distinctions made between forest wat and urban wat, the wat always stands as an invitation into the forest—that is, into the world of the imagination, out of everyday life. This is one manifestation of the paradoxical situation in which Buddhist societies find themselves structured around a principle of social renunciation.

The contrast between apparent village poverty and wat wealth can be shocking to the outsider. It is wise to avoid hasty interpretations of this apparent discrepancy, which can often mask quite complex systems of relations among various segments of society. One should note, to begin with, that the wat is traditionally financed principally by community residents or returning members, so in many instances the contrast indicates more an investment in the collectivity through Buddhist merit making than any simple disparity between clerical and lay wealth. Further, a variety of community members, from monks to laywomen practitioners, to aspiring students, to orphaned children, to the mentally or physically handicapped or the abused (including political rebels or refugees) traditionally live or find temporary shelter in the wat grounds. In this way, the wat can be thought of as the expression of a sort of collective ideal, built, maintained, and operated by all for the benefit even—or especially—of those who are otherwise marginal to society. Of course, we should remember that the ideal remains by definition more or less unobtainable. The trickle-down theory of wealth redistribution, mentioned previously in reference to Sihanouk's post-independence project for Buddhist Socialism, has often seemed a cruel joke in the modern era of war-associated corruption and vast income disparity. Likewise, post–Khmer Rouge diasporic contributions to wat renewal—which are in some important ways a modern embodiment of a traditional practice whereby people having left their native village periodically return to invest in "home"—often prove problematic. The multifaceted disparity between people who remained in the village and those who return for short visits (including the diaspora but also the wealthy political/business elite) can today be so great as to disrupt rather than encourage renewal. When, for example, local monetary contributions are so massively dwarfed by those of outsiders, traditional local responsibility for defining and implementing communal goals can be supplanted, such that "renewal" projects appear to fulfill personal political goals oriented around self-gratification, with relatively little practical benefit to local development.

These constantly shifting borders between the inside and the outside of community are of particular importance. Even in the previous examples of modern transformation, we can discern traditional organic relations between the social and cultural roles of the wat. For it is precisely as the locus of culture that the wat incorporates representation of the uncultured—that is, of the outside-of-society. The word "representation" is to be taken here, first, in its sociopolitical connotation, with reference to the composition of resident populations in the wat. The marginal community members taken in by the wat include those in need of personal support, as mentioned, but also spirits—in short, those who are defined by their liminal position between the wild and the civilized. The wat harbors outcasts within: those who are not fully integrated into the society. Their position inside is in a certain sense as an outsider. The logic of such a statement—and others that inform our discussions here—has been aptly labeled koanlike, with reference to Zen Buddhist textual strategies characterized by contradiction and/or circularity. Such thinking can be difficult to grasp in part because it flies in the face of the Western Enlightenment tradition of linear logic and the ultimate goal of the resolution of contradiction. Here, as in the koan text, circularity is celebrated and contradiction is set forth in the absence of a dialectical move toward synthetic resolution. Certain forms of Buddhist practice and philosophy encounter so-called postmodern thought in this interest in the unresolved, this embrace of the possibility of the coexistence of two apparently opposing forces free of any pressure, theoretical or otherwise, to ultimately establish a hierarchy of one over the other. This is what has been previously referred to as the "noncontradiction" of apparently opposed terms: the modern and the traditional, the concrete and the abstract, the universal and the local, rupture and continuity, and so on.

The wat is indeed something like a marginal space, or a system of marginal spaces, collected at and functioning as something like the center of the village. But of course if this is true, the center is not simply a center, and the margin not simply a margin. In other words, the social topography of such a community is a paradoxical one, to say the least. Many misunderstandings on the part of ethnographers and historians can be traced to this impossible, unrepresentable topography, which proves difficult to interpret according to standard Western models of the centered community.

A brief survey of the types of spirits—these paradigmatic inside-outsiders—that are sheltered or otherwise resident on wat grounds may help to give these abstract considerations a somewhat more palpable feel. Spirits are often spotted in tall trees, around the stupas, or in some otherwise nondescript area of the wat. These can be malevolent or benevolent spirits. Perhaps the most commonly sighted appear as female heads with long hair and dangling entrails, or hovering balls of light. Powerful and sometimes dangerous female spirits reside in ritual rowboats owned by many wat around the country. One genre of benevolent female spirit frequently resides in the pedestal of the central Buddha worshipped inside the vihara. These spirits can be associated with the Earth Goddess, who is frequently represented pictorially on the central Buddha pedestal with reference to the canonical "Calling the Earth to Witness" episode in the Buddha's life story. They can also be associated with malevolent though powerful female spirits, and they are thought to enhance the Buddha's power (Guthrie 2004a, 106; Ang 1986, 131). Local territorial ancestral spirits (neak ta or, in the rarer female guise, yiey deb) are frequently housed in the wat (Ang 1986, 1988). These spirits can be represented metaphorically in the form of rocks or ancient statue fragments, roof tiles or pottery shards; but they can also be given anthropomorphic representation. Associated with a particular locality, the neak ta/yiey deb generally appear to be the modern Khmer form of animist entities central to what has been called an indigenous "cadastral religion" proper to ancient monsoon Asia in which territorial (or cadastral) management is inseparable from religious practice (Mus 1933). Another type of secondary spirit worshipped on wat grounds also seems to have its origins in pre-Theravadin Cambodia. These are divinities bearing names indicative of Brahmanical Hindu origins—Neak Ta of the Iron Rod seems to be a reincarnation of Vishnu, for example, while Neang Khmau, the "Black Woman," is likely a descendant of Durga. One hesitates to classify these ancient gods rejected by Buddhism yet reincorporated into the wat and the religious lives of Cambodian Buddhists as spirits or divinities. Suffice it to say that their liminal position with regard to Buddhism is manifest in their marginalized location in the wat—outside the vihara but nonetheless within the demarcated Buddhist confines of the monastery grounds—and also makes manifest the fundamental prei/srok (forest/culture) division operated by the wat investigated here. With the recycled Brahmanic divinities as with recuperated social outcasts, we see the wat as a matrix for establishing, transgressing, and reestablishing divisions between the inside and the outside—as a matrix, that is, for imagining a certain kind of community.

It is important to note the complexity of the imagining process here. The cultural production of a division between the civilized and the wild that the wat operates inherently transgresses that very division. For, in providing a space for expression of the wild, the wat effectively brings the wild into the civilized world. In other words, the wat's very demarcation of cultured space is dependent on a representation of the impossibility of maintaining that absolute demarcation. If the wat contributes to the conception of the srok as distinct from the prei, the prei is nonetheless and inevitably present—represented—inside the srok within the boundaries of the wat.

Another concrete realization of this koanlike abstraction is evidenced in the debris so often conserved in the modern Khmer wat, most notably behind the central Buddha altar within the vihara. Fragments of old statues or other cult objects can be found displayed on the central altar itself. More often, however, this debris is collected, along with layers of dirt and dust, as well as funerary urns, behind the central Buddha—on the back of the Buddha pedestal itself, in the small space between the back of the pedestal and the western vihara wall, or on shelves lining that wall. The material is conserved but not cared for. There are many ways to interpret this remarkable practice of conserving debris as debris, all referring in one way or another to the cult of the relic (Thompson 1998). For the present purposes, one may simply posit this as another expression of the perpetual (re-)establishment of the srok/prei division—the debris is the remains and in a sense the excessive overflow, the illicit incursion of the dead, the wild, the other world, and is accordingly rejected; yet it is recuperated as such, behind the Buddha's back.

Turning now to artistic representation of the srok/prei division within the wat, the wat can be seen as a cultured representation of the forest. This can take on more or less explicit and elaborate forms. Some wat are veritable forest monasteries set atop wooded mountains or otherwise isolated in vegetation.

Others are simply more wooded than the surrounding community. Some feature natural formations such as caves or waterfalls reminiscent of the wild. Others figure the forest in artificial landscaping. Typically sculpted or painted with stylized vines and branches, wat entrance gates suggest the transition into the wild. One of the most common iconographic emblems on the entrance gate gives further insight into the domain represented by the wat. This is Rahu, an Indian astrological divinity explicitly associated in Khmer tradition with death, and in a sense with all that is uncultured and thus a threat to the cultured diurnal world of the human community (Ang 2004). This remarkable culturing of the wild, or perhaps this savaging of culture, is frequently reiterated on a smaller scale in the wat itself, as a specific more or less wooded or isolated area within the monastery grounds can be designated as prei. It is here that human remains are buried or that people take retreat for meditation.

The srok/prei division is further manifest in narrative representations sculpted and painted across monastery grounds. Though some form of local legend is usually depicted somewhere within the wat, Buddhist stories remain predominant. The repertoire generally includes the story of the Buddha's life, certain Jataka tales, and representations of Theravadin cosmology. With the Buddha alternately retreating into the forest and begging alms in towns, or with the ever-present depictions of sinners suffering in one of many Buddhist hells, these narratives show the tension between srok and prei to be more than an exclusively Khmer concern. Yet the ways in which Buddhist legend is localized is telling. Through the process of localization, well documented in Buddhist practice, distinctions between local and Buddhist legend are indeed obscured. Local legend is, in varying ways, depicted through the Buddhist narrative frame.

Episodes in the Buddha's life or past lives are, for example, frequently set in a Khmer geographical setting (Thompson 2003). Srok scenes can be situated through the depiction of local landmarks—such as Angkor Wat or Wat Phnom. Forest scenes are frequently associated with the Phnom Kulen, a range of mountains in Siem Reap Province just north of the central Angkor complex. Myriad practices and beliefs, which will be considered in the last section of this essay, show these mountains to be conceived, or even experienced today, as the cradle of Khmer culture. The Angkorian empire was apparently ritually founded here in the early ninth century. Subsequent politico-religious foundations in the region demonstrate the sacred nature of the Phnom Kulen. In mythological terms, and within the Angkorian Shaivite complex, as the source of the Siem Reap River, which was itself assimilated with the Ganges, the Kulen Mountains were and still are the Khmer actualization of the Himalayas. Today the Kulen are explicitly associated with the fantastical Himavanta forest of Indian lore. The Himavanta (*Himapean* in Khmer), and so the Kulen, are the quintessential cultured wild. For Cambodians they are the paradigmatic prei contrasting with the srok, and yet, in keeping with notions of ongoing process outlined above, the Kulen are also the origin of culture itself.

Another relatively common form of localization of Buddhist lore deserves mention here. This is the association of Khmer Rouge torture with that meted out to sinners in Buddhist hells. The genocidal regime of the 1970s can be seen as the ultimate transgression of the srok/prei division, as society was ultimately constructed on savagery. What can seem unimaginable is in effect imagined in traditional cosmological imagery. In this way, post–Khmer Rouge representations of Buddhist hells can be seen as an important psychotherapeutic aid for trauma victims. At times the assimilation is made explicit: in the artwork, for example, with Buddhist torturers dressed in Khmer Rouge uniforms; in accompanying legends; or by caretaker commentary offered to monastery visitors. At others, the association remains latent. In any case, through this Buddhist iconography, Khmer Rouge savagery is exteriorized, at once from the memory of the victim and from the worldly domain of the living.

Yet this artistic expression is something of a double-edged sword. One can only speculate on ways in which Khmer Rouge perpetrators may have drawn—consciously or not—from Buddhist imagery in designing torture techniques. If a principal Khmer Rouge goal was to eradicate traditional Cambodian society and, ultimately, its Buddhist base, never did they eradicate fundamental Buddhist formulations from within their own movement (Hinton 2002, 71; Harris 2005, 181–189). This is, of course, the risk and the very concept of revolution—that which is purported to be radically overturned inevitably has a way of coming back around in the gestures of the revolutionaries themselves. The law of karma, for example, continued to govern Khmer Rouge logic. In a repressed and frighteningly twisted interpretation of Buddhist tenets, Khmer Rouge executioners saw themselves to merit the power to inflict punishment on those whose accumulated demerit merited descent into living hell. Likewise, the prei/srok division was not simply eradicated in the Khmer Rouge plan for creating a wholly new Cambodia liberated of tradition as of history and thus founded at Year Zero. The terms of the opposition were unwittingly maintained but in effect inverted, with the fundamental division of society into old and new people. It was old people—the unschooled, the illiterate rural poor, including children, who were to organize society. The new people, the cultured population, were to be at best decultured (i.e., reeducated) or simply killed. This inversion was made strikingly manifest in the wat itself. Under the Khmer Rouge, wat were used for a variety of purposes, as storage grounds or hospitals, for example. But most notably in the context of the present study, they were also made into execution centers. This was a particularly efficient method of desacralizing Buddhist space. It also points up the pivotal role of the wat in imagining Khmer reality. To radically transform or literally destroy the wat was to destroy the very possibility of imagining the Cambodian community prior to Year Zero.

Painting of Khmer Rouge torture near Buddha altar, Wat Kompong Thom, Kompong Thom province, Cambodia. (Photo by Caroline Nixon, courtesy of Ian Harris)

The Cambodianness of Buddhism in Cambodia

This final section will consider the general scholarly assumption that there is something specifically Cambodian about Buddhism in Cambodia. Of course this is a commonplace and seemingly self-evident hypothesis, which might even be seen to be at work in the present volume, organized as it is around the modern nation-state. The structure of this book, containing separate essays on Buddhism in Burma, Thailand, and so on, undoubtedly responds to practical concerns at several levels, but it also necessarily involves an ideological presupposition that in its extreme form could be described as the assumption that the ensemble of Buddhist practices and beliefs prevalent in a given nation-state can be somehow defined and understood as a function of that particular contemporary geopolitical entity. It must be stressed that this assumption provides an important and in many ways necessary basis from which to begin considering Buddhism in our times. Yet at least insofar as one salient aspect of Buddhism, highlighted in particular ways within modern practice, is the religion's cosmopolitan reach, such a hypothesis seems problematic. This may resonate oddly, coming after commentary on the localizing process characteristic of Buddhist narrative practices. However, here again we must appeal to a koanlike logic in which universalization and localization are not antithetical; they are better understood to function in tandem within the microcosmic-macrocosmic representational schema. Just as Cambodians give Buddhism specific inflection, so has Buddhism long served as a vehicle for Cambodians to cross borders—be they cultural, linguistic, or national. This situation suggests one approach to resolving the dilemma previously outlined, whereby Buddhism itself only exists in specific historically contingent manifestations. Viewed from within the microcosmic-macrocosmic frame, this would not constitute a paradox or a dilemma at all. One might even say that the very function of the microcosmic-macrocosmic schema is to deconstruct any strict binary opposition between, on the one hand, the universal, the atemporal, the abstract, and, on the other, the local, the historical, the contingent.

While keeping these theoretical questions in mind, one must nonetheless ask, in accordance with this volume's foundational assumption: What is specifically Cambodian about Buddhism in contemporary Cambodia? History appears to offer the most obvious path to exploring this question. Viewed within the framework of a linear historical model of cause and effect, the idea appears simple: Cambodia's specific past has given rise to its specific present. Contemporary Cambodian Buddhist practice is a result of historical factors. Yet, as mentioned earlier with reference to Walter Benjamin and Buddhist notions of cyclical time, this essay also seeks to cast this particular historical model as a problem. In suggesting that only certain moments of history can be seized by the historian, and that these past moments can only be seized at certain present moments, Benjamin proposes a critique of the Western post-Enlightenment historiographical narrative (Benjamin 1970). Benjamin inverts the dialectical view of history, by which the present is contingent on the past, to posit the past as itself contingent on the present. In this Benjaminian model, a constellation forms between past and present, the one rendering the other manifest. This provides a useful way of conceptualizing Buddhist notions of cyclical time, in which the past is actualized in the present. As evidenced in the Maitreya story summarized previously, certain present conditions make possible the appearance of certain moments of the past. In other words, it is through the present that the past is made visible. These various models will be explored through a series of case studies of modern Buddhist practice that both illuminate and are illuminated by historical factors.

The first point to be made with reference to the brief overview of Cambodia's politico-religious past provided in the opening to this essay concerns syncretism. The living heritage of this history, Buddhism practiced in Cambodia today is a hybrid mixture of related, nondiscrete traditions, including a variety of beliefs and practices generally grouped under the umbrella headings of an-imism, Brahmanism, Mahayana, and Theravada Buddhism. There is of course a diachronic, historical relationship among these religions in Cambodia—first there was animism, then Brahmanism, and so on. And yet, such a linear narra-tive is misleading, because each tradition grew out of (or at the very least, in re-lation to) the others—even as one may have, in doctrinal, theoretical, or ritual terms, attempted to define itself in contradistinction to another. Linga worship may, for example, have been formulated and perceived as a higher, organized form of animist cadastral religion, from which it nonetheless was born; similar relations could be traced between Buddhism and Brahmanism, or Theravada and Mahayana. This is not to say that the distinctions are unimportant; on the contrary, it is important to highlight the crucial role of such distinctions in the narrative of Cambodian religious history. Indeed, in this context one may begin to examine official conceptions of Buddhism as they have evolved in Cambodia over the nineteenth and twentieth centuries, as reform movements have largely been concerned with defining modern Theravada within the larger narrative of religious history. As has already been noted regarding the wat, this ongoing, circular process of distinction/re-fusion is at the heart of Cambodian community formation.

One might ask why this essay emphasizes the political aspect of Cambodian religious history. An initial response would be to recall the supposition that Cambodian religion has never been distinct from the Cambodian state. This is true to such a degree that the associated distinction frequently made between official or elite religious practice and popular religious practice requires much qualification. Though this is not the orthodox scholarly view, one may argue that, as a rule, differences between elite and popular practices remain formal, and that relations between the two should themselves be conceived within the macrocosmic-microcosmic schema. A possible exception to this rule can be found in modern reform movements that explicitly aim to rid Cambodian Bud-dhism of popular unorthodox practice and elitist nondemocratic structures. In many ways, these movements end up recreating the very distinctions they aim to eradicate.

The elite/popular relation is perhaps most clearly defined in reference to the monarchy, though it is in no way limited to the royal sphere. That modern Cambodia's national motto reads "Nation–[Buddhist] Religion–King" points up the enduring importance of the Khmer monarchy as mediators in the on-going assimilation of Cambodian and Buddhist. Notions only suggested in the first section of this essay regarding the conceptual assimilation of the body of the king with the body politic composed of its individual members have been examined in detail elsewhere (Thompson 2004a, 2004b). The following mod-ern examples aim to demonstrate this assimilation, along with a certain conti-nuity in tradition that is curiously enhanced by the radical nature of twentieth-century rupture. For, if the Khmer Rouge nearly succeeded in eradicating Buddhism in Cambodia during their years of rule, this very extremism engendered an extreme commitment to the rehabilitation of Buddhism in the post–Khmer Rouge era.

In 2002, an elaborate ceremony was performed to transport and enshrine a Buddha relic in the new Sakyamuni Chedei, or stupa of Sakyamuni, built for the occasion on a mountain near the old Royal Palace in Oudong. In terms of both attendance and attention paid by all sectors of society, this was arguably the most important Buddhist event to have been held in Cambodia in the post–Khmer Rouge era. Nearly fifty years earlier, in preparation for the 2,500th anniversary of the birth of Buddhism, the relic had been ceremoniously transported from Sri Lanka and enshrined in another Sakyamuni Chedei, also built for the occasion, in Phnom Penh. The decision to transport the relics from Phnom Penh to Oudong was publicly initiated by King Sihanouk, who had likewise presided over earlier ceremonies and who now expressed indignation at the unsightly contemporary surroundings of Phnom Penh's Sakyamuni Chedei. The urban landscape had changed significantly over time. The original Sakyamuni Chedei was built in the eastern axis of the train station, an icon of national unity and modernity. Trains run only rarely now, and the station, once buzzing with activity, has become a site of urban decay and dereliction. It is perhaps also significant that the railway yards served as the site of early Khmer Rouge gatherings during the Sangkum Reastr Niyum period. Initial plans had the relics reenshrined at a new stupa on the northern flank of Wat Phnom. Construction was begun and halted for a variety of reasons, undoubtedly including political and commercial maneuverings. Rumor held that, at this site, the Sakyamuni Chedei would inappropriately compete, in aesthetic and symbolic terms, with that of Wat Phnom. New plans were drafted to erect the stupa on Phnom Preah Reach Troap, the "Mountain of the Royal Treasury" in Oudong.

Some 40 kilometers northwest of Phnom Penh, Oudong has been a sacred site since ancient times. It was the capital of the kingdom for relatively brief periods after the foundation at Wat Phnom summarized previously and before a return to Phnom Penh at the instigation of the French Protectorate in the nineteenth century. Virtually nothing remains of the Royal Palace grounds at Oudong. As at Angkor and Phnom Penh, the stupas serve as the principal landmark. Phnom Preah Reach Troap Mountain is in fact dotted with royal stupas dating to the premodern and early modern periods. The Sakyamuni Chedei is the latest to be constructed on the mountain—and the tallest. This removal of the Buddha's relics from the train station at the center of Phnom Penh in the mid-twentieth century to what is effectively the royal Theravadin cemetery at the beginning of the twenty-first century says a good deal about the shifting relations among nation, religion, and king in modern Cambodia.

King Sihanouk (right), *assisted by the Minister of the Royal Palace, transporting the Buddha relic to the new Sakyamuni Chedei in Oudong, Cambodia, 2002. Prime Minister Hun Sen is pictured behind the king. (Courtesy of Preap Chanmara)*

In this same context, one can best understand King Sihanouk's concomitant campaign to incinerate and enshrine the bones recovered from Khmer Rouge mass graves. Since his return to the throne in the early 1990s, King Sihanouk has made repeated appeals to perform a national ceremony to incinerate remains found in mass graves of the period in view of enshrining them in a national stupa. Objections have been repeatedly raised to this royal proposition from many quarters, perhaps most vociferously from those intent on commemorating the genocide otherwise. These include the caretakers and sponsors of a genocide museum located in the Khmer Rouge Tuol Sleng execution center, which displays among other gruesome remains a map of the country composed of human bones, as well as the caretakers and sponsors of the killing fields at Choeung Ek, a site outside of the capital where skulls are displayed in a commemorative monument adjacent to the mass graves from which they were exhumed. This monument, often called a *stupa*, was erected at the site by the ex–Khmer Rouge, ex-communist, current Prime Minister Hun Sen in the late 1980s as part of political and religious liberalization campaigns. Around this time, the ruling party was claiming genealogical affiliation with Sihanouk's Sangkum Reastr Niyum. Yet, displaying the unincinerated remains behind glass in a pavilion stylistically resembling other civil monuments throughout the country built by the communist state, this stupa bears little resemblance to that proposed by Sihanouk. Likewise, proponents of the international tribunal to try Khmer Rouge leaders, an initiative similarly dependent on the conservation and public display of archives, have typically opposed the mass incineration of the remains of those assassinated by the Khmer Rouge. From a traditional Buddhist perspective, the royal project would conserve the remains symbolically, as ashes, to commemorate the dead and thereby also the genocide itself, offering the individual deceased as well as the nation the possibility of rebirth. Yet from other competing and purportedly secular points of view, the erection of a national stupa would accomplish precisely the opposite. Rather than conserving the remains, the stupa would require the destruction of evidence, and thus it would inhibit commemoration and weaken memory.

In this example, two diametrically opposed relations to the past and to its remains (burn them ritualistically; conserve them museographically) are both wholly concerned with the future. The Buddhist cremation ceremony would finally allow the dead to reenter samsara—the cycle of death and rebirth—on the road to enlightenment. The Western ceremony of museographical conservation obeys promises that are no less ideological; it would be seen as a pedagogical initiative to oblige future generations to remember what took place in hopes that never again will such horror occur.

Another example demonstrates the present and future role of the royal Buddhist cult in conceiving the Khmer nation. This concerns the cult of Maitreya, which in contemporary Cambodia is intimately associated with Khmer royalty. The very popular image of the crowned Buddha is systematically identified today as Maitreya, yet he is also frequently a figure of the modern monarch, or perhaps better put, a sort of postmodern figure of monarchy. The Maitreya legend is clear on this point. The presence of a moral monarch is a precondition to the arrival of the future Buddha; the moral monarch is, moreover, in many people's eyes, a future Buddha himself. This somewhat startling fusion of political and spiritual power is conveyed in the paradoxical image of the adorned Buddha, displaying all the attributes of enlightenment (the ultimate release from the suffering caused by all forms of worldly attachment) yet dressed in royal garb and crowned. The image can be read as an anticipation of the king as Buddha, or a recollection of the Buddha-once-prince. This association of the Buddha and the monarch as the embodiment of a future prosperous and morally pure state is manifest in myriad forms, from ritual practice to everyday expressions to monastery art. This may be illustrated with a seemingly minor event, recorded in local newspapers as one more royal foundation, but which, when read against the backdrop of the historical context outlined above, constitutes a telling manifestation of the particularly Cambodian nature of Buddhist practice in modern Cambodia.

In 1998, Prince Norodom Sihamoni, one of the contenders to the throne, stood in for his ailing father King Sihanouk in the inauguration ceremony of a provincial office of Phnom Penh's Buddhist Institute. The ceremony took place in a worship hall on the Institute's new grounds. At the center of the hall was a curious Buddha statue: a complex image composed of four Buddhas sitting back to back on a single pedestal, placed directly under a pyramidal roof. The royal archives record, in a somewhat uncanny echo of sixteenth-century epigraphy at Angkor Wat, that at this ceremony, Sihamoni's Mother, Queen Monineath, expressed her joy and satisfaction before the pious accomplishment of her son. Now, we should recall that since its foundation in 1930 the Buddhist Institute has been the pillar of twentieth-century initiatives to assimilate Cambodian and Buddhist in the nation-building process (Edwards 1999, 2004; Hansen 2004, forthcoming). This latter-day rehabilitation of the Institute, with an extension into the provinces, participates in attempts to reestablish Buddhist principles across the land, of course, but also, in line with the politico-religious relations outlined earlier with regard to Wat Phnom and Angkor Wat, to refound Cambodia itself on the basis of Buddhism. This renaissance of the political body is realized in the body of the Buddha-stupa-monarch. Sihamoni's foundation could be likened to many over time, including, of course, to those at Angkor Wat and Wat Phnom, but also to the four-faced towers of Jayavarman VII, the paradigmatic rebuilder of Cambodia anew following near destruction. The provincial Buddhist Institute foundation is also, of course, a rehearsal if not a reenactment of the Maitreya story, in which Buddhism and state can only grow together. A few years later, Prince Sihamoni did indeed become king.

Testimony to the prevalence of the Angkorian reference in modern religious practice across the country is abundant. A notable example is the proliferation in recent years of Angkorian-style construction projects directed by messianic leaders and attracting significant followings (Marston 2004; Marston forthcoming). While they are often organized outside the wat, these cults are typically posited as Buddhist, or at the very least as being at the periphery of Buddhist practice. Other examples can be found in the particular articulations of those uniquely Cambodian Theravadin esoteric practices documented primarily by Bizot (Bizot 1976, 1980, 1981). In a 1996 interview with an elderly woman participating in a Buddhist ceremony to prolong her life in Siem Reap province, we find a striking metaphoric representation of the Kulen Mountains as the womb from which the ritual participant is herself reborn. The ritual was part of a larger nonreformed or traditionalist collective parivas retreat, in which monks perform various ascetic practices in view of purification (de Bernon 2000). In the periphery of this event a pansukul ritual was performed, a traditionalist practice in which participants, crouching in a fetal position, are covered in a white cloth (called *pansukul,* or "shroud") that is then slowly pulled off by chanting monks. The cloth is understood to be at once a shroud and the placenta; through the ritual act, the participant is reborn (Bizot 1981). At the ceremony's conclusion, the woman in question recounted her experience in no uncertain terms: she was in the Kulen, emerging from the womb, as she felt the Siem Reap River's waters rushing over her (Thompson personal interview, Wat Adhvea, March 1996). For this woman, as for so many others like her today, simply being is inseparable from being Buddhist and being Khmer.

In Conclusion

This essay has largely focused on continuity as a salient characteristic of contemporary Cambodian Buddhism. In attempting to demonstrate the noncontradiction of modernity and tradition, it has (1) posited the contemporary imagination of the nation as an ongoing process of Buddhist commemoration; (2) interpreted contemporary Buddhist practice in Cambodia as participating in the (re)construction of seemingly timeless principles, and (3) tracked a series of practices and beliefs over time. While this insistence on continuity undoubtedly reflects this author's professional experience of contemporary Cambodian Buddhism, this experience itself reflects a range of contemporary Cambodian relationships to and readings of the present with regard to the future, in which Buddhism is experienced as a means of overcoming otherwise unfathomable rupture. But, as we have been reminded throughout, this reading of continuity paints only a fragmentary picture of Buddhism in contemporary Cambodia—be it a picture of religious practices that strive to render wholeness. And even then, the striving for continuity becomes conceivable only in relation to the awareness of rupture, which is also a salient characteristic of contemporary Cambodian Buddhism.

References

Ang, Chouléan. 1986. *Les êtres surnaturels dans la religion populaire khmère.* Paris: Cedoreck.

———. 1988. The Place of Animism within Popular Buddhism in Cambodia: The Example of the Monastery. *Asian Folklore Studies* :47:35–41.

———. 1990b. La communauté rurale khmère du point de vue du sacré. *Journal Asiatique* 278(1–2):135–154.

———. 2004. La mort-renaissance en abstraction iconographique. *Udaya* 5:85–98.

Ang Chouléan and Tan Yinh Phong. 1992. Le monastère Khemararam: Espace identitaire de la communauté khmère. In *Habitations et habit d'Asie du sud-est continentale: Pratiques et représentations de l'espace,* ed. J. Matras-Guin and C. Taillard, 285–302. Paris: Harmattan.

Benjamin, Walter. 1970. *Illuminations*. London: Cape.

Bernon, Olivier de. 2000. Le ritual de la grande probation annuelle (*mahapari-vasakamma*) des religieux du Cambodge. *Bulletin de l'Ecole Française d'Extrême-Orient* 87(2):473–510.

Bizot, François. 1976. *Le figuier à cinq branches*. Recherches sur le bouddhisme khmer. Paris: EFEO.

———. 1980. La grotte de la naissance. *Bulletin de l'Ecole Française d'Extrême-Orient* 67: 221–273 (Recherches sur le bouddhisme khmer 2).

———. 1981. *Le don de soi-même* (Recherches sur le bouddhisme khmer 3). Paris: EFEO.

———. 1988a. Les origins du Theravada de la péninsule. *Premier Symposium Franco-Thaï: la Thaïlande du début de son histoire jusqu'au XVe siècle*. Bangkok: Silpakorn University: 45–57.

———. 1988b. *Les traditions de la pabbajja en Asie du Sud-Est* (Recherches sur le bouddhisme khmer 4). Göttingen: Vandenhoeck and Ruprecht.

———. 1989. *Ramaker ou l'amour symbloqiue de Ram et Seta* (Recherches sur le bouddhisme khmer 5). Paris: EFEO.

———. 1992. *Le Chemin de Lanka*. Paris; Chiang Mai, Thailand; and Phnom Penh, Cambodia: EFEO.

Chandler, David. 1996. Songs at the Edge of the Forest. In *Facing the Cambodian Past*, ed. David Chandler, 76–99. Chiang Mai, Thailand: Silkworm Books.

Coedès, George. 1908. Les inscriptions de Bat Cum (Cambodge). *Journal Asiatique* 12: 213–254.

———. 1933. Études cambodgiennes, XXX: À la recherche du Yaodharasrama. *Bulletin de l'Ecole Française d'Extrême-Orient* 32(1): 84–112.

———. 1937. Études cambodgiennes, XXXII: La plus ancienne inscription en pâli du Cambodge. *Bulletin de l'Ecole Française d'Extrême-Orient* 36(1): 14–21.

———. 1952. Un yantra récemment découvert à Angkor. *Journal Asiatique* 240(4): 465–477.

Dalet, R. 1936. Dix-huit mois de recherches archéologiques au Cambodge. *Bulletin de l'Ecole Française d'Extrême-Orient*, 35(1):117–145.

Ebihara, May. 1966. Interactions between Buddhism and Social Systems in Cambodian Peasant Culture. In *Conference on Theravada Buddhism*, ed. Manning Nash, 175–196. New Haven, CT: Yale University Press.

———. 1968. *Svay, a Khmer Village in Cambodia*. PhD dissertation, Columbia University, New York.

Edwards, Penny. 1999. *Cambodia: The Cultivation of a Nation, 1860–1945*. PhD dissertation, Monash University, Australia.

———. 2004. Making a Religion of the Nation and Its Language. In *History, Buddhism and New Religious Movements in Cambodia*, ed. J. Marston and E. Guthrie, 63–85. Honolulu: University of Hawai'i Press.

Freud, Sigmund. 1918. *Totem and Taboo*. Trans. A. A. Brill. New York: Random House.

Giteau, Madeleine. 1966. Les peintures du monastère de Kompong Tralach. *Etudes Cambodgiennes* 5:34–38.

———. 1975. *Iconographie du Cambodge post-angkorien*. Paris: EFEO.

————. 1997. Les représentations du *Ramakerti* dans les reliefs modelés de la région de Battambang (Cambodge). In *Living Life According to the Dhamma: Papers in Honour of Professor Jean Boisselier on His Eightieth Birthday,* ed. R. L. Brown and N. Eilenburg, 229–243. Bangkok, Thailand: Silpakorn University.

Glass Palace Chronicle of the Kings of Burma. 1960. Trans. Pe Maung Tin and G. H. Luce. Rangoon: Burma Research Society.

Guthrie, Elizabeth. 2004a. *A Study of the History and Cult of the Buddhist Earth Deity in Mainland Southeast Asia.* PhD dissertation, University of Canterbury, New Zealand.

————. 2004b. Khmer Buddhism, Female Asceticism, and Salvation. In *History, Buddhism and New Religious Movements in Cambodia,* ed. J. Marston and E. Guthrie, 133–149. Honolulu: University of Hawai'i Press.

Hansen, Anne. 2004. Khmer Identity and Theravada Buddhism. In *History, Buddhism and New Religious Movements in Cambodia,* ed. J. Marston and E. Guthrie, 40–62. Honolulu: University of Hawai'i Press.

————. Forthcoming. *How to Behave: Buddhism and Modernity in Colonial Cambodia, 1860–1930.* Honolulu: University of Hawai'i Press.

Harris, Ian. 2005. *Cambodian Buddhism: History and Practice.* Honolulu: University of Hawai'i Press.

Hinton, Alexander Laban. 2002. Purity and Contamination in the Cambodian Genocide. In *Cambodia Emerges from the Past: Eight Essays,* ed. J. Ledgerwood, 60–90. DeKalb: Northern Illinois University, Center for Southeast Asian Studies.

Hughes, Caroline. 2001. Mystics and Militants: Democratic Reform in Cambodia. *International Politics* 38:47–64.

Kalab, M. 1968. Study of a Cambodian Village. *Geographical Journal* 13(4):521–537.

Ledgerwood, Judy L., and Kheang Un. 2003. Global Concepts and Local Meaning: Human Rights and Buddhism in Cambodia. *Journal of Human Rights* 2(4): 531–549.

Lewitz, Saveros. 1970. Inscriptions modernes d'Angkor 2 et 3. *Bulletin de l'Ecole Française d'Extrême-Orient* 57:99–126.

————. 1971. Inscriptions modernes d'Angkor 4, 5, 6 et 7. *Bulletin de l'Ecole Française d'Extrême-Orient* 58:105–123.

Löschmann, Heike, ed. 1995. *Proceedings of the First Conference on the Role of Khmer Buddhist Don Chee and Lay Women in the Reconciliation of Cambodia.* Prek Ho, Kandal Province, Cambodia: Center for Culture and Vipassana, May 1–4.

Marchal, H. 1954. Note sur la forme du stûpa au Cambodge. *Bulletin de l'Ecole Française d'Extrême-Orient,* 53(2): 581–590.

Marston, John. 2004. Clay into Stone: A Modern-Day "Tapas." In *History, Buddhism and New Religious Movements in Cambodia,* ed. J. Marston and E. Guthrie, 170–192. Honolulu: University of Hawai'i Press.

————. Forthcoming. Constructing Narratives of Order: Religious Building and Moral Chaos. In *Songs on the Edge of the Forest: Narrative and Problems of Meaning in the Work of David Chandler,* ed. A. Hansen and J. Ledgerwood. Cornell University Southeast Asia Program.

Marston, John, and E. Guthrie. 2004. Introduction. In *History, Buddhism and New*

Religious Movements in Cambodia, ed. J. Marston and E. Guthrie, 1–5. Honolulu: University of Hawai'i Press.

Mus, P. 1933. L'Inde vue de l'Est: Cultes indiens et indigènes au Champa. *BEFEO,* 33:367–410. Trans. and ed. I. W. Mabbett and D. P. Chandler under the title "India Seen from the East: Indian and Indigenous Cults in Champa." Monash paper on Southeast Asia no. 3, Centre of Southeast Asian Studies, Monash University, Australia, 1975.

Nafilyan, Jacqueline, and Guy Nafilyan. 1997. *Peintures murales des monastères bouddhiques au Cambodge.* Paris: Maisonneuve et Larose/UNESCO.

Phim, Toni Shapiro, and A. Thompson. 1999. *Dance in Cambodia.* Kuala Lumpur, Malaysia: Oxford University Press.

Poethig, Kathryn. 2004. Locating the Transnational in Cambodia's Dhammayatra. In *History, Buddhism and New Religious Movements in Cambodia,* ed. J. Marston and E. Guthrie, 197–212. Honolulu: University of Hawai'i Press.

Rohanadeera, Mendis. 1988. The Noen Sa Bua Inscription of Dong Si Maha Bo, Prachinburi. *Journal of the Siam Society* 76: 89–99.

Skilling, Peter. 1999. A Buddhist Inscription from Go Xoai, Southern Vietnam, and Notes Towards a Classification of *Ye Dharma* Inscriptions. In *80 pi satsadachan dr. prasert na nagara: ruam bot khwam vichakan dan charuk lae ekasan boran* (80 years: A collection of articles on epigraphy and ancient documents published on the occasion of the celebration of the 80th birthday of Prof. Dr. Prasert Na Nagara), 171–187. Bangkok, Thailand: Archaeology Department of Silpakorn University.

Thompson, Ashley. 1998. The Ancestral Cult in Transition: Reflections on Spatial Organization of Cambodia's Early Theravada Complex. In Marijke J. Klokke and Thomas de Brujin, eds., *Southeast Asian Archaeology 1996. Proceedings of the 6th International Conference of the European Association of Southeast Asian Archaeologists, Leiden, 2–6 September 1996,* Centre for Southeast Asian Studies, University of Hull.

———. 2000. Lost and Found: The Stupa, the Four-Faced Buddha and the Seat of Royal Power in Middle Cambodia. In Jan Christie, ed., *Southeast Asian Archaeology 2000. Proceedings of the Seventh International Conference of the European Association of Southeast Asian Archaeologists.* Berlin: Centre for Southeast Asian Studies, University of Hull.

———. 2003. Drawing Cambodia's Borders: Notes on Buddhist Temple Murals in Kampuchea Krom (Vietnam). *Udaya* 4:21–40.

———. 2004a. The Future of Cambodia's Past: A Messianic Middle Cambodian Cult. In *History, Buddhism and New Religious Movements in Cambodia,* ed. J. Marston and E. Guthrie, 13–39. Honolulu: University of Hawai'i Press.

———. 2004b. "The Suffering of Kings": Substitute Bodies, Healing and Justice in Cambodia. In *History, Buddhism and New Religious Movements in Cambodia,* ed. J. Marston and E. Guthrie, 91–112. Honolulu: University of Hawai'i Press.

———. 2004c. Pilgrims to Angkor: A Buddhist Cosmopolis in Southeast Asia? In *Indokitaya: Tendentsii razvitiya* (Indochina: Trends in development), ed. N. Bektimirova and D. Valentina, 201–222. Gumanitarii, Russia: Moscow State University, Institute of Asian-African Studies.

———. 2005. *Calling the Souls: A Cambodian Ritual Text.* Phnom Penh, Cambodia: Reyum.

Vann, Molyvann. 2003. *Khmer Cities of the Modern Period.* Phnom Penh, Cambodia: Autorité pour la sauvegarde et l'aménagement de la region d'Angkor (Authority for the Protection and Management of the Angkor Region).

Winichakul, Thongchai. 1994. *Siam Mapped.* Chiang Mai, Thailand: Silkworm Books.

Chapter Six

Buddhism in China and Taiwan
The Dimensions of Contemporary Chinese Buddhism

STUART CHANDLER

At 7:00 a.m., Vice-abbess Yanci leads the sixty resident nuns as they conclude their morning service at Fuhu Temple, one of five nunneries on Mount Emei, the sacred Buddhist pilgrimage site of Sichuan Province. They have been reciting a portion of the Amituo Jing, a primary scripture of Chinese Pure Land Buddhism. In the closing stanzas, the women renew their hope that through their faith they can be reborn in Sukhavati, the pure land presided over by Amitabha Buddha, so that they will be able to continue their practice until attaining enlightenment. As the melodious tones of their chanting drift outside the monastery walls, a family of Tibetans pauses briefly in appreciation of the prayer. The Tibetans have taken the arduous pilgrimage from a Tibetan autonomous region in the western part of Sichuan because Mount Emei is considered to be the abode of Samantabhadra—who in addition to being regarded by Chinese as the bodhisattva of practice, is also honored by Tibetans as a primordial buddha. The family of pilgrims is not the only group to tarry. Several Chinese tourists have also halted briefly, not only to listen to the chanting but also to gawk at the Tibetans.

Halfway around the world in Los Angeles, Ven. Xingyun has promptly begun his Dharma talk at 7:00 p.m. The setting is Hsi Lai Temple, the $30 million monastery constructed in 1989 by Ven. Xingyun's organization, Foguangshan. The topic for the evening is "Establishing a Pure Land on Earth." Ven. Xingyun shares with Ven. Yanci a deep devotion to Amitabha. Unlike the nun, however, he would prefer that people exert their energies on transforming our world so

A visitor stands beneath the footstep of the Buddha in Leshan, Sichuan province, China. Located in the Mount Emei region, the statue measures 71 meters high and is the tallest Buddha statue in the world. (China Newsphoto/Corbis)

that it can become as pure and ideal a place for Buddhist practice as Sukhavati is described to be. Some 800 people are in the audience to listen to Ven. Xingyun. Most are Chinese. In fact, nearly all hail from Taiwan, where Foguang headquarters is located. Since there are about a dozen Euro-Americans in the audience (as well as some second- and third-generation Chinese Americans), a nun standing beside Ven. Xingyun translates the lecture from Mandarin into English.

These two scenes give a glimpse into the complexity of the contemporary Chinese Buddhist universe. This is a universe with at least six overlapping dimensions. The first of these is the form of the tradition practiced by Han Chinese Buddhists living in the People's Republic of China (PRC). Scholars, the PRC government, and the practitioners themselves generally identify this form as Mahayana. There are other Buddhist votaries in the PRC, however, who belong to one of the fifty-five minority groups recognized by the government and who adhere to alternative traditions. Most conspicuous in this second Buddhist sphere would be the Tibetans who follow Vajrayana Buddhism and the Dai peoples of Yunnan Province (just north of Vietnam), who engage in Theravada

Buddhism. Such Buddhist communities, whether of Han Chinese or other ethnic groups, make up only a small portion of the PRC population.

The vast majority of people, especially among the Han Chinese, have not taken the Triple Refuge and know little if anything of Buddhist teachings or practices. Thirty years of religious repression and iconoclasm by the Chinese Communist Party (CCP) nearly succeeded in wiping out a tradition that had been part of Chinese culture for two millennia. Since 1978, however, the government has both relaxed laws proscribing religious practice and has recognized what a strong draw prominent Buddhist temples and pilgrimage mountains can be for domestic and foreign tourism. Such tourists have not grown up engaging in any Buddhist practice, yet even they can recognize the persistence of Buddhist language and assumptions in Chinese culture. The third dimension of Chinese Buddhism, then, includes those Chinese who know little of the tradition and rarely if ever engage in its practices, yet whose mind-set and habits continue to be influenced by it on a more or less conscious level. For example, although the specific Buddhist meanings of terms such as *kuhai,* "the bitter sea" (often used to describe the difficulties of life), and *wuming,* "ignorance," that have been incorporated into daily Chinese language may be lost on many, the general assumptions about the nature of life and how one acts in it continue to shape the Chinese psyche. Buddhist influence is also notably present in certain strains of contemporary Chinese art and literature.

Just as there are non-Han who practice Buddhism in mainland China, there are Han Chinese residing outside of the PRC who practice the various forms of Mahayana Buddhism. Most of these live in the fourth Sino-Buddhist realm, that is in the Chinese ethnic communities of Southeast Asia that trace their expatriate roots as far back as the fifteenth century. Only in Taiwan are Chinese the ruling majority and do Chinese Buddhists form a sizable portion of the population, but smaller enclaves may also be found in Vietnam, Thailand, Malaysia, Indonesia, and Singapore. Given the difficulties encountered by Buddhists at the hands of the Communist Party in the PRC from 1950 until 1978 and the relative influence and affluence of several Buddhist groups in the Republic of China (ROC), one could argue that, at the moment, Taiwan constitutes the center of the Chinese Buddhist universe. The fifth realm of Sino-Buddhism includes those Chinese devotees of the Dharma who live elsewhere around the world. This Chinese Buddhist diaspora dates initially from the mid-nineteenth century, when some of the thousands of laborers from southeast China who ventured abroad to join gold rushes in the United States, Australia, and South Africa brought with them their Buddhist images (along with a panoply of Daoist and folk images). Most contemporary Chinese Buddhist organizations outside Asia, however, are very young. A few date from the 1960s, when immigration laws were loosened in various nations, and the vast majority have been started only since the late 1980s. The sixth and final

A figure of Buddha, carved into the rock at the Beijing Caves, China. There are numerous Buddhist archaeological sites of significance found throughout the People's Republic of China. (John Slater/Corbis)

dimension of Chinese Buddhism refers to the extension of the tradition beyond ethnic Chinese. This especially includes those non-Chinese elsewhere in the world who practice Chan and/or Pure Land Buddhism, having been exposed to them through expatriate Sino-Buddhist organizations.

This essay examines certain salient aspects of three of the six dimensions of Chinese Buddhism—Han Buddhism in the PRC, ROC, and Chinese diaspora. I focus especially on certain rhetorical devices that have shaped Chinese Buddhist discourse over the past century: (1) the notion that Chinese Buddhism is undergoing a great revival; (2) the distinction made by practitioners and scholars between traditionalist and modernist approaches to practice; and (3) the evolution of such concepts as Humanistic Buddhism (rensheng Fojiao/renjian Fojiao) and establishing a pure land in the human realm (renjian jingtu). Through this analysis, the present essay makes several observations concerning the main contours of contemporary Chinese Buddhist self-identity. First, the declaration of a revival gives much more insight into Chinese Buddhist self-understanding than it does into any increase in either numbers of devotees or sociopolitical influence of the tradition. Second, although the majority of practitioners appear to accept a more traditionalist approach to Buddhist teachings rather than a modernist one, those who espouse the latter have set much of the agenda of contemporary practice, especially in Taiwan. And third, Humanistic Buddhism and establishing a pure land in the human realm—the key concepts devised by the modernist camp—have been the most important phrases shaping the character of contemporary Chinese Buddhism, although their connotations are colored differently by traditionalists and modernists.

The Chinese Buddhist Revival

When speaking to Chinese Buddhists, whether in the PRC, ROC, or elsewhere, one is immediately struck by their optimism. The vast majority agree that their tradition is enjoying a tremendous resurgence (fuxing). In the mainland, Buddhist clergy and laity proudly point to the massive construction and restoration projects under way that are returning many of the country's most prestigious temples and pilgrimage sites to their former glory. In Taiwan, not only Ven. Xingyun, but also such Buddhist leaders as Vens. Zhengyan, Shengyan, and Weijue have founded dozens of temples, halls, and offices around the island, and their multitudinous charitable and educational endeavors frequently make news. Overseas Chinese Buddhists need simply point to the emergence of temples and lay Dharma societies in lands that heretofore had no Buddhist heritage. Vens. Xingyun and Zhengyan have played seminal roles in this process, each having established a significant network of outposts that extends not only throughout Asia and the Pacific Rim but through Africa, Europe, North America, and South America.

The sense of experiencing a revival may, in fact, be considered a key, unifying characteristic of modern Chinese Buddhism. Already 100 years ago, when the language of modern Buddhism (xiandai Fojiao) first entered Chinese discourse, references to an incipient revival simultaneously began to be heard in the conversations and lectures of Vens. Xuyun, Yinguang, Yihong, and especially Ven. Taixu, as well as in accounts of the tradition's current state given by such scholars as Karl Ludvig Reichelt and C. Yates McDaniel (Chan 1953, 56–57). The general assertion was that, after having suffered a period of decline that stretched back some six centuries, Chinese Buddhism was undergoing a remarkable upturn and that the number of people, particularly young people, interested in the Dharma was multiplying exponentially over the first decades of the twentieth century.

There is reason for caution in accepting the glowing accounts given by scholars and Chinese Buddhists of the tradition's return to halcyon days. Through careful analysis, Holmes Welch (1968, 222–269) revealed that the rhetoric of revival lacked any concrete supporting evidence. The tradition, Welch discovered, had neither suffered such terrible decline in recent centuries as Buddhist monks and Christian missionaries had depicted, nor did it undergo any substantial growth or revitalization during the Republican era (1912–1949). Contemporary Chinese Buddhists indirectly confirm Welch's appraisal for, though they regard themselves as perpetuating the movement initiated by their mentors in the early twentieth century, they have subtly altered the time frame for the revival and consequently the status of its founders. It is now said that the leaders of Republican-era Buddhism laid the seeds for a revival through their teachings and plans, but did not experience their blossoming. Such fruition only occurred in the closing decades of the twentieth century.

When contemporary Buddhists of mainland China speak of a revival, they are referring to the tradition's rebirth after the Mao era. The putative upturn during the Republican period was in any event cut short with devastating effect once the CCP came to power in 1949. As Welch (1972) has chronicled in detail, Buddhist institutions were controlled through ever-stricter governmental policies, and practitioners suffered mounting persecution through the 1950s and 1960s, culminating in the Cultural Revolution (1966–1976), when the tradition was nearly extirpated. Welch (1972, 340–363) describes how beginning in 1966 virtually all temples were shut down, numerous temples were vandalized or destroyed, and monks and nuns quietly disappeared back into the general populace. Only with the more liberal policies initiated in 1978 under Deng Xiaoping did Buddhist institutions begin to rebound. Especially important in this regard were the Third Plenum of the Eleventh Central Committee of the CCP, which in late 1978 reinstated a policy of freedom of religious belief, and the 1982 revision of the national constitution, which thereafter in article 36 gave specific protection to religious activities (Luo 1991, 146). According to statistics gathered by the World Christian Database, as of 2000 there were approximately 105,829,000 Buddhists, 68,000 monks and nuns, and 13,000 Buddhist temples in mainland China, including Tibet (Melton and Baumann 2002, 237–238). Four years later, the number of Buddhists had climbed to 107,393,511 (worldchristiandatabase.org). Considering that Buddhism was decimated almost to extinction, the swelling of the monastic numbers through the return of elderly clerics, the renunciation of young men and women, and the concomitant increase of lay participation in rituals represent tremendous growth for the tradition. Such a rapid blossoming has instilled an optimistic sense of Buddhism's vitality and promise for the future. Such optimism is buttressed by the significant state-sponsored reconstruction projects of larger temples and pilgrimage centers throughout the country.

Given the hardships experienced by their Buddhist compatriots in the PRC during the latter half of the twentieth century, Buddhists in the ROC argue that only with the tradition's transplantation from the mainland to Taiwan have conditions truly coalesced for the revival prematurely proclaimed by Ven. Taixu and others in the Republican era to shift from hopeful anticipation to actuality. They support this claim by pointing to the growing percentage of people associating themselves with Buddhist organizations. According to one report (Hsiao 2002, 63), in the mid-1980s, just under 5 percent of Taiwan's population identified themselves as practitioners of Buddhism (i.e., 800,000 people out of a population of 20 million). Subsequent statistical data collected by the Buddhist Association of the ROC in 1990, however, showed that 13.3 percent of the population in Taiwan had taken Triple Refuge and 22.2 percent had stated that they frequented Buddhist temples (2.68 million and 4.48 million people, respectively). Two years later, the percentages jumped even higher, to 18.4 percent and 23.9 percent, respectively (3.76 million and 4.86 million people). Statistics concerning numbers of Buddhist and Daoist temples give a similar picture: 5,531 such establishments were reported by the *Revised Edition of the Taiwan Provincial Gazetteer* (*Chongxiu Taiwan sheng tongzhi*) in 1981; but 9,707 temples were identified by the Ministry of the Interior in 2001 (Katz 2003, 90).

Vens. Xingyun and Zhengyan supplement these statistics by pointing to the impressive numbers and growth rates of their own organizations at the turn of the millennium. The former claims for the Buddha's Light International Association (BLIA; Foguangshan's lay society) a membership topping 3 million; the latter asserts a roster of more than 5 million for her Buddhist charitable organization, Ciji Gongde Hui. These two and other prominent monastics attribute Buddhism's increased prestige and affluence to the success of their efforts to make the Dharma more accessible. There is some truth to this, for the tradition would not have gained wider appeal without suitable "marketing." The public stature of Vens. Xingyun, Zhengyan, Shengyan, and Weijue cannot be denied, nor can the influx of wealth to Buddhist groups that has allowed for the construction of ornate temples around the island.

Assuming for the moment that Taiwan's Buddhists are correct and their religion has experienced an upsurge on the island in recent decades, what could have effected such a phenomenon? A repackaging of Buddhist teachings only provides part of the picture. A constellation of sociological, political, and economic factors seems to have spurred on the sense of revival. Most notably, Buddhism has benefited from the search for appropriate vehicles to symbolize social integrity in the aftermath of the removal of the Republic of China's seat from the United Nations in 1971 and the severing of official ties by the United States six years later. The decrease in missionary work by Christian churches since that time, coupled with a search for cultural roots and legitimacy by Taiwan's populace, created for Buddhist organizations and such folk traditions as Yiguandao an opportunity for increased prestige and growth. These groups therefore profited from an overall trend toward localization (bentuhua)—that is, toward a higher valuation of indigenous culture. The scholar Jiang Canteng (1997, 2) points to Taiwan's rapid urbanization as another important factor in the skyrocketing popularity of Buddhism and of religion in general, for the isolation of city life increased people's sense of alienation (shuligan).

The lifting of martial law in 1987 and the promulgation of the 1989 Revised Law on the Organization of Civic Groups may have further contributed to Buddhism's spread. The former meant that restrictions on large public assemblies were discontinued. The effects of the 1989 law were even more significant, for the new legislation broke the hegemony of the Buddhist Association of the Republic of China (BAROC), the government's semiofficial liaison office for Buddhist monasteries (Jones 1999). Henceforth, clerics would no longer have to receive ordination at a BAROC-sponsored ceremony or to gain permission from that body to study abroad, and associations such as BLIA and Ciji Gongde Hui could legally form. Supplementing these cultural, sociological, and political factors was Taiwan's economic boom, which through the 1980s and 1990s allowed a wide range of devotees regularly to offer generous donations to build facilities and to support monastics.

The hot economy impelled by Taiwan's successful entrance into the global marketplace also led to the internationalization of the island's Buddhist community, having done so by catalyzing the establishment of "Little Taiwans" throughout the world and ensuring the necessary funding to establish branch organizations overseas. The vast majority of Chinese clerics who have journeyed outside of Asia have been content to serve one local community. Some, however, have been more ambitious. After arriving in the United States in 1959, Ven. Xuanhua eventually founded a total of six monasteries in the United States and Canada (including the 237-acre City of Ten Thousand Buddhas in Talmage, California). Even his accomplishment, however, pales in comparison to the successes of Vens. Zhengyan and Xingyun in planting so many centers over such a broad geographical range. In less than a decade Ciji Gongde Hui and Foguangshan each went from having virtually no overseas branches to embracing nearly 100.

As of 2001, Ciji Gongde Hui included 79 offices in 28 countries (excluding Taiwan). Similarly, Foguangshan oversaw 95 temples in a total of 29 countries outside the ROC. The Foguang network was supplemented by BLIA, which included 111 chapters spread over 55 countries. Ciji and Foguang outposts therefore may be found in Asia, Africa, Australia, Europe, North America, and South America—virtually anywhere that even small communities of emigrants from Taiwan have coalesced.

Contemporary Chinese clerics therefore may be on firmer ground for asserting a Buddhist revival than were Republican-era observers of the tradition. Several caveats must nonetheless be kept in mind. First, the statistics available for Buddhist activity are suspect in both the PRC and ROC. As Paul R. Katz (2003, 90), Raoul Birnbaum (2003, 429), and others have observed, the amorphous quality of participation in Buddhist organizations and activities and the questionable methodology used in compiling much of the data renders the usefulness of most of the statistical reports dubious at best. The numbers given for monastic and lay Buddhists in the PRC are very suspect. One especially wonders who exactly falls under the rubric "Buddhist"—is simply visiting a temple enough? Similarly, it seems very unlikely that the percentage of people in Taiwan participating in Buddhist activities had climbed so steeply from the mid-1980s to 1990 or that more than a million people took refuge in the subsequent two years. Hence, the apparent growth during this period probably reflects a change in computational method or a more efficient collection of data rather than such a large increase in affiliation. One must also be careful using the statistics provided by individual organizations. If both BLIA and Ciji Gongde Hui had the millions of members that they claimed in 2000, they would have had to account for virtually all of Taiwan's Buddhists plus a sizable contingent of overseas Chinese Buddhists.

Second, even if there had been an increase, the overall numbers remain small: If one grants the number of 107 million practitioners in mainland China, that still only accounts for 8.5 percent of the population for 2004. Even in Taiwan, less than one-quarter of the island's population engages in Buddhist practice.

Finally, there is evidence that whatever revival had occurred on Taiwan may have peaked by the close of the 1990s. ROC Interior Department statistics for 2000 record that 4.8 million people identified themselves as frequenting Buddhist temples, virtually the same number as eight years earlier. The number of overseas Chinese who engage in Buddhist activities may also have reached a steady state. Foguangshan essentially ceased constructing new overseas temples after 1998, and the number of Ciji overseas offices also appears to have stabilized.

What, then, has slowed or even stopped the momentum in the ROC and abroad? The single greatest factor, ironically, appears to have been the tradition's phenomenal success. The proliferation of Buddhist organizations in the late 1980s and early 1990s stretched the resources of devotees. Once Taiwan's economy slowed, contributions also dropped. The revival, which had been as much a financial as a spiritual phenomenon, stagnated. This downward trend was exacerbated by a series of scandals involving Buddhist and folk Buddhist organizations that corroded the tradition's image. The autumn of 1996 was especially hurtful. The prominent Chan monastery Zhongtaishan received months of adverse press coverage and criticism after its founder, Ven. Weijue, tonsured 158 novices without gaining parental approval. Just as this scandal was simmering down, it came to light that the popular folk Buddhist Ven. Song Qili had swindled devotees out of millions of New Taiwan dollars. Investigators revealed how he had employed trick photography and other stunts to impress the credulous and had then diverted temple funds into his own bank accounts. Numerous other cases of fraud involving self-proclaimed Buddhist masters soon hit the papers, leading the government tax bureau to review the financial books of all Buddhist organizations. Not surprisingly, donations tumbled. This sudden drop in funding intensified what was already a downward trend in donations, which has been noted anecdotally by clerics from many temples.

The significance of the revival may, in fact, lie outside of statistics about membership, finances, or temple construction. Instead, I would argue that its importance derives from what such rhetoric says about Chinese Buddhist self-understanding in the late twentieth and early twenty-first centuries. Contemporary discussions of the revival of Sino-Buddhism hinge around the conceptual dyad of modernity and tradition, so it is to this topic that we now turn.

Chinese Buddhist Perspectives on Tradition and Modernity

Contemporary religious leaders who have used the rhetoric of history to galvanize public support for their revivalist agendas have generally fallen into one of two camps—traditionalists or modernists (Chandler 2004, 66–68). Traditionalists declare that the vast majority of changes in social relations that have occurred as an epiphenomenon of modernity have proved to be unnecessary and detrimental to morality and communal stability. Innovations in worldview or custom that have directly challenged religious symbols and praxis are especially anathema, but even those with no such apparent implications are often viewed with skepticism. Meanwhile, modernists have considered such adaptations as necessary for their tradition's survival in the present and have openly espoused them as holding positive benefits. The difference in perspective between these two groups is not as simple as one may think at first, for both have argued that they are the ones who carry on the work initiated by the religion's founder. To understand how not only the traditionalists but the modernists can make such a claim, we must look more closely at the rhetoric of tradition.

The noun "tradition" and adjective "traditional" describe practices and doctrines that have been passed down through time. Edward Shils (1981, 15) has observed that three generations of cohorts is the minimum requirement for something to be regarded as a tradition. The time scope for various traditions may therefore vary widely, anywhere from a few years to several millennia. A particular cultural group inherits a wide range of such traditions, and the sum total of these elements constitutes that group's cumulative tradition as a singular whole. Members within the group are rarely clearly cognizant of the relative antiquity of the various components making up their cumulative tradition. In other words, people tend to experience their cumulative tradition as a monolithic mass that they assume has remained largely undisturbed through the flow of history. Based on readings of certain passages in canonical texts and on observations of the practices, beliefs, and values inherited from their parents' and grandparents' generations, inferences are made about the religion's general character as it is presumed to have been passed down over the centuries. Tradition is typically associated more with stability than with dynamic transformation.

Both traditionalists and modernists establish their understanding of their religion's traditional worldview in this way. The two differ, however, in the significance they give to the data. Traditionalists typically assume that, until very recently, all mainstream devotees since the religion's founding viewed the world in essentially the same way. While there have been heterodoxies, these were perpetrated by fringe elements and soon thwarted. Only in recent times have pernicious aberrations threatened to undermine the faith's core structure itself, and these deviations are intimately linked to the modern worldview. In other cases, traditionalists largely ignore the religion's history during those centuries just preceding modernity. The contrast given is between classical authority and modern aberration. In either case, the religion is said to have passed through two main stages of history: traditional, characterized by genuine faith; and modern, in which spurious forms of faith and antagonistic secular worldviews threaten the religion's very existence.

Modernists similarly construct their image of tradition through reference to personal and communal memory. Unlike traditionalists, however, they are more likely to question both the continued viability of certain interpretations and customs associated with inherited practice and whether certain aspects of cumulative tradition, even some legitimized in canonical texts, were central elements of the religion or even date back to its founding. Hence, they base their view on two arguments: relevance and authenticity. First, while their predecessors' worldview may have been appropriate for their own time, it is no longer deemed adequate for the present, modern world. Reformers therefore wish to shed these perceived fetters. Second, many of the assumptions and beliefs shaping the practice of immediate predecessors are said to only date back to relatively recent periods (in some cases even only having arisen within the past several centuries) and hence are an aberration from the original faith. More importantly, recent forebears are criticized for having strayed away from the dynamic spirit that characterized the early community. Unlike the founder and his initial disciples, who recognized the importance of engaging contemporary society, later followers are castigated for having mistakenly latched onto literal interpretations of certain inherited notions. It is claimed that in their stubborn adherence to particular elements, they have lost the creative, vivifying spirit that led to the establishment of such beliefs, practices, and values in the first place. Modernists are not seeking a revolution, they aver, but a revival. Claiming that ancient practice was itself modernist for its time, they argue that one must also be a modernist to actualize that tradition. Modernists therefore posit a three-stage historical schema: original, genuine tradition as practiced in the early community; spurious tradition that was promoted in subsequent, especially recent, centuries; and modern tradition, which contravenes the false practices of spurious tradition to regain the underlying spirit of genuine faith.

How, then, does such rhetoric play out in contemporary Chinese Buddhism? According to the scholar Jiang Canteng, the vast majority of Buddhist practitioners—both during the Republican era and more recently—have held to more traditionalist language (Jiang 1989, 168–169). Venerable Yanci of Fuhu Temple, Ven. Weijue at Zhongtaishan, and Ven. Hsuan Hua of the City of Ten Thousand Buddhas all exemplify such traditionalism—the first perpetuating the antimodernist Pure Land approach of Ven. Yinguang and the other two laying more stress on the traditionalist Chan approach of Ven. Xuyun. Traditionalist rhetoric is especially noticeable in the PRC, where those attracted to Buddhism are drawn to it at least partly as an alternative to the rigid modernism of communist ideology (Qin 2000, 2–3). Because the current revival in mainland China has only occurred after such recent catastrophic political events, the general tendency is to regard any pre–Cultural Revolution Buddhist practice as traditional. Those elderly clerics who by grit and luck persisted in adhering to the Dharma through decades of persecution are regarded as living treasures and as the tenuous links keeping authentic tradition alive. Hence, when Ven. Yanci compiled *Buddhist Rites of Mt. Emei* (Emeishan Foshi), she did so not by consulting canonical texts, of which few were available, but by interviewing elderly monks on the mountain (Qin 2000, 169). Ven. Yanci and other nuns at Fuhu Temple are especially proud that they fully perform all of the required monastic daily rituals (unlike most of the monks in monasteries on the mountain) and consider themselves to be guardians of authentic, traditional Pure Land practice.

According to Jiang Canteng (1997) and Charles Brewer Jones (2003, 139), the majority of devotees in Taiwan also think in more traditionalist terms. These are the teachings espoused not only at the Chan center Zhongtaishan and the Pure Land monastery, Lingyan Temple (named after the establishment in Soochow made famous in the Republican era by Ven. Yinguang), but by the leadership of BAROC (Laliberte 1999, 174–175) and in myriad smaller establishments such as Xilian Temple outside the town of Sanxia (Jones 2003, 128). And yet, despite the preponderance of traditionalist practitioners, the leaders of the island's largest, most influential organizations—i.e., Vens. Xingyun, Zhengyan, and Shengyan—have all appropriated the modernist rhetoric initially laid down early in the twentieth century by Ven. Taixu and subsequently amplified through the scholarly analyses of Ven. Yinshun. This is the rhetoric that very much sets the tone in Taiwan and throughout the Chinese Buddhist diaspora and against which traditionalists find themselves having to respond. Even in mainland China, the legacy of Ven. Taixu continues, although in a

Taiwanese Buddhist monk collects alms as pedestrians pass by the Lung-Shan Temple of ancestor worship in Taipei, Taiwan, 1991. (Bohemian Nomad Picturemakers/Corbis)

more muted form. It therefore will be helpful to consider in some detail the line of reasoning and the modus operandi of contemporary Chinese Buddhist modernists.

The Venerable Xingyun tells audiences that the Buddha was very innovative and modern in his techniques for spreading the Dharma. He notes that even the Buddha's living quarters took advantage of the latest technology. "According to archeological relics found in India," observes Ven. Xingyun, "the Buddha's place of residence was very progressive, no matter whether in terms of sanitation, ventilation, etc., so it was very 'modern'" (Shi Xingyun 1995, vol. 10, 429). Venerables Xingyun, Shengyan, and Zhengyan agree that the Buddha's immediate successors maintained this spirit of innovation and engagement, as did the early Chinese patriarchs. Ven. Zhengyan especially emphasizes that the social services provided by monasteries during the Northern Wei dynasty (424–532) and the Fields of Compassion Institutes (beitian yuan) of the Tang dynasty (618–905) used creative new methods to fulfill their humanistic mission.

Modernist Buddhists attribute the start of Chinese Buddhism's gradual and steady decline to specific historical, non-Buddhist sources that took place at the advent of the Ming dynasty. The general argument is that Zhu Yuanzheng, the founding emperor of the Ming dynasty (1368–1644), feared Buddhism's influence over society and therefore instituted a variety of government policies designed to minimize contact between the Sangha and laity. Ever since, monks and nuns retreated to the forests and mountains, and laity only summoned them to conduct funerary rites so that the resulting merit could aid the deceased in attaining a better rebirth, perhaps even rebirth in Amitabha's Sukhavati Pure Land. People therefore increasingly associated Buddhism with seclusion, escape, self-concern, individualism, otherworldliness, old age, and death. The tradition, in other words, is said to have lost its Mahayana spirit so that by the early twentieth century, it was lifeless and out of touch.

Fortunately, the modernists continue, at the advent of the twentieth century a small vanguard of young, progressive monks under the leadership of Ven. Taixu began to actively bring the Buddha's message to urban society. They established printing presses, monastic colleges, and other innovative techniques to attract intellectuals and to reach the masses. Ciji Gongde Hui, Foguangshan, and Ven. Shengyan's Fagushan regard themselves as inheriting this leadership role, using the even more effective techniques developed since Ven. Taixu's time so that his initial efforts can now bear fruit. The key to the revival, assert contemporary Chinese Buddhist modernists, has been the balancing of modern techniques with traditional wisdom. Ven. Xingyun states:

> Buddhism must use the most effective means to serve the needs of each age so that Buddha's spirit of compassion can be spread throughout society. This is what is meant by being "modern" for each age. Hence, the Buddhist modernism that

we promote is not something new, but rather is a revitalization of the ancient, carrying on the great heritage of the buddhas and great worthies of the past through methods that will be accepted easily and willingly by modern people. (Shi Xingyun 1995, vol. 10, 429)

The Chinese Buddhist revival, in other words, is both a modern revival and a revival of modernism. For the spirit to remain constant, the techniques, it is argued, must ceaselessly change. Modernist Buddhists therefore see themselves as instituting a modernization that revives Buddhism's original spirit. Hence, it is a modern revival that requires the perpetuation of genuine tradition, the sloughing off of spurious tradition, and the adoption of those modern innovations that can aid in spreading the Dharma. Fagushan and Foguangshan take great pride in organizing what they consider to be model, canonical Dharma functions and in providing orthodox training for clerics. The facilities in which these activities take place and the process through which leaders are selected and decisions made, however, take full advantage of twentieth-century advances.

Proponents of Chinese modernist Buddhism focus on three areas: (1) enthusiastic appropriation of new technology, (2) the appropriation of modern organizational methods to Buddhist endeavors, and (3) the secularization of practice to give it a more humanist tone. Technological innovations are embraced if they are judged to do one of two things: materially improve people's lives or directly facilitate the spread of the Dharma. For those in Ciji Gongde Hui, technological advances in the field of medicine have been of utmost importance in aiding the Buddhist goal of alleviating suffering. Hence, considerable funds are devoted to keeping Ciji hospitals equipped with the latest, most advanced medical equipment. Modernists have also enthusiastically appropriated modern means of communication and transportation. Foguang clerics proudly point to the fact that Ven. Xingyun was among the first Chinese Buddhist monastics to use an automobile, slide projector, and radio and television transmission. Meanwhile, computers and the Internet have received an especially eager reception, with Ciji Gongde Hui, Fagushan, and Foguangshan all publishing CD-ROMs and DVDs and developing sophisticated Web sites.

As Jones has pointed out (2003, 127–128), the difference between modernists and traditionalists is not whether modern technological advances are used, but rather the attitude toward such advancement itself, with modernists being much more likely to sing the praises of technology's virtues. Even among modernists, however, not all technology is uniformly embraced. Whether monasteries should use air conditioners, for instance, is a topic of debate. At Foguang temples, such cooling devices may be found in all offices and in the lodgings for lay practitioners and visitors. Jingsi Hermitage (the headquarters of Ciji Gongde Hui) and Fagushan—as well as such traditionalist centers as

Zhongtaishan—prefer to do without. Detractors cite Foguangshan's usage as another example of the group succumbing to the easy life. Ven. Xingyun's response is twofold. First, as we saw previously, he claims that the Buddha himself took advantage of the most up-to-date means to provide proper ventilation in his dwelling. If the Buddha could do it, why cannot modern clerics? Second, Ven. Xingyun states that the critics have mistakenly assumed that because Foguangshan's public facilities have air conditioning and other comforts, so do the private quarters for monastics. This is not the case, he assures people. Living quarters for Foguang clerics are very simple, with neither air conditioning nor soft beds. If anything, he contends, they are even more austere than the monastic lodgings found elsewhere around the island.

The second area of focus by Chinese modernist Buddhists is the adaptation of modern organizational patterns to Buddhist practice. This is particularly noticeable in the impulse to establish charitable foundations, lay associations, and Buddhist academies and in the growing tendency to use democratic voting methods to select temple leadership. Ven. Zhengyan has been especially successful in giving an institutional basis for applying the Buddhist virtue of compassion, leading many to refer to her as the Mother Teresa of Taiwan. Ciji Gongde Hui and its affiliated foundation support a very impressive medical center in Hualien (eastern Taiwan) that includes a first-rate hospital, cutting-edge nursing school, and sophisticated medical school. The group has also opened several other facilities around Taiwan and each year provides millions of dollars in relief in response to natural disasters around the world. Fagushan and Foguangshan also engage in medical and relief efforts (the latter running a large orphanage as well), but neither approaches the scale of Ciji Gongde Hui's programs. Only recently have temples in mainland China had the financial wherewithal to undertake any such philanthropic endeavors, so their achievements have been more modest. Nonetheless, since 1995, Nanputuo Monastery, the temple in Xiamen for which Ven. Taixu once served as abbot, has had a charitable organization that supplies disaster relief and that supports the elderly, the sick, the weak, and children in underfunded schools. The Shishi Chanyuan nunnery, a close affiliate of Nanputuo Monastery, founded a similar charitable organization in 2000 (Birnbaum 2003, 444).

Modernist Buddhist organizations have also undertaken institutionalization through the adaptation of contemporary political ideals and administrative techniques to monastic life. Fagushan, Foguangshan, and Ciji Gongde Hui all have clearly defined institutional hierarchies with codified guidelines for promotion, transfer, taking leaves of absence, and so on. Because Foguangshan's monastic contingent is so much larger than that of the other organizations—comprising some 1,300 monks and nuns—that Sangha has especially emphasized administrative innovations as evidence of its modernist approach. Each year, the Foguang headquarters sponsors a three-day conference on temple administration that is attended by several hundred clerics, approximately two-thirds of whom come from temples not part of the Foguang network. Integral to modern administration, emphasizes Ven. Xingyun, is the democratization of the decision-making process, especially through the election of temple leadership. Ven. Xingyun and his disciples are very proud of Foguangshan's balloting method for selecting both the Foguang headquarters' abbot and the nine members of the Religious Affairs Committee (the committee that, according to Foguang bylaws, is responsible for setting all of the organization's policies).

A key aspect of institutionalizing monastic life has been the establishment of academies to train clerics (and to a lesser degree lay leadership), an innovation that reflects the influence of both Western liberal arts pedagogy and methods of Christian seminary education. Ven. Taixu and an array of other Republican-era modernists all experimented with the creation of Buddhist schools in which both monastic and lay students could take a wide range of classes in Buddhist ritual, doctrine, and history (Pittman 2001, 54–56, 235–236). Although very few of the early academies survived more than a few years, the method itself has flourished. In fact, as Raoul Birnbaum (2003, 438–440) has observed, the creation of seminaries is the one component of the Republican-era modernist Buddhist agenda that has subsequently permeated traditionalist Sanghas as well. Hence, not only can one visit the Minnan Buddhist Academy (associated with Nanputuo Monastery of Xiamen and one of the few schools founded by Ven. Taixu that has been revived), Fagushan Buddhist Academy, and Foguangshan Buddhist Academy, but also Fuhu Temple's Emei Buddhist Academy for Nuns, the Zhongtaishan Buddhist Academy, and the Dharma Realm Buddhist University (founded by Ven. Hsuan Hua as part of the City of Ten Thousand Buddhas). The curricula of schools associated with modernist and traditionalist monasteries are quite similar in many respects; the same rituals and scriptures are taught at both kinds of schools. The two types of institutions primarily differ in the degree to which they advocate direct engagement with secular society or, as the issue is phrased by Chinese Buddhists, whether they advocate a form of Humanistic Buddhism.

Humanistic Buddhism

Ven. Taixu was the first to employ the concept of rensheng Fojiao. In Ven. Taixu's opinion, the deterioration of Chinese Buddhism over the past several centuries had been mostly due to an overemphasis on funerary and other rites devoted to transferring merit for the benefit of the deceased. He therefore devised the term *rensheng Fojiao* to remind people that, as it is living humans (rensheng) who are in the best position to cultivate the necessary merit and wisdom to attain enlightenment, Buddhists should devote their energies to maximizing this opportunity, both for themselves and others (Pittman 2001, 169–181). It was Ven. Taixu's most famous disciple, Ven. Yinshun, who first fully explored the concept's assumptions and implications, although he preferred renjian Fojiao over rensheng Fojiao to give even more emphasis to the fact that Buddhism should not only focus on the living, but also that its practice must occur through active participation in human society (*renjian:* "in the human domain," "in the midst of people"). It should not be inordinately devoted to worshipping buddhas as though they were deities, a tendency that in his opinion has plagued the Mahayana tradition since its inception (Shi Yinshun 1993, 1–63).

In Taiwan, both Ven. Xingyun and Ven. Zhengyan have followed Ven. Yinshun's terminology. Ven. Shengyan, in contrast, refers to both rensheng Fojiao and renjian Fojiao, so as to show his indebtedness to both Ven. Taixu and Ven. Yinshun. In mainland China, where Ven. Yinshun's work is not as well known, those who employ the language of Humanistic Buddhism—such as the monks of Nanputuo Monastery and the nuns at Shishi Chanyuan—generally maintain the wording coined by Ven. Taixu. All of these clerics qualify the word "Buddhism" with adjectives approximating the English "humanistic" so as to redirect people's attention back from other realms and lifetimes to present existence in this world. Shakyamuni Buddha, they remind people, was no spirit or god, but a person who was born in this world, cultivated himself in this world, and attained enlightenment in this world. Buddhists should therefore model their practice on him, and not devote so much of their time and energy to participating in abstract discussions, performing rites on behalf of the deceased, or seeking a better rebirth in some far-off pure land. To follow in the footsteps of the Buddha simply means to tread the middle path, neither succumbing to the temptations of desires nor stubbornly insisting on rigorous asceticism. Hence, one will not find at Foguangshan, Fagushan, or Jingsi Hermitage such practices as fasting or the use of one's own blood to copy sutras.

Along with downplaying asceticism, Humanistic Buddhists believe that treading the middle path implies a certain openness to altering aspects of Buddhist practice, especially those concerning monastic life that, having been rendered outmoded by current circumstances, have become obstacles to benefiting others. Any literalist interpretation of the Vinaya or of tradition, in fact, is said to contradict the founding teacher's exhortation that each person is to think for himself or herself so as to respond appropriately to every new situation. This understanding of how to emulate the Buddha has the advantage of allowing for flexibility. The hermeneutical challenge is to determine the degree to which such flexibility is permissible.

What Foguangshan, Fagushan, and Ciji Gongde Hui monastics claim as the acceptable adaptation of precepts and custom in light of current conditions, other clerics assert to be feeble excuses for lax practice. Those advocating Humanistic Buddhism are therefore accused of undermining Buddhist monastic ethics. Foguangshan, Fagushan, and Ciji Gongde Hui clerics counter that it is easy to claim complete purity for oneself when one remains behind shut doors and therefore has almost no interaction with others. As one nun explained to me, purity is a matter of intention and suitability of action. Furthermore, she continued, the middle path requires that one balance the cultivation of wisdom (zhi) with the accumulation of merit (gongde) and blessings (fu). Those who do not follow Humanistic Buddhism have become so engrossed in nurturing the former that they have forgotten that the latter can only occur through helping and nurturing others, and this requires flexibility in approach. Advocates of Humanistic Buddhism argue that, far from vitiating monastic ethics, their more pliant interpretation has buttressed the Buddha's instructions on morality, not only for those who have "left home" (chujia), but for laity as well. Much attention is therefore given to broader Buddhist ethical teachings, e.g., the four all-embracing virtues, five precepts, and six paramitas. Humanistic Buddhist cultivation is seen to be first and foremost about learning how to be fully human. As Ven. Taixu often intoned, "Relying upon the Buddha, perfection lies in human character; 'humanness' perfected is buddhahood attained; This is called true reality" (Shi Xingyun n.d., 6).

The this-worldly pragmatism that serves as the focal point of Humanistic Buddhism affects its votaries' interpretations of Chan and Pure Land teachings. Humanistic Buddhists are ambivalent about the role that meditation should play in daily practice. The several dozen nuns who have tonsured under Ven. Zhengyan meditate very seldom, if at all, for to spend time in a Chan Hall is regarded as selfishly attending only to one's own liberation and hence as being contrary to the bodhisattva spirit of serving all beings. Each day at Jingsi Hermitage begins and ends with half an hour of recitation. Most of the time in between these sessions is devoted to running Ciji Gongde Hui's charitable programs. Ven. Shengyan, alternatively, is regarded as one of Taiwan's preeminent meditation teachers, as well as a first-rate scholar. In his view, meditation is the most effective expedient means to aid all people, both monastic and lay, in eradicating the deep-rooted afflictions (fannao) that are the sources of suffering. Ven. Xingyun's position on meditation is midway between these two. Although a forty-eighth-generation holder of the Linji Dharma scroll, only in recent years has he encouraged devotees to make formal meditation an important part of their cultivation. Up through the 1980s, he considered Pure Land recitation a more suitable expedient means to attract lay followers, given their busy lives, relatively low education level, and scant understanding of the Dharma. Clerics were also dissuaded from spending too much time in meditation so that they could actively fulfill their bodhisattva vows. Only in the early 1990s, when many lay Buddhists (and even non-Buddhists) were turning to meditation as a means to relieve stress, did Ven. Xingyun more actively discuss the benefits of such practice, backing up his rhetoric by constructing Foguang-shan's beautiful Chan Hall. The monks and nuns of Nanputuo Monastery and Shishi Chanyuan appear to take essentially the same position as the monastics at Foguangshan; meditation is not part of the curriculum of the two-year sem-inary program, but fully ordained clerics are encouraged to sit regularly as a way to calm down and reduce anxiety (MacInnis 1989, 136).

Despite the differences in the degree of emphasis given to sitting medita-tion, those advocating Humanistic Buddhism all agree that Chan only has any worth if it is integrated into one's approach to every task, especially one's work. As Ven. Xingyun phrases it, formal sitting is worthless unless one is able to ex-perience "a taste of Chan in daily life." Ven. Baizhang's maxim "a day without work is a day without food" has been broadened radically so that, rather than merely justifying farm work as suitable for monastics, it has become a paean ex-alting various forms of social engagement as an essential part, and potentially the highest form, of religious practice at Fagushan, Foguangshan, Jingsi Her-mitage, Nanputuo Monastery, and Shishi Chanyuan. In the view of Humanistic Buddhist monastics, it is they, and not clerics, who sit in absolute silence for hours on end in some isolated monastery, who practice to attain the most pro-found level of Chan realization.

The Humanistic Buddhist perspective interprets Pure Land teachings in a new way as well. Following Vens. Taixu and Yinshun, contemporary modernist Buddhists have made renjian jingtu (establishing a pure land in the human realm; building a pure land on earth) a central slogan for their activities (cf. Shi Taixu 1953; Shi Yinshun 1992, 1993). In Chinese Buddhist tradition, a pure land, in the broadest sense, is any place where one may engage in unhindered spiritual cultivation. Drawing from various sutras, Pure Land votaries often de-scribe the remarkable features of such pure lands as Amitabha's Sukhavati, Bhaisajya-guru's Vaidurya Pure Land, and Maitreya's Santushita. Those reborn in such realms suffer no deprivation or distractions; their surroundings of beauty and peace afford an optimal setting for learning the Dharma. In addi-tion to such a literal understanding of the notion of pure lands, many Chinese Buddhists, having been influenced by the Chan and Consciousness-Only schools, have articulated that whether a person finds himself or herself in a pure land ultimately depends on the degree of that person's own inner purity of intention and thought. A place rife with defilements for one person remains fully compatible for self-cultivation for someone else farther along the bod-hisattva path. Hence, even our saha world (i.e., the realm of suffering and de-filement in which humans live) can be a serene pure land so long as the mind is tranquil. There is no need, according to this view, to await rebirth to experi-ence the bliss of a pure land; one need only fully realize the ultimate sanctity of mind and hence of all reality.

Those who issue the call to establish a pure land in the human realm do not

deny that there are pure lands elsewhere in the cosmos or that through meditation one can experience the present world as already pure. Nonetheless, they
deemphasize such metaphysical and psychological cosmologies, especially the
former, preferring instead to encourage people to follow the examples set by
Amitabha, Bhaisajya-guru, and Maitreya to create a pure land actively and literally through their own vows and deeds. This approach assumes that optimal
spiritual cultivation relies on purifying both external environment and internal
intention. Vens. Xingyun and Zhengyen emphasize the former, stressing that
the calmness of mind necessary for meditation and recitation depends on the
satisfaction of certain basic health and material needs, and so attending to
those needs for oneself and others is an ineluctable part of Buddhist practice.
Ven. Xingyun has been especially likely to extol the role of technological advancement and political democratization in fostering circumstances that are
conducive to spiritual realization, an optimism that at one point even led him
to posit that the United States already satisfied some of the fundamental criteria for a pure land (Shi Xingyun 1994, entry for October 14, 1989). Ven.
Shengyan regards such alterations in external conditions as holding limited significance for meaningful spiritual progress. Instead, purification of the mind
through rigorous concentration must be primary, although as an aid to help
people attain such inner purity, he calls for the preservation of this world's
beauty through protecting natural resources. Hence, he is closely associated
with environmentalism. While the specifics diverge, all leaders of Humanistic
Buddhism stress that they do not want people to passively accept their present
conditions while awaiting rebirth.

The exhortations to experience a taste of Chan in daily life and to establish
a pure land in the human realm underscore a defining characteristic shaping
all interpretations of Humanistic Buddhism: the secularization of Buddhist
practice. In other words, the divisions between supramundane and mundane
and between monastic and lay life are blurred. The otherness of buddhas as sacred beings and of pure lands as radically distinct realms is minimized in favor
of accentuating the possibility of enlightenment for all and the accessibility of
purity even in our saha world. Secularization also incorporates an element of
laicization; that is to say, lay and monastic spheres of performance merge. Clerics are urged to return their focus to this mundane world, primarily by instructing lay devotees how to bring an element of the sacred into their lives. The holy
life of monastics is secularized while the secular life of laity is sacralized. Humanistic Buddhists assert that doing so is an extremely effective strategy for
transcending the dichotomy of sacred and profane. Their traditionalist critics
contend that Humanistic Buddhists have merely succeeded in trivializing the
supramundane.

The placement of religious duties in the hands of nonspecialists has been especially noticeable in Taiwan, where the 1989 Revised Law on the Organization

of Civic Groups—a bill whose primary intent was to loosen governmental control over voluntary associations—had the unintended, fortuitous consequence for Buddhist organizations of granting a more formal institutional recognition of lay participation. Of the approximately twenty Buddhist and Buddhist-affiliated associations that were founded over the subsequent decade, Ciji Gongde Hui and BLIA have without a doubt been the most influential. These two and the other Buddhist associations were formed as a means to better organize Taiwan's lay Buddhist population and to give it a greater leadership role. Lay devotees therefore fill not only the Ciji Gongde Hui and BLIA rosters, but most of the organizations' leadership positions as well. As of 1998, the three vice chief executive officers (CEOs) of Ciji Gongde Hui and five out of six vice CEOs for BLIA were laypeople. In both associations, virtually all positions of authority on the local level—chapter president, vice president, secretary, treasurer, and so on—are filled by laity (for BLIA, the only exception to this being the consultative post of guiding cleric).

It should be noted, however, that Ven. Xingyun has been much more wary than Ven. Zhengyan of handing over the reins of spiritual leadership to the laity. The actual policymakers of BLIA continue to be Ven. Xingyun and his most senior disciples. The influence of monastics is also considerable at the regional and local levels, since every BLIA chapter's guiding cleric plays a major part in shaping activities. For Ven. Xingyun, although monastic and lay life need not be so radically separated as occurs in many monasteries, clerics as specialists in religious affairs nonetheless perform certain services that cannot be accomplished by laity. BLIA therefore does not regard itself so much as a lay organization as an association through which lay devotees can play a greater role in cooperation with and usually under the supervision of monastics. Ven. Zhengyan has taken a more radical step toward laicization, for despite the fact that Ciji Gongde Hui has a much larger lay membership than does BLIA, Ven. Zhengyan only has 100 nuns to support her efforts, all of whom are stationed at Jingsi Hermitage. The Ciji Gongde Hui offices elsewhere in Taiwan and around the world are led by laity. Ven. Xingyun feels that Ven. Zhengyan has gone too far in laicizing her organization and hence predicts that in the future Ciji Gongde Hui will completely lose its Buddhist character, evolving into a secular philanthropic society. Ciji Gongde Hui devotees counter that the greater distinction in roles between laity and clerics at Foguangshan reflects a continued entrapment in dualistic thinking and hence does not represent the apex of Humanistic Buddhist thought.

As the most prominent organizations promoting Humanistic Buddhism, Ciji Gongde Hui, Fagushan, Foguangshan, Nanputuo Monastery, and Shishi Chanyuan share important traits, but they also differ in significant ways. As we have seen, Ven. Xingyun and Ven. Zhengyan both emphasize compassionate service over rigorous meditation or abstract study. This also appears to be the case with the monks and nuns of Nanputuo Monastery and Shishi Chanyuan, since both have established charitable foundations, and the two-year training of novices does not include meditation (MacInnis 1989, 136). Ven. Shengyan, alternatively, is regarded as a preeminent meditation teacher as well as a first-rate scholar. Although Ven. Xingyun and Ven. Zhengyan share an emphasis on service, they differ in focus and method. For instance, Ven. Zhengyan stresses relieving the physical and psychological suffering of life through organizing medical works. Ven. Xingyun's efforts have centered more in the area of creating joy through Buddhist education. Ciji Gongde Hui members argue that their willingness to confront and alleviate suffering is more in line with the Buddha's teachings. Foguangshan devotees counter that Ciji Gongde Hui's programs are noble but only supply temporary relief. Ultimate liberation from suffering can only occur through realizing the joy of the Dharma, and providing people with this opportunity, they say, is the mission of Foguangshan's multifaceted educational enterprises.

The differences in method employed by those associated with the various modernist, humanistic organizations are a matter of emphasis rather than cut-and-dried distinctions. Foguangshan, Ciji Gongde Hui, Fagushan, Nanputuo Monastery, and Shishi Chanyuan all engage in charitable and educational efforts. The financial foundation of the two temples in mainland China remains relatively weak, so their programs have been on a smaller scale. Each of the groups in Taiwan, having benefited by the island's burst of prosperity, has been able to sponsor ambitious endeavors on several fronts. The Dharma education activities provided by Ciji Gongde Hui's television station, Internet sites, and magazines rival, if they do not surpass, those offered by Foguangshan. Fagushan is in the midst of founding a very ambitious Buddhist university that will be open to monastic and lay Buddhists. At the same time, both Foguangshan and Fagushan engage in medical relief and other social service enterprises. The differences in focus nonetheless set the tone for each organization: Ciji Gongde Hui is Taiwan's Buddhist group famed for its compassionate service, Fagushan is regarded as the foremost place to learn meditation, and Foguangshan is known for its educational endeavors. Having staked their claim in the spiritual marketplace, each organization staunchly guards its domain. There is little cooperation or even interaction among the three communities. They are rivals more than allies—generally polite rivals, but rivals nonetheless, for they are all vying to attract a limited population: those Buddhists on Taiwan who find the rhetoric of Humanistic Buddhism appealing.

Of the various leaders who employ the phraseology of Humanistic Buddhism and establishing a pure land in the human realm, Ven. Shengyan interprets these concepts in a way most in line with traditionalists' understanding of practice. This is especially evident in his characterization of establishing a pure land in the human realm as a task whose starting and ending points must be the purification of one's own mind. In such an interpretation, "establishing a pure land in the human realm" can become little more than a modernist re-phrasing of the centuries-old doctrine of "consciousness-only pure land." This more traditionalist rendering is, in fact, quite common among rank-and-file clerics at temples espousing Humanistic Buddhism. Jones (2003, 136–137) cites a discussion that took place at a conference in 1990, for instance, in which a nun from Foguangshan agreed with a monk from Nungchan Temple (which is an affiliate of Fagushan) that individual minds must first be purified before social action could elicit any true benefit. The difference between more traditionalist-leaning Humanistic Buddhists and Buddhists who are fully in the traditionalist camp, continues Jones (2003, 138), is that the former consider purification of the mind as a prelude to social activism, while the latter deem purification of the mind as sufficient in and of itself. Hence, if traditionalists use at all the terminology "establishing a pure land in the human realm," they do so as a synonym of "consciousness-only pure land."

This is very much the case in mainland China. Ven. Yanci and other nuns in Fuhu Temple, for example, occasionally quote Ven. Taixu's slogan, but never as a call to social action. Instead, they give it a traditional reading, understand-ing it simply to paraphrase the assertion in the Vimalakirti-nirdesa Sutra, "As the mind is pure, so is the world pure." According to the scholar Wen-jie Qin, this is the interpretation held by the vast majority of contemporary monastic communities in the PRC. "In mainland China," Qin states, "due to the political restraints on religion, this notion [of renjian jingtu] has so far remained largely a guide for meditation rather than for social campaigns" (Qin 2000, 405). Hence, while the philanthropic endeavors of Nanputuo Monastery and Shishi Chanyuan reflect a modernist understanding of the process necessary to estab-lish a pure land in the human realm, such an interpretation is an exception to the general conservative trend. The more widespread understanding, exempli-fied by Fuhu Temple, deems that, by bringing to mind the pristine qualities of Sukhavati, recitation not only prepares one for rebirth in that land of bliss but acts to purify one's mind here and now, thereby allowing one to realize this very world as inherently pure.

Conclusion: The Interpenetrating Dimensions of Chinese Buddhism

Is the pure land to the west in Sukhavati; in the West in the United States; or present everywhere, although our cluttered, tainted minds don't allow us to recognize this fact? Similarly, is the center of the Chinese Buddhist universe in the PRC, despite the relatively small numbers of devotees; in the ROC, where its public face is more evident; in the Chinese Buddhist communities scattered around the world; or in the consciousness of anyone who has come into contact with the tradition, even if the person is not ethnically Chinese and only received that knowledge through an occasional lecture or through books? Has the tradition experienced a revitalization? Or has the revival really been essentially a transformation in self-awareness? If there has been a revival, have the traditionalists or the modernists been the driving force?

Current trends indicate that the revival to which practitioners so proudly point has occurred, but not in nearly so grand a fashion as they claim. Much of the revitalization appears to be essentially a shift in demographics allowing for the emergence of new centers. The new institutional centers that have garnered the most attention are those with modernist leanings, although in sheer numbers, the traditionalists appear to hold the edge. While the scale of resurgence may be disputed, the fact that this is a tradition in flux cannot be denied.

Practitioners within Chinese Buddhism would most likely observe that, if the language of "center," "revitalization," "tradition," and "modernity" is appropriate or useful at all, it is so only on the mundane level. From the supramundane perspective, all facets of Buddhism—regardless of spatial location or basic outlook—are radically interdependent. The historical center of mainland China, the institutional center of Taiwan, and the myriad cognitive centers of devotees around the world ceaselessly create one another, just as the notions of traditionalism and modernism only subsist in dynamic interrelation. The historical center of today was the institutional center of yore, and it one day may return to that status (or that center may move elsewhere entirely), just as the bedrock components of contemporary tradition were once controversial innovations. Similarly, the institutional center of today will become the historical center for the practitioners of tomorrow, and at least some of the present modern advances will be elements of future tradition. The Sino-Buddhist universe is as multivalent and complex as Pure Land cosmology. The nuns at Fuhu Temple, the Tibetan pilgrims and Chinese tourists who climb Mount Emei, and the Chinese and non-Chinese visitors to Hsi Lai Temple live in distinct yet overlapping dimensions of that universe.

References

Birnbaum, Raoul. 2003. Buddhist China at the Century's Turn. *China Quarterly* 174, 428–450.

Buddhist Association of the ROC. 1990. Buddhist Association of the ROC and Buddhism in the Taiwan Area. Taipei, Taiwan: Buddhist Association of the Republic of China.

Chan, Wing-tsit. 1953. *Religious Trends in Modern China.* New York: Columbia University Press.

Chandler, Stuart. 2004. *Establishing a Pure Land on Earth: The Foguang Buddhist Perspective on Modernization and Globalization.* Honolulu: University of Hawai'i Press.

Hsiao, Hsin-Huang Michael. 2002. Coexistence and Synthesis: Cultural Globalization and Localization in Contemporary Taiwan. In *Many Globalizations: Cultural Diversity in the Contemporary World,* ed. Peter L. Berger and Samuel P. Huntington, 48–67. New York: Oxford University Press.

Jiang Canteng. 1989. *Renjian Jingtu de zhuixun—zhongguo jinshi fojiao si xiang yanjiu* (Pursuit of a pure land in the human realm: A study of contemporary Chinese Buddhist thought). Taipei, Taiwan: Daoxiang.

———. 1997. *Taiwan Dangdai Fojiao* (Modern Buddhism in Taiwan). Taipei, Taiwan: Nantian Shuju.

Jones, Charles Brewer. 1999. *Buddhism in Taiwan: Religion and the State, 1660–1990.* Honolulu: University of Hawai'i Press.

———. 2003. Transitions in the Practice and Defense of Chinese Pure Land Buddhism. In *Buddhism in the Modern World: Adaptations of an Ancient Tradition,* ed. Steven Heine and Charles S. Prebish, 125–142. Oxford, UK: Oxford University Press.

Katz, Paul R. 2003. Religion and the State in Post-war Taiwan. In *Religion in China Today,* China Quarterly Special Issues New Series No. 3, 89–106. New York: Cambridge University Press.

Laliberte, Andre. 1999. *The Politics of Buddhist Organizations in Taiwan, 1989–1997.* PhD dissertation, University of British Columbia.

Luo, Zhufeng. 1991. *Religion under Socialism in China.* Trans. Donald E. MacInnis and Zheng Xi'an. Armonk, NY: M. E. Sharpe.

MacInnis, Donald E. 1989. *Religion in China Today: Policy and Practice.* Maryknoll, NY: Orbis Books.

Melton, J. Gordon, and Martin Baumann. 2002. *Religions of the World: A Comprehensive Encyclopedia of Beliefs and Practices,* vol. 1. Santa Barbara, CA: ABC-CLIO.

Pittman, Don Alvin. 2001. *Toward a Modern Chinese Buddhism: Taixu's Reforms.* Honolulu: University of Hawai'i Press.

Qin, Wen-jie. 2000. *The Buddhist Revival in Post-Mao China: Women Reconstruct Buddhism on Mt. Emei.* PhD dissertation, Harvard University.

Shi Taixu. 1953. *Taixu Dashi Quanshu* (Compete Works of Master Taixu). Hong Kong: n.p.

Shi Xingyun. 1994. *Xingyun Riji* (Xingyun's diary), vol. 1. Kaohsiung, Taiwan: Foguang Press.

———. Undated. Zenyang Zuo Ge Foguangren" (How to be a Foguang Buddhist), pamphlet 7502. Kaohsiung, Taiwan: Foguang Press.

Shi Xingyun, ed. 1995. *Fojiao Congshu* (Anthology of Buddhism), 10 volumes. Kaohsiungm, Taiwan: Foguang Press.

Shi Yinshun. 1992. *Jingtu yu Chan* (Pure Land and Chan). Taipei, Taiwan: Zhengwen Press.

———. 1993. *Huayu Ji,* vol. 4. Taipei, Taiwan: Zhengwen Press.

Shils, Edward. 1981. *Tradition.* Chicago: University of Chicago Press.

Welch, Holmes. 1968. *The Buddhist Revival in China.* Cambridge, MA.: Harvard University Press.

———. 1972. *Buddhism under Mao.* Cambridge, MA: Harvard University Press.

Chapter Seven

Buddhism in Korea
Decolonization, Nationalism, and Modernization

PORI PARK

After the Korean Peninsula was liberated from Japanese colonial rule (1910–1945), Korea was soon caught up in cold war ideological strife and then plunged into the Korean War (1950–1953). The present celibate Chogye (Jogye) order of South Korea—which is the predominant sect, possessing both the most monastic members and the majority of traditional Buddhist monasteries and properties—was formed during the so-called Purification Movement, which lasted from 1954 to 1970. During this time, the minority celibate clerics staged a war against the majority of married monks who had appeared during the colonial period.

The leaders of the Purification Movement initiated a Dharma war against the "evil" married monks, who they believed ruined the pure Dharma. In addition, they used the rhetoric of decolonization because monk marriage had first been introduced to Korea during the colonial era by Japanese Buddhist clerics, most of whom had already adopted it after the Meiji Restoration (1868–1912) in the name of modernization. The celibate leaders accused the married monks of being collaborators with the Japanese regime and thus a social evil to be eradicated. They also argued that their fight for celibacy was to restore the tradition that had wrongly been altered by the "Japanized monks."

The monks who adopted marriage were mostly the recipients of modern education in Korea or Japan, and some of them were politically influential at the time of the initial conflict. The nationalist polemic won over the mind of the general population and thus put the celibate monks in a favorable position. To bring to an end the chapter of colonial history and bring justice to the people who had lived under Japanese rule, the celibates targeted victims they could easily find, namely, the married clerics. The government sided with the celibate camps, which ultimately led to the victory of the celibates.

The issue of decolonization is closely interwoven with the nationalist fervor of this transitional period. "Buddhism for the state" (*hoguk Pulgyo*) became the catch phrase of the celibate Buddhists, while the married monks insisted on the continuation of Buddhism modern reforms. During a prolonged fight, the march for the modernization of Buddhism, which had provided a rallying point for the Buddhists during the colonial era, yielded to the issue of decolonization and the nationalist ideology.

Internal dissension intensified during the Purification Movement and continued even after 1970, carried forward by diverse lineage groups that appeared soon after the hegemonic struggle. The confrontations among these lineage groups were tenacious and violent. Because the Sangha was thus occupied, it easily became a willing partner of, or was manipulated by, the succession of authoritarian Korean regimes that had held sway since the independence of Korea.

The Sangha returned to the task of modernization in the 1980s. With the passage of time, Korean Buddhists renewed their interests in attuning their practices to their rapidly Westernizing society. While the Sangha emphasized the institutional reforms of monastic education and propagation, younger generations reintroduced the idea of minjung Pulgyo (Buddhism for the masses), which already had been integrated into the modern reforms of the Sangha during the colonial period. It was a way for monks to become involved in the march for social and political justice, which had been persistently undermined by a succession of authoritarian regimes.

By looking at the complex interplay of Buddhism, politics, modernization, and nationalism, this essay examines the ways in which contemporary Buddhists shaped their traditions. It will present the many shades of meaning in the term "modernization," starting from the colonial period and then moving to the postindependence era and to recent times.

Modern Reforms during the Colonial Era

The Japanese rule brought an end to 500 years of persecution of Buddhism under the staunchly Confucian Choson dynasty (1392–1910), and the colonial regime attempted to curry favor with the Buddhists by appearing as a protector of the religion. The Japanese regime announced the seven articles of the temple ordinance (sach'allyong) in June of 1911 and, in the following month, declared eight articles of "regulations for administering the temple ordinance." The regime claimed that this ordinance was intended to secure the sustenance of Buddhism and to protect Buddhist monasteries and properties (Toru 1973, 887–888). It encouraged Buddhist reforms so that Korean Buddhism would become strong enough to support its policies on the peninsula. The government's support of Korean Buddhism also was prompted by the rapid growth of Christianity, serving as a way to curb Christian expansion (So 1988, 119).

Under the temple ordinance, the Korean Sangha was restructured into a system of thirty main monasteries and embarked on the reform movement under the scrutiny of the Japanese regime. The main areas of the reforms were in Sangha education and methods of propagation to make the Sangha more accessible to the public. Monasteries attempted to implement a modern educational system for Buddhist clerics as both independent and cooperative projects. The curriculum included secular subjects to make Buddhist clerics conversant with society. By 1915, the Buddhist order appeared to have completed a three-step modern education system, starting with primary schools, local preparatory schools, and a central postsecondary school as the highest educational institution at Seoul (Nam 1988, 255).

As well as attending their own Buddhist schools, young clerics went to public secondary schools in Seoul and colleges in foreign countries, mostly in Japan. The magazine Haedong pulbo (Buddhist Journal of Korea) reported that there were thirteen students in Japan in 1913, only three of whom were studying with monastery funds, while five students were reported to be in Seoul, with four supported by monastery funds. The first three graduates returned from Japan to Korea in 1918, finishing their studies at Soto-shu College. These monks received a hearty welcome from their fellow Buddhists. In 1924, about thirty students studied in Japan and six at universities in Pei-ching. In 1928, twenty-two graduated from Japanese colleges. Until liberation in 1945, Buddhist clerics continued to go mostly to Japan to study. These educated monks emerged as the leaders of the youth movement and later assumed the central positions of the Sangha.

Besides paying attention to the education of the clerics, each monastery district also opened branch temples for proselytization (p'ogyo-so) in villages and towns to make the religion accessible to the general public. The Central Propagation Office of Korean Buddhism was established in 1910 by the cooperative investment of main monasteries. In 1912, the Central Propagation Office of Korean Son Buddhism was opened in Seoul by nine monasteries, including Pomo-sa, T'ongdo-sa, Paegyang-sa, and Taehung-sa. By 1913, 18 propagation branches had opened, including the 2 central propagation offices just mentioned. According to the Sangha's report, the numbers of p'ogyo-so had increased to about 40 and Buddhist lay followers numbered 100,000 in 1915. By the end of 1924, there were 72 p'ogyo-so with 72 p'ogyo clerics and 200,000 laypeople. In 1930, there were 117 p'ogyo-so, with 122 p'ogyo clerics. These figures show the Buddhists' effort to reach out to Korean society.

After the March First Movement, which demanded Korean independence from Imperial Japan in 1919, the Buddhist reforms, which had been apolitical in nature, took on a political dimension as Buddhists joined the nationalist march for the restoration of sovereignty. After the independence movement, the Japanese acceded to the outcry of the Korean people and changed their coercive policy into a so-called cultural one. Young clerics launched the youth movement, advocating the separation of religion from politics and the abolition of the temple ordinance on account of the abuses it spawned. Under the temple ordinance, each main monastery had been made an independent unit of operation, and there was thus no way to control a corrupt monastery. Further, the arbitrary imposition of the main monastery system had been a constant source of strife between the main and branch temples. For these reasons, young clerics urged the colonial government to abolish the temple ordinance and give the Korean Sangha independence to manage its own affairs, as had been the case before the advent of Japanese rule.

The youth also criticized Bureaucratic Buddhism (kwanje Pulgyo), which was subservient to the Japanese government. Han Yongun (1879–1944), a leading monastic reformer, pointed out that the general public and other religions disdained Buddhism through the use of the term *kwanje Pulgyo* (Han 1931a, 144–145). This term was used in a negative sense to mock the close ties between the Sangha and the colonial regime. Young monks instead advocated minjung Pulgyo (Buddhism for the masses) to sever the ties of Sangha with the powerful Japanese state and to serve the general public. The focus of the reformation became minjung (the masses). In this sense, minjung Pulgyo was not only a way of reaching out to people socially, but it was also a form of resisting state intervention.

The socialist influence in the term *minjung* is apparent. Kang Man'gil of Koryo University notes that the first use of minjung as the leaders of the nationalist movement appeared in Sin Ch'aeho's (1880–1936) "Declaration of the Korean Revolution" (Choson hyongmyong sonon so), written in 1923 (Kang 1995, 32–34). Kang infers that Sin used the term *minjung* to refer to the proletariat of the oppressed colonial nations in Asia. It has also been argued that movements of peasants and laborers became rampant during the mid-1920s (An 1980, 68).

Prior to Sin's usage, the term *minjung*, which appeared in the latter half of the nineteenth century, simply indicated the general populace. Korean Buddhist clerics used the concepts *minjung* and *taejung* interchangeably—*minjung* thus probably referred to a wider range of people who are the governed, in contrast to those who do the governing. During the latter part of the 1920s, the term *minjung* seemed to have been used widely by society and among Buddhists. In 1928, a monk stated that, at that time, no one failed to mention minjung. The term *minjung Pulgyo* was also used by Buddhists in Japan. It was spread widely by the introduction of democracy during by the Taisho era (1912–1925), referring to the larger segment of the general populace (Taijo 1967, 399–406). Meanwhile, Han Yongun defined *minjung Pulgyo* as follows:

> *Taejung Pulgyo* [*minjung Pulgyo*] means to practice Buddhism for *minjung*. Buddhists neither abandon human society nor deny close, loving relationships with people. They instead attain enlightenment through defilement and achieve nirvana in the midst of the stream of life and death. Being aware of this truth and getting involved in action are the practices of *Taejung Pulgyo*. (Han 1931b, 167)

Han argued that everything had to be changed for the minjung, including the doctrine, system, and properties of the Sangha. Buddhist doctrines and canons should be made simple and accessible to the minjung. Buddhist institutions and properties had to be open to, and used for the benefit of, the minjung. In his article "Record on the Reformation of Korean Buddhism" published in 1931 (quoted in Han 1931b), Manhae argued that Buddhism should be involved in making secure the lives of the minjung. Thus, Buddhists should participate in social activities by establishing Buddhist libraries, welfare institutions for laborers and farmers, and educational facilities for the general public.

Overall, the Sangha's investment in both education and proselytization suffered from financial crises. Evidence of financial problems is seen in the journal Pulgyo, which reported in 1924 that the monastery treasures of Haein-sa, one of the largest main monasteries, were subject to seizure because of huge debts due to the failed ventures of the abbot. A Buddhist cleric lamented in 1927 that all monasteries, whether main or branch ones, were burdened by crushing debt (Kim P. 1927, 226). Moreover, under the scrutiny of the temple ordinance, the reforms suffered from serious restrictions. The temple ordinance and the government's intervention in the affairs of the Sangha persisted, however, until the end of Japanese rule in 1945.

Korean Buddhism was severely Japanized during the occupation and was secularized in the name of modernization. Korean monasteries were reorganized according to the Japanese main monastery system. Buddhist clerics were bureaucratized and competed for the limited number of abbot positions. Most of them adopted the practices of Japanese Buddhism, wearing Western-style clothes, taking wives, eating meat, and drinking wine. Clerical marriages already had become prevalent when the government officially approved them in 1926. Those monks began to observe Japanese national rites, incorporating the Imperial rites among the regular ceremonies conducted at Korean monasteries. Under the heavy influence of Japan, the internal conflict between pro-Japanese clerics and the independent-minded young clerics persisted.

Korean monk of the Haein-sa Temple displays one of 80,000 wood block volumes that comprise the tripitaka—that is, the "three baskets" of Buddhist scriptures: Vinaya (monastic discipline), Abhidharma (psychology), and Sutra (discourses) believed to originate from the teachings of Sakyamuni Buddha himself. (Leonard de Selva/Corbis)

The Purification Movement and Clerical Marriage

When the Korean peninsula was liberated from Japanese rule in 1945, Korean Buddhists felt obliged to purge themselves of the remnants of colonialism, which included identifying and punishing the so-called traitors and eliminating the Japanese product of the temple ordinance. The ideological confrontation and political chaos immediately following liberation frustrated the initial effort to decolonize the Buddhist order. Korea was divided in two by the "liberating" forces of the Soviet Union and the United States, and the nation was soon engulfed in civil war from 1950 to 1953.

The Purification Movement was the second attempt to purge the order. This time, however, the focus was restricted to the issue of clerical marriage. With the aid of the first president, Yi Sungman (Syngman Rhee, president from 1948 to 1960), who abruptly ordered the married monks' resignation, the celibate monks embarked on a campaign to get rid of married monks as a way of cleansing away the colonial memories. During the colonial period, Korean monks adopted the practice of clerical marriage, which also was widely practiced by Japanese monks at that time. They regarded clerical marriage, fewer regulations, and city living as more convenient than living in monasteries as celibate monks for relating to and assisting laypeople. By the time of liberation, about 7,000 monks were married and only 700 monks remained celibate (Mok 1993, 105).

During the Purification Movement, clerical marriage began to appear as a product of Japanized Buddhism, and married monks were thus deemed collaborators in Japanese rule. As reported in a newspaper, President Yi stated that his nation, which was in the process of restoring the freedom and independence of Korean people, should not tolerate those who were pro-Japanese (the married monks) and who did not care about the crisis of national sovereignty. He further insisted that everyone should cherish patriotism by abandoning Japanese customs and habits: Those who were monks in a Japanese fashion should thus gradually return to lay life and help restore the sacred celibate tradition.

Taking advantage of these favorable social and political currents, the celibate clerics focused on religious justification for the restoration of celibacy of the Sangha. Kim Iryop (1896–1971), a nun at Kyonsong-am, argued that celibacy was the most decisive precept of Buddhist clerics (Han'guk 1995, 207–209). She stated that great awakening requires great restriction, and one cannot enter the right path of life without giving up the self. Being a Buddhist cleric meant that one first had to leave his or her home, then leave his or her own body, and, finally, transcend the world of birth and death (Han'guk 1995, 273–277). Arguing thus, Kim affirmed the validity of the Purification Movement.

Yi Ch'ongdam (1902–1971), the de facto leader of the Purification Movement, saw the movement as a Dharma war (popchon) between good and evil. According to him, there should be no compromising with the opposing party, and even common sense and majority opinions should not wield any influence in this process of restoring the truth, because the truth is beyond the boundaries of time and space and is not made by consensus among people (Han'guk 1995, 381).

President Yi Sungman issued an order on May 20, 1954, commanding that married monks leave the Buddhist order. This had a great impact on both the married and celibate monks, given the almost absolute power of the president in the fledgling democracy of Korea. Yi not only ignited the fight, but he also became the main force behind the prolonged battle between these two factions of the Korean Sangha.

As an immediate response, the married faction convened a general meeting in June 1954, allotting fifty monasteries to the celibates and designating the Three Jewel monasteries, the largest monasteries, for the celibates. The celibate leaders also convened in Seoul in August 1954 and held a conference of the celibates on September 27, 1954, where they passed their version of the constitution of the Chogye order. This constitution stated that married monks should be removed from the monk registry and that they instead should be known as Dharma protectors (hobopjung), who would only take care of the official duties of the order for the public. The celibates also decided that they would assume the power of the administration and that the married monks would leave the monasteries within the span of ten years. The married faction, however, denounced the celibates' decisions, stating that they could not be just Dharma protectors, and decided to establish a separate sect. Tensions grew between the two, and there were no compromises made by either side.

President Yi issued then a second order on November 4, 1954, affirming his position favoring the celibates. Encouraged by this second order, the celibates entered and occupied the headquarter temple T'aego-sa on November 5, 1954, and changed its name to Chogye-sa. On November 11, a bloody confrontation erupted as the married faction tried to retake the temple. The married monks did not concede to this coercive action without putting up a fight. This violent conflict became deadlocked, and the president issued a third order on November 19, 1954, making it firm that the Japanized married monks should yield and resign gradually and that the Buddhists had to end the fight among themselves. If Buddhists did not concede, he threatened, the government would intervene and punish them.

In response to this third order, the married faction convened at T'aego-sa on November 20–23, 1954, and decided that they would resign from central administration positions and abbot posts. The married faction then appointed the celibate monks, who belonged to their own camp, to major positions. Filling such positions with their own celibate monks was the strategy of the married monks to retain their power while fulfilling the presidential order and the demands of the opposite camp. The married monks elected celibate scholar monks, as opposed to Son meditation monks in the other faction.

These emergency measures, however, did not satisfy the broader celibate faction. When the married faction handed over the official duties to the elected members on November 3, 1954, the celibate faction intervened in the process and demanded that the transition procedure should be open to the public. Physical fights among those involved followed the confrontation.

At the beginning of the conflict, the celibates earned not only the support of the government, but also of the general public because of their seemingly moral cause of liquidating the product of the colonial past—married monks. As the chaotic confrontation persisted, however, the general public became increasingly upset by the violent exchanges between the two factions and rebuked this battle as a fight over Buddhist property, which included 800 jongbo of forest (approximately 1,960 acres), 700 jongbo of land (approximately 1,715 acres), 900 temples, 9 colleges, 15 middle and high schools, and small and medium enterprises. The daily paper Tonga reported that the total annual income of the enterprises of the Buddhist order reached several million hwan (Korea's currency introduced in 1953 at 1/60 U.S. dollar). Several weeks earlier, the Choson Ilbo (Choson Daily newspaper) had ridiculed the celibates for their heavy dependence on presidential orders and criticized the bloody fighting.

As a result of this impasse, the government directly intervened to mediate between the two factions. On February 4, 1955, the minister of education arranged a meeting among the ten delegates from both camps. Therafter, they agreed on the eight conditions of Buddhist clerics, which include shaving one's hair, wearing monk robes, maintaining a single life, abstaining from meat and liquor, living in the community, and being older than twenty-five years of age. On May 18, 1955, in the room of the minister of education, delegates from both camps formed the Special Committee for Purification of Buddhism and decided to hold a nationwide abbot election. They would then report the election results to the ministers of education and the interior by the end of June 1955.

This agreement, however, never materialized because of the resistance of the married monks, who thought that these measures threatened their survival in the order. No further discussion took place, and the married faction still dominated the order. In response, 200 celibate monks, representing Son Hagwon in Seoul, a center temple for celibates, fasted for seven days from June 9 through June 15 in 1955 to protest the administrative delay of the government. During this event, about 360 married monks attacked the fasting monks and injured about 30 of them (Han'guk 2002, 81).

On August 2–3, 1955, the celibates convened without government permission. They passed a revised constitution and elected the Supreme Patriarch (Chongjong) and central posts. The next day, August 4, President Yi held news briefings with reporters and again made it clear that monks who were collaborators of the Japanese government should leave the order. He added that the married monks were the ones who had attempted to become good citizens of the Japanese regime. Yi regarded clerical marriage as a way for some monks to please the colonial rulers. On August 5, the day after the news conference, Yi summoned the ministers and told them to resign their positions if they could not promptly resolve the Buddhist conflict.

Encouraged by Yi's support, and this time with the approval of the government, the celibate monks gathered at Chogye-sa on August 12 and passed the constitution of the Sangha. They elected 56 Sangha assembly members and filled the administrative positions. The celibate faction filled all the ecclesiastical positions. Thus, with the Conference of Buddhist Clerics and the passing of the constitution, the resignation of the married monks could no longer be avoided. The celibates began to take over major monasteries. This process of seizing monasteries was difficult due to the resistance of those who operated them. With the help of police, the celibates forced the married monks out.

Those who were kicked out of monasteries went to the street and became a social problem, as well as a symbol of Buddhist strife.

By October 1955, the celibates had taken over from the married faction about 450 monasteries out of 1,000. They gave only the right of operation of the remaining monasteries to those married monks who agreed with the Purification Movement. In reality, however, these monasteries remained under the ownership of the married monks, as the minority celibates simply did not have sufficient manpower to take over so many monasteries (Minjok 1986, 59). The celibates employed thugs and street boys for their fights and later transformed them into clerics without much discretion or training. Despite all these inventions, they still could not operate many of these monasteries by themselves.

Meanwhile, the married monks resorted to the judicial system and filed lawsuits. Additionally, they did not give up the operation of enterprises, schools, companies, and Buddhist foundations. The Sangha was engulfed in a succession of legal battles with the married faction. In June 1956, the married monks won a victory in district court. The court announced that the constitution proclaimed by the celibates was not effective. In July 1956, the married monks also won their lawsuit against the T'aego-sa temple. After these judgments, the married monks reassumed power over the Sangha (Han'guk 1995, 257).

In response, the celibate monks appealed to a high court of justice and won their lawsuit on September 17, 1957. Additionally, the district court recalled its decision on the ownership of T'aego-sa in August 1956. Thus, the situation again was favorable for the celibates. The government's support of the celibates was the major force for this judicial victory. In the end, both the government and the judicial system protected the celibates.

With this litigation, both parties had consumed the wealth and resources of the Sangha, and still more than seventy lawsuits over the ownership of temples were in process. Many married monks got divorced in order to acquire single status and to thus preserve their rights over their monasteries (Han'guk 1995, 236–237).

Political Turmoil and Monastic Strife

Student and popular protest put an end to the corruption and dictatorship of Yi Sungman's regime in April 1960. Along with this political change, the Buddhist order again went through a period of great upheaval. Now the celibate monks' fate was at the mercy of politics. Following this popular revolt and the loss of their major supporter, Yi Sungman, the situation changed for the worse for the celibates.

The married faction took full advantage of the situation and began to reoccupy monasteries, while accusing the celibates of being both adherents of Bureaucratic Buddhism and parasites of the corrupt regime (Taehan 2001, 208). On April 27, 1960, married monks attempted to retake Chogye-sa, and a bloody fight ensued. In May 1960, the married monks reassumed control of major monasteries such as Haein-sa, Hwaom-sa, Sonam-sa, and T'ongdo-sa, as well as ten other monasteries (Minjok 1986, 60).

With the change in government, the judicial system also turned unfavorable to the celibates. The Supreme Court sent the case back to the high court, before which the married faction had contested the efficacy of the decision of the Conference of Buddhist Clerics held in August 1955 and had won. This ruling frustrated the celibate faction, and seven celibate monks went to the Supreme Court and protested the decision by attempting to cut their abdomens with a knife. Upon hearing about this incident, several hundred celibate clerics broke into the court, and 133 of them were arrested for illegal entry. Legal and physical fights over the ownership of temples erupted everywhere, and Buddhists were involved in seventy-five lawsuits during this period. Both factions further consumed temple property in litigation. Under these chaotic circumstances, some monks hid temple property for personal use and sold it before returning to lay life.

A faction of the military elite staged a coup d'état on May 16, 1961. A young general, Pak Chonghui (Park Chung Hee, who served as president from 1961 to 1980), rose in power and began to implement sweeping social reforms to make up for the lack of legitimacy of the coup. After one year of tasting democracy, Korean people again lost their political freedom. Under the exigent situation, not much freedom was left, even for the Buddhists. The Chogye order of the celibate faction decided to aid the military coup and end the purging of the Sangha. It handed a petition to the interim government, which asked for its assistance in completing the takeover of the order (Taehan 2001, 217).

General Pak issued two orders urging Buddhists to reach a prompt agreement to end the social disturbance. Adhering to the request of the military government, the Supreme Court ordered all seventy-five Buddhist lawsuits pending in court to stop. This command benefited the celibates because the court appeal had been the major means of winning lawsuits for the married faction (Kim K. 2000b, 409).

Following the suggestion of the Department of Education, both parties formed the Committee of Rebuilding Buddhism in January 1962. The committee held four meetings and prepared the foundation for the unified Sangha. It elected members and developed operational rules of the Emergency Sangha Assembly of Rebuilding. The assembly members consisted of fifteen monks from each faction, with fifty total. They confronted each other, however, on the issue of qualifications of clerics. The celibates insisted that Buddhist clerics had to be single, and the married faction emphasized that the married monks also should be recognized as legitimate clerics.

Pushed by the government's request to end the conflict, both factions had to abandon their disagreement and agree to adopt the constitution, leaving to the government revision of the phrases in the constitution and the clerical qualification issues. The constitution was revised so that those who stayed alone without a family at a temple would be regarded as monks. The previous constitution defined monks as single people who stay at a temple (Taehan 2001, 222–223). Due to government pressure, the married faction agreed to accept the revised constitution, although they still did not like it. On March 25, 1962, the Sangha finally passed the revised constitution.

On April 11, 1962, the unified Sangha officially began under the name of the Chogye Order of Korean Buddhism (Taehan Pulgyo Chogyejong). Both factions filled the administration. For example, the Supreme Patriarch was Hyobong Sunim from the celibate camp, and the chair of the administration was Im Sokjin from the married faction. The unified Sangha, however, soon faced another conflict regarding the ratio of the two factions among the numbers of the assembly. The celibate faction outnumbered the married faction thirty-two to eighteen. The married faction wanted to be represented equally, yet its opinion was ignored. Further, the government backed the celibates in leading the Sangha.

The dejected married faction declared its separation and established its own administrative headquarters. Within less than a year after the Sangha was supposedly unified, Korean Buddhism again faced dissension and division. The government and the general public did not approve of the separation. The married faction thus again turned to the judicial system. The Seoul district court announced victory for the married faction on October 4, 1962. The celibate administration made an immediate appeal to the high court, and so the court battle resumed. By this time, approximately 90 percent of the Korean monasteries belonged to the celibate Chogye order. The court battles spread to local monasteries, where individuals fought over abbotships. In September 1965, the celibate order won the case in the higher court and was legally recognized. Nevertheless, the local legal battles continued long after this victory (Taehan 2001, 226).

In March 1965, the celibate order tried to win over some married monks by dropping the court appeals and following the Sangha's constitution and rules. With this conciliatory attitude, the Chogye order took more monasteries, which belonged to the married monks, and let those monks known as hwadongpa (the conciliatory faction) take charge of some main and branch monasteries. In October 1969, the Supreme Court dropped the appeal of the married faction regarding the legitimacy of the celibate order. This final court decision facilitated further submission of the married monks to the celibate order.

Married monks who rejected the compromise with the celibate order criticized the hwadongpa monks and declared their official separation from the

Lantern Festival at the eve of the Buddha's birthday (April 8 in the lunar calendar) near Jogye-sa in Seoul, Korea. (Courtesy of Pori Park)

celibates. However, they could not secure legitimate status due to the Law for the Control of Buddhist Property. This law allowed only one Sangha—that is, the celibate order as registered by Chogye-chong. To protect the few monasteries that belonged to them, the married faction decided to create a new denomination and registered as the T'aego order in May 1970. The two administrations thus went their separate ways, and the long battle over control of the Sangha officially ended after more than two decades. Nevertheless, the disputes over local monasteries continued long after this separation.

Thus, the celibates became the final victors in the battle over the hegemony of the Korean Sangha. From this strife, the Chogye order, the largest Buddhist denomination in numbers of clerics and the possession of traditional monasteries, emerged as a celibate order. The determining force behind the triumph of the minority faction was the intervention and support of the government. The Purification Movement began with the Yi Sungman's issuance of an order against the married monks. Throughout Yi's rule, he showed consistent support to the celibates and offered legitimacy to them by identifying the married as Japanized monks. His administration provided moral support and police force in taking over the monasteries of the married monks.

Other major political aid came from Pak Chonghui, who rendered the final victory for the celibates with the enactment of the Law for the Control of Buddhist Property in 1962. These two presidents, popularly regarded as dictators, favored the minority faction, possibly for political reasons. Yi ruled the nation for thirteen years and Pak for eighteen years. Yi wanted to use the rhetoric of decolonization to boost his weak political foundation and regarded the purging of the married monks as a way of purging the colonial past. Also, to divert people's attention away from the unlawful revision of the constitution of the nation in November 1954, he ignited and exacerbated this unusual battle among monks. Similarly, Pak needed the people's support for his military takeover. He regarded the purging of the Buddhist Sangha as a means for the betterment of society.

With the aid of dictatorial governments, the celibates were able to attain final victory. Their commitment and dedication to the cause were admirable, yet their use of violence and their dependence on dictatorial regimes left them exposed to doubts and cynicism among later generations of Koreans. They also had to pay a price for their close relationship with the government. The Chogye order was under heavy political control and was not able to operate the Sangha independently. In addition, the Sangha earned the name "Bureaucratic Buddhism" and was widely scorned by the public for its close ties to politicians.

Internal Division in Dharma Families

Soon after the separation of the married faction, the celibates dove into another whirlpool of conflict, this time among themselves. Instead of rebuilding the Sangha from the ruins, the clerics banded together among their own Dharma family members. Major families were formed surrounding those celibate leaders in the battle against the married clerics (Yo 1985, 396). The two most powerful families, the Pomosa and Togsung families, were associated with the monks Tongsan and Kumo, respectively. As a reward for their bloody engagement in the Purification Movement, these families came to take charge of the main monasteries in greater numbers and thus assumed great power. In the ferocious hegemonic fights among these Dharma families, we can see patterns of violence and legal battles similar to those that had happened repeatedly during the earlier celibate-married conflict.

After the Purification Movement, the Chogye order was divided over the issue of which faction would represent the Sangha. During the late 1960s and early 1970s, the conflict erupted between the monks Ch'ongdam and Kyongsan, who were backed by their respective Dharma lineages of Togsung and T'ongdo-sa. In the mid-1970s, the Sangha chose Soong as the Supreme Patriarch (chongjong) because of his neutral stance in the conflict about Dharma lineage. But Soong took a drastic turn in strengthening his own position as the Supreme Patriarch by revising the Sangha constitution. Monks Wolsan and

Hyejong of the powerful Kumo (Togsung) family sided with Soong, while Wolju and Wolso of the same family opposed this abrupt seizure of power. The powerful Kumo lineage was divided, backing either the Sangha administration or the Sangha's Central Council. This division resulted in the establishment of two administration offices in Seoul, one in Chogye-sa and the other in Kaeun-sa (Yo 1985, 397). Each party appealed its case to the court. Finally, the Kaeun-sa faction won the case before the Supreme Court in 1980. The two then finally drew up an agreement on a united Sangha.

The newly established administration, with Wolju as the executive director, was abruptly interrupted by the infamous October Incident on October 27, 1980, when the junta that emerged after the fall of President Pak in 1979 carried out a military campaign and raided the compounds of 3,000 monasteries before dawn in the name of rooting out communist sympathizers and criminals. Due to this external blow, both the Sangha administration and the Central Council were disbanded. Within a year of the October Incident, the executive director of administration had been replaced four times (Tonguk 1997, 58–59). On the surface, the conflict was between the central administration and the local main monasteries. Beneath the surface, the conflict of lineage interests was the driving force. The central administration passed a law placing several financially important monasteries (due to their function as tourist attractions), such as Pulguk-sa, Woljong-sa, and Sinhung-sa, under its direct control.

This action brought about violent resistance from the local monasteries, which wanted to run the monasteries within their own Dharma families. Bloody fights erupted when the centrally appointed abbots arrived at Pulguk-sa and Woljong-sa and faced the resistance of the local monks. The most serious confrontation was over Pulguk-sa, which is situated at the ancient Silla capital Kyongju, a major city for tourism. Pulguk-sa appealed its case to the local court and won. The central administration soon had to give up its direct operation of Pulguk-sa and Woljong-sa. A similar confrontation broke out in Sinhung-sa in 1983 between the local monks and those monks accompanied by the abbot who had been appointed by the central administration (Tonguk 1997, 60–61). One monk was murdered and six were seriously injured during the clash. As a result, nineteen monks were arrested.

This succession of contention led to a protest among progressive younger clerics who were concerned about the future of the order, and 1,000 such clerics gathered at Chogye-sa, demanding Sangha reforms. An emergency council was formed and prepared for a new election for executive director. In 1984, a reform council announced reform proposals that reflected the demands of the progressive clerics. These proposals included the abolition of the main-monastery system, the opening of management of temple finances to the laity, and inclusion of lay propagators in the Sangha membership (Taehan 2001,

261–264). These progressive measures were, however, bitterly opposed by Supreme Patriarch Solch'ol (1912–1993), who tendered his resignation. This opposition generated another violent confrontation and frustrated the efforts for change.

Internal conflicts continued to plague the Sangha. In 1988, the order was divided again over the appointment of the abbot at Pongun-sa in south Seoul (Taehan 2001, 274–275). The central administration appointed a new abbot to Pongun-sa, yet the current abbot, Mirun, did not accede to the decision. Mirun, a political rival of the Chogye director Uihyon, established a separate administration at Pongun-sa in defiance of the Chogye-sa headquarters. The new administration was backed by those monks whose reform plans had failed in 1984, and this opposition group convened a rally of monks at T'ongdo-sa. Each group invaded the other's headquarters, armed with iron pipes and baseball bats. This violent confrontation was ended through compromise; nevertheless, it severely harmed the prestige of the Sangha in general.

In the early 1990s, the Sangha was again divided over the election of the Supreme Patriarch. Two major Pomo and Togsung families supported their own candidates—Pomo supported Songch'ol and Togsung supported Wolsan (Taehan 2001, 275). Each camp held separate rallies of monks in 1991. They established two separate headquarters, the Chogye-sa in north Seoul and the Pongun-sa in south Seoul. They began legal battles, as had repeatedly happened before. In 1992, the Chogye headquarters in north Seoul won the court battle.

In this context, another generation of young reform-minded clerics began to band together to rescue the divided, conflict-ridden Sangha. The Cleric Association for Engaged Buddhism began a movement to gather signatures for the Sangha reformation (Tonguk 1997, 74–76). Seven other clerical associations soon supported the movement. These progressive clerics formed the Executive Council for the Sangha Reforms and criticized the corruption of the administration of Uihyon, the director, including Uihyon's illegal donation to the political fund for presidential candidate Kim Yongsam (president from 1993 to 1997), demanding his resignation (Taehan 2001, 299–303). Uihyon responded by retaliating against the clerics with an assault by hired thugs, forcing them to disband with the aid of the government. He then made himself director for a third term.

Outraged by his actions, not only the progressive clerics but also the senior clerics and laypeople joined together in defending the monastic order from further abuses under the administration. In April 1994, a rally consisting of 2,500 clerics and 1,000 laypeople was held at Chogye-sa. The administration fought back with the support of the police. Those present at the rally engaged in a violent skirmish, and many of them were injured and taken to the police. After three days of confrontation, the police withdrew and Uihyon resigned. The rally finally dissolved the Central Council and replaced it with the Reform Council. The Reform Council promised a drastic turn of the administration, emphasizing the independence of the Sangha from government, democratic operation of the Sangha, and the restoration of the "purity" of the order.

The high hopes that Buddhists had for this reformed administration were again dashed in 1998 and 1999, the most recent incidents of the Sangha conflict. The Sangha was divided again between those who supported reelection of Wolju, the director, and those who opposed it, including the Supreme Patriarch Worha (Taehan 2001, 318–323). The opposition camp held a rally of clerics at Chogye-sa and forcibly occupied the Sangha headquarters. The administration appealed its case to the court and asked the government's aid. It took forty-three days to restore the headquarters, with the aid of 5,000 policemen. The opposition clerics made a violent scene, and the media broadcast violent fights throughout the nation and the world.

Even after the Purification Movement, the Sangha could not distance itself from power struggles. It continually repeated the patterns of resorting to violence, court battles, and collective actions in the form of clerical rallies, just as the previous generations had done in their battles with the married clerics. The hegemonic strife among Dharma families was largely responsible for the conflicts between the Supreme Patriarch and the director of administration, between the administration and the council, and between the administration and the main monasteries. The fate of the Sangha was largely dependent on secular court rulings, as the clerics could not find ways to resolve their own conflicts by themselves.

Meanwhile, as its internal chaos deepened, the Sangha was further subordinated to the government. During Pak's regime, which was the main force for the final victory of the celibates, the Sangha became a willing partner of the dictatorial regime. For example, it aided government policies by participating in the rallies against the North Korean communist regime, supporting the constitutional changes for extending presidential terms, participating in the government-initiated new-village movements, and establishing armies of patriotic monks (Kim K. 2000b, 371). Further, since May 1962, the Sangha has operated under the Law for the Control of Buddhist Property. This law provided the government with a means to supervise the Sangha through the appointment of abbots and the management of Buddhist property. The celibate clerics at that time actively sought the government's supervision to protect their property from being lost to greedy individual clerics and to acquire the government's sanction for their order (Taehan 2001, 226).

The Revival of Minjung Buddhism

In response to the authoritarian rules of Pak Chonghui (president from 1961 to 1980) and Chon Tuwhan (president from 1981 to 1987), a new generation of Buddhists developed a socially conscious movement by forming an allegiance with the growing antigovernment movements among the intellectuals, college students, and the populace. These younger clerics and lay Buddhists began to address the people's political and economic plight and reappropriated minjung Pulgyo as the catchword for their movement. Just as the young clerics during the colonial period had advocated this populist Buddhism as a way to oppose Bureaucratic Buddhism and the Japanese regime, this new generation attempted to challenge the idea of hoguk Pulgyo and the dictatorial regime in particular. While focusing on the common people (minjung) rather than the privileged (and the regime, in particular), they participated in the larger movement for democratizing the nation.

In the mid-1970s, a minjung Pulgyo study group was formed among lay Buddhists (Kim K. 2000b, 354–355). Another study group was established by both lay and cleric members in 1980. Among college students, Buddhist associations also sprang up and tried to connect Buddhist doctrines with social science (i.e., history, politics, economics) in order to explore theoretical bases for minjung Buddhism. In addition, college students initiated a sawonhya (monasticization of society) movement that aimed to pattern society after an ideal type of monastic community (Kim K. 2000a, 171–172). With the support of temples such as Ch'ilbo-sa, Myogak-sa, and Kaeun-sa in Seoul, they made temples the centers for their activities, which included forming study groups and opening night schools for children from underprivileged homes. At the end of 1981, however, the government arrested about 150 Buddhist youth for their alleged socialist activities, and several of them suffered imprisonment.

In the mid-1980s, the progressive Buddhist movement began to gain momentum, as lay and cleric Buddhists together formed the League for the Promotion of Minjung Buddhism in May 1985 (Taehan 2001, 267–273). The major founding members of this association were Yo Iku, publisher of the league's official journal; poet and former monk Ko Un; and the monks Chin'gwan, Song'yon, and Hyon'gi. The league vowed to participate in democratization and antigovernment movements and pledged to advance minjung Pulgyo. The police, however, took all 150 people who attended the inaugural meeting for the league into custody. The league's official journal, People's Dharma Hall (Minjung Poptang), faced political censorship, and its publisher, Yo Iku, was incarcerated each of the five times that a new edition was published (Tonguk 1997, 441). In 1989, the government accused the league of being sympathetic to socialism because of its involvement in labor issues and antigovernment protests. The league was finally dissolved in 1991.

Inspired by the activities of the League for the Promotion of Minjung Buddhism, progressive clerics formed their own associations as a way to join the social movement. In June 1986, the National Association of Buddhist Clerics for the Realization of the Pure Land was formed by twenty-two progressive clerics, including Chison, Ch'onghwa, and Chin'gwan. It aimed at promoting engaged Buddhism and political independence for the Sangha. These reform-minded and politically progressive clerics staged a rally of 2,000 clerics at Haein-sa in 1986, demanding social democratization and Buddhist freedom from political intervention. This was a watershed event for the minjung Pulgyo movement, as it struck a shocking blow to the traditionally conservative Sangha (Taehan 2001, 265). Some of its members left, however, due to differences in political views, and formed a separate group. In 1993, the Cleric Association for Engaged Buddhism reunified the two associations. The intervention of progressive clerics into the internal affairs of the Sangha enabled the incorporation of the reform proposals into the Sangha's policies, and the progressive clerics came to occupy important positions in the central administration.

The minjung Pulgyo ideology helped to repair the broken image of the Sangha, which had maintained close ties with authoritarian regimes, by participating in the societal movement for democratization. But despite some of the social and political gains of politically engaged Buddhism, the minjung Pulgyo could not be fully accepted by the conservative Sangha. Moreover, an independent thinker and critic within the Sangha, the Son master Hyuam Song (1941–1997), criticized the progressive monks for their political ambitions. According to him, the younger factions were not that different from those who sought hegemony within the order. His contention turned out to be fairly accurate, given the aftermath of the two reform efforts in 1984 and 1994. Previously, in 1979, Hyuam was the first one who denounced the hoguk Pulgyo and the internal disputes based on the lineage/Dharma family interests. He felt that the adoption of foreign slogans, either hoguk or minjung, were the same in that they were a mere imitation, not the original way of dealing with Buddhist issues. He then argued that Buddhists needed to make an effort to solve their problems in uniquely Buddhist ways, drawing from the pool of Buddhist teachings. And he raised questions regarding what could be the differences between politically oriented monks and the secular political activists.

More recently, the minjung Pulgyo lost its ideological ground as advocates for democratization after Korea faced political changes, beginning in 1988 and culminating in the presidencies of Kim Yongsam (1993–1997) and Kim Taejung (1998–2002), who had long been the leaders of the opposition party. Buddhists began to redirect their engagement in society and in propagation methods, catering to changed circumstances. The meditation movement and community movement were among those Buddhist activities that gave great incentive to the Buddhist communities and also produced a positive response from the general public.

City temples established free meditation programs open to anyone, providing a quiet place to meditate (Tonguk 1997, 275–282). This program is called the Citizen Meditation Halls (simin sonpang) movement. Temples open meditation halls any time for the meditator's convenience and hold training sessions and guided sitting programs on weekends. This program has great appeal to those who lead busy, stressful lives. In tandem with this daily meditation practice, traditional monasteries have been successful in offering summer retreats at their beautiful mountain sites. This summer meditation program has become so popular that monasteries have problems accommodating all the applicants, who even include non-Buddhists, such as those from Christian backgrounds. One of the head monasteries, Songgwang-sa, the first monastery to begin a retreat program in 1969, now holds retreats for meditators six or seven times each summer.

Some city mission temples made great strides in attracting people by building a Buddhist community that gives them a sense of belonging. In the 1980s and 1990s, mission-oriented temples in big cities began to appear as model cases for generating effective community involvement. Temples like Kuryong-sa, Nungin sonwon, Jungto hoe, Hanmaum sonwon, and Sogwan-sa have developed various social and cultural programs for the laity, forming a community not only among the Buddhist laity but also among the local population at large (Tonguk 1997, 113–117). They operate welfare programs including clinics, kindergarten, marriage counseling, and job training. They also run their own grocery market, dealing directly with farmers to benefit both consumers and producers. The Jungto hoe temple, in particular, is concerned with the preservation of the environment, social justice, and the unification of North and South Korea. Silsang-sa in South Cholla province engages in organic farming, provides alternative education, and is concerned with environmental issues. In other words, these groups try to create Buddhist versions of community involvement and establish working relationships with other socially active organizations outside the contested sphere of politics.

Conclusion

During the course of the modern Purification Movement, Korean Buddhism's dependency on the government led the Buddhist order to fall under the control of a secular power. The repeated internal disturbances within the Sangha, even up to recent times, increased the government's control of Buddhism.

Buddhist clerics requested the government's aid in getting rid of the opposition groups, and the police were called on in most confrontations to restore order. The involvement of Korean Buddhists in the Purification Movement left them with almost no time for the reform issues they had addressed during the colonial period. Because of the prolonged confrontations and litigations between clerical groups, the Sangha almost exhausted its financial resources. Moreover, the separation of the married faction depleted human resources, given the fact that the majority of the monks who had received a modern education were married.

In the late 1970s and early 1980s, Korean Buddhism experienced a resurgence due to the nationwide movement of discovering a national and cultural identity through Korean traditions. The hoguk Pulgyo ideology, which had been employed in earnest since the Purification Era, had caught the attention of the Sangha. It further rationalized and promoted the Sangha's close ties with the state. The hoguk propaganda was, however, seriously challenged by younger clerics, who began to participate in the societal movement for democracy. These progressive clerics adopted the idea of minjung Pulgyo, under which the Sangha had previously galvanized the youth in its protest against the Japanese regime and the bureaucratic nature of Buddhist institutions controlled by the state. In the name of socially engaged minjung Buddhism, the progressives began to voice their political stance and participated in the national march of the antigovernment movement.

Yet even the advocacy of minjung Pulgyo became a target for criticism. Korean Buddhists began to raise questions about the adoption of the minjung ideology and tried to develop uniquely Buddhist ways to deal with social issues. Such activities as the meditation movement, environmental preservation, and community-based networking are examples of Buddhist involvement in social activities. The Sangha in Korea has opened its doors to the laity and members of the general public who seek quiet places to recuperate from noisy city environments. City temples and countryside monasteries offer daily or seasonal meditation programs, whose popularity has skyrocketed as increasing numbers of individuals have focused on well-being, health, and quality of life. Buddhists also are concerned with environmental issues and engage in organic farming, recycling, the use of environmentally safe products, and the protection of natural resources. Further, Buddhists form a sense of belonging by establishing a community in which not only religious needs, but also economic and social functions, are fulfilled. In other words, the Sangha is now eager to develop ways to connect with the laypeople, and the laity becomes an important participant in these enterprises.

The Chogye order, however, has not fully recovered from the 1998 and 1999 incidents, and the internal divisions among the different Dharma families will

Buddha's birthday celebration at a local temple in Namyangju-si, Kyonggi province, Korea. (Courtesy of Pori Park)

most likely persist in the near future. Under these circumstances, the laity, who had been largely alienated from the Sangha politics, began to function as a pressure group for Sangha reform. In 1999, approximately forty lay Buddhist groups came together to form Buddhist Solidarity for Reform and embarked on its function as a watchdog for the Sangha administration in 2001. The Sangha is thus no longer immune from the watchful eyes of about ten million laypeople (about 50 percent of the religious population of South Korea).

References

An Pyongjik. 1980. Manhae Han Yongun ui tongnip sasang. In *Han Yongun sasang yon'gu*, ed. Manhae Sasang Yon'guhoe. Seoul: Minjoksa.

Han Yongun. 1931a. Chong-gyo rul pullip hara (Do separate religion from politics). *Han Yongun chonjip* 2:144–145.

———. 1931b. "Choson Pulgyo kaehyok an." *Han Yongun chonjip* 2:160–169.

Han'guk Pukgyo Kunhyondaesa Yon'guhoe, ed. 1995. *Sinmun uro pon Han'guk Pulgyo kunhyondaesa*. 2 vols. Seoul: Sonudoryang Press.

———, ed. 2002. *22in ui chung'on ul t'onghae pon kunhyondae Pulgyosa*. Seoul: Sonudo-ryang Press.

Kang Man'gil. 1995. Contemporary Nationalist Movements and the Minjung. In *South Korean's Minjung Movement: The Culture and Politics of Dissidence*, ed. Kenneth Wells, 31–38. Honolulu: University of Hawai'i Press.

Kim Kwangsik, ed. 2000a. *Han'guk Pulgyo paengnyon: 1900–1999*. Seoul: Minjoksa.

———. 2000b. *Kunhyondae Pulgyo ui chaechomyong*. Seoul: Minjoksa.

Kim Pyogon, 1927. Choson Pulgyo kiu-ron (Article on worrying about Korean Buddhism), *Pulgyo* 33:20–25.

Minjok Pulgyo Yon'guso, ed. 1986. *Han'guk Pulgyo chongdan chojik silt'ae chosa pogoso*. (Report on the organization of the Korean Buddhist Sangha). Seoul: Han'guk Ch'ongnyon Sungga Hoe.

Mok Chongbae. 1993. Kun Hyondae. In *Han'guk Pulgyo ch'ongnam*, ed. Han'guk Pulgyo Ch'ongnam P'yonch'an Wiwon Hoe. Seoul: Taehan Pulgyo Chinhung Won.

Nam Toyong. 1988. Kundae Pulgyo ui kyoyuk hwaltong. In *Kundae Han'guk Pulgyo saron*, ed. Pulgyo Sahakhoe. Seoul: Minjoksa.

So Kyong-su. 1988. Ilche ui Pulgyo chongch'aek. In Kundae Han'guk Pulgyo saron, ed. *Pulgyo Sahakhoe*. Seoul: Minjoksa.

Taehan Pulgyo Chogyejong Kyoyukwon, ed. 2001. *Chogyojong sa: kun/hyondae py'on*. Seoul: Chogyejong Press.

Taijo, Tamajuro, ed. 1967. *Nihon Bukkyo shi* III. Kyoto, Japan: Hozokan.

Tonguk taehak Songnim tongmun hoe, ed. 1997. *Han'guk Pulgyo Hyondae sa*. Seoul: Sigongsa.

Toru, Takahashi. 1973. *Richo Bukkyo*. 1929. Reprint. Tokyo: Kokusho Kankokai.

Yo Ikgu. 1985. Han'guk Pulgyo ui inmaek/chimaek. *Sintong'a* (May): 386–398.

Chapter Eight

Buddhism in Japan
The Creation of Traditions

STEPHEN G. COVELL

Today, Buddhist schools, sects, denominations, branches, and movements combined represent the largest form of organized religion in Japan. There are more than 70,000 temples, 250,000 clergy, 95 million lay believers, and numerous lay and professional societies and institutions. A trip to almost any bookstore in Tokyo turns up books on Buddhism ranging from sectarian household ritual how-to manuals to the works of the Dalai Lama. A stroll through nearly any town or neighborhood brings one in contact with a Buddhist temple. What is more, many Japanese people purchase amulets for traffic safety or success in school exams at Buddhist temples every year, or they seek answers to life's quandaries in Buddhist lay movements. Finally, Buddhist organizations can be found developing nongovernmental and nonprofit organizations and are involved in politics at a variety of levels.

The modern period in Japan has been one of the most tumultuous periods in Japanese Buddhist history, and it is clear from even a cursory examination that Buddhism is a vibrant part of contemporary Japanese religious life. Some of the major developments in Japanese Buddhism that have occurred over the past century, including clerical marriage, legal reform, new lay movements, and ritual adaptations, will be considered here.

Modern Japanese History: A Brief Overview

The twentieth century was one of great and rapid change in Japan. In the space of 100 years, Japan metamorphosed from a primarily premodern agricultural society under self-imposed near-total exclusion from the outside world to a major industrial power, to a colonial power, to a devastated failed empire, to a democracy boasting one of the most powerful economies in the world. Furthermore, it is no coincidence that Japan's various incarnations throughout the modern period came about amidst constant interaction with Western powers, which were themselves creating and experiencing modernity at nearly the same time and pace as Japan.

Japan's modern period is dated from the beginning of the Meiji period (1868–1912), when a new government came to power and Japan embarked on a course of rapid nation building and industrialization. Japan's leaders planned an aggressive program of modernization when faced with internal turmoil surrounding the restoration of Imperial power and the end of the previous regime (the Tokugawa regime, which had held power for nearly three centuries) and external pressure from Western powers seeking to force open Japan's ports to trade.

During the first several decades of Japan's modern period, the Japanese government created what would become known as the "emperor system"—a combination of institution and ideology that used the emperor as a unifying symbol for the fledgling state (Gluck 1989, Fujitani 1996). Additionally, the government instituted compulsory education and military conscription, conducted massive campaigns to instill common values, separated Buddhist and Shinto institutions, and created a national "secular religion" in State Shinto. All of these measures were implemented as part of a vast program to catch up with the Western powers, which Japanese leaders feared as having colonialist designs on Japan. They were also designed to facilitate the birth of a national consciousness to create, for the first time, a modern nation-state of individuals self-consciously aware of themselves as citizens. The education system and military conscription were extremely effective devices for disseminating state ideology, but the Meiji government also instituted a system of doctrinal instructors (kyodoshoku) that drew on Shinto and, later, drew on Buddhist priests to preach the state's message (Hardacre 1989).

The leaders of the fledging Meiji state were aware that Western constitutional governments based their authority on a consensus over history and religion (Beasely 1989). Understanding this concept, Meiji leaders sought to make the emperor, whom they promoted as descendant from the gods (the perfect link between the mythic past and the historic present), Japan's point of consensus. To this end, it was argued early on that the state should sever its long-standing ties to Buddhism, a "foreign" religion, and promote the indigenous Shinto.

In the aftermath of World War II, scholars portrayed the emperor system as a plan that was consciously designed, implemented, and forced on the Japanese people by the state. However, this view of Japan's modern history silences the many competing voices that shaped Japan's path. Sheldon Garon (1994,

A thirteenth-century bronze statue of Daibutsu (the Great Buddha) at Kotokuin Temple in Japan. Buddhism has been a prominent religion of Japan since its arrival in the sixth century CE. (Corel)

1997) points out that inculcating loyalty to the emperor was only a small part of the state's effort to manage its citizens. Garon shows how the rapidly growing middle class and government bureaucracy held a stake in modernity. Citizens cooperated with government efforts to improve daily life. Together with religious institutions, including most Buddhist sects, citizens actively participated in government "moral suasion" and other campaigns. When the campaigns switched to austerity drives as the war with China dragged on for more than a decade (1931–1945), the people continued to support them because of their appeal to maintaining the previous gains of modernization. In a similar vein, the efficacy of state efforts to curb new religious movements, including

Buddhist lay movements, stemmed from the belief that they were an irrational, backward-looking reaction to modernity. The popular press and the Buddhist establishment persecuted new religious movements for fear that they represented the reappearance of a premodern worldview and a corruption of proper doctrine.

Modernity played an important role in scholars' construction of this period. The fact that modernity could result in bitter fruits was generally overlooked. Given their positive view of modernity, scholars could only see the politics of the war era as an aberration. They could sweep questions of wider agency under the rug by asserting that average citizens lived in fear of a runaway regime. More recently, scholars have begun to demonstrate that Japan's direction during the war years, far from being instigated by a small clique, was the result of rational decisions by a well-informed state bureaucracy in consultation with a wide array of interest groups, including Buddhist sects.

The Modern Study of Japanese Buddhism

Scholarship on modern Japanese religion and on the modernization process itself has played an important role in shaping how we view Japanese Buddhism during the modern period. Unfortunately, there has been little cross-fertilization between scholars of Japanese Buddhism and scholars of Japanese religions more broadly, a topic that has been covered extensively elsewhere (Covell and Rowe 2004, Gomez 1995, Sharf 1995a). To summarize, Buddhist studies scholars have long been more interested in the study of texts than the study of the creation and interpretation of teachings as practiced in the modern period. Because of this emphasis on the past and on classical doctrine, premodern and modern Buddhism were seen as degenerate forms of a pure original. On the other hand, anthropologists and sociologists, whose work focuses on the modern period, have expressed little interest in textual development or historical analysis. Only in the past decade or so have scholars started to bridge the gap by approaching the subject of traditional Buddhist texts and teachings as used in the contemporary period by Buddhist practitioners (Reader and Tanabe 1998, Rowe 2003, Riggs 2004).

This problem, or division of labor (Sharf 1995a), in scholarly practice led early on to the impression that the object of study, too, is divided along these lines: Buddhism is seen as a textual tradition, with "real" Buddhism located sometime in the distant past; modern forms are viewed as degenerate, as completely new religions, or as folk corruptions that perhaps have borrowed from or misunderstood real Buddhism. The bifurcation of Japanese Buddhism into traditional (dento) or established (kisei) Buddhism and new religions (shinko shukyo, shin shukyo, shinshin shukyo) is a major stumbling block to the inter-

pretation of modern Japanese Buddhism. This divide is one used in Japanese
sectarian scholarship as well as Western scholarship. The term "traditional Buddhism" refers to the various forms of Buddhism or Buddhisms founded in
Japan before the modern period. The term is used to distinguish such Buddhisms from more recent forms in a move to elevate certain schools or sects of
Buddhism above their contemporary rivals. The term "new religion," therefore, is applied to nontraditional forms of Buddhism. They are not referred to
as "New Buddhism"—a term that, as we shall see, is used to refer to a specific
movement with ties to traditional Buddhism. Thus, Buddhist new religions are
deprived of their very identity as Buddhist by the term used to describe them.
Furthermore, as Jamie Hubbard (1998) points out, the scholarly division of
labor and the implied distinction between real Buddhism and new religions
have also led to the almost complete lack of study of the doctrines of the new
religions. This is because they are understood as popular religions lacking serious tradition and doctrine and because those studying them are rarely trained
in Buddhist textual or doctrinal analysis. The continued use of the terms "traditional Buddhism" and "new religions" by scholars only continues to exacer-
bate the problem by implying that there is some form of traditional or real Buddhism, and it thus implicitly partakes in a sectarian worldview. Here I will use
the term "Temple Buddhism" to refer to traditional Buddhism to avoid participation in the sectarian debate over traditional and new. Thus, Temple Buddhism refers to all sects, subsects, and branches of Buddhism established by the
seventeenth century (Tendai, Shingon, Rinzai, Soto Zen, and so on), their institutions, teachings, and practices. I use this term because the religious, cultural, social, and economic life of so-called traditional Buddhism in Japan is
centered on the temple.

Sociological approaches to the study of religion also made strong inroads
into nineteenth and twentieth century Japanese scholarship. Early scholarship
on religion and the process of modernization tended to center on the work of
Max Weber. Japanese scholars often followed Weber's view regarding the critical role of religion in the development of a modern ethos, and like Weber, they
found that ethos lacking in Japan (the following discussion is drawn from Shimazono 1981, Davis 1992, and Hayashi and Yamanaka 1993 and appears in
Covell 2005). This trend continued following World War II, when Japanese religions were seen as a reflection of the magic-oriented nature of Japanese society. The magic-oriented nature of Japanese society could be traced in part to
the dominance of esoteric Buddhism, which in Japan enjoyed wide popularity
throughout history due to the perception that esoteric rituals could produce
abundant this-worldly benefits.

By the early 1970s, Japanese scholars began to react to Western theories of
modernization and evolutionary histories in which Japan always played catch-
up to the West, which served as the "ideal." The roots of Japan's successful

Monks meditating in a temple at Hachioji, Tokyo, Japan. (Michael S. Yamashita/Corbis)

modernization and democratization, it was argued, need not be transplanted from the West. During the 1950s and 1960s, Japan enjoyed a period of high economic growth. Japan's success, in spite of its assumed lack of a magic-denying religion that could provide a modern ethos, encouraged scholars to reconsider how they had viewed Japanese religions. As Hayashi and Yamanaka (1993) show, Shimazono Susumu positively evaluated the role of magic through the concept of vitalistic salvation (seimei shugi), which he found central to the many new religious movements flourishing in modern Japan, including lay Buddhist movements (Shimazono 1999). Shimazono writes:

> In vitalistic religious thought the Buddha, *kami* and other such religious objects of worship are portrayed as the source of life, and humans and other forms of life are thought to have been born from this fundamental life power and caused to live through a sharing of their existence with it. Thus the true form of humanity is both to be completely merged in the natural internal life function and to be in a state of harmony with nature and all other creatures, all of which share the same life existence. (Shimazono 1981, 218–219)

According to Shimazono, Japan's modernization was enabled by a popular ethos acting in combination with the vitalistic concept of salvation. The dissolution of traditional and communal social bonds in modernity led to a situation in which

> [P]eople began searching anew for a clear intellectual symbol of the ties between themselves and others, and between themselves and nature; these were ties that had been evident until that time. . . . This precedes questions such as wholistic, rationalistic interpretations of the world, or of social order or of ways of implementing social justice, and can be identified as an intellectual question existing at the most fundamental level of human life. (Shimazono 1981, 220)

In this sense, Japanese vitalistic thought reflects an attempt to resolve the intellectual problem facing those who experienced a rupture in their traditional relationships as a result of modernization.

Shimazono (1981) asserts that Temple Buddhism possesses similar characteristics. However, he notes, such characteristics are not highlighted in practice to the extent that they are highlighted in the new religions (cf. Hardacre 1986). Nevertheless, my research has shown that such characteristics are found actively taught in contemporary Temple Buddhism. Because of the problematic way in which Buddhist studies scholars have avoided the contemporary popular teachings of the sects and schools of Temple Buddhism, notions similar to the vitalistic concept of salvation have not been observed in practice (Covell 2004). Also, while not speaking specifically to the concept of vitalistic salvation, Ian Reader and George Tanabe (1998) demonstrate that Buddhist temples play a significant role in the everyday life of many Japanese through offering this-worldly benefits. Typically, this-worldly benefits include healing, material gain, peace of mind, success in education, and other such awards that can be reaped in this life. Often, such benefits are linked to living an ethical life in which one recognizes one's ties to the deity and expresses gratitude in all actions. While more diffuse than the teachings of new lay movements, which are often narrowly focused on the themes that Shimazono identified, the teachings of Temple Buddhism regarding practical, this-worldly benefits are very similar in nature to Shimazono's vitalistic concept of salvation. The this-worldly benefits are practical, physical expressions of one's relationship to the deity and, it can be argued, are often turned to by Japanese in order to overcome or accept the anomie brought about by modernity. Such benefits are so important in the religious life of most Japanese that Reader and Tanabe (1998) view the quest for and provision of them as Japan's "common religion."

Buddhism on Trial: Buddhism and the State

While it is clear that Buddhism continues to play an array of roles in all aspects of modern Japan and the modernization process itself, there was some doubt early on in the modern period if Buddhism, or at least established forms of Buddhism, would survive. In the waning years of the premodern period, Buddhism came under increasing attack by Shinto and nativist scholars. As the old regime passed and the new Meiji government came to power in 1868, persecution of Buddhism became a matter of policy. Buddhism had become so thoroughly integrated with the previous regime that the act of separating it from the institutions of state led to severe financial and political difficulties for the Buddhist establishment. This led to a popular movement to destroy Buddhism and throw out Shakyamuni (haibutsu kishaku) in which Buddhist temples across Japan were ransacked.

The physical separation of Buddhism from its positions of privilege created many hardships for Buddhist institutions. In addition to losing state financial support for certain temples, the 200-year-old temple registration system (tera-uke seido), under which all Japanese were required to register at their local temple (a system in which Buddhist priests effectively became state functionaries), was replaced with a civil registration system (koseki seido) in which people registered at their local town offices. This severely weakened the coercive power that Buddhists had held over local populations. Buddhist temples had used the temple registration system to enforce their own temple membership system (danka seido), in which people who were registered at the temple were required to have all of their religious needs met by the temple. While at first a certain level of coercion was not uncommon, over the centuries temples became fully integrated into local life, serving as the religious and often the social center of towns and villages. It was under this system that temples came to provide funerary and memorial services for most Japanese. The withdrawal of legal support for the system in the modern period led many in the Buddhist establishment to fear for the future of the majority of Buddhist temples since they relied on temple members for their financial support. As it turns out, the Buddhist role as caretaker of the dead had become so thoroughly ingrained in the ritual life of the Japanese that the system carried on with little trouble for another century. It is only recently—with dramatic changes in the traditional family system, ancestor veneration, and views of the afterlife, as well as with the increasing number of new lay movements—that the temple membership system has begun to collapse.

Probably no single act was as devastating to Buddhism as the forceful separation of Buddhism from the indigenous Shinto religion that is directed to the worship of native deities called *kami*. Buddhism possessed a large corpus of texts and a mature ritual-philosophical system that could address issues related to death and the afterlife. Shinto grew out of local traditions of worshiping kami to seek divine assistance for more immediate, worldly needs. For centuries, Buddhism and Shinto had existed in a state of symbiosis. Shinto practices were a part of everyday life at most Buddhist temples, and Buddhist thought permeated even those schools of Shinto that developed a distinct identity as purely Shinto (Teeuwen 1993, Grapard 1984). Furthermore, in most cases, practitioners turned to Buddhism and Shinto for the benefits of specific rituals and not with a preconceived notion of the two as separate religions. Buddhist temples had Shinto shrines, Shinto shrines housed Buddhist ritual implements and objects of worship, and Buddhist priests officiated at Shinto rites. The separation of the two, which was spurred on by Shinto conservatives and by political leaders who sought to create a native religion around which to establish a national identity, created the modern myth that Buddhism and Shinto in Japan are two wholly separate religions. For Buddhist temples, the separation was devastating. Shrines housed on temple grounds were removed, or the temples themselves were destroyed. Buddhist ritual equipment used at shrines was confiscated, Buddhist priests were defrocked, and Buddhist influence in the halls of power was weakened severely.

As James Ketelaar (1990) points out, the treatment received by the Buddhist establishment, though it was often portrayed as the just deserts of a religion that was no more than the corrupt agent of an oppressive premodern regime, was in fact part of a much larger project of resignification that the new state embarked on to legitimate its rule and fashion a modern state on a par with the Western powers. Rather than allowing the continued persecution of Buddhism, however, leading Buddhist intellectuals were able to turn the process of resignification to their own needs, creating new understandings of Buddhist history and thought that were more in line with the demands of the modern state. Critiques of Buddhism as "foreign" were reconfigured to demonstrate Buddhism as a modern, transnational, cosmopolitan, and universal force of "global relevance" (Stone 1993). The view that Buddhist sectarianism demonstrated the degeneration of Japanese Buddhism was countered with the argument that a transcendent truth existed over historical adaptations. Sectarian divisions were explained to be the particular manifestations of the universal designed to respond to the needs of specific historical moments. Drawing on contemporary science, Buddhist intellectuals portrayed Japanese Buddhism as the cutting edge of the Buddhist evolutionary process. Once Buddhist intellectuals including Shimaji Mokurai, Watsuji Tetsuro, and Daisetsu Teitaro (D. T.) Suzuki had reconfigured Buddhism as global, transcendent, rational, and scientific, they were able to overcome their critics and once again demand that Buddhism be restored to its position of privilege in Japan (Suzuki's work on Buddhism and Japanese culture has come under considerable scrutiny recently; see, for example, Sharf 1995b).

The strong turn toward the creation of a modern Buddhism (rational, scientific, universal) was successful in countering the early assaults on Buddhism. However, within Buddhist circles there were numerous competing views as to how Buddhists should best respond to the demands of modernity. For example, priests and lay Buddhists formed the New Buddhist Friends' Association (Shinbukkyoto Doshikai) and published the magazine *New Buddhism* (Shin Bukkyo). This group lashed out at the Buddhist establishment and its close association to the state (including widespread Buddhist support for militarism) and advocated that Buddhists become more engaged in society. On this last point, they were inspired by the growing socialist movement in Japan, which was spurred on by the increasingly harsh conditions faced by many Japanese in the rapidly industrializing nation. In fact, although most members of the New Buddhist Friends' Association did not advocate violent change, several members were implicated along with a leading socialist in an alleged plot to assassinate the emperor. One, a Soto Zen priest named Uchiyama Gudo, was executed (Victoria 1997, Ishikawa 1998).

In contrast with the New Buddhist Friends' Association and its emphasis on worldly engagement, another leading voice in modern Buddhism was Kiyozawa Manshi (1863–1903), who believed that reform could only come from a very intense personal spirituality. Kiyozawa trained at the Imperial University in Tokyo (now called Tokyo University) and was versed in Western philosophy including Hegel, Spinoza, and others (Bloom 2003). He was also renowned for his intense austerities. He believed that the Buddhist establishment had become marginalized because it no longer provided personal meaning for people. And his "intense quest for religious authenticity led Kiyozawa to recognize the need for change in the sect if it were to realize its spiritual meaning in modern society" (Bloom 2003, 23). Sect officials resisted his reform attempts, but he was eventually given the task of modernizing the Jodo sect college (later Otani University), where he exerted significant influence on later generations of priests.

The concerted but diverse efforts to redefine Buddhism in order to stress its relevance to modern society and ensure its survival had lasting implications. Among these were the indelible critiques that the ritual practices of Buddhism were premodern and, especially, that the Buddhist preoccupation with funeral rites represented a degenerate form of practice. Today, images of the Buddhist priesthood as purveyors of expensive and increasingly meaningless funeral rituals dominate popular and scholarly works on Japanese Buddhism. For example, Itami Juzo's now famous film *Ososhiki* (*The Funeral*) is a raucous portrayal of a family burying their father in which the priest arrives in a Rolls Royce and salivates over the family's French-tile garden table. Although the term "funeral Buddhism" (*soshiki Bukkyo*) was not coined until Tamamuro Taijo's critical work by the same name appeared in 1963, the view that "real" Buddhism should not be involved in such rites found dominance early on in the modern period. In particular, the efforts of Meiji Buddhist intellectuals to describe Buddhism as a universal rational philosophy or as an introspective personal faith undermined the authority and legitimacy of the ritual practices of the vast majority of temple priests. This critique, advanced by Buddhist intellectuals as well as by outside critics of Buddhism, left many priests in an existential bind: Buddhism, they were now finding out, was supposed to be a rational philosophy, not a system of ritual practices for such things as securing a positive postmortem life for the dead; however, such ritual practices were the spiritual and financial heart of temple life. The battle to reconcile these conflicting understandings of Buddhism continues to the present.

From Nationalism to War

As we have seen, Buddhist intellectuals pursued many strategies to reconfigure Buddhism for the modern period. Some of the most powerful of these concerned (re)identifying Buddhism with the state and Japanese ethnicity. Such moves call to mind the long relationship between Buddhism and the state characterized by the doctrines of King's Law–Buddha's Law (Obo-Buppo) and nation defending (chingo kokka), in which Buddhist teachings were described as essential to the maintenance of peace and order within the state. Such teachings characterized the relationship between Buddhism and the state for centuries. In the modern period, a renewed emphasis on Buddhism's unique relationship with the state was promoted by many, including Inoue Enryo (1858–1919), Tanaka Chigaku (1861–1939), and leading figures in all sects who supported Japan's militarism.

Inoue Enryo is best known for the phrase "defend the nation and love the truth" (*gokoku airi*) (Staggs 1983). Inoue drew on the rising interest in rationalism and science to demonstrate that Buddhism was an expression of the same Truth that modern science sought to identify. Moreover, Buddhism was the best expression of that Truth. Christianity, Inoue argued, was based on emotion and was irrational by nature. Through linking Buddhism to science and at the same time attempting to show Buddhism's superiority to Western philosophy and science, Inoue demonstrated how Japanese could defend their nation from Western encroachment through reliance on a Japanese religion. This struck a chord with nationalists and elevated Inoue's teachings to prominence.

Like Inoue, Tanaka Chigaku taught an aggressive form of Buddhist nationalism. Basing his teachings on the writings of Nichiren (1222–1282), Tanaka identified Japan's national essence (*kokutai*, literally "nation-body") with the Lotus Sutra and linked the teaching of aggressive proselytization (shakubuku) with what he saw as Japan's unique role as unifier of the world. Tanaka supported the efforts of Japan's leaders to expand Japan's control throughout the world. He believed force was justified in this mission because only through the spread of the Lotus Sutra, which was embodied by Japan, could world peace be realized (Tanabe 1989).

Nationalism and support for Japan's militarism were espoused by Buddhist intellectuals such as Inoue and Tanaka; however, they were not alone in supporting Japan's expanding empire. Harada Daiun Sogaku, a renowned Soto Zen priest, makes clear that proponents of the war were found in the Zen sect as well:

> If you see the enemy you must kill him; you must destroy the false and establish the true—these are the cardinal points of Zen. . . . Isn't the purpose of the *zazen* (sitting meditation) we have done in the past to be of assistance in an emergency like this? (cited in Victoria 1997, 138)

Buddhists did not, however, universally support the Imperial government or Japan's many wars. Yet, priests who protested were few in number and were denounced as a whole by the established Buddhist sects for opposing Japan's wars. For example, the Youth Alliance for New Buddhism (Shinkobukkyo Seinen Domei), founded in 1931, sought to recreate Buddhism for the modern world. Buddhism, its members felt, had become set in its ways and had strayed from the teachings of Shakyamuni. They called for a return to those teachings and for the application of Buddhist teachings of equality to reform capitalist society (Covell 2005). Their call for equality was interpreted as a direct attack on the divinity of the emperor, and the alliance eventually ceased to exist after all its leaders were jailed.

In the postwar period, Buddhists have slowly come to recognize publicly the role they played in Japan's militarism both before and during the war. Many sects formed study groups to investigate the root causes of their support for the war, and they have issued some form of apology for the roles they played in support of militarism, though these often are couched in terms of "being used" by the state. The current Critical Buddhism (hihan Bukkyo) movement, which claims that Japanese Buddhism is not Buddhism, developed out of the questions raised by Japanese scholars regarding Buddhist support for Japan's wars and for discrimination against minority groups such as the Burakumin and ethnic Koreans (on Criticial Buddhism, see Hubbard and Swanson 1997; on discrimination, see Bodiford 1996). The Japanese scholars Hakayama Noriaki and Matsumoto Shiro, both of whom are also Zen priests, advanced the idea that only the teachings of nonself and dependent arising are the true teachings of the Buddha. Of course, this assertion, when carried to its logical conclusion, undermines most forms of Buddhism, but especially Mahayana and the ideas of original enlightenment that came to be integral to Japanese Buddhism.

The intimate relationship between Buddhism and the state in modern Japan is one source of ongoing critiques of Buddhism in Japan today. The image of Buddhism as part of wartime nationalism plays a role in how Buddhists are looked on now. This image is linked to larger concerns regarding the proper role of the priesthood and the so-called "true" teachings of Buddhism.

Law and the Shaping of Contemporary Buddhism

Another productive approach to studying modern Japanese Buddhism through the state-religion nexus is to examine the ways in which the development of a modern legal system influenced Buddhist practice. While many important developments in Buddhism can be approached in this manner, a few notable ones include clerical marriage, the religious juridical persons law, and the development of Buddhist nongovernmental organizations and nonprofit organizations.

Today, it is common for Japanese Buddhist priests to marry and for their children to succeed them as the head priests of their temples. Although the precedent for clerical marriage existed in the past—most notably within the True Pureland Sect (Jodo Shinshu), which from its founding in the thirteenth century recognized clerical marriage—it was not until the modern period that clerical marriage became the norm. According to Richard Jaffe (2001), the main reason for this is the repeal of laws banning clerical marriage. As part of its efforts to modernize the legal system, the Meiji government sought to weed out laws that advantaged Buddhism and to eliminate the Confucian-based status system (in which the priesthood occupied a position of privilege), replacing it with the modern notion of equality of all priests and laypeople as citizens of a nation-state. In 1872, the Meiji government repealed laws that enforced Buddhist precepts, such as those forbidding marriage or eating meat.

Leading Buddhist figures fiercely debated the state's decision. Some argued in favor of the repeal and even helped the state in the decision-making process. They argued that Buddhism was failing because its practices, including views on clerical marriage, were no longer suitable to the times. Despite resistance from many leaders in the Buddhist establishment, clerical marriage quickly spread. By 1880, nearly half of all priests were married. The rapid growth in married clergy indicates that, in all likelihood, many priests previously had common-law wives. Surveys of the Buddhist priesthood in Japan today reveal an 80–90 percent rate of marriage.

While views concerning clerical marriage were liberalized, the actual practice of marriage was long considered something to be done discreetly. It was not until after World War II that most sects of Buddhism began to formally recognize the fact that priests could marry and were marrying. Previously, the wives of priests were forced to live in quarters separate from the temple or otherwise to keep a low profile. Although having children—especially boys, who could eventually join the priesthood and take over their fathers' temples—was encouraged by sect leaders, the children were expected not to draw attention to themselves. Even today, the wives of priests occupy a precarious position in the temple world. In most cases, the incoming priest expels the wife, should her husband die without a male heir, from the temple with little or no compensation (Kawahashi 1995; Covell 2005). Many sects have now come to recognize the insecure nature of the wives' position and have begun programs to openly accept temple wives in temple and sect institutions. However, these programs, including the creation of special ordinations for temple wives, have met with stiff resistance from conservative priests, and it will probably be decades before temple wives enjoy security and status in Buddhist sects.

Within clerical marriage, views concerning gender remain extremely conservative. Temple wives are chiefly called on to play the roles of good wife, wise mother, and model of faith and faithfulness to temple lay members. The first two of these reflect ideals of female identity as promoted by the Japanese state throughout the modern period in school classrooms and moral campaigns. As Gail Bernstein (1991) notes, the family was the cornerstone of the state's ideology and practical policy, and it was thought that "as women go, so goes the family." To prevent the deleterious effects of modernization on the family, the state took steps to bolster the middle-class family by promoting the ideal wife as one who remained at home. Buddhist sects promoted this model of the ideal family type throughout the modern period. Moreover, the temple family is held up as a role model for lay families. Thus, as the result of laws passed at the end of the nineteenth century and the coincidence of traditional Buddhist views on women with conservative-values campaigns by the state, Japanese Buddhism in the twentieth century is marked by clerical marriage in which priests, who still consider themselves renunciates (shukkesha), marry and lead a family that is to act as a role model to the laity.

Much as with the modern critique of ritual practice, the existence of clerical marriage in the face of priests' self-proclaimed identity as world renouncers has created an existential crisis for the modern Buddhist priesthood. Critiques of clerical marriage can be heard coming from within Temple Buddhism establishments (Kumamoto 2004). However, lay members of Temple Buddhism do not often lodge such complaints. Indeed, they frequently prefer their local priests to marry. This is because temple members have a preference for continuity in the caretakers of what they consider to be their temple. Passing on the temple within the temple family assures members that the temple will be cared for and invested in their community. In this regard, many temple members express great interest in the upbringing of the temple family's children.

Clerical marriage is but one example of the effects the creation of a modern legal system had on Japanese Buddhism. The manner in which the 1951 Religious Juridical Persons Law served to shape Buddhist institutions is another. Following the difficulties faced by Buddhists in the early years of the modern period, the Buddhist establishment sought to use the developing legal system to its advantage. In 1927 and 1929, Buddhist sects supported bills presented before the House of Peers that would have resulted in greater levels of state interference in their internal affairs. The sects supported the passage of these bills because in return for letting the state gain some control, they received a strong, centralized, and legally enforceable administrative system to help them maintain internal control. As the problem of clerical marriage demonstrates, the established Buddhist sects feared the loss of their previously close relationship with the state because they questioned their own ability to maintain internal cohesion without legal coercion. The bills failed to pass, but in 1939, the Religious Organizations Law was finally passed and included provisions for strong centralized sect control over internal affairs.

Following Japan's defeat in World War II, laws governing religions were repealed. In 1945, the occupation authorities imposed the Religious Organizations Ordinance. This ordinance was very similar in content to the previous laws but, through the removal of various restrictions on incorporation, greatly enhanced the freedom of organizations to gain legal recognition. Restrictions were so light that new religious organizations exploded in number, including many that were clearly incorporated solely to take advantage of the tax exemptions granted incorporated religions. The Religious Organizations Ordinance was replaced in 1951 by the Religious Juridical Persons Law, which closed loopholes but still allowed for comparatively easy incorporation. These laws had obvious and dramatic effects on Buddhism in the contemporary period, including enabling the boom in new lay movements, as well as a less obvious but very substantial impact on temple operations.

Changes in the legal structure reflected the postwar belief shared by government bureaucrats and the average citizenry that religious organizations should not suffer state interference as they had in prewar and wartime Japan. This new tolerance helped spur on a boom in new lay Buddhist movements. During the early postwar years, lay movements such as Rissho Koseikai and Soka Gakkai expanded exponentially, growing from small organizations with memberships numbering in the thousands to giant organizations claiming millions of members worldwide. By the 1970s, many other new religious movements based primarily on esoteric Buddhism, such as Agonshu and Aum Shinrikyo, developed and attracted substantial followings. Aum Shinrikyo, for example, was seen by some at that time as an authentic form of practice because of its emphasis on meditation, austerities, and withdrawal from the secular world.

The minimal government oversight of religious corporations came to an end following the 1995 poisoning of thousands of commuters with sarin gas by Aum Shinrikyo. Aum was based on an eclectic mix of yoga, Tibetan Buddhism, and

Christianity (Reader 2000). This act dramatically focused attention on the manner in which the government monitored religions, and changes were made to the legal code to allow a modest increase in government oversight. The increased public scrutiny of religious organizations brought about by the Aum incident exacerbated ongoing criticism of the tax exemptions enjoyed by temples and of the financial activities many temples engaged in to support themselves.

The events of 1995 led to increased scrutiny of religious organizations, but the Religious Juridical Persons Law was already a powerful force in shaping Buddhism at the national and local institutional levels. On the national level, the law placed temples and sects on equal footing as religious juridical persons. This meant large, wealthy temples could break away from the sect more readily than under prewar and wartime law, when the sects had enjoyed strong centralized control. Many temples took advantage of this opportunity. The 1951 law also had a lasting effect on the day-to-day operations of temples. For example, to assure religious organizations freedom from state interference, the law required incorporated religions, such as temples, to establish boards of directors in charge of all secular affairs (generally defined as those having to do with financial matters). Ideally, by establishing such a board of directors, the government could hold a religious establishment accountable for legal transgressions without interfering in the "religious" aspects of the organization. Of course, in practice the dividing line between secular and religious is not easily determined. The law has thus been the source of numerous disputes between, for example, temple priests and lay members of the temple. Moreover, creation of a board of directors added a new administrative position to traditional temple operations. This, too, led to disputes, as lay members and temple priests sought to clarify the boundaries between new and old administrative duties.

Another area in which modern laws have influenced temple operations is in public welfare. The Japanese Buddhist priesthood has been involved in welfare activities for centuries, but the rapid onset of modernization in Japan, together with competition from Christian missionaries, created an increased need for engagement in welfare activities. Postwar laws concerning nonprofit organizations also created new opportunities and new demands for engagement in welfare activities.

In the modern period, Buddhist welfare activities were developed in response to the advent of industrialization and capitalism. The long relationship between Buddhist institutions and the state and the need of those institutions to overcome persecution served as the impetus for a rapid expansion of welfare activities, which were both helpful to the state and seen as the proper role of a modern religion.

In the mid-1800s, Buddhist priests were called on by the government to preach against abortion and the killing of unwanted children in poor areas. Later, they began to open shelters and schools for unwanted children and became involved in a variety of other efforts including prison chaplaincies. As industrialization advanced, the problems facing Japanese society changed, inducing a corresponding change in Buddhist efforts. Temples, for example, began offering day care for children whose mothers worked in factories. When Japan went to war, temples played important roles in caring for Japanese war orphans. The teachings drawn on in support of welfare activities changed as well, from the notion of equality found in the teaching that all possess Buddha-nature to a stronger stress on the teachings of compassion that highlight helping others.

By the 1920s, welfare came to be understood in social rather than mainly individual terms. In other words, whereas previously welfare activities were understood as personal religious practices aimed at the salvation of the practitioner, they now came to be seen as acts the primary purpose of which was the betterment or salvation of society. During this period, the number of Buddhist facilities and welfare groups greatly expanded. In 1926, for example, social welfare education became part of the official curriculum at Taisho University, a major Buddhist university affiliated with the Tendai, Jodo, and Shingon sects. Also around this time, Buddhist priests who were engaged in efforts to care for children began to develop national transsectarian networks.

During World War II, welfare activities were part of a national public effort to support the country. Buddhists were called on to develop programs to care for families of the war-bereaved and to care for orphans. However, as the war in the Pacific dragged on, funding, supply, and staff shortages led to temporary shutdowns of many facilities.

Following Japan's defeat in World War II, Buddhist activities revolved around helping those in immediate need. Perhaps the best-known form of welfare activity was the operation of kindergartens and schools. However, the prevalence of kindergartens, which serve to generate income for the temples as well as to care for and educate children, opened the way for critics to claim that many of these facilities were begun out of a need to generate income to overcome the economic hardships of postwar Japan.

During Japan's period of sustained high economic growth (1950s–1960s), Buddhist sects developed broad social welfare programs, such as the Soto sect's Soto Volunteer Association and the Tendai sect's Light Up Your Corner movement (Covell 2001, 2005). These programs, designed in large part to increase lay member involvement in the sect, also significantly expanded the scope of Buddhist welfare activities. Through these programs, Buddhist sects became involved in international relief and national emergency response efforts, peace movements, and other matters. These programs often mirrored similar programs developed by the large lay Buddhist movements such as Rissho Koseikai's Brighter Society movement.

By the 1980s, a new phenomenon began to emerge: Facilities developed by individual temples or sects began to break off and to establish themselves independently as private welfare or educational organizations. The most famous of these was the Soto Volunteer Association, which became the Shanti Volunteer Association. Sect officials have greeted this trend with a measure of alarm, questioning whether a specifically Buddhist element will continue. It is also conceivable that sect leaders fear a loss of control over their organizational resources.

Recently, some priests have begun to develop welfare activities that are organizationally separate from (though often spatially contiguous with) the temple. The 1998 Non-Profit Organization Law (Tokutei Hierikatsudo Hojinho) opened the door to increased involvement in welfare activities outside of the bounds of the temple by making donations to nonprofit organizations tax deductible. Buddhist priests from many sects, now seeking to take advantage of this new law, have begun holding conferences to research how to best use the new opportunity. One avenue being explored is the creation of welfare organizations on and off temple grounds that are organizationally separate from the temple and that employ professionals such as counselors who are not priests and are not members of the sect.

Many temples, moreover, have begun to address the problems of Japan's aging society. In addition to individual priests visiting retirement homes to give lectures or sing songs, temples now open their facilities for use by the elderly, or they build new facilities on temple property that are registered separately as nonprofit organizations. Other temple priests now participate in a Buddhist hospicelike movement called the Bihara Undo (Vihara Movement). This movement seeks to provide care to the dying and the bereaved on the basis of Buddhist principles, much like the hospice movement in the West is based on Christian principles. Many young priests believe this movement offers the best way to combine traditional Buddhist death ritual roles with contemporary needs and to overcome the stale funeral-Buddhism image (Covell 2005).

Although Buddhist sects and lay movements have put considerable effort into welfare programs in the modern period, such programs have not always enjoyed the full support of the membership, particularly in the case of temples and sects of Temple Buddhism. The temple membership system of the premodern period shaped contemporary Buddhism and continues to ensure that local needs are paramount. By emphasizing the needs of members first, the system inhibits sects' efforts to implement centralized social welfare programs. Also, there is often a lack of interest in social welfare activities on the part of members who would rather avoid change and leave the temple a secure place for the care of their ancestors. Because the livelihood of the priesthood is based on maintaining good relations with temple members, many priests have little interest in pushing beyond the immediate ritual needs of the temple membership.

Other priests, however, are less concerned about offending temple members than they are about what they see as the primary role of the temple. Many hold the sincere belief that they serve as defenders of local and national traditions. To move away from traditional ritual duties, festivals, and temple maintenance would obscure what they see as the original meaning and importance of the temple as a place of practice and local tradition.

Priests are left trapped between two religious ideals. On the one hand, modern notions of the religious life assume that religious professionals should be engaged in aiding society in some way. (This is why the Religious Juridical Persons Law treats religious juridical persons as a form of public welfare corporation.) On the other hand, temple members and many priests demand the continuation of traditional roles such as providing care for ancestors. The challenge for priests who wish to engage in social welfare activities is to find ways to do so within their traditional roles.

Lay Buddhism

As we have seen, Temple Buddhism has often been trapped in the modern period between traditional ritual roles and idealistic views of "real" Buddhism and between internal and external strains caused by modern views of religion and the demands of modern society. In contrast to Temple Buddhism, the many lay movements that have appeared during the modern period have not been hampered in the same fashion by the demands of institutional tradition, though they have often been attacked for a lack of tradition.

In the prewar period, numerous lay movements arose, some in conjunction with disaffected priests. These were largely intellectual movements, such as the New Buddhism movement. In the postwar period, relaxation of laws governing religious organizations, combined with a desire to move away from the heavy-handed state control of religions that marked prewar Japan, led to a dramatic increase in the number of new movements. The teachings of these new lay movements tend to be marked by the vitalistic concept of salvation discussed previously. While there is great diversity in their practices, religions that prospered early in the postwar period (1950s–1960s) were marked by an emphasis on the traditional family, ancestor veneration, and this-worldly benefits such as healing. One of the best-known practices of these earlier forms of Buddhist practice is a type of group counseling (hoza) in which lay members, often led by a senior member, break into small groups and discuss the problems each person is facing—offering mutual counsel and advice for spiritual development. The largest groups were generally based on the teachings of Nichiren and the Lotus Sutra (Reiyukai, Rissho Koseikai, Soka Gakkai).

Of the many new movements, perhaps Soka Gakkai is the most controversial. The source of much of that controversy lies in its political involvement. In Soka Gakkai, personal salvation is linked to the salvation of others. The creation of

Believers of the Soka Gakkai chant prayers to start an evening gathering at a small apartment in Tokyo, Japan, in 2004. An election is just days away, and, as these Buddhists see it, it is the moral duty of each true believer to get out the vote. Repeated in the homes of millions of members all over the country, the gathering is typical of the Soka Gakkai, one of Japan's most influential religious organizations. (AP Photo/Itsuo Inouye)

a Buddhist democracy based on human socialism, which is seen as an ideal combination of socialism and capitalism, became a critical part of Soka Gakkai's mission. To this end, a political arm, Komeito, was created. Popular fears about a religious movement gaining political power, inflamed by strident attacks on Soka Gakkai and its aims by members of the Temple Buddhism establishment, led to an acrid atmosphere. Members of Temple Buddhism were (and in most cases still are) enraged with Soka Gakkai not only because of its involvement in politics but also because of its extreme sectarianism in which all other forms of Buddhism are attacked. Soka Gakkai eventually separated from Komeito, at least institutionally, which helped to ease some people's concerns about Soka Gakkai's intents. Today Komeito is part of the ruling coalition in Japan's parliament.

Like Soka Gakkai, Rissho Koseikai is a very successful Buddhist lay movement founded in the modern period. The founder, Niwano Nikkyo, was originally a member of another lay movement, Reiyukai, which was based on Nichiren's teachings on the Lotus Sutra. A prolific writer and tireless teacher,

Niwano built Rissho Koseikai into a major religion in a few short decades. Rissho Koseikai is similar to other modern lay movements in its use of the hoza practice, stress on the importance of the traditional family, and the like. But, under Niwano's direction Rissho Koseikai has become well known for its involvement in peace activism and its vocal advocacy of Buddhist ecumenism. In addition to early work building an association for new religions, Niwano also reached out to Temple Buddhist sects, especially Tendai, which was portrayed as the source of Rissho Koseikai's teachings on the Lotus Sutra.

Following the oil shock of 1973 and the decline of Japan's economy in the early 1990s, a new form of religious expression came into prominence. Unlike the earlier lay movements, with their stress on ancestor veneration and group counseling, these so-called new new religions tended to be much more focused on individual introspective practice. One example is the previously mentioned Aum Shinrikyo; another, Agonshu, was founded by Kiriyama Seiyu and emphasizes practices based on esoteric Buddhism (Kiriyama himself was ordained as a priest in the Shingon sect of Temple Buddhism). These religions tend to attract a younger, more urban following than their predecessors and often make use of modern technologies for teaching and propagation, such as videos and CDs.

Ritual Adaptations

The new lay Buddhist movements were not alone in creating practices or adapting them to modern needs and tastes. The priests of Temple Buddhism, too, adjusted to the times, as seen in the discussion of the development of modern Buddhism and welfare activities. Another area in which we see a response to the exigencies of modernity is in ritual adaptation. Old rituals were modified or wholly new ones created to meet the spiritual needs of the faithful. Ritual adaptation also played an important part in temple economics. Following Japan's defeat in World War II, occupation authorities implemented land reform measures that deprived temples of income-producing properties. Temples were forced to shift from a land-based income (rent, crop production) to a ritual-based income.

Reflecting changes in modes of transportation, temple priests adapted longstanding ritual practices to ensure the safety of travelers to include such modern inventions as trains, planes, and automobiles. Perhaps more significant, however, are ritual adaptations that reflect changes in the population. As Japan has developed, its population has lived longer and longer. Today, Japanese have one of the longest life expectancies in the industrialized world. Combined with declining birth rates, this has led to an aging population. Buddhist temples have begun providing innovative rituals for the elderly. These include pokkuri-dera, temples where the elderly can wish for a quick death and thereby find

Nichiren Calming the Storm *by Utagawa Kuniyoshi, circa 1835, portrays the Japanese Mahayana master as one capable of influencing natural events. Nichiren initiated the practice of chanting an obeisance to the Lotus Sutra, "Namu Myoho Renge Kyo," as the singular means of attaining enlightenment. (Historical Picture Archive/Corbis)*

peace of mind as they live out their final years knowing they will not burden family members (Wöss 1993). In a similar vein, there are temples dedicated to Yomeirazu Kannon, or the "no-need-for-a-daughter-in-law Avalokitesvara" (the bodhisattva of compassion). Yomeirazu Kannon assures those who call on her a timely death so that they need not rely on their daughter-in-law for caretaking in their old age, which would only strain further the famously strained relationship between mother-in-law and daughter-in-law. Another example, aimed at reassuring the elderly about a different fear, is the Boke yoke Jizo, or senility-preventing Kshitigarbha. Some temples also offer new forms of protective devices, such as underwear that prevents incontinence.

Another modern innovation is the mizuko kuyo rite, or rite for fetuses that do not survive to term or children who have not come of age. This rite is linked to a much broader set of memorialization rites and to ancestor veneration and, as such, has a long history. However, in the modern period it has become closely identified with abortion. The modern deritualization of pregnancy and childbirth, and the passage of the Eugenics Protection Law in 1948, which permitted abortion on grounds of economic hardship, helped create a market for this ritual, as did aggressive advertising by unscrupulous religious organizations that published advertisements warning of the retributive spirits of fetuses

(Hardacre 1997). While not always viewed in a positive light, especially because of its notoriety as an income-generating ritual, many Buddhist temples offer the rite, and many people avail themselves of it. The rite has probably caused more controversy in Western scholarship, where the debate over abortion is far more heated (see LaFleur 1992, Hardacre 1997) than it has been in Japan.

Conclusion

Ritual innovation, the rise of lay movements, and institutional changes brought about by new laws and state actions mark Japanese Buddhism in the modern period. In particular, the massive state programs to modernize Japan in the late nineteenth and early twentieth centuries forced rapid and often severe changes in the institutions of Temple Buddhism. Such state actions, in confluence with changing social structures brought about by the modernization process and combined with cycles of economic boom and bust, have led to the creation and recreation of practices on an unprecedented scale. As is shown by the development of new religious movements such as Agonshu and the trend toward temples beginning nongovernmental organizations and nonprofit organizations, Buddhism in Japan is likely to continue experiencing major changes stemming from the effects of modernization in the years to come.

References

Beasely, W. G. 1989. Meiji Political Institutions. In *The Cambridge History of Japan: The Nineteenth Century*, ed. Marius B. Jansen, 5:618–673. Cambridge, UK: Cambridge University Press.

Bernstein, Gail Lee, ed. 1991. *Recreating Japanese Women, 1600–1945*. Berkeley: University of California Press.

Bloom, Alfred. 2003. Kiyozawa Manshi and the Path to the Revitalization of Buddhism. *Pacific World* 3(5):19–33.

Bodiford, William M. 1996. Zen and the Art of Religious Prejudice: Efforts to Reform a Tradition of Social Discrimination. *Japanese Journal of Religious Studies* 23(1–2):1–27.

Covell, Stephen G. 2001. Lighting Up Tendai: Strengthening Sect-Parishioner Bonds through the Light Up Your Corner Movement. *Asian Cultural Studies* 27:35–47.

———. 2004. Learning to Persevere: The Popular Teachings of Tendai Ascetics. *Japanese Journal of Religious Studies* 31(2):255–287.

———. 2005. *Japanese Temple Buddhism*. Honolulu: University of Hawai'i Press.

Covell, Stephen G., and Mark Rowe, eds. 2004. *Traditional Buddhism in Contemporary Japan. Japanese Journal of Religious Studies*, 31(2):245–487.

Davis, Winston. 1992. *Japanese Religion and Society: Paradigms of Structure and Change*. Albany: State University of New York Press.

Fujitani, Takashi. 1996. *Splendid Monarchy: Power and Pageantry in Modern Japan*. Berkeley: University of California Press.

Garon, Sheldon. 1994. Rethinking Modernization and Modernity in Japanese History: A Focus on State-Society Relations. *Journal of Asian Studies* 53(2):346–366.

———. 1997. *Molding Japanese Minds: The State in Everyday Life*. Princeton, NJ: Princeton University Press.

Gluck, Carol. 1989. *Japan's Modern Myths: Ideology in the Late Meiji Period*. Princeton, NJ: Princeton University Press.

Gomez, Luis O. 1995. Unspoken Paradigms: Meandering through the Metaphors of a Field. *Journal of the International Association of Buddhist Studies* 18(2):183–230.

Grapard, Allan G. 1984. Japan's Ignored Cultural Revolution: The Separation of Shinto and Buddhist Divinities in the Meiji and a Case Study: Tonomine. *History of Religions* 23(3):240–265.

Hardacre, Helen. 1986. *Kurozumikyo and the New Religions of Japan*. Princeton, NJ: Princeton University Press.

———. 1989. *Shinto and the State: 1868–1988*. Princeton, NJ: Princeton University Press.

———. 1997. *Marketing the Menacing Fetus in Japan*. Berkeley: University of California Press.

Hayashi, Makato, and Yamanaka Hiroshi. 1993. The Adaptation of Max Weber's Theories of Religion in Japan. *Japanese Journal of Religious Studies* 20(2–3):207–228.

Hubbard, Jamie. 1998. Embarrassing Superstition, Doctrine, and the Study of New Religious Movements. *Journal of the American Academy of Religion* 66(1):59–92.

Hubbard, Jamie, and Paul L. Swanson, eds. 1997. *Pruning the Bodhi Tree: The Storm over Critical Buddhism*. Honolulu: University of Hawai'i Press.

Ishikawa, Rikizan. 1998. The Social Response of Buddhists to the Modernization of Japan: The Contrasting Lives of Two Soto Zen Monks. *Japanese Journal of Religious Studies* 25(1–2):87–116.

Jaffe, Richard. 2001. *Neither Monk nor Layman: Clerical Marriage in Modern Japanese Buddhism*. Princeton, NJ: Princeton University Press.

Kawahashi, Noriko. 1995. Jizoku (Priests' Wives) in Soto Zen Buddhism: An Ambiguous Category. *Japanese Journal of Religious Studies* 22(1–2):161–183.

Ketelaar, James Edward. 1990. *Of Heretics and Martyrs in Meiji Japan: Buddhism and Its Persecution*. Princeton, NJ: Princeton University Press.

Kumamoto, Einin. 2004. Shut Up, Zen Priest: A Review of Minami Jikisai's *The Zen Priest Speaks* and Other Works. *Japanese Journal of Religious Studies* 31(2):465–487.

LaFleur, William R. 1992. *Liquid Life: Abortion and Buddhism in Japan*. Princeton, NJ: Princeton University Press.

Reader, Ian. 2000. *Religious Violence in Contemporary Japan: The Case of Aum Shinrikyo*. Honolulu: University of Hawai'i Press.

Reader, Ian, and George Tanabe. 1998. *Practically Religious: Worldly Benefits and the Common Religion of Japan*. Honolulu: University of Hawai'i Press.

Riggs, Diane. 2004. Fukudenkai: Sewing the Buddha's Robe in Contemporary Japanese Buddhist Practice. *Japanese Journal of Religious Studies* 31(2):311–356.

Rowe, Mark. 2003. Grave Changes: Scattering Ashes in Contemporary Japan. *Japanese Journal of Religious Studies* 30(1–2):85–118.

Sharf, Robert H. 1995a. Sanbokyodan: Zen and the Way of the New Religions. *Japanese Journal of Religious Studies* 22(3–4):417–458.

———. 1995b. The Zen of Japanese Nationalism. In *Curators of the Buddha: The Study of Buddhism under Colonialism,* ed. Donald S. Lopez Jr., 107–160. Chicago: University of Chicago Press.

Shimazono, Susumu. 1981. Religious Influences on Japan's Modernization. *Japanese Journal of Religious Studies* 8(3–4):207–222.

———. 1999. Soka Gakkai and the Modern Reformation of Buddhism. In *Buddhist Spirituality: Later China, Korea, Japan, and the Modern World,* ed. Yoshinori Takeuchi, James W. Heisig, Paul L. Swanson, and Joseph S. O'Leary, 435–454. New York: Crossroad Publishing.

Staggs, Kathleen M. 1983. "Defend the Nation and Love the Truth": Inoue Enryo and the Revival of Meiji Buddhism. *Monumenta Nipponica* 38(3):251–281.

Stone, Jacqueline. 1993. Book Review: Of Heretics and Martyrs in Meiji Japan: Buddhism and Its Persecution. *Harvard Journal of Asiatic Studies* 53(2):582–598.

Tamamuro, Taijo. 1963. *Soshiki bukkyo.* Tokyo: Daihorinkaku.

Tanabe, George J. 1989. Tanaka Chigaku: The Lotus Sutra and the Body Politic. In *The Lotus Sutra in Japanese Culture,* ed. George J. Tanabe and Willa Tanabe, 191–208. Honolulu: University of Hawai'i Press.

Teeuwen, Mark. 1993. Attaining Union with the Gods: The Secret Books of Watarai Shinto. *Monumenta Nipponica* 48(2):225–245.

Victoria, Brian A. 1997. *Zen at War.* New York: Weatherhill.

Wöss, Fleur. 1993. Pokkuri-Temples and Aging: Rituals for Approaching Death. In *Religion and Society in Modern Japan,* ed. Mark R. Mullins, Shimazono Susumu, and Paul L. Swanson, 191–202. Berkeley: Asian Humanities Press.

Chapter Nine

Buddhism in Tibet and Nepal
Vicissitudes of Traditions of Power and Merit

NICOLAS SIHLÉ

By way of introduction, a few words may be said about the dual focus of this essay on Tibet and Nepal. Whereas "Nepal" in its contemporary sense refers to a small, ethnically diverse, multicultural state in the central Himalayas, what entity does "Tibet" refer to? In the context of the disputed issue of Tibetan independence or autonomy, this question is inescapably political. But culturally Tibetan (or closely related) societies, home to Tibetan Buddhist traditions, are also situated outside of the area under dispute—namely, in northern areas of India and Nepal and in the major part of Bhutan.

The term "Tibetan" will be used here in two ways. With regard to sociocultural features, it will refer to the large cultural area that straddles the borders of these various states. However, as the name of an ethnic group, or an "ethnonym," it will refer to those people, including exiles, whose homelands lie within the Tibetan areas of the People's Republic of China (PRC). These areas occasionally will be designated as Tibet for the sake of convenience. Finally, since the 1959 flight into exile of the Dalai Lama, followed by some 100,000 Tibetans, Tibetan Buddhism has been exported very successfully across the world and has spawned somewhat modified, often modernist, forms. Unless stated otherwise, "Tibetan Buddhism" will refer in this essay to those forms of Buddhism found in Tibetan societies.

Within this culturally and religiously highly diverse region, do Tibetan and Nepalese forms of Buddhism have anything fundamental in common? Nepal, a predominantly Hindu state, is home to a variety of Buddhist traditions, not all of them closely related to Tibetan Buddhism. The Buddhism of the Newar people in the Kathmandu valley is of Indic character and is profoundly intertwined with Hinduism. Its texts are written in Sanskrit, and it fits within a complex socioreligious caste organization. It has been devoid of celibate monasticism since the fourteenth or fifteenth century (Gellner 1992, 22), and its hereditary clergy is found exclusively in one high caste. In contrast, Tibetan Buddhism and the traditions it has influenced in the Himalayas are all based on Tibetan texts. They are found in societies with a simpler stratification that generally comprises at least some celibate monastic clergy. Finally, Theravada Buddhism, based on Pali texts, established itself in Nepal in the 1930s, primarily among the Newar. It has produced no massive conversions until the turn of the twenty-first century, but it is slowly gaining in importance.

Tibetan and Nepalese Buddhist traditions do share, however, at least two fundamental features. First, if we omit momentarily Theravada Buddhism, they are all thoroughly tantric. That is, although they remain based on Mahayana conceptual foundations (emphasis on the ideal of universal altruism; a broad pantheon of enlightened beings—Buddhas and bodhisattvas—that historically was further expanded by tantric theologians; and a view of the nature of reality according to which all phenomena are ultimately empty or devoid of inherent existence), these traditions are also highly ritualistic. They give a central place to ritual practices that typically involve the visualization of transcendent deities, the repetition of their mantras, and sometimes particular hand movements (mudra), all of which enable the practitioner to mobilize the power of these deities (Snellgrove 1987). Quite commonly known examples of large tantric rituals are the Tibetan masked dances (cham). These are often performed as a communal exorcism at the end of the year, for instance in a monastery. The dances themselves, which attract large crowds of lay spectators, are preceded by several days of textual recitations in which the main tantric deities are invoked, receive offerings, and are enjoined to take action (to grant blessings, to repel or subdue harmful agents, and so on). During the dances, the monks wear masks of various deities, such as transcendent and worldly protectors. The latter are commonly fierce warrior deities. The former, who often have both benign and wrathful forms, are represented here in their wrathful modes, in accordance with the violent, exorcistic nature of the ritual. The climax is reached when anthropomorphic and other effigies symbolizing demonic forces are destroyed by a strongly empowered officiant. The ritual then concludes, as always, on a final auspicious note, and the following year can then begin with the assurance that all has been done to keep harmful agents at bay.

Another very well known practice that has a tantric character is the simple recitation of the Mani—the mantra *Om mani peme hung*—which is associated with Avalokiteshvara, the bodhisattva of compassion. Some Tibetans recite it

A pious stonecutter carves the Tibetan Buddhist mantra "Om Mani Padme Hum" (often pronounced by Tibetans as "Om mani peme hung"), a task he has dedicated himself to for 40 years, on a monastery grounds in Sikkim. (David Leskowitz)

thousands of times each day almost as second nature, or, when they are more mindful, focusing mentally on Avalokiteshvara. Religious specialists may accompany its recitation with a precise visualization of the deity. In Buddhist theology, the benefits of this practice are limitless; in actual practice, the most common motivations are the accumulation of merit, the virtuous focus on religious activity (beneficial in itself), and some expectation of blessings (chinlap) that would result from the invocation of the compassionate deity.

A second common feature of Tibetan and Nepalese Buddhist traditions is that the development of modernist trends in all of these areas is fairly recent, which may be related in part to the relative absence of colonial history (recent developments in Tibet excluded). Theravada Buddhism in Nepal is still in a formative stage, and the appearance of modernist discourses in Tibetan Buddhism, primarily in the Tibetan diaspora, is largely an indirect consequence of the recent Tibetan exile. Somewhat paradoxically, the current Dalai Lama has since the start of his exile in 1959 become the most prominent proponent of Buddhist modernism (Lopez 1998, 185).

Beyond these important commonalities, there is a tremendous diversity of sociopolitical contexts among these Buddhist traditions. In the PRC, only half of the ethnic Tibetans live in the Tibetan Autonomous Region, which corresponds roughly to the territory of the central Tibetan state in the early twentieth century. The other half are found in Chinese provinces more to the east in areas that constituted, prior to 1950 and the beginning of the Chinese takeover of Tibet, a complex mosaic of small, largely autonomous polities of varied types. The larger river valleys in central and eastern Tibet were characterized by relatively dense agricultural populations and relatively centralized polities that could support large monastic institutions. Such institutions were characteristically absent from the higher pastoralist areas, as well as from most of the small agricultural Himalayan societies practicing Tibetan or similar forms of Buddhism.

Three particular cases were the two small and one medium-sized Himalayan kingdoms of Ladakh, Sikkim, and Bhutan. Ladakh, situated at the far western end of the Tibetan cultural area, is now part of the Indian state of Jammu & Kashmir. It remains today a stronghold of Geluk monastic institutions—the same order as the one that, notably through the line of incarnation of the Dalai Lamas, was associated with temporal power in the central Tibetan state. Sikkim, today also integrated within the political boundaries of India, was a multiethnic state ruled by a line of culturally Tibetan kings with strong links to the Nyingma order. Bhutan, itself linguistically and culturally very diverse, remains to this day a kingdom in which Vajrayana Buddhism is the state religion; the state is intimately associated with the Drukpa Kagyu order of Tibetan Buddhism. The high degree of interrelatedness between Tibetan Buddhism and major sociopolitical institutions is a striking feature of this region.

Finally, the Kathmandu valley constitutes a highly complex, ethnically diverse sociopolitical realm in itself. Historically, the main Buddhist tradition of the valley is that of the indigenous Newar. Some of the valley's major collective rituals and cults are strongly linked to the former Newar kingdoms. The last Newar kingdoms were conquered in the late eighteenth century by the rulers of Gorkha (a small town in the center of present-day Nepal) during the military "unification" of what has become the Nepalese state. Apart from the presence of Newar Buddhism, the valley has also had links with Tibetan Buddhism for centuries. Tibetans have had, for instance, a long-standing interest in certain sacred sites in the valley. And since 1959, the arrival of Tibetan refugees and the establishment of Tibetan monastic institutions on the periphery of Kathmandu have had a profound religious and economic impact well beyond the confines of the valley, both in other Buddhist societies of Nepal and in the larger, transnational web of Buddhism. It is also in the context of the development of this transnational web of relations that we must understand the recent emergence of a Theravada movement in Nepal.

Buddhism in the Tibetan Cultural Area

Three interrelated and interpenetrating ritual complexes are commonly distinguished in the Tibetan context: Buddhism, Bon, and a third category sometimes called "folk religion." In its contemporary doctrinal, ritual, and sociological forms, Bon is a religious tradition extremely similar to Buddhism, and in particular to the Nyingma order (the tradition of the "Ancients," based on the early translation of the tantras). These two traditions share the existence of a sizeable nonmonastic clergy; the historically rather late development of large monastic institutions (seventeenth century); and an orientation that, particularly among the nonmonastic clergy, emphasizes tantric practice over scholastic learning. As a result of extensive creative appropriations, mainly though not exclusively from Buddhism by Bon, roughly from the eleventh century onward, many deities, texts, and rituals of Buddhism have formal equivalents in Bon, albeit bearing different names (Kvaerne 2000). In their institutions and actual practices, the two religions are largely separated, although common ritual practice in a pragmatic or ecumenical spirit occasionally happens in certain areas. Numerous Bonpo, or followers of Bon, take part in large collective initiation rituals carried out by prominent Buddhist masters, such as the renowned Kalachakra initiations given by the Dalai Lama. Some Bonpo monks have also traditionally pursued further studies in philosophy in the large Gelukpa monastic centers situated around the city of Lhasa. As a rule, however, Buddhists and Bonpo remain separate and to quite some extent ignore each other.

Bon and Buddhism are distinguished notably in terms of notions of religious affiliation, perceptions of hierarchy between the two traditions, and historical narratives. The Bonpo constitute a small minority that has historically known episodes of persecution. As a result, the bulk of them are now found mostly in peripheral areas, notably in eastern Tibet. Many Tibetans are aware of important commonalities between the two religions in ritual practices, institutional forms, and central tenets, but Bon is also looked down on by many Buddhists, who hold that it constitutes a worldly, ritualistic tradition devoid of soteriological value. These Buddhists consider Bonpo as non-Buddhists, literally "outsiders" (*chipa*), a designation that Bonpo reject.

From a Western historical perspective, the existence of a religion called Bon cannot be ascertained before the eleventh century (Stein 1988). However, according to both Tibetan Buddhist and Bonpo historiography, Bon was the indigenous Tibetan religion prior to the introduction of Buddhism into Tibet (seventh century onward). Furthermore, Bon is understood by many Tibetans to be older than the religion established by the historical Buddha. In sum, the two traditions, having constituted themselves by drawing quite extensively from the same (primarily Indic and Tibetan) materials (albeit through different processes), show now considerable similarities. To the extent that we can

Tibetan Bon iconography from the Yungdrung Kundrak Ling Bonpo monastery in Gyalshing, Sikkim. The deity on the right is Sherab Chamma, the Loving Mother who is worshipped as the primordial source of wisdom. The yungdrung (or swastika in Sanskrit) held by the deity on the left is an ancient Bon symbol of the permanence of truth in the Bon teachings. Its iconographic function is similar to the use of the vajra in other Tibetan Buddhist art. (David Leskowitz)

disregard native notions of religious affiliation, as Tibetological scholarship has occasionally done, Bon could be seen as a form of Buddhism, albeit with idiosyncratic, Tibetocentric historiographical traditions (Germano 1998, 165, n. 4). Recently, such a view has found a form of echo in modernist ecumenical discourses in the Tibetan diaspora. Bon has started to be called, for instance by the Dalai Lama, one of the five major Tibetan orders (or traditions)—an innovative shift from the traditional designation of the four major Buddhist orders. Currently, however, this notion remains alien to most Tibetan understandings.

The third major component of Tibetan religion has been called the nameless religion (Stein 1972) or folk religion (Tucci 1980, Samuel 1993). There are, however, multiple difficulties with these terms. First, the notion of "a religion" may be somewhat inappropriate for this diverse, relatively unorganized, and seemingly rather composite set of practices and conceptions—even though one can arguably observe a degree of continuity in terms of several basic assumptions about the order of the world: the nature of the invisible forces that surround man, the principles that govern man's interaction with them, the pervasive notions of auspiciousness and inauspiciousness, and so on. This component of Tibetan religion is generally not conceived of by Tibetans as an entity in itself. Second, referring to this component as "folk" or "popular" is also problematic, primarily because it suggests that social and religious elites do not share these views and practices. Third, one should beware of equating "non-Buddhist" and "pre-Buddhist" (very little is known about pre-Buddhist Tibetan religion, or religions); rather than privileging a speculative historical dimension, it is more sound and highly important to consider the relations between this "folk" religious component and Buddhism.

What appears immediately is the considerable degree of interpenetration between these two components of the Tibetan religious sphere. "Popular" fumigation rituals (sang) performed at the domestic or collective levels, which aim primarily at purification, have been formally integrated into all major Buddhist or Bonpo liturgical contexts. The Tibetan notion of la (soul), which the person may lose or which demons may carry away—hardly a doctrinal Buddhist notion—is at the center of soul-calling (laguk) therapeutic rituals, the main specialists of which are most often the Buddhist or Bonpo clergy, whether monks or tantrists (nonmonastic householder religious specialists). The rituals themselves, in their form and content, are basically pragmatically oriented tantric rituals (Karmay 1998).

Another feature typically associated by scholars with the "folk religion" is the somewhat diverse set of specialists known as spirit mediums or oracles. Yet their paraphernalia, the preliminary ritual acts of a séance, the pantheon the mediums interact with, or the deities' discourse during the séance (Berglie 1976) could in no way be all described as non-Buddhist. There are also considerable institutional aspects in this interpenetration. Mediums (lhapa, lhamo, and so on) are often formally recognized and legitimized by a member of the Buddhist clergy. Their transition to full medium status often necessitates repeated purifications and blessings, if not actual training, by members of the higher Buddhist clergy. Some mediums are monks themselves and officiate primarily in the monastic context, for example during important collective rituals (Brauen 1980). The main state oracle of the central Tibetan state, himself a monk, interacts with the highest levels of the religious and political hierarchies. He is often consulted by the Dalai Lama on questions of policy or even questions of religious import for the high Buddhist clergy, like the recognition of high reincarnate masters (trulku).

Obviously, associating Tibetan mediums with the so-called folk religion (especially when the latter is opposed to Buddhism) may reify boundaries and hinder understanding of these phenomena. Focusing on the relations among the various religious components—for instance, on the processes and vicissitudes

Tibetan refugees from the Kathmandu valley hoisting prayer-flags on a hill top on the important occasion of the Dalai Lama's sixtieth birthday; the gathering continued with a large fumigation (sang) ritual, led by members of the Buddhist clergy (an example of the interpenetration of "Buddhist" and "folk" religious elements). (Courtesy of Nicolas Sihlé)

of "buddhacization," notably on the boundaries of the Tibetan cultural area— is more relevant and productive. "Buddhacization" refers to the establishment of Buddhist institutions and the adoption of Buddhist practices and ideas; the Buddhist clergy's efforts in many places to obtain more widespread conformity to Buddhist orthopraxy can be seem as a continuation of that process. A concern with socioreligious dominance and control also appears clearly in some of these instances. The most crucial foci of these attempts have been (and still are) sacred geographies and the cults of the local place gods (a major component of Tibetan religion; e.g., Gyatso 1987, Blondeau & Steinkellner 1996, Macdonald 1997) and death rituals.

Tantric origin myths present great sacred mountains of tantric practice and pilgrimage as sites of the subjugation of Hindu gods by tantric Buddhist deities. In a similar vein, hagiographical literature and myth emphasize the dramatic subjugation, conversion, and binding by oath of local deities in Tibet, as in the narratives surrounding Padmasambhava, an eighth-century Indic master considered by Tibetan tradition as the great introducer of tantric Buddhism to Tibet. In actual ethnography, a recurrent pattern is the transformation (or attempted transformation) of communal animal sacrifices to place gods into acceptable Buddhist practices by prestigious masters traveling through an area (Mumford 1989). Typically, white dough offerings are substituted for the red sacrificial offerings and are backed by the charisma of a textual ritual composed ad hoc by the master. Only the high religious authority of qualified masters, as charismatic representatives of the prestigious Buddhist tradition, can modify the long-established, binding relationships of sacrifice to the powerful and irritable local place gods. This activity of the high clergy is obviously a struggle against the practice that most clearly undermines claims to the establishment of the Buddhist reign, namely the taking of life for the worship of deities. In this struggle, lesser representatives of the Buddhist clergy may not have the necessary charisma or clout; human sacrifice in the cult of a place god came to an end in Nyishang, in the north of Nepal, only around 1950, after centuries of Tibetan Buddhist monastic presence (Sihlé 2001, 159).

The association of death rituals with the Buddhist clergy, and in particular with the Buddhist monastic clergy, seems to have some universal character, from Theravadin to Vajrayana Buddhist societies and from small-scale, mostly nonliterate to complex, modern societies. In Baragaon, or Lower Mustang, in the north of Nepal, local monastic communities have been trying to increase the laity's adherence to Buddhist orthopraxy in funerary matters. Local traditional patterns included, for instance, at the end of the mourning period, the family of the deceased hosting large-scale feasting of co-villagers and relatives of the deceased, accompanied by complex patterns of gifts and countergifts, amounting to substantial economic exchanges. Although in theory the consciousness principle of the deceased is reincarnated within forty-nine days, annual commemorative ceremonies were held, sometimes for up to three years after the death, each time with similar, substantial exchanges. These practices were condemned by the monastic clergy, as a result of which some villages actually banned these repeated, extensive interlaity exchanges and instead started following patterns of increased sponsoring of Buddhist merit-producing rituals.

Another interesting feature in this society is that monastic dominance in death rituals is precisely codified and institutionalized. Performing several major rites in the long sequence of funerary rituals, notably the crucial rite of ejection of the consciousness principle (p'owa), is a duty and a prerogative of the local monk communities. Partly as a result of this, the specialists competent in the performance of the p'owa tend to be monks. In past generations, very few of the Baragaon tantrists (nonmonastic specialists) were qualified to perform it. This situation of quasimonopoly has given the monastic clergy substantial power in its dealings with the local society (Sihlé 2001).

The emphasis here on buddhacization and power relations should not conceal the existence of numerous syncretic local traditions. Thus the relations among Buddhism, Bon, and the widely shared set of practices and conceptions often termed "folk religion" are complex. Historical processes of adaptation and mutual influence have resulted in a high degree of interpenetration. The contemporary boundaries would seem almost to dissolve, were it not for elements like the Tibetan understandings of Buddhist and Bonpo religious affiliations and history, the contested hierarchy of religious traditions defined by the dominant Buddhist discourse, and the ongoing opposition of the high Buddhist clergy with regard to the remaining sacrificial practices.

Some Central Conceptions and Practices

The members of the Buddhist clergy in Tibet are the main, and often sole, specialists for the entire spectrum of religious activities. The main exceptions are specific forms of divination and therapeutic ritual, performed by mediums (where these are present), and the cult of the local place gods, performed, according to the areas, either by specific priests, by mediums or, more commonly, by laymen. One of the main reasons for this unusual preponderance of the Buddhist clergy is the profoundly tantric character of Tibetan Buddhism. In effect, tantric ritual provides highly powerful techniques that can be applied both to ultimate soteriological aims (of Enlightenment and liberation from the rebirth cycle) and to an extremely broad spectrum of this-worldly aims—prosperity, health, longevity, the propitiation of deities, the warding off of all kinds of misfortune, exorcism, victory in battle, or just plain sorcery.

Tibetan notions of misfortune and of the means to prevent or respond to it illustrate how widely tantric rituals may be applied. Karma is often presented as the (logically and ethically) primary and underlying cause of any form of misfortune, and many Tibetans, if asked, would subscribe to such a view. In practice, however, a person may spontaneously refer to his or her karma as the ultimate cause of a given experience of misfortune, but generally not before other, more proximate possible causes have been considered. This is done through personal speculation or through consultation with mediums or specialists (most often monks or tantrists) of divination (mo) or astrological calculation (tsi), to name but the most important techniques. Importantly, the other levels of interpretation in these techniques generally allow for the possibility of remedial action in ways that explanations in terms of karma do not.

A basic level of interpretation of misfortune that does not involve consultation with religious specialists resorts to what could be called natural processes such as landslides, floods, or hail, at least when such events are not interpreted as having been caused by some powerful agent. With regard to meteorological phenomena, even when no intentional agent is commonly posited, it is still held that they may be controlled by ritual means, provided the officiant is sufficiently qualified. The prevention of the most common of these phenomena, hail, is actually institutionalized in many Tibetan agricultural areas. Villages or groups of villages entrust the protection of their crops from summer hailstorms to a tantrist, a specialist in powerful tantric rituals. Interestingly, these rituals often treat hail as caused by spirits and are in effect forms of exorcism (Nebesky-Wojkowitz 1956), even if many villagers may have a more naturalistic view of the phenomenon.

A somewhat similar and highly important category of misfortune is illness (natsa), understood here as an affliction that, beyond notions of contagion, is not caused by outside intentional entities—in which case the illness would be categorized rather as harm. For illness, it is rather physiological, environmental, and psychological factors that are understood to be at play. Treatment is typically medicinal but may include substances charged with a blessing-power (chinlap) derived from contact with a sacred site or person or from a variety of tantric rituals, ranging from the simple recitation of mantras to highly powerful and complex rituals. These means may be complemented typically by rituals addressing either vital attributes of the person or nonhuman entities, such as protective deities or harmful demons.

A second major level of the interpretation of misfortune concerns relations with the complex pantheon of deities, spirits, and demons. Misfortune may be seen as having been caused by a local place god or household deity who is irritated by (supposedly) inadequate worship. Another very common reason is that improper behavior—urination on a place associated with a subterranean deity, spilling food on a hearth—may have caused the defilement of such deities and thus provoked their retaliation. Less predictable spirits and demons may yet have inflicted harm in a totally unprovoked way. All of these forms of misfortune are addressed primarily through ritual means, ranging from propitiation, placation, and purification rituals to exorcisms displaying various degrees of ritual violence.

In the case of unprovoked demonic harm, further meaning may be conferred, for instance by reference to the weakness of one of the person's vital attributes (which explains the person's vulnerability), a set of notions that constitutes in itself a third fundamental level of possible interpretation. The notion of la, a soul that can be lost or seized by a demon, has already been mentioned. Other vital attributes include the sok, or life force on which life itself depends, and the ts'e, or longevity. Tantric rituals can call back the soul, or may even attempt to call back the life force, through the propitiation of the deities held responsible, the offering of ransoms and symbolic substitutes, and so on. Various ritual means also aim at enhancing longevity, including longevity consecrations (ts'ewang), a much sought-after ritual service provided typically by members of the high Buddhist clergy, often publicly, to assemblies that may number in the hundreds, if not in the thousands. Yet another attribute of the person, the lungta (literally "wind horse," associated with invulnerability to misfortune and

The senior tantrist of a community, throwing a sor ("ritual weapon") during the climax of a tantric exorcism ritual. (Courtesy of Nicolas Sihlé)

meeting with success when the attribute is high), can be raised through relatively simple ritual means when it is diagnosed as low. For instance, one performs a fumigation (sang) on a high hill and throws over the hot air small squares of paper, themselves called lungta, which are printed with Buddhist text and representations of a flying horse and which then rise into the air. Importantly for our discussion, these notions are largely devoid of any Indic Buddhist pedigree but are addressed by a very wide spectrum of textual tantric rituals, ranging from modest, simple manipulations to highly prestigious ritual events often held to necessitate the services of a master (lama).

A fourth level of interpretation of misfortune concerns more social or interpersonal relationships. Jealous looks and envious talk are held to bring harm to the envied household. In Bhutan, one seeks to avert them by hanging oversized wooden phalluses from the edges of the roof; but in various parts of the Tibetan world, textual tantric rituals have the same aim. Similar rituals may also be performed to protect oneself or one's household from sorcery, against which there exist both simple lay procedures and more complex, tantric rituals. Yet another mode of misfortune is possession either by a living person (a witch) or a deceased person. This mode is characterized by abnormal behaviors or states of mind in the victim, and the move toward a resolution of the crisis often involves engaging in some form of dialogue with the possessing agent, who will speak through the victim. Rituals of purification and exorcism may complement this.

A fifth level of interpretation, which is often complementary to the other levels already evoked, can be termed astrological. Misfortune may be at least partly interpreted by reference to the effects of planets or the inauspicious nature of certain days or particular times; for example, the completion of every twelve-year cycle in one's life is marked by the passage through a dangerous "obstacle-year." All of these astrological factors constitute, in effect, a variety of independent systems.

As has already been suggested, attempts at interpretation and possibly resolution, including explanations in terms of karma, may combine (or move back and forth among) several of these levels. For several of these possible causes of misfortune, we have noted that there exist specific ritual, and in particular tantric, means to address and to attempt to overcome or repel them. Finally, beyond such specific ritual means, most tantric rituals, whatever their particular aims, comprise within the larger ritual sequence sections of repelling (dokpa) that address large, ideally exhaustive, arrays of ills. Apotropaic concerns are thus built into the very structure of tantric rituals.

The preceding discussion, through its focus on conceptions and practices linked to misfortune, illustrates some important features of Tibetan religious worldviews and of the Tibetan ritual sphere. It leaves out, however, important nontantric elements of the ritual sphere (often interwoven with tantric rituals), such as the circumambulation of sacred architectural elements or sacred mountains (Huber 1999), the manipulation of texts, or, importantly, the reading of canonical scriptures—besides tantric ritual, one of the major modes of ritual services provided by the clergy. These acts may also have apotropaic functions; they are primarily, however, forms of virtuous activity that enable one to accumulate merit and to receive life-enhancing blessings (chinlap).

We have started to identify central features of the ritualism of Tibetan Buddhism, particularly the importance of tantric ritual. These rituals constitute, fundamentally, techniques for mobilizing powers both formidable and of virtually unlimited applicability: They are understood to enable specialists to influence to some degree (if not control) precipitation and the effects of planets, wealth and power, health and the very forces of life and death—as well as to advance, for the most serious and dedicated practitioners, on the difficult path to Enlightenment. Importantly, in the actual practice of Tibetan Buddhism, these wide-ranging powers are not just understood as a by-product of advanced stages of the path to Enlightenment. The specialists thus empowered are not just highly realized masters—as Samuel's (1993) more doctrinally inspired model seems to suggest—but a far wider set of more or less powerful religious specialists, including common monks and, of particular importance in many village contexts, tantrists. The master (lama), however, as the preeminent figure of the soteriological sphere, remains the most powerful (and ideal) specialist in the realm of worldly, pragmatic ritual activity (Samuel 1993). All of this helps us understand the central place that tantric ritual occupies in Tibetan religion. In Tibet, unlike in Theravadin societies, the members of the Buddhist clergy, notably through their specialization in the powerful arsenal of tantric ritual, are by far the main, if not the exclusive, specialists in applying ritual power to worldly, pragmatic aims.

Tibetan tantric rituals, particularly those not based centrally on Buddhist ethical principles, have often been called magical. It is important to realize that violent exorcisms, or even rituals of sorcery that explicitly aim to destroy one's enemies, are built on very much the same model as other more "respectable" tantric Buddhist rituals (Sihlé 2002). They are typically framed by preliminaries and concluding acts through which the officiant at least theoretically generates anew in himself, or states, the ethical and soteriological perspective of Buddhist practice. The central ritual procedure involves invoking enlightened Buddhist deities (possibly under their wrathful manifestations) and their retinue of worldly deities; offerings are made, blessings and realizations are requested, and the deities are finally summoned to take action (Beyer 1973). The killing of an enemy is clothed typically under the terminology of destroying "enemies of the Dharma." The term "magical," stripped of its derogatory connotations of irrationality, applies in effect quite well to a major mode in Tibetan Buddhist ritual, characterized by the aim of achieving a variety of pragmatic effects, the frequency of a coercive thrust (albeit alongside other modes of relationship to deities and spirits), and the manipulation of powerful substances and imagery, combined with powerful utterances such as mantras. The magical character of tantric techniques is also found in central practices of the soteriological sphere (for example, consecrations) and the actual mental creation of high, enlightened deities in the adept's practice.

The strong magical emphasis in Tibetan Buddhism compels us to reconsider critically classic anthropological theories of religion, such as Weberian and other models that postulate a general evolutionary trend from more magical, local, oral religious traditions to more ethical so-called world religions or religions of the book. The case of Tibetan Buddhism, as a product of the emergence of the Vajrayana out of the fold of Mahayana Buddhism, suggests that, in Weberian terms, processes of intellectual and ethical rationalization need not be incompatible with the development of a highly magical outlook. Rather than a general opposition, one finds in Tibetan Buddhism the coexistence and even the intimate combination of this magical character with several other important orientations: the practice of meritorious acts (circumambulations, recitations of the Mani mantra, prostrations) aiming at the accumulation of positive karma; a fundamental ethical dimension; a devotional tone with regard to high masters and deities like Padmasambhava, Avalokiteshvara, and Tara; occasionally a properly mystical character, with deities appearing in visions and dreams, and still today ongoing scriptural revelations by charismatic masters (Germano 1998); and, importantly, a highly rational, intellectual orientation, particularly developed or emphasized within the higher clergy and prominent monastic traditions (Dreyfus 2003). These various orientations interact in complex ways. Life within institutions of scholastic learning remains framed by tantric ritual activities, such as the daily worship of high deities and protectors. Some Tibetan scholar-monks have produced extensive exegetical literature on tantric practice and have left autobiographical accounts of mystical experiences. These magical and mystical elements combined with a highly rational intellectual tradition are assuredly major factors of the fascination felt for Tibetan Buddhism by many non-Tibetans, be they Westerners, Indians, Chinese, Newar, or others.

Specialists and Institutions

Monasticism is a major institution in Tibet, but it is not the only form of Tibetan Buddhist clergy. There are numerous and relatively fluid types of religious specialists, but one relatively clear-cut distinction is that between the monastic clergy (monks [tr'awa] and nuns [ani or jomo]) and specialists most often called ngakpa (tantrists) who do not pronounce monastic vows. Sometimes improperly designated as married monks, the ngakpa are generally male householders who typically specialize more exclusively than their monastic counterparts in tantric rituals—thus the name tantrist. They often constitute family lines, typically with the eldest son succeeding the father. These family lines are most often somewhat isolated. In a typical central Tibetan village, one would not expect to find more than one ngakpa household. In other areas, however, notably in northeastern Tibet or in some Himalayan societies, one may find considerable concentrations of tantrists, with possibly even entire villages constituted of ngakpa families (Sihlé 2001). In such places, the tantrists of a given community generally carry out collective rituals in a village temple. Some mixed religious communities of monks and tantrists are also known; while they are in residence, the tantrists then also follow the monastic rule.

In terms of the major categories of specialists, one may also mention the hermit (gomchen or ritropa). As opposed to the previous types, this is, however, generally not a lifelong status. The yogi Milarepa, famous among others for having lived off nettles during his prolonged retreats in isolated caves, would come somewhat close to being an exception, but his eremitic lifestyle was interrupted by periods of wandering and teaching. The term "hermit" thus refers less to a socioreligious status like the preceding categories and more to a mode of religious activity. A hermit may actually be a monk, a nun, a tantrist, a non-monastic itinerant practitioner like Milarepa, or even for instance an elderly layperson seriously engaged in religious practice.

A final, polysemous category is that of the lama. The term refers primarily to someone's personal religious master (in the sense of the Sanskrit guru), to the master of a religious community, or, more generally, to persons of high religious status. The term will be used here in these primary senses. It also has, however, some looser uses. In many Himalayan Tibetan Buddhist societies devoid of monasticism, the tantrists (who constitute, in effect, the local Buddhist clergy) are often called lama. Importantly, a lama in the primary senses just given is not necessarily a monk, but he may also be a tantrist. Although this is not commonly the case, the master of a monastic community may be a tantrist and vice versa. Lama are generally male, with but a few exceptions.

Masters are fundamental figures in many ways. They are essential for transmitting the teachings (tantric practices, in particular, require initiation by a qualified master and cannot be learned from books); their high religious power is a precious source of blessings (chinlap) and other religious services for the laity; and their prestige is unequaled. The great masters are, for their disciples and the laity alike, living embodiments of the ultimate truths of the Buddhist Dharma; they are surrounded by devotion and awe (Aziz 1978, ch. 10). They may be, however, somewhat inaccessible for the common laity, and many places do not have any lama. Some scholarly accounts (such as Samuel 1993), with their overriding emphasis on the lama figure, may suffer from a somewhat elitist bias. One may argue that, in some ways, the monk remains in Tibet the religious specialist par excellence. Monks make up by far the most numerous category; monkhood has profound historic and symbolic associations with the Buddhist doctrine; and the most prominent seats of religious learning and transmission are monasteries. Indeed, the most common definition of "tantrists" is that "they marry"—in other words, in people's minds, they are defined in opposition to the central figure of the monk.

A striking feature of Tibetan monasticism is its demographic dimension. In some areas, before the Chinese takeover in Tibet, 10 to 15 percent of all adult males were monks, justifying the designation "mass monasticism" (Goldstein 1998). The figures for females are lower, due notably to the lack of economic support that has affected the nunneries (Havnevik 1989). The modalities of monastic recruitment are quite diverse. Many parents, with a whole range of economic and religious motivations, send children to the monastery while they are still very young. Before 1950 in some areas, monasteries had the right to levy various taxes, including monks; one spoke of a "monk tax." In other areas—in some Tibetan societies of the Himalayas, for instance—customary law prescribes that if a household has at least three sons (or daughters), the second is to be sent to the local monastery. Due to the effects of restrictive Chinese policies, this phenomenon of mass monasticism has been strictly curtailed in Tibetan areas in the PRC, in particular in the Tibetan Autonomous Region. It continues to some extent in exile, where the ranks of monks born in exile are greatly increased by the ongoing arrival of monks fleeing Tibet.

In the most recent book-length synthesis on Tibetan religion, Samuel (1993) bases his analysis in part on a distinction between shamanic and clerical Buddhism. Samuel's shamanic category is defined very widely, in terms of alternate modes of consciousness, which enables him to address under one heading two (substantially different) realms—spirit mediums and tantric ritual. Clerical Buddhism, in contrast, is the domain of monastic discipline and scholarship. Despite certain problems, such as a somewhat elitist bias in Samuel's emphasis on the figure of the tantric lama and on the mastery of tantric yoga and the ambiguities that surround his uses of the shamanic terminology (Ray 1995, Bjerken 2004), the duality he examines—between meditative practice and discursive study, between experience and wisdom—is fundamental far beyond the case of Tibetan Buddhism (Tambiah 1984).

In a highly schematic way, this duality may serve to distinguish roughly between historically dominant emphases or orientations in the four main orders of Tibetan Buddhism and in Bon. The Geluk order—which, notably through the reincarnation lineage of the Dalai Lamas, has been closely associated with state power in central Tibet since the seventeenth century—constitutes an almost exclusively monastic tradition and places great emphasis on scholastic learning. This order is the closest to Samuel's clerical Buddhism. One must note, however, that religious life in Geluk monasteries, as in monasteries of all Tibetan orders, is profoundly permeated with tantric ritual. High Geluk masters, beyond their profound knowledge of doctrinal matters, are tantric masters as well.

On the other end of this schematic spectrum, the Nyingma order is the one that historically has laid the strongest emphasis on meditative practice and the least emphasis on monasticism. Thus, most tantrists are associated with the Nyingma. This order developed large monastic institutions (largely on the Geluk model) later than the other orders, starting in the seventeenth century. It has, however, also produced some of the greatest philosopher figures of Tibetan Buddhism, and today the more prestigious Nyingma monastic communities generally have a scholastic curriculum not unlike those of their Geluk counterparts. Tantrists, however, as part of a much less structured and less centralized form of clergy with far looser links to the main centers of learning, remain, generally speaking, far more exclusively focused on tantric practice.

The Bon tradition, as already mentioned, strongly resembles the Nyingma order in its sociological and religious features. The two remaining Buddhist orders, Sakya and Kagyu, can be placed roughly between the Geluk and the Nyingma on the schematic spectrum outlined previously. One may note that the

Sakya order, apart from some of its hierarchs, is exclusively monastic and in that sense somewhat closer to the Geluk, whereas some Kagyu ritual traditions are in effect hardly distinguishable from the Nyingma traditions.

Neither the word "order" used here, nor the terms "sect" or "school" used by other scholars (Lopez 1997, 24), convey perfectly the Tibetan notion of choluk (literally, tradition, or way, of Dharma). Each order is a more or less loosely federated set of religious, and notably ritual, traditions, based in monasteries and followed sometimes also by tantrist lineages and communities. The central defining factor of such traditions is a transmission lineage of tantric ritual practice that may be associated with a given central monastery or with a given master or lineage of masters. The basic units that make up these ritual traditions are tantric cycles, which are collections of rituals all centered on a given meditational deity (yidam). Thus, orders, suborders, or traditions of individual monasteries can be characterized by reference to a certain set of major meditational deities, the name of the central practices, the main monastery of that tradition, or the name of a master who developed a particular version of such a tradition.

The distribution of tantric practices across the orders of Tibetan Buddhism shows on the one hand concern for sectarian continuity and separation and on the other hand eclecticism, fluidity, and change. Some practices are shared by virtually every Tibetan order. In eastern Tibet in the nineteenth and early twentieth centuries, a series of prominent Nyingma, Kagyu, and Sakya masters led the Rime (ecumenical) movement, in which they composed large arrays of materials ranging from the academic to the visionary (with quite an emphasis on the supreme meditative practices of Dzokchen, or Great Perfection) and authored vast collections of well-known and more obscure tantric practices, as well as scholarly editions of canonical and exegetical literature. These were to become highly influential throughout Tibetan areas and religious traditions (the Geluk order excluded), determining to quite some extent the face of much of Tibetan Buddhism today (Smith 1970; Samuel 1993).

The lineages through which teachings have been transmitted are in many ways another fundamental feature of the strongly tantric Tibetan tradition. One may engage in a given practice only after having been duly initiated into the practice by a qualified master. These transmission lineages (lop-gyu) are combined under multiple modalities with two striking socioreligious institutional features of Tibetan Buddhism: hereditary and reincarnation lineages. Hereditary lineages (dung-gyu or ru-gyu, literally bone lineage) are found primarily among tantrists, as monks in principle have no descendants. The term *dung-gyu* refers primarily to patriline (i.e., a line of descent through males) or to an entire lineage, but such a patriline is understood as a vehicle for the transmission of social status and, importantly, of a form of religious potential that results from the accumulated ritual power of the previous practitioners of the patriline. This potential needs to be activated through the usual techniques for the acquisition of tantric power, namely engaging in retreats devoted to the ritual service of meditational deities (yidam), which, notably, involves repeating each deity's mantra tens or even hundreds of thousands of times. In addition to status and religious potential, religious teachings and functions (such as those of the hierarch at the head of an order or of a monastery's main lama or abbot) may also be transmitted in such a lineage, typically from father to son or uncle to nephew. In the latter case, the uncle and nephew may be monks.

Succession through incarnation lineages (ku-gyu) has become a major Buddhist and state institution in Tibetan history. Theoretically, reincarnate masters (trulku) are the reincarnations of highly advanced practitioners who, following the model of the bodhisattva, choose to be reborn in order to continue to benefit sentient beings. In practice, the reincarnations of hosts of greater and lesser lama have been sought, found, and in some cases officially recognized by hierarchs of the various orders. Over time, hundreds of reincarnation lines, including several of the most exalted Tibetan religious figures and others of purely local significance, have thus appeared. The question of the authenticity of reincarnate masters may be left to the believer (and this is a question some Tibetans definitely do discuss); it has been pointed out that many trulkus are quite effectively trained to assume the role of Buddhist masters, but that becoming focal points for the demand of religious services may not be to everyone's taste (Ray 2001, Kapstein 2002).

Beyond questions of spiritual significance and the politics of religious legitimacy, the institution of reincarnation lineages involves centrally economic considerations. Reincarnate masters drain considerable patronage and offerings. In Tibet prior to 1950, many were at the head of large landed estates called *labrang*, with peasants and pastoralists providing substantial resources and corvée labor. Succession by reincarnation in effect provided economic and institutional continuity to socioreligious networks of teaching, practice, patronage, and religious services constituted around the figure of a lama when the latter did not belong to a hereditary lineage formally associated with a monastery (Snellgrove and Richardson 1986, 136). In many cases, however, the two institutions of hereditary and reincarnation lineages overlapped in a complex interweaving with family lines of the religious nobility.

Buddhism and the Sociopolitical Order

The situation of Buddhism in pre-1950 Tibetan sociopolitical and institutional life is unique. Tibet has often been called a theocratic state, with reference to the fact that the Dalai Lamas are identified with Avalokiteshvara, the patron bodhisattva of Tibet. However, both theologically and historically, this is only partly accurate. The Dalai Lamas, rather than direct emanations of the deity, are primarily the reincarnations of their direct historical predecessors (Stein 1972, 138–139). Besides, only a few of them actually ruled the central Tibetan state. In the mid-seventeenth century, the great Fifth Dalai Lama, with the help of his Mongol supporters, was the first of his line of incarnation to accede to temporal power over central Tibet. His reign, a moment of flowering in Tibetan cultural history (Pommaret 2003), was followed by political turmoil. Then, with just one very brief exception, the state was ruled continuously from the mid-eighteenth century to 1950 by lines of incarnation—nominally by that of the Dalai Lamas, but as most of them died young and many never ruled, the actual political power was held for most of this period by eleven successive regents belonging to six lines of incarnation of the Geluk order (Goldstein 1973).

Before 1950, half of the government's officials in Lhasa were monks, and a common formulation of the state's political ideology was cho-si sung-drel, religion and politics conjoined. Other major but less institutionalized political forces in the central Tibetan state were the three large Gelukpa monastic seats (Drepung, Sera, Ganden) that surrounded the capital. They "exercised an almost vetolike power over major government policy" (Goldstein 1998, 19). With their total of 20,000 monks, these institutions, together or individually, could constitute significant threats, and some have actually taken part in violent political struggles. The monks of Drepung were also officially given control over Lhasa during the annual three-week-long Great Prayer festival, which since the time of the Fifth Dalai Lama has become a major political ritual of the Lhasa state. The complex and diverse ritual sequence was centered primarily on the Dalai Lama, the state protective deities, the representatives of the Geluk monastic order, and the central temple of Lhasa—the Jokang, a most potent politicoreligious symbol. This holiest of all Tibetan sacred sites was founded by the seventh-century king Songtsen Gampo, who was considered by later Tibetan historiographical tradition to be an incarnation of Avalokiteshvara (and thus a predecessor of the Dalai Lamas); he was said to have melted at his death into the statue of the same deity housed in the temple. During the festival, the Dalai Lama resided not in his Potala palace, but in the Jokang (Richardson 1993).

The Lhasa- and Geluk-centered picture given here should not be generalized to all Tibetan societies. However, several more or less autonomous Tibetan polities, such as Sakya in central Tibet or Derge in eastern Tibet, were ruled by lines of reincarnation or noble families of very high social and religious status, while yet other large, semiautonomous estates were headed by monasteries (Cassinelli and Ekvall 1969). Religious institutions (monasteries and the labrang estates of incarnation lines) were also major socioeconomic forces: They possessed between 37 percent and 50 percent of all arable land in central

Tibet, as well as substantial pastoral holdings (Goldstein 1998, 19). It definitely seems appropriate to call the central Tibetan state, as well as several other Tibetan polities, not theocratic, but ecclesiastical (Stein 1972, 138–139).

The recent political history of Tibet shows the ongoing, intimate association of religion and state politics. Today the Dalai Lama still heads the government in exile established at Dharamsala in northern India, albeit in a more limited role—but the current prime minister of the government in exile, for instance, is also a Gelukpa reincarnate lama. Within Tibet, both the Chinese authorities and those who resist them have clearly recognized the political potency of religious symbols, be they places, ritual events, or masters. Major political demonstrations in Lhasa between 1987 and 1990 and the Chinese state's subsequent displays of military power focused on the Great Prayer festival and the Jokang temple (Barnett 1994). In these demonstrations, fumigation rituals (sang) became a mode of political protest and were then specifically outlawed (Schwartz 1994). With varying degrees of success, the Chinese authorities have also attempted to control the major Tibetan masters still living in the PRC and their reincarnations—a policy the roots of which arguably predate the establishment of the PRC (Kapstein 1998, 147–148).

Many Buddhist masters throughout the Tibetan areas in the PRC have been given positions in the political and administrative structures, more in order to control them than to empower them. In 1995, the six-year-old reincarnation of the Panchen Lama, the second dignitary of the Geluk order, was abducted as soon as the Dalai Lama officially recognized him, and the Chinese authorities organized their own ceremony of designation of the Panchen Lama shortly afterward. The boy who was nominated in that way has now been receiving a thorough political education, and his public statements of faithfulness and gratitude to the Chinese state have been broadcast on television. In exile, the Buddhist religion and the figure of the Dalai Lama in particular have become central foci in the political struggle and in the construction of a Tibetan nationalism (Goldstein 1978).

The substantial involvement of Buddhist institutions, charismatic figures, ritual, and ideology in the political life of Tibet is paralleled by their strong interrelations with the socioeconomic sphere. In anthropological studies of Tibetan monasticism (not to mention nonmonastic forms of clergy), it has become increasingly clear that the potential usefulness of the notion of renunciation is very limited. Before 1950, most monks were not fully supported by their institutions and had to rely on the support of their families and had to make themselves available for requests for ritual services or had to engage in other economic activities such as trade. Entering the Buddhist order most generally does not entail a radical rupture of socioeconomic ties with one's family. For instance, in many areas, a monk's or nun's monastic quarters are juridically and economically part of the person's native household (Mills 2003). In many

Tibetan contexts, monastic or other religious institutions play a fundamentally communal role—for householders, taking part in sponsoring the collective ritual activity, whether the officiants are monastic or not, is very often an important condition of community membership (Fürer-Haimendorf 1964). Numerous instances have been described of rituals with strong communal dimensions being taken over by monks (Ramble 1993).

Recent Transformations and Trends

Transformations in the Tibetan religious landscape have been profound in the past fifty years. The first decades of Chinese rule have brought highly traumatic experiences. The quickly suppressed Lhasa uprising of 1959 led to the flight into exile of the Dalai Lama, followed by some 100,000 people, including a large proportion of the Tibetan high clergy. The launching of the Great Leap Ahead (1959–1961) then ushered in a period of violence and starvation. The suffering and violence culminated with the Cultural Revolution (1966–1976), which visited on Tibet—as indeed throughout the PRC—a decade of devastation and alienation during which the (Han Chinese, but also Tibetan) Red Guards systematically desecrated and destroyed monasteries, temples, and all signs of religion. They violated the bodies and minds of thousands, in particular monks and nuns, whose shaven heads and red robes made them the most visible of Tibet's persons of religious status. Tantrists of the northeastern Amdo province, many of whom keep several-foot-long locks of hair, sometimes matted dreadlocks, coiled around their heads, were also highly recognizable. Many others, though, with less conspicuous hairstyles, were able to blend somewhat more safely—to the extent that anybody was safe—into the anonymous ranks of the householder society. The social and religious history of this period remains very largely to be written, and the ethnography of the post-Mao period and of the traces, scars, and memories of the preceding decades is just starting to be conducted (Goldstein and Kapstein 1998, Schrempf 2001, Makley 2003).

At the height of religious oppression during the Cultural Revolution, some masters and dedicated practitioners managed to pursue their practice and even to continue giving and receiving teachings, either by living in remote pastoral areas, possibly with the complicity of local cadres, or by hiding or conducting their practices at night. Folios of religious texts were concealed in belts and in the lining of clothes. Series of thousands of full-length prostrations, as part of the preliminary tantric practices, were performed in silence at night, the practitioner cautiously changing place regularly within the room so as not to leave telltale traces in the form of the characteristic wear of the floor's wooden planks.

Then, in the 1980s, the PRC authorities embarked on a course of cautious religious liberalization, allowing the rebuilding of monasteries and temples and the resumption of private religious practice. However, draconian restrictions were maintained on monastic recruitment and collective religious performances. This was, however, interrupted by the cycle of demonstrations that erupted in Lhasa in 1987 and spread somewhat across the Tibetan areas. A major feature of these demonstrations, besides the religious symbolism mentioned previously, was that they were often staged by monks and nuns. As a consequence, the Chinese authorities intensified political repression and surveillance, as well as the apparatus of political indoctrination, notably within the monasteries (Schwartz 1994). Faced with restrictive regulations, the partially interrupted transmission of teachings, a dearth of qualified teachers, and at times the intense pressures that ensue from the political vicissitudes, a large number of monks and nuns live in a state of relative alienation. The monastic clergy is substantially overrepresented in the hundreds of Tibetans who, still today, flee every year into exile.

However, for the Chinese authorities, the great Tibetan monasteries represent both threats and opportunities. They are at once potential sources of political unrest, conspicuous institutions that cannot be fully hidden from the scrutiny of foreign human rights organizations, and a fundamental asset for international tourism. Tourism, both domestic and international, is becoming an important force in the post-Mao reshaping of large religious institutions and certain large-scale religious activities. As a potentially important economic resource, there is the risk that tourism may lead to more folklorized forms—exotic, colorful displays that could lose some of their local religious and cultural relevance (Epstein and Peng 1998).

The critical issues that face the Buddhist clergy in the PRC more largely are just one face of the current situation, which is characterized also by resistance and even by revival and the (re)invention of tradition. In eastern Tibetan areas outside of the politically more tense Tibetan Autonomous Region, the Nyingma order in particular has experienced a powerful institutional revival. Khenpo Jigme Puntsok or Jikpun (1933–2004), possibly the most charismatic Nyingmapa master living in the PRC in recent decades, established a religious center in 1980 known as Larung Gar in the Golok area in eastern Tibet. Political involvement has been cautiously avoided at this center, which has become one of the largest contemporary Tibetan religious communities. This is not a monastery with a fixed membership and rigid, sectarian adherence to a certain set of practices, but a more open type of community, headed until his death by Khenpo Jikpun, with attendance fluctuating between 1,400 and 2,000 practitioners (monastic and nonmonastic, male and female) and rising to 10,000 at times of major initiations. This institution has started producing impressive numbers of highly trained teachers. One hundred khenpo (a title that could be translated as doctors or masters of theology—the requirements were initially "somewhat relaxed") graduated in its first decade (Germano 1998, 56, 62–65). Khenpo Jikpun also attracted a large Han Chinese following, both at Larung Gar and during his travels in China. This phenomenon is probably an important aspect of the current religious dynamics surrounding Tibetan Buddhism in the context of the Chinese state. It seems to have been one of the factors that led to the authorities' recent crackdown on, and forceful reduction of, the master's ever-expanding religious community.

Beyond his fame as the head of Larung Gar, Khenpo Jikpun's considerable charisma also very importantly derived from and was manifested in his being an active terton—a revealer of hidden treasures, or terma. These are objects or teachings considered to have been concealed typically by Padmasambhava in order to be rediscovered at an appropriate time by a reincarnation of one of the great master's disciples. The terma tradition, which appeared historically in Nyingmapa and Bonpo circles, constitutes a mode of creative reappropriation and to some extent invention of religious artifacts, ideas, and practices. An alternative, but contested, mode of religious legitimacy was devised within this tradition, based on the recognition of lines of reincarnation and the claims to authenticity of particular revelations rather than the usual direct master-to-disciple transmission lineages (Thondup 1986). Germano argues that the current, mainly eastern Tibetan revival of the terma tradition manifests similarities with its period of historical emergence in the eleventh and twelfth centuries. Similarities include a context of sociopolitical conflict and resistance to exogenous sources of authoritative knowledge and the aim of opposing the latter through the establishment of authoritative materials grounded in Tibet, in the sense that these terma, which are often physically excavated, were initially taught and concealed by exalted masters such as Padmasambhava in Tibet itself (Germano 1998, 88–89). This mode of ongoing revelation is a sign of vitality and Tibetocentric renewal. The question remains whether the terma tradition will successfully integrate modernity, be it Western, Chinese, or Tibetan, in its contents and forms—a challenge that seems presently to remain beyond its powers (Germano 1998, 94).

Looking beyond the borders of the PRC, Tibetan Buddhism today is in a unique position in which a significant proportion of the clergy—including a major part of the religious elite and most religious hierarchs—is currently found outside of Tibet, scattered across the Tibetan diaspora, mainly in India and Nepal, but also in various parts of East Asia and the West. In the increasingly globalized spaces of the Kathmandu valley and Dharamsala, complex cultural encounters occur, mediated and informed by the tourism industry, the business and "culture of Dharma" (Moran 2004), and new media such as the Internet. Several of these interactions can be dissociated from the political context only with difficulty, as discourses on Tibet are inescapably caught up at least somewhat in a web of political relations. These highly complex developments go far beyond the scope of this discussion. It must be realized, though, that they have important implications with regard to the spread of Tibetan Buddhist practices, notions, values, and institutional patterns in non-Tibetan areas (or even in the Tibetan Himalayas, as we shall see), as well as in terms of the adoption of novel features within these exile contexts. The words of the Dalai Lama and other masters are reaching ever-wider Tibetan and global audiences through a combination of modern, traditional, and hybrid medias, such as tantric initiations conferred to wealthy Western converts to and sympathizers of Tibetan Buddhism from the most prestigious stages of Western capitals.

It has been said that modernist Buddhism, at least prior to 1980, did not appear in Tibet (Lopez 1998, 185). The Buddhist intellectual Gedun Chopel (1903–1951), who directed a modernist critique at his society and religion, was a precursor more than the founder of a movement. In this respect, there remain today significant differences between the PRC Tibet and the diaspora. Starting in the 1960s, a distinctly modernist Tibetan Buddhist trend has emerged in exile, with the Dalai Lama as one of its main proponents—possibly one of the most prominent proponents of modernist Buddhism today as a whole. This trend has been at the core of the Dalai Lama's discourses addressed to non-Buddhists or non–Tibetan sympathizers, but it has also penetrated the sermons he delivers to Tibetans. These modernist discourses emphasize ecumenism and extremely simple ethical, universalist definitions of religion or Buddhism. They also stress the rational and scientific character of Buddhist understandings of the mind or of the nature of reality, and they express concerns for world peace, the environment, and human—or specifically women's—rights (Lopez 1998, 185–186; 2002, xxxi). The Dalai Lama and Tibetan Buddhist masters in general remain at the same time, if not necessarily in the same breath, masters of tantric ritual and practitioners of protective deity worship. Many aspects of these latter practices hardly fit with the simple ethical, ecumenical, and rationalist aspects of these masters' modernist discourses, and in effect the practices remain mostly unknown to the non-Tibetan audiences to which these modernist discourses are mainly directed.

Since the mid-1970s, however, a dispute has emerged among the Geluk exiles over the worship of the protective deity (cho-kyong) Shukden. The dispute has caused a deep rift in the Geluk order between those who worship the deity and those who, in accordance with the strong public pronouncements of the Dalai Lama, do not. The crux of the problem lies in the opposition between some of the Dalai Lamas (such as the present one) favoring and integrating into official state practice certain Nyingma ritual elements and the extreme concern of another part of the Geluk establishment for sectarian purity. Powerful, worldly (that is, not enlightened) protective deities like Shukden are held to be capable of causing severe harm when propitiated with evil intent by their followers, and this probably prompted the public statements of the Dalai Lama. The dispute reached a climax in 1997 with the murder of three monks in Dharamsala, apparently by Tibetan followers of Shukden. Since the 1970s, this conflict has sent repeated waves of shock and dismay throughout the Tibetan exile community and has caused quite some puzzlement beyond, not the least among Western audiences more accustomed to modernist depictions of Buddhism (Dreyfus 1998; Lopez 1998, 188–196).

Echoes of these modernist discourses are reaching PRC Tibetan, exile Tibetan, and Himalayan societies with varying intensities and degrees of clarity, brought by attendees of Kalachakra initiations and other teachings or by the flow of cassettes containing sermons of the Dalai Lama. These and other processes of globalization among the exile communities—such as the historically unprecedented but also somewhat volatile levels of mostly Western and East Asian patronage to the major exile monastic institutions—are having repercussions even in the most remote Tibetan valleys of the Himalayas. In Baragaon, also known as Lower Mustang, a region well connected with the Nepalese lowlands, the vitality and prestige of local Sakya monastic communities was bolstered in the 1990s by their increased links with the major monasteries of their order. At the same time, in a Nyingma tantrist village community that had developed what one could call a culture of strong exorcistic practice, the ethical basis of this activity was being increasingly questioned, including by the tantrists themselves (Sihlé 2001).

In other areas, such as the neighboring Nyishang and Nubri, monks have been sent in increasing numbers to the well-endowed Tibetan institutions of the Kathmandu valley or India, and the local laity fall back to some extent on nuns for religious services (Watkins 1996). In Dolpo, a land of high arid valleys, scarce resources, and a substantial but almost exclusively nonmonastic clergy, the local tantrists are also increasingly sending their sons to become monks in the Tibetan exile institutions. According to information collected in 1997, not less than seventy-three young Dolpo monks were enrolled at that time in the sole monastery of Penor Rimpoche (possibly the most prominent Nyingmapa master living in exile) in climatically, linguistically, and culturally alien faraway southern India. The first Dolpo monks were then starting to complete their long monastic curriculum, but after enjoying the comfort of a decade or more of full economic support, none so far had made the choice to come back to live in Dolpo, where the near absence of economic surplus is a major obstacle, at the least for institutional monasticism. Thus the tantrist lineages of Dolpo were to some extent depleting themselves, without any clear prospect of the local society being able to create an alternative resident clergy.

Finally, beyond the previously mentioned aspects of globalization or the development of a modernist trend within Tibetan Buddhism, localized forms of

A tantrist from the Dolpo district of Nepal carrying out a powerful tantric meditation practice in a funeral context; among other ritual implements he carries notably a human thighbone trumpet, an emblem of powerful tantric practices. (Courtesy of Nicolas Sihlé)

globalization and modernity are also directly affecting the societies of Tibetan Buddhism, which in turn has effects on religion (see, for instance, Ortner 1995). The spread of modern education in state-sponsored schools challenges long-held understandings or assumptions about the authoritative sources of knowledge. Status ascription by birth, for instance—a highly significant feature of tantrist hereditary lineages—is increasingly challenged by modern claims of achieved status. In this sense, the encounter between Tibetan Buddhism and modernity is well under way throughout the Tibetan world.

Buddhism in Nepal

Tamang and Other Forms Influenced by Tibetan Buddhism

This section presents some striking general features of forms of Buddhism found in non-Tibetan societies of Nepal, in which various Tibeto-Burman tongues are spoken—primarily the Tamang (who live mainly in areas surrounding the Kathmandu valley), the Gurung (who live more to the west, around

Pokhara), and the Thakali (whose homeland, the Thak Khola valley, lies to the north of Pokhara). Apart from Newar Buddhism and the emerging modernist Theravada movement, these Buddhist traditions of Nepal are all influenced by Tibetan Buddhism. These traditions are also centered on tantric ritual, a feature also shared with Newar Buddhism.

A first important caveat regards the tendency to assume that one can speak of the Buddhism of a given ethnic group or ethnic category (for example, Thakali Buddhism, Gurung Buddhism, or Tamang Buddhism) as if it were a homogenous and clearly distinct entity sealed off from the larger Buddhist world. To assume that significant ethnic specificities exist is a valid and sound presupposition, but one should not overlook the very real possibility of both considerable intraethnic variation—the Thakali and their geographic, socioeconomic, and religious divisions are a case in point (Fisher 2001)—and substantial religious interactions across ethnic boundaries. These boundaries may be crossed, for instance, in the master-to-disciple relations, in occasional or even regular ritual practice, or in relations of patronage. In forms of Buddhism influenced by the Tibetan model, the official recognition of the reincarnate lama, which may be guided by concerns for strengthening alliances of a not purely religious nature, can lead to the designation of a boy from a different ethnic group (Vinding 1998, 305–306). Continuity with Tibetan notions and ritual forms is also found outside of the more Buddhist sphere, for instance in the cults of the local place gods (Höfer 1997).

Importantly, the traditions influenced by Tibetan Buddhism all interact with masters (and other representatives) of the Tibetan tradition. In some cases, these contacts have been sporadic and rare; in others, relations with Tibetan centers of learning have been maintained over generations. Some of these were interrupted with the closure of the Tibetan border by the Chinese in 1959. In recent decades, though, new relationships have been emerging in the Kathmandu valley, in Pokhara, and elsewhere in the subcontinent with Tibetan monastic institutions that were reinstituted in exile. Many liturgical texts used in Tamang, Gurung, or Thakali Buddhist rituals are the same as those used in Tibet, although this does not mean the rituals in themselves are identical. The local understandings of the concepts and deities mentioned in the texts may vary significantly from their standard Tibetan equivalents. The social contexts in which these rituals are performed—for instance, the fact that these Himalayan societies are strongly organized by relations of matrimonial exchange between clans, whereas Tibetan societies are more typically organized around households—may also have crucial implications on the form of the rituals. A fundamental, overarching feature is the fact that the interactions between Tibetan masters or other religious specialists and the Tamang, Thakali, or other similar traditions are often strikingly asymmetrical. The latter are all practiced within relatively small ethnic groups devoid of major centers of formal religious learning (if not of monastic institutions altogether) and, sometimes, devoid of major religious personalities. The philosophical and soteriological dimensions of Buddhism are less present in these traditions than in the Tibetan tradition—the overriding concern, in the collective and private rituals carried out by the local ritual officiants, is primarily with obtaining worldly benefits. This can be the case in local Tibetan traditions, too, but Tibetan Buddhism is also well known for its large monastic institutions and its numerous highly charismatic masters. It is typically associated, in local understandings by the Tamang and others, with higher levels of literacy (in the literary Tibetan of the texts) and of ritual power. Thus, in these encounters, the representatives of Tibetan Buddhism, especially when they are prestigious masters, are endowed with the authority of religious charisma, textual and ritual mastery, and the historical precedence of their tradition. These masters occasionally use this religious authority to push for changes, in a missionary spirit, as the local traditions often diverge from the Tibetan orthopraxy. It appears, however, that these efforts were sometimes only temporarily successful (Ramble 1990) and that the influence of Tibetan Buddhism in local Himalayan traditions could wax and wane.

It should be emphasized that in Tamang and other Buddhist traditions in Nepal that are influenced by Tibetan Buddhism, the local religious field as a whole can in no way be seen as dominated by Buddhism. An important consequence of this is that, for instance, the Tamang cannot be called "Buddhists" in any simple way. In these Himalayan cases, as opposed to the Tibetan one, the term "Buddhism" refers to just one of several interrelated religious complexes. The Buddhist religious specialists are most commonly nonmonastic householder priests often called *lama* in these societies, whatever their degree of ritual (or doctrinal) competence. They generally enjoy relatively high prestige, for reasons similar to those that explain the even higher prestige of outside Tibetan masters—they, too, represent traditions associated with written texts. But beyond this superior prestige of the Buddhist specialists and texts, the religious field as a whole is neither subordinated to nor integrated within the Buddhist fold, as it is to quite some extent in Tibet. The other local religious complexes are typically centered around various shamanic specialists, and sometimes sacrificers, whose rituals and myths (generally in the local Tibeto-Burman tongue or archaic versions thereof, sometimes also with Tibetan or Nepali influences) are transmitted orally and independently of the local Buddhist institutions.

Beside, and interacting with, these complexes, one finds also Hindu Brahmans and other specialists belonging to castes of the politically dominant ethnic category of Nepal, the Nepali-speaking Parbatiya. Although they may live in the same villages as the Tamang or Gurung, these specialists, through their belonging to the dominant caste hierarchy of Nepal—and for the Brahmans due also to their strong concerns with maintaining ritual purity, which places limits on their interactions with members of other groups—retain quite an alien identity in the eyes of the local villagers. It may be noted that the Hindu Brahmans and the indigenous Buddhist lama, beyond the striking differences between them, actually share an important trait: As representatives of religions strongly based on written texts, they are all endowed with a prestige that local shamans or sacrificers of oral traditions generally do not possess. Finally, this already rather complex picture would not be accurate if we failed to mention the presence of Christian converts, among the Tamang notably, a result of missionary activities deployed in Nepal increasingly since 1990. These conversions have been either individual or collective, with economic disparities and local political strategies as some of the factors in play. The global picture is definitely one of considerable flux across ethnic, social, and linguistic boundaries. Complex religious systems are here the norm.

Generally speaking, the relations among the various complexes that traditionally comprise Tamang or similar varieties of religion are marked both by a certain degree of complementarity and by some overlap in the ritual functions. A primary responsibility of the Buddhist specialists is typically that of conducting the funerary rites. Gurung or Thakali shamans are also commonly called to officiate for funerals, but their Tamang counterparts, the bombo, are barred from participating in the major death feasts, ritual events of considerable social importance conducted by the Buddhist lama (Pignède 1993; Fisher 2001; Holmberg 1989). In other parts of the ritual sphere, the contrast between these two types of specialists appears much reduced: Thus, some of the basic assumptions underlying the therapeutic exorcism rituals of the Tamang lama and bombo shamans are quite similar (Steinmann 1997; see also Balikci 2002). A myth found in various forms throughout Tibet and the Buddhist Himalayas recounts a contest of magical powers between a Buddhist master and a rival belonging to another religious tradition: a Bonpo in the standard Tibetan versions, a bombo shaman among the Tamang. The identity of the protagonists changes, but the different versions of the myth all convey similar patterns of (contested) hierarchy and tension, of complementarity and partial overlap between the Buddhist and other religious traditions.

Newar Buddhism

With the Newar case, we come to a very different sociocultural context. The Newar, the indigenous inhabitants of the Kathmandu valley, have had a sophisticated urban and agricultural civilization documented by more than 1,500 years of historical sources. The Newar count just over a million people; half live in the Kathmandu valley and half in outlying bazaar towns. The religion of the Newar, in which Hinduism and Buddhism are interwoven, is intimately linked with the particular caste structure of the society. The Newar caste organization is characterized by its double-headed hierarchy—a Hindu segment headed by a small caste of Brahmans and a Buddhist segment headed by a larger caste of Buddhist priests (consisting of two subgroups, the Vajracharya and Shakya). Hindu (shivamargi) or Buddhist (buddhamargi) affiliation is defined by the identity of one's household priest (a Brahman for the former, a Vajracharya for the latter). Other sometimes conflicting notions of religious affiliation are also present. A relatively clear-cut Hindu or Buddhist affiliation is to be found mainly among the higher castes. The Vajracharya and the Shakya can be said to constitute two caste subgroups. They are both patrilineal descent groups with a preference for endogamy, but they often intermarry with each other; and they have distinct surnames and, as we shall see, distinct socioreligious identities (Gellner 1992, ch. 2).

A striking feature of traditional Newar Buddhism is the absence of celibate monasticism and the hereditary recruitment of the religious specialists. The Vajracharya and Shakya men are married householder priests, but their religious identity contains elements of a monastic character. Thus, they are organized in religious communities based on institutions called baha or bahi (cf. *vihara* or "monastery") that in their architecture and in their ritual life show similarities with ancient Indic monasticism. Many Shakya until recently used surnames such as Shakyabhikshu (Buddhist monk), and Vajracharya and Shakya priests receive alms yearly in ritual contexts. Most notably, their caste initiation ritual is derived from the ancient Buddhist monastic ordination rite. During the ritual, Vajracharya and Shakya boys are in effect monks for four days. As stated previously, this is however, fundamentally, a hereditary priesthood. Only the sons of Vajracharya or Shakya fathers and mothers can undergo this caste initiation ritual, which functions as a rite of entry into the priesthood of their particular "monastic" community (baha or bahi). After their initiation into the caste, the Vajracharya and Shakya will be in charge of ritual duties in their religious community, such as the daily worship, on a rotating basis. They have thus only a part-time priestly activity (Locke 1989; Gellner 1992).

Priesthood is also very importantly differentiated within the caste: Only the Vajracharya may receive the consecration of a (vajra-)master (acha luyegu, acharya abhisheka), which entitles them, and them only, to perform certain tantric rituals such as fire oblations (homa) and to act as household priests for others. Thus the Vajracharya priests are at the same time monks (in local perceptions), householders, and tantric priests; this last status is at the top of the religious hierarchy of Newar Buddhism. It should be mentioned that the Newar tradition is based on ritual and worship (Gellner 1992; Lewis 2000), not on scholasticism, as is one strand of the Tibetan tradition.

In the tantric context of Newar Buddhism, women hold very particular roles. Tantric practices, apart from the more restricted ones like the fire oblations, are open to male and female members of all high Buddhist castes. To enter

A Newar woman bows toward the hand of the statue of a great Buddhist deity that has been carried in procession through Kathmandu on the occasion of a large religious festival. (Courtesy of Nicolas Sihlé)

into a given tantric practice, one must first obtain tantric initiation (diksha). This can be imparted only by a Vajracharya priest, himself duly initiated and married to a Vajracharya woman. During the ritual of tantric initiation, which is held in secret, the initiates are paired in couples (it may be a married couple, if husband and wife take the initiation together), which are led together through the sequence of consecrations that constitutes the initiation. In that process, the woman is occasionally given precedence over her male partner, the couple are made to hold hands at times (a symbolic substitute of the ritual intercourse prescribed by tantric texts), and at certain points the participating women often start shaking, possessed by tantric deities. The inversions, the acts carrying sexual symbolism, and the possession are all taboo in everyday life. Their practice in the context of the secret initiation ritual is an example of the transgressive features often associated with tantric traditions; these are, however, controlled and highly codified transgressions.

Another very particular female role in Newar Buddhism is that of the Kumari. This name refers primarily to a tantric goddess whose cult is generalized throughout the Newar society both among Hindus and Buddhists, although these may understand the deity to have differing identities. Kumari is also the name given to young girls of (generally high) Buddhist castes, found in the three ancient Newar capitals of Kathmandu, Patan, and Bhaktapur. These girls are considered as incarnations of the goddess and are worshiped as such, as long as they are prepubescent; they are then reintegrated into their human status and are replaced by younger girls. The so-called Royal Kumari, in particular, are at the center of large collective cults in the three former royal capitals. In Kathmandu, the capital of the present-day Nepalese state, one observes the striking situation in which the ethnically Parbatiya Hindu king of Nepal pays worship to the Royal Kumari, a young Newar girl of the Vajracharya and Shakya Buddhist caste, considered by Hindus as the high Hindu goddess Taleju or Durga, the main protector of the Hindu kingdom (Allen 1996).

In a situation characterized by the relatively strong dominance of Hinduism (the present-day state religion) over Newar Buddhism, the Kumari cult is one of the few cases of Buddhist preeminence. Another is the cult of Karunamaya-Matsyendranath, a local form of the great bodhisattva Avalokiteshvara that is associated, under very localized identities, with particular temples in the valley. These deities are at the center of major and highly popular chariot festivals, notably in Patan and Kathmandu, that attract the participation of virtually all Newars of the city and are directed by the Vajracharya and Shakya priests of the deity. These popular cults have been important factors in maintaining the status and income of the Newar Buddhist priests (Locke 1980; Gellner 1992, 87–88, 260; Owens 1989).

This status, and with it a centrally defining feature of Newar Buddhism, is now, however, increasingly undermined from all parts. The Vajracharya and

Shakya, as well as others, have come to doubt the legitimacy of a monastic status accessible only to sons of Vajracharya and Shakya fathers and mothers. The economic basis of the Vajracharya and Shakya's collective religious activity has also been severely reduced, notably in connection with land reform and the decline of the stipend (dakshina) that household priests receive for their ritual services. Most young Vajracharya and Shakya now look to other economic opportunities. In this context of a tradition perceived by many Newar Buddhists as in decline, a major challenge comes also from the recent development of a modernist Theravada tradition in Nepal (Locke 1989, 111–114; Gellner 1992, 166–167, 322).

Buddhist Modernism in Nepal

Buddhist modernism started spreading in Nepal, particularly among the Newar population, in the 1930s. This movement, which appeared first in Sri Lanka in the nineteenth century, is characterized by its emphasis on social activism, education, and meditation for all Buddhists; its rationalism (Buddhism is presented as a philosophy, not a religion); a nationalistic dimension; and its advocacy of a return to the "true" teaching of the Buddha (Gombrich and Obeyesekere 1988). The main founding figure of Sri Lankan Buddhist modernism, Anagarika Dharmapala (1864–1933), who established his Maha Bodhi Society in Calcutta in 1902, had a strong influence on the emergence of a Nepalese Theravada movement. The rise of this movement is linked both to Newar cultural resistance to the Hindu state (Leve 1999) and to the modernist, rationalist critique that some of the movement's adherents have directed at traditional Newar Buddhism, which is characterized in their eyes by its ritualism, the decline of Buddhist knowledge, and the absence of proper monasticism. Yet this critique, initially expressed in heated debates, was also perceived as an attack on traditional Newar values, which alienated part of the laity. The adherents of the movement then learned to place more emphasis on the values they shared with the laity, and some adaptations to Newar customs have taken place. Today, the movement is attracting increasing support from the Newar laity.

One may ask why the critics of Newar Buddhism turned to the Theravada tradition and not to Tibetan Buddhism, which had had contacts with the Kathmandu valley for centuries. Actually, the founding figures of the Nepalese Theravada movement first became monks in the Tibetan tradition. A Tibetan master known to the Newar as Kyangtse Lama came on pilgrimage to the valley in 1925 and preached to huge crowds. His sermons were translated in the Newar tongue (known as Nepal bhasha). The next year, five of his Newar followers, among which were three Shakya and one Shrestha (a caste generally perceived by the rulers of Nepal as Hindu), were ordained by another Tibetan master. This act and the subsequent going on alms rounds by the monks led to their expulsion from the country on charges of causing communal disturbances. In India, they met with a Shakya disciple of Dharmapala, an activist working for a modernist revival of Buddhism in Nepal and for the use of Nepal bhasha and, more generally, Newar cultural and linguistic nationalism. Ultimately the Shrestha monk, Mahapragya, was converted to Theravada Buddhism. He studied in Burma and then returned to Nepal. Two of his disciples, Amritananda and Pragyananda, became highly influential figures of the new Theravada movement, which started obtaining some official legitimacy only in the 1940s. Mahapragya's ultimate choice of the Theravada tradition over the Tibetan tradition in which he was first ordained was probably linked primarily to linguistic and pragmatic reasons. The Pali language of the Theravada texts was close to Nepali, and translations in Hindi and English were readily available through the Maha Bodhi Society, whereas learning Tibetan and obtaining the texts of the Tibetan tradition were substantial obstacles. Other reasons may have included the wider role available for the laity or the greater simplicity of Theravada Buddhism as compared with the complex ritualism of both the Tibetan and the Newar traditions. Modernist arguments per se may have not been determinant at that moment, although they definitely became influential later in attracting lay support (Gellner 2002).

Today, Nepalese Theravada monks and nuns, including novices, number approximately 300, a third of whom are currently abroad (in Thailand, Burma, Sri Lanka, and so on) mostly for study purposes. The movement was initially exclusively Newar, but it is slowly expanding to include other ethnic groups; only three-fourths of the novices are currently still Newar. Among the Newar, the movement has recruited primarily from the Buddhist castes, particularly from the Shakya and Uday castes, which are more open to alternative Buddhist traditions than the Vajracharya. There are today approximately 100 Theravada vihara (monasteries and nunneries), half of which are located outside of the Kathmandu valley. Only two vihara at this point possess a sima enclosure within which full ordinations can take place, and institutions of monastic learning are still lacking. The Nepalese Theravada tradition is therefore still dependent on (and enriched by) its links with the outside.

Although the movement has been relatively successful in finding lay support, monkhood is experienced as a life of restrictions, and many monks ultimately disrobe. Males of upper castes are more attracted by the possibilities of secular education that are offered to them; the bulk of the new Theravada monks are young men of lower socioeconomic levels, often from the Newar bazaar towns outside of the Kathmandu valley. Nunhood however is experienced as a life of lesser restriction, and disrobing is rare. Many nuns are from higher castes, and some of them even have higher university degrees. They engage in many health and education programs (LeVine 2002).

Is a specifically Nepalese form of Theravada Buddhism emerging? This tradition is probably still in its formative stage, but a few elements may be suggested. It appears from the data summarized previously that the context of Newar caste identities conditions the nature of monastic recruitment. The practice of going on alms rounds is sometimes problematic, due to the purity concerns of supporters belonging to higher castes. On the whole, the Nepalese Theravada movement has adopted a modernist, rationalist stance, but it also provides ritual services where requested, for instance the chanting of paritta, sections of canonical text that are recited for apotropaic purposes. These can be performed in connection with lifecycle rites, in cases of illness or death, on birthdays, and so on. In response to lay requests, a Buddhist marriage ceremony has been devised. In line partly with traditional Vajracharya and Shakya caste initiation rituals, boys but also men have been able to undergo temporary novicehood or monkhood at a Theravada vihara for a few days or for the entire summer rain retreat (Kloppenborg 1977, 312, 315). This is in a way quite reminiscent of traditions in southeast Asia, where monkhood is often a social rite of passage. The traditional Newar lifecycle rites constitute a domain within Newar religion that, generally speaking, shows a very strong Hindu influence and a substantial degree of continuity with non-Newar Hindu practices. Now, virtually all of these rites (or newly invented equivalents thereof) can be performed in Theravada vihara. Today, approximately one boy out of ten undergoes his puberty initiation ritual in a Theravada vihara, but virtually all Buddhist (and even some Hindu) girls are sent to a nunnery for their prepuberty initiation rite (Gellner and LeVine 2005). In a social context marked by strong gender inequalities, a specifically Newar or Nepalese version of Theravada Buddhism is emerging, marked somewhat paradoxically by a certain preeminence of the nuns.

References

Allen, Michael R. 1996 (1975). *The Cult of Kumari: Virgin Worship in Nepal.* 3rd rev. ed. Kathmandu, Nepal: Institute of Nepalese and Asian Studies, Tribhuvan University Press.

Aziz, Barbara Nimri. 1978. *Tibetan Frontier Families: Reflections of Three Generations from D'ing-ri.* New Delhi: Vikas.

Balikci, Anna. 2002. *Buddhism and Shamanism in Village Sikkim.* PhD dissertation, School of Oriental and African Studies, University of London.

Barnett, Robbie. 1994. Symbols and Protest: The Iconography of Demonstrations in Tibet, 1987–1990. In *Resistance and Reform in Tibet,* ed. R. Barnett, 238–258. London: Hurst.

Berglie, Per-Arne. 1976. Preliminary Remarks on Some Tibetan "Spirit-Mediums" in Nepal. *Kailash, a Journal of Himalayan Studies* 4(1):87–108.

Beyer, Stephan. 1973. *The Cult of Tara: Magic and Ritual in Tibet.* Berkeley: University of California Press.

Bjerken, Zeff. 2004. Exorcising the Illusion of Bon "Shamans": A Critical Genealogy of Shamanism in Tibetan Religions. *Revue d'Etudes Tibétaines* 6:4–59.

Blondeau, Anne-Marie, and Ernst Steinkellner, eds. 1996. *Reflections of the Mountain: Essays on the History and Social Meaning of the Mountain Cult in Tibet and the Himalayas.* Vienna: Verlag der Österreichischen Akademie der Wissenschaften.

Brauen, Martin. 1980. *Feste in Ladakh.* Graz, Austria: Akademische Druck-u. Verlagsanstalt.

Cassinelli, C. W., and Robert B. Ekvall. 1969. *A Tibetan Principality: The Political System of Sa-sKya.* Ithaca, NY: Cornell University Press.

Dreyfus, Georges B. J. 1998. The Shuk-den Affair: History and Nature of a Quarrel. *Journal of the International Association of Buddhist Studies* 21(2):227–270.

———. 2003. *The Sound of Two Hands Clapping: The Education of a Tibetan Buddhist Monk.* Berkeley: University of California Press.

Epstein, Lawrence, and Peng Wenbin. 1998. Ritual, Ethnicity, and Generational Identity. In *Buddhism in Contemporary Tibet: Religious Revival and Cultural Identity,* ed. Melvyn C. Goldstein and Matthew T. Kapstein, 120–138. Berkeley: University of California Press.

Fisher, William F. 2001. *Fluid Boundaries: Forming and Transforming Identity in Nepal.* New York: Columbia University Press.

Fürer-Haimendorf, Christoph von. 1964. *The Sherpas of Nepal: Buddhist Highlanders.* London: John Murray.

Gellner, David N. 1992. *Monk, Householder and Tantric Priest: Newar Buddhism and Its Hierarchy of Ritual.* Cambridge, UK: Cambridge University Press.

———. 2002. Theravada Revivalism in Nepal: Some Reflections on the Interpretation of the Early Years. *Studies in Nepali History and Society* 7(2):215–237.

Gellner, David N., and Sarah E. LeVine. 2005. All in the Family: Money, Kinship, and Theravada Monasticism in Nepal. Paper presented at international workshop *Monastic Life in the Mirror of Kinship,* Univ. Paris X Nanterre, Feb. 2–3.

Germano, David. 1998. Re-membering the Dismembered Body of Tibet: Contemporary Tibetan Visionary Movements in the People's Republic of China. In *Buddhism in Contemporary Tibet: Religious Revival and Cultural Identity,* ed. Melvyn C. Goldstein and Matthew T. Kapstein, 53–94. Berkeley: University of California Press.

Goldstein, Melvyn C. 1973. The Circulation of Estates in Tibet: Reincarnation, Land and Politics. *Journal of Asian Studies* 32(3):445–455.

———. 1978. Ethnogenesis and Resource Competition among Tibetan Refugees in South India: A New Face to the Indo-Tibetan Interface. In *Himalayan Anthropology: The Indo-Tibetan Interface,* ed. J. F. Fisher, 395–420. The Hague, Paris: Mouton.

———. 1998. The Revival of Monastic Life in Drepung Monastery. In *Buddhism in Contemporary Tibet: Religious Revival and Cultural Identity,* ed. Melvyn C. Goldstein and Matthew T. Kapstein, 15–52. Berkeley: University of California Press.

Goldstein, Melvyn C., and Matthew T. Kapstein, eds. 1998. *Buddhism in Contemporary Tibet: Religious Revival and Cultural Identity.* Berkeley: University of California Press.

Gombrich, Richard F., and Gananath Obeyesekere. 1988. *Buddhism Transformed: Religious Change in Sri Lanka.* Princeton, NJ: Princeton University Press.

Gyatso, Janet B. 1987. Down with the Demoness: Reflections on a Feminine Ground in Tibet. *Tibet Journal* 12(4):38–53.

Havnevik, Hanna. 1989. *Tibetan Buddhist Nuns: History, Cultural Norms and Social Reality.* Oslo: Norwegian University Press.

Höfer, András. 1997. *Tamang Ritual Texts II: Ethnographic Studies in the Oral Tradition and Folk-Religion of an Ethnic Minority in Nepal.* Stuttgart: Franz Steiner Verlag.

Holmberg, David H. 1996 [1989]. *Order in Paradox: Myth, Ritual, and Exchange among Nepal's Tamang.* 2nd ed. Delhi: Motilal Banarsidass.

Huber, Toni. 1999. *The Cult of Pure Crystal Mountain: Popular Pilgrimage and Visionary Landscape in Southeast Tibet.* New York: Oxford University Press.

Kapstein, Matthew T. 1998. Concluding Reflections. In *Buddhism in Contemporary Tibet: Religious Revival and Cultural Identity,* ed. Melvyn C. Goldstein and Matthew T. Kapstein, 139–149. Berkeley: University of California Press.

———. 2002. The Tulku's Miserable Lot: Critical Voices from Eastern Tibet. In *Amdo Tibetans in Transition: Society and Culture in the Post-Mao Era,* ed. T. Huber, 99–111. Leiden: Brill.

Karmay, Samten G. 1998. *The Arrow and the Spindle: Studies in History, Myth, Rituals and Beliefs in Tibet.* Kathmandu, Nepal: Mandala Book Point.

Kloppenborg, Ria. 1977. Theravada Buddhism in Nepal. *Kailash, a Journal of Himalayan Studies* 5(4):301–321.

Kvaerne, Per. 2000. The Study of Bon in the West: Past, Present, and Future. In *New Horizons in Bon Studies,* ed. S. G. Karmay and Y. Nagano, 7–20. Osaka, Japan: National Museum of Ethnology.

Leve, Lauren G. 1999. *Contested Nation/Buddhist Innovation: Politics, Piety, and Personhood in Theravada Buddhism in Nepal.* PhD dissertation, Princeton University.

LeVine, Sarah E. 2002. *The Evolution of the Theravada Nuns' Order of Nepal.* PhD dissertation, Harvard University.

Lewis, Todd T. 2000. *Popular Buddhist Texts from Nepal: Narratives and Rituals of Newar Buddhism.* Albany: State University of New York Press.

Locke, John K. 1980. *Karunamaya: The Cult of Avalokitesvara-Matsyendranath in the Valley of Nepal.* Kathmandu, Nepal: Sahayogi Prakashan.

———. 1989. The Unique Features of Newar Buddhism. In *The Buddhist Heritage,* ed. T. Skorupski, 71–116. Tring, UK: Institute of Buddhist Studies.

Lopez, Donald S., Jr. 1997. Introduction. In *Religions of Tibet in Practice,* ed. D. S. Lopez Jr., 3–36. Princeton, NJ: Princeton University Press.

———. 1998. *Prisoners of Shangri-La: Tibetan Buddhism and the West.* Chicago: University of Chicago Press.

———. 2002. Introduction. In *A Modern Buddhist Bible: Essential Readings from East and West,* ed. D. S. Lopez Jr., vii-xli. Boston: Beacon Press.

Macdonald, Alexander W., ed. 1997. *Mandala and Landscape.* New Delhi: D. K. Printworld.

Makley, Charlene E. 2003. Gendered Boundaries in Motion: Space and Identity on the Sino-Tibetan Frontier. *American Ethnologist* 30(4):597–619.

Mills, Martin A. 2003. *Identity, Ritual and State in Tibetan Buddhism: The Foundations of Authority in Gelukpa Monasticism*. Richmond, UK: Curzon Press.

Moran, Peter K. 2004. *Buddhism Observed: Travelers, Exiles and Tibetan Dharma in Kathmandu*. Richmond, UK: Curzon Press.

Mumford, Stan Royal. 1989. *Himalayan Dialogue: Tibetan Lamas and Gurung Shamans in Nepal*. Madison: University of Wisconsin Press.

Nebesky-Wojkowitz, René von. 1956. *Oracles and Demons of Tibet: The Cult and Iconography of the Protective Deities of Tibet*. The Hague: Mouton.

Ortner, Sherry B. 1995. The Case of the Disappearing Shamans, or No Individualism, No Relationalism. *Ethos* 23(3):355–390.

Owens, Bruce M. 1989. *The Politics of Divinity in the Kathmandu Valley: The Festival of Bungadya/Rato Matsyendranath*. PhD dissertation, Columbia University.

Pignède, Bernard. 1993 [1966]. The Gurungs: A Himalayan Population of Nepal. Kathmandu: Ratna Pustak Bhandar

Pommaret, Françoise, ed. 2003. *Lhasa in the Seventeenth Century: The Capital of the Dalai-Lamas*. Leiden: Brill.

Ramble, Charles. 1990. How Buddhist Are Buddhist Communities? The Construction of Tradition in Two Lamaist Villages. *Journal of the Anthropological Society of Oxford* 21(2):185–197.

———. 1993. A Ritual of Political Unity in an Old Nepalese Kingdom: Some Preliminary Observations. *Ancient Nepal* 130–133:49–58.

Ray, Reginald A. 1995. Tibetan Buddhism as Shamanism? *Journal of Religion* 75(1):90–101.

———. 2001. *Secret of the Vajra World: The Tantric Buddhism of Tibet*. Boston: Shambhala Publications.

Richardson, Hugh E. 1993. *Ceremonies of the Lhasa Year*. London: Serindia.

Samuel, Geoffrey. 1993. *Civilized Shamans: Buddhism in Tibetan Societies*. Washington DC: Smithsonian Institution Press.

Schrempf, Mona. 2001. *Ethnisch-religiöse Revitalisierung und rituelle Praxis in einer osttibetischen Gemeinschaft im heutigen China*. PhD dissertation, Institute for Ethnology, Free University of Berlin.

Schwartz, Ronald D. 1994. Buddhism, Nationalist Protest, and the State in Tibet. In *Tibetan Studies*, ed. P. Kvaerne, 728–738. Oslo, Norway: Institute for Comparative Research in Human Culture.

Sihlé, Nicolas. 2001. *Les tantristes tibétains (ngakpa), religieux dans le monde, religieux du rituel terrible : Etude de Ch'ongkor, communauté villageoise de tantristes du Baragaon (nord du Népal)*. PhD dissertation, Paris X Nanterre.

———. 2002. Lhachö [Lha mchod] and Hrinän [Sri gnon]: The Structure and Diachrony of a Pair of Rituals (Baragaon, Northern Nepal). In *Religion and Secular Culture in Tibet: Tibetan Studies II*, ed. H. Blezer, 185–206. Leiden: Brill.

Smith, E. Gene. 1970. Introduction. In *Kongtrul's Encyclopaedia of Indo-Tibetan Culture*, parts 1–3, ed. Lokesh Chandra, 1–87. New Delhi: International Academy of Indian Culture.

Snellgrove, David L. 1987. *Indo-Tibetan Buddhism: Indian Buddhists and Their Tibetan Successors*. Boston: Shambhala Publications.

Snellgrove, David L., and Hugh E. Richardson. 1986. *A Cultural History of Tibet*. Boston: Shambhala Publications.

Stein, Rolf A. 1972 (1962). *Tibetan Civilisation*. Stanford, CA: Stanford University Press.

———. 1988. Tibetica Antiqua V: La religion indigène et les Bon po dans les manuscrits de Touen-Houang. *Bulletin de l'Ecole Française d'Extrême-Orient* 77:27–55.

Steinmann, Brigitte. 1997. Shamans and Lamas Exorcise Madness. In *Les habitants du toit du monde: Etudes recueillies en hommage à Alexander W. Macdonald*, ed. S. G. Karmay and P. Sagant, 419–440. Nanterre: Société d'Ethnologie.

Tambiah, Stanley Jeyaraja. 1984. *The Buddhist Saints of the Forest and the Cult of Amulets: A Study in Charisma, Hagiography, Sectarianism and Millenial Buddhism*. Cambridge, UK: Cambridge University Press.

Thondup Rinpoche, Tulku. 1986. *Hidden Teachings in Tibet: An Explanation of the Terma Tradition of the Nyingma School of Tibet*. London: Wisdom.

Tucci, Giuseppe. 1980 (1970). *The Religions of Tibet*. London: Routledge and Kegan Paul.

Vinding, Michael. 1998. *The Thakali: A Himalayan Ethnography*. London: Serindia.

Watkins, Joanne C. 1996. *Spirited Women: Gender, Religion and Cultural Identity in the Nepal Himalaya*. New York: Columbia University Press.

Chapter Ten

Buddhism in the West
Transplantation and Innovation

ELLEN GOLDBERG

Over the past several decades, there has been an explosion in the popularity of Buddhism in the West. This is most obvious in North America and Europe, where literally thousands of centers and groups are appearing and having an impact on local mainstream culture. Buddhist meditation centers, social justice movements, eco-Buddhists, Buddhist Internet sites, and university courses in Buddhism are flourishing. There can be no doubt that Buddhism has arrived and is here to stay, although not without significant adaptations made to its Western contexts.

The processes through which Buddhism has been introduced and established in North America and Europe may be understood through the application of Martin Baumann's strategic theory of "transplantation." This term signifies a complex interplay between reinterpretation—as a result of events such as modernization and globalization—and tradition. Baumann outlines a useful five-stage adaptation process that includes contact, confrontation and conflict, ambiguity and adaptation, recoupment (reorientation), and innovative self-development to describe the Western adaptation of Buddhism. In this essay, Baumann's model will be extended for a revised analysis of Buddhism in the West. Since recoupment and innovative self-development are overlapping categories, they will be replaced by the single phrase "reorientation and innovation." For each of these stages in the adaptation process, this essay will show how specific schools, teachers, and teachings of Dharma articulate more thoroughly the dynamics involved in the transplantation of Buddhism to the West. The stages, one might add, do not necessarily proceed sequentially or chronologically. Instead, the categories are fluid and the actual transplantation process is variable and complex.

Furthermore, since many features of Asian traditions are discussed in the preceding essays, this essay focuses primarily on non-Asians drawn by the proselytizing impulse within Buddhism, rather than on ethnic Buddhist traditions that were transplanted to the West through Asian immigration beginning in the late eighteenth and early nineteenth centuries. It is evident, however, that in the West there has been a bifurcation of the tradition into two distinct Buddhisms that, according to Charles S. Prebish, may be broadly designated as (1) ethnic Asian–North American Buddhism (sometimes referred to as immigrant, hereditary, or baggage Buddhism) and (2) non-Asian, North American convert Buddhism (sometimes referred to as elite, white, or neo Buddhism). (See, for example, Prebish 1979, 1999; Nattier 1998.) Baumann questions the relevance of this binary classification for consecutive generations and renames the two types of Buddhism "traditionalist" and "modernist," respectively (he has also used the categories canonical, traditional, modern, and global). He argues that by renaming them, we avoid placing undue emphasis on "ethnic ancestry, skin color difference, and citizenship" (Baumann 2002, 59; see also Baumann 2001).

Still another option is to refer to so-called Asian immigrant Buddhism as the Buddhist diaspora community. This reference parallels the transplantation of other diaspora communities such as Judaism and Hinduism, and it also resists the implications associated with Enlightenment and Protestant mentality that engaging in religious ritual somehow signals traditionalism, whereas the practice of meditation or social engagement is distinctly modern. It is the latter convert tradition, or what Victor Hori (1994) has fittingly called "sweet and sour Buddhism," that will be addressed as the primary theme in this essay. A secondary organizing theme will revolve around the Buddhist diaspora community. In both traditions, it is increasingly clear that modernity and globalization have become the dominant paradigms necessary to understand the change and development that have taken place in the spread of Buddhism to the West.

The Contact Stage

The first stage in the transplantation process involves contact between the foreign and host cultures through, for example, the media of Buddhist teachers and texts. The 1893 meeting of the World's Parliament of Religions in Chicago is often cited as the date of first contact between Buddhism and North American culture. However, this moment of contact can be seen as the natural culmination of a process of Orientalism that had begun much earlier. For instance, Indian themes deriving from the pioneer writings of Orientalists such as William Jones, Charles Wilkins, and Brian Houghton Hodgson are evident as early as the 1830s and 1840s in the literary works of the American transcendentalists such as Henry David Thoreau (1817–1862), Ralph Waldo Emerson

(1803–1892), and Walt Whitman (1819–1892). Emerson called Whitman "an American Buddha" after reading the publication of *Leaves of Grass* in 1855, and Rick Fields (1981, 64–65) said Thoreau was "like a priest of Buddha." The popularity of their writings made Buddhism a household word nearly 50 years before the arrival of the first Buddhist teachers at the World's Parliament of Religions in 1893 (Fields 1981, 69). What is significant here in the North American context is that Orientalism is already present in the self-identification of Buddhism in the West. Whitman, for example, may have used Buddhist themes in *Leaves of Grass*, but the origins and antecedents of these themes require further analysis. In other words, North American contact with Buddhism is derived first from European sources.

These sources of Eastern wisdom are a product of Orientalism and colonial history in the sense that they are text-based. As Edward Said (1994, 52) puts it, "The Orient studied was a textual universe by and large; the impact of the Orient was made through books and manuscripts." According to Said, Western scholars made "the Orient" more of a "real thing" through essentializing it in texts. These textualized Oriental cultures appeared in ways that Western authors thought they should, and thus they imposed complete transformations on Asian cultures in Western writings beginning in the eighteenth century. Written accounts of the Orient made it present and visible to Western readers. As a result, the various representations of Oriental cultures depended more on the imagination of Western authors than on actual life in so-called Oriental lands (Said 1994, 21–22).

Initially, then, contact between Buddhism and the West took place through a process of translation and retranslation of texts, as seen in, for instance, the scholarly works of French philologist Eugene Burnouf (1801–1852), British scholar T. W. Rhys Davids (1843–1922), Hermann Oldenberg (1854–1920), Émile Senart (1847–1928), Max Müller (1823–1900), Louis de La Vallée Poussin (1869–1938), Étienne Lamotte (1903–1983), the literary contributions of Sir Edwin Arnold (1832–1904), the philosophical writings of Arthur Schopenhauer (1788–1860), and the Romantic work of German Sanskritist Friedrich Schlegel (1772–1829). The representation of the East through translated texts is seen as authoritative or the "real thing," and as such it represents a formidable resistance to lived reality (Said 1994, 116; Lopez 1995, 4, 7). This tendency is permeated by a pervasive neglect and indifference among early Buddhologists to texts written in Asian vernaculars (living languages), because lived reality challenges the West's cultural hegemony over its subject (Jong 1998; Hallisey 1995). The Orientalist reifies the category "Buddhism" as an object dislocated from modern life. Living Buddhism disrupts this reified image, but it is the reified image that appeals to the West. Consequently, converts to Buddhism in the West did not contact Buddhism as such, nor did they contact Buddhism via members of the Asian Buddhist immigrant communities who arrived in North America beginning in the 1800s. Instead, they encountered Buddhism as represented in and controlled by these European textual sources.

The same is true of the first Buddhist teachers and missionaries who arrived in Chicago, Illinois, in 1893 for the World's Parliament of Religions. Buddhist teachers such as Soyen Shaku, a Rinzai Zen master from Japan, and Anagarika Dharmapala (born Don David Hewavitarne, 1864–1933), a Sinhalese Christian convert who reverted to Buddhism, came from Asia to propagate a repackaged form of Buddhism to North Americans. To this end, Shaku brought thousands of Buddhist works translated into English, thereby making Buddhist texts readily available. Three years later, Shaku sent D. T. Suzuki, his most promising disciple, to North America to promote Rinzai Zen Buddhism. Suzuki later became one of the most significant figures in the emerging North American Zen presence.

This same Orientalized ideology can be observed in the work of Dharmapala. Charles Hallisey points out that Edward Said wrongly assumes that Orientalism is embedded only in European culture. Orientalism, in Hallisey's view, may also be rooted in the native culture's self-representation (Hallisey 1995, 49–50). Revival and reform initiatives inspired in part by Orientalism surfaced in the indigenous Asian cultures in protest of hundreds of years of colonial domination. This can be seen in the nineteenth century's so-called Protestant Buddhism movement in Sri Lanka. Dharmapala and Henry Steel Olcott (1832–1907), two influential spokespersons for Protestant Buddhism, became influential propagators of modern Buddhism in the West (Obeyesekere 1972; Gombrich and Obeyesekere 1988; Prothero 1996). Their homespun revivalist notions of Theravada Buddhism, which emphasized meditation, and the deritualized, scientific, and rational origins of their religion, provide evidence not only of initial contact between Buddhism and the West but a preference for a particular kind of modern Buddhism.

Socially engaged Buddhism, which is an emergent discourse in Asia and the West today, is a derivative form of the modern nineteenth-century revivalist Buddhism of Dharmapala and Olcott. This movement has an intricate history. In early twentieth-century Sri Lanka, it served as a protest movement against— as well as a synthesis of—the Christian and colonial presence in this country. And it functioned as a precursor to the more contemporary, global formulations of Buddhist social engagement. In India, the Dalit social protest movement against untouchability under the leadership of Bimrao Ramji Ambedkar (1891–1956) is another distinct example of socially engaged Buddhism in modern Asia (Ambedkar 1989; Doyle 2003). Other Asian Buddhist reformers and political activists such as A. T. Ariyaratne (1931–) in Sri Lanka; Thich Nhat Hanh (1926–), living in exile in France from his native Vietnam; Aung San Suu Kyi (1945–) in Myanmar (formerly Burma); and Tenzin Gyatso (1935–), the

Participating in the "Mind and Life" discussion series, His Holiness the Fourteenth Dalai Lama operates a pipette containing mouse DNA in the laboratory at MIT's Genome Institute in Cambridge, Massachusetts, in 2003. The exiled spiritual leader of Tibet frequently takes part in such interdisciplinary conferences to share his expertise in Buddhist psychology with eminent Western scientists. (Jim Bourg/Corbis)

Fourteenth Dalai Lama, currently living in exile in India from his native Tibet, are examples of reformers and peace activists who seek within their own particular schools of Buddhism the impetus for revitalization, change, and liberation. The popular form of Engaged Buddhism that is characteristic of and necessary to the reorientation of Buddhism in the West is certainly not exclusive to the West. Both Asian and Western expressions of Engaged Buddhism consider their versions of applied Buddhism to be consistent with the original Dharma.

Likewise, both Asian and non-Asian forms of Engaged Buddhism are text-based, and their tendency toward scientific and rational thought proceeds from this dependency on texts as in the European Protestant world from which it emerged. Dharmapala and Olcott composed *Gihi Vinaya* and *Buddhist Catechism* based on Christian missionary manuals. The latter has been published in 40 editions in 20 languages since it was first published in 1881, and it is still in use in Buddhist communities. This is equally true of B. R. Ambedkar and his *The Buddha and His Dhamma,* originally published in 1957. As Christopher Queen writes, "Each sentence is versified, and the style imitates that of the English Orientalist T. W. Rhys Davids, whose renderings of the Pali scriptures were featured in Max Müller's *Sacred Books of the East*" (Queen 1996, 26). Specifically, however, this Protestant and Enlightenment influence can be most clearly seen in the struggle for social justice and reform, the emphasis on science and rational epistemology, the repudiation of ritual and traditionalism, and the revival and redefinition of classical religion—for example, privileging ethics and meditation. This has had widespread implications, for as Christopher Queen (1996, 30) says, "The Buddhism that attracted Americans was not one of pessimism, resignation, and retreat, but a vigorous religion of optimism and activism."

The story of D. T. Suzuki (1870–1966) and his importance to the contact stage of Zen Buddhism in the West and a whole generation of North Americans referred to as the Beat Generation is discussed in numerous studies (McMahan 2002; Sharf 1995; Batchelor 1994; Tweed 1992; Fields 1981). In general, Suzuki is another example of a "curator of the Buddha" to the West whose teachings reflect an Orientalized understanding of Buddhist Dharma (see Lopez 1995). On his arrival in the United States in 1897, Suzuki resided with Paul Carus (1852–1919) in La Salle, Illinois. Carus, who was editor of *The Open Court* and *The Monist* (two journals dedicated to the unification of religion and science), was a significant figure in Suzuki's life and deeply influenced his understanding of Buddhism. Carus's form of Buddhism—clearly derived from the Orientalist impulse—was apologetic, positivistic, and scientific. Moreover, he saw the Buddha himself as the "first positivist, the first humanitarian, the first radical freethinker, the first iconoclast, and the first prophet of the Religion of Science" (cited in Sharf 1995, 118). Carus's Buddhism resounds with Protestant overtones, the likes of which are reflected in the title of his 1894 text, *Gospel of the Buddha.*

His hands held in the gesture of a Buddhist mudra while grasping Hindu prayer beads, Beat Generation poet Allen Ginsberg performs a Sanskrit chant on July 24, 1967, in Hyde Park, London, during the "summer of love." Ginsberg was later arrested for allegedly "violating park rules." Ginsberg became a student of Chogyam Trungpa Rinpoche in the 1970s, leading some from the hippie movement toward a more serious approach to spirituality. (Bettman/Corbis)

The influence of Carus on Suzuki was substantial. Suzuki translated *Gospel of the Buddha* into Japanese, and his work with Carus helped to transform Suzuki's understanding of Buddhism and his presentation of the tradition to the West. Robert Sharf asserts that the strategy Suzuki used to present Zen Buddhism to lay audiences in Japan and the West was shaped as much by his exposure to Western currents of thought while a philosophy student in Tokyo and as an assistant to Carus as by his necessarily limited involvement in Zen training (Sharf 1995, 121). As a prolific writer, lecturer, and translator, Suzuki was a major figure in (if not singularly responsible for) the initial Zen explosion in North America and, to a lesser extent, in Europe. The list of those he influenced includes Alan Watts, Erich Fromm, Philip Kapleau, John Cage, Thomas Merton, Carl Jung, Jack Kerouac, Allen Ginsberg, and Gary Snyder, to name just a few ("sympathizers" and "night-stand Buddhists" according to Tweed [2002]). Through Suzuki and the writers of the Beat Generation, Zen became a popularized form of Buddhism that had been made accessible to non-Asian Westerners.

This Buddhism that the West encountered and inherited from Suzuki was thoroughly Orientalist and modernized. For instance, Suzuki's Buddhism harbors characteristics of mystification. That is, he valorizes pure, nondual, direct experience over ritual, theology, and doctrine. His generalization of Buddhism can be found in a kind of perennialist or universalist approach to Buddhism and world religions. Finally, Suzuki's preoccupation with the categories "Orient" and "Occident" finds expression in a reversal of the polarization of geopolitical designations. Suzuki, like other modern Asian Orientalists such as Indian poet Rabindranath Tagore (1861–1941), contrasts the essential spirituality of Asia with Occidental materialism. These structures of Orientalism, as defined by Said, came to typify the bohemianism of early North American Zen Buddhism (or Beat Zen) in the 1950s and early 1960s. By being depicted as exotic, disembodied, transcendental, ahistorical, and essentially mystical, Buddhism was falsely characterized; and this misrepresentation lingers still in some Western forms of Zen Buddhism (McMahan 2002, 218, 221).

Although it is difficult to pinpoint the precise moment of contact between Buddhism and the West, it is nevertheless certain that the contact was initially textual, followed by the teachings of eminent Buddhist individuals representing various forms of Asian Orientalist Buddhism. In this way, the Buddhism with which the West had initial contact was an already modernized and reconstituted form of Buddhism tailor-made for its Western audience.

The Confrontation and Conflict Stage

Martin Baumann (1994, 40) postulates that, during the adaptive stage of conflict and confrontation, deficiencies in the host culture become evident because of the presence of the foreign culture. In turn, the foreign culture, because of its otherness, proposes strategic alternatives to solve these cultural deficiencies. In addition, according to Baumann, the host culture must be tolerant of and willing to admit the foreign culture into its domain. Baumann's model overlooks, however, the hybrid structures already present in the foreign culture's self-representations. It is these very elements in Asian Buddhist cultures that offer a corrective to the deficiencies in the Western host cultures, for they are precisely what the Western imagination is nostalgically longing for in Buddhism.

Thomas Tweed, who examines the emergence of Victorian-era Buddhism, found that Western convert Buddhists are attracted to issues and practices that posed a distinct alternative to mainstream Christian values, such as theism and the failure of Christianity in the modern West to respond to social, political, and ideological changes. The image of Buddhism, for instance, as exotic and mystical was a panacea for the prevailing social ills in the West or host culture. To illustrate, in the 1960s there was enormous social and political protest in the United States and, to a lesser extent, in Canada, because of the war in Vietnam. Racial and political unrest swept major American urban centers. The foreign idea of ahimsa or nonviolence, the then-exotic practice of vegetarianism, the possibility of personal enlightenment, and so forth, attracted many non-Asian North Americans and helped Buddhism spread throughout the West. To those who were part of a decade of widespread experimentation with psychedelics, Buddhism also offered the practice of meditation as a viable alternative to drug use. In addition, this pacified form of Buddhism seemed to provide options to the militaristic and aggressive sociopolitical problems that the United States faced, problems that many Christian traditions failed to address. In response to the social dissonance in the United States, courses in Buddhism were developed at North American universities such as the University of Wisconsin, Harvard University, Columbia University, and the University of Toronto, and books on Buddhism became quite popular and fashionable. It is by virtue of its exotic otherness, expressed primarily in the highly attractive practice of meditation, that Buddhism offered a romanticized emancipatory vision of social reform to increasing numbers of non-Asian Westerners.

This can also be seen in the West's attitude toward Tibetan Buddhism. Donald S. Lopez Jr. (1995, 10) writes, "Tibet is seen as the cure for an ever-ailing Western civilization, a tonic to restore its spirit. And since the Tibetan diaspora that began in 1959 there seems an especial urgency about taking this cure, before it is lost forever." In 1959, approximately 70,000 Tibetan refugees (some estimates are as high as 100,000) followed the Dalai Lama into exile after the People's Republic of China asserted its claim to Tibet. Most of the exiled Tibetans settled in India on land donated by the Indian government specifically for the Tibetan refugees. Numerous problems, such as dramatic climate change, lack of food, and so forth, seriously threatened the survival of the Tibetan refugee community in India. The monasteries and the lineages of monks were in serious danger of extinction. In response to these critical conditions, countries such as Canada, England, and the United States offered the Tibetan Buddhists refuge. Shortly after the refugees' arrival, Tibetan Buddhist centers took root in many Western locales including North America, England, France, Germany, and the Netherlands.

Adaptation to the West represents not only the second phase of conflict and confrontation, as outlined by our transplantation model, but also a movement within Buddhist ideology itself away from a more Protestant reading to one that is decidedly exotic and less like what is typically found in the West. This preoccupation with the alien and exotic, as well as the mystical and timeless, is seen especially in Western forms of Tibetan Buddhism. For example, Robert Thurman's photographic exposé *Inside Tibetan Buddhism* (1995) shows non-Asian practitioners performing sacred Buddhist rituals, prostrating before Tibetan images, sitting in meditation, and making mandala offerings alongside Tibetan Buddhist practitioners and monks. It also documents in visual splendor the development of a distinctly Western Tibetan Buddhist Sangha composed of Tibetan monks and Western laypersons. Thus Thurman's photographic essay captures nicely the Western idealizations of and fascination with Tibetan Buddhist exotica. This can also been seen in popular Hollywood (also referred to as "Dalaiwood") films such as *Lost Horizon* (1933), *Little Buddha* (1995), *Seven Years in Tibet* (1997), and *Kundun* (1998). Even Dharamsala, the principal home of the Tibetan refugee community in India, holds an otherworldly allure for the traveling Western Buddhist. As Lopez explains, "Tibetan Buddhist culture has been portrayed as if it were itself another artifact of Shangri-La from an eternal classical age, set high in a Himalayan keep outside time and history" (Lopez 1994, 16). As such, Tibetan Buddhism in the West offers an irresistible, prepackaged form of New Age Orientalism ready for the spiritual marketplace and the Western consumer.

The Adaptation and Ambiguity Stage

The adaptation (also referred to as acculturation) of a foreign religion to another geocultural context is an intricate process. Ambiguity seems unavoidable in such instances. Baumann (1994, 41) explains that "for members of the host culture, it is only possible to interpret and understand symbols, rituals or ideas of the imported religious tradition on the basis of their own conceptions." Thus, the foreign culture borrows jargon and terminology from the host. This pattern is already familiar to Buddhism in its earlier adaptation to Asian countries outside its Indian birthplace such as Sri Lanka, China, Tibet, and so on. Buddhism in China, for example, looked to the indigenous religion of Taoism for adaptive terminology, while Buddhists in the West have turned, for example, to Christianity and the language of Western psychotherapies. Examples of this process can be seen in the adaptation of Buddhist teachings and practices to modernity. As stated earlier, many Buddhist countries during the late nineteenth and early twentieth centuries were transformed by colonialism, and, as a result, people found it necessary to remythologize their Buddhist heritage to fit in with the modern institutions and forms of knowledge imposed on them. In many countries, this revival of Buddhism based on its encounter with Christianity became a source of national pride and identity (Baumann 2001, 9). The founding of Buddhist schools, the renewed interest in and reliance on scriptures, the deritualization of Buddhist practice, and an emphasis on reason and science were just some of the ways that Buddhism was modernized and adapted. This, however, was only part of the inheritance of modern Buddhism.

Chinese and Japanese migrant workers who emigrated to the United States and Canada during the mid-1800s to pursue economic opportunity provide another look at how the process of adaptation owed much to Christianity. On arrival of the immigrants, temples were built and missionary priests were brought from China and Japan to North America to minister to the needs of the growing immigrant population. By 1921, there were 76 Japanese Jodo Shinshu (or True Pureland) temples in the United States alone and hundreds of "joss houses," or Chinese temples with some Buddhist component. These growing immigrant communities faced severe marginalization and racial discrimination. For example, they had to face anti-Asian legislation that made them ineligible to apply for citizenship; to struggle with segregation; and, in the case of thousands of Japanese Americans in 1941, to submit to being relocated to internment camps (Williams 2002). In response to this hostility, Japanese leaders urged their members to adapt to Christian North America. Temples became "churches" to appear less foreign. English become the primary language. Services and meetings were conducted at "Sunday schools," the community sat in pews, the ministers used pulpits, organs were purchased, hymns were written, and a Young Men's Buddhist Association (YMBA) was created to parallel the Young Men's Christian Association. In 1948, the Jodo Shinshu community officially changed its name from North American Buddhist Mission to Buddhist Churches of America (BCA) (Tanaka 2002, 5–6), and the Buddhist Churches of Canada (BCC). At the same time, many Japanese and Chinese immigrants converted to Christianity.

Asian Buddhist diaspora communities have also adapted to the West by augmenting the roles of women and the laity in their organizations as a symbol of increased democratization. For instance, the Toronto temple of the BCC currently employs the first female kaykyoshi (minister), and Tam Bao temple in Montreal installed a nun, Reverend Thich Pho Tinh, who administers, teaches meditation, and sits on the board of directors (Boisvert 2005). Nuns also serve as teachers, accountants, translators, and cooks (Tsomo 2002, 255). Janet McLellan (1999) reports that Thich Thien Nghi, head monk of the Vietnamese Zen temple Hoa Nghiem (Flower of Serenity) in Toronto, encourages the spiritual capacities of nuns in their community. Other examples that illustrate Asian Buddhism's adaptive strategies include electing a board of directors or board of governors; registering as a nonprofit organization; chanting and providing instruction in Western languages (e.g., Foguangshan's Hsi Lai temple in Los Angeles); installing Euro-American-born monks (e.g., BCC);

teaching meditation classes to laity; burning candles to mark periods of zazen (e.g., ABC Zen Center); government lobbying (e.g., the Tibetan community protesting against visiting Chinese government officials); endowing Buddhist studies chairs at universities (e.g., the Numata Center for Translation and Research); developing an evangelical spirit (e.g., Soka Gokkai); providing yoga, meditation classes, and Dharma camps for children; and emphasizing the compatibility between science and Buddhism (e.g., Mahabodhi Society of the United States of America).

At the same time, the forms of Buddhism practiced by Asian immigrants in Western countries typically balance a desire for assimilation with equally strong interests in maintaining the cultural traditions and identities of their homelands. It has been noted that Asian Buddhists in Western societies tend to see Buddhism as something to be preserved and passed along to younger generations rather than as a radical departure from societal and religious norms in the West (Seager 1999, 234–235). For some Asian Buddhist immigrants, temples offer important and comforting networks within which to reinforce one's cultural identity and establish ties with others in one's ethnic community. For second- and third-generation immigrants, the impetus to adapt to Western culture may decrease as the forces of increased immigration and multiculturalism lessen the need to assimilate into North American culture by abandoning one's native traditions or imitating Christian ones.

Nevertheless, Buddhist communities in the West have generally remained open to innovation. For example, some Buddhist teachers have used the language of Western psychotherapy to adapt Buddhism to the West. This is appropriate, since many of the teachings of Buddhism are psychological or even physiological—the five skandhas relating to cognition and perception, the six sense doors and six sense organs, the 75 mental states outlined in Abhidharma, and so on. The process of observing the mind (or states of mind) has long been deemed crucial to Buddhist practice. Teachers such as Chogyam Trungpa (1940–1987), who heavily influenced the image of Tibetan Buddhism in the West, understood the necessary role of psychology as a way to integrate his "crazy wisdom teachings" (Trungpa 1991). The Buddhist Vihara Society in Surrey, British Columbia, offers meditation alongside psychological counseling. The Dharma Vijaya Buddhist Vihara in Los Angeles also makes counseling formally available to the local Asian community. Other groups provide marital, refugee, and trauma counseling.

Not only do Asian Buddhist teachers make use of this adaptive mechanism, Western (convert) Buddhist teachers also rely on it as a way to communicate with their students. For instance, Jack Kornfield, cofounder of the enormously successful Insight Meditation Society in Barre, Massachusetts, and of Spirit Rock Center in Marin County, California, integrates his training as a monk in

Great Stupa of Dharmakaya at the Shambala Mountain Center, Red Feather Lakes, Colorado. (Julie Dunbar)

Burma under Mahasi Sayadaw (1904–1982) with his training as a clinical psychologist. As a lay teacher of vipassana meditation, Kornfield focuses on the practical needs of everyday life and insists that meditation without psychotherapy is often not enough to heal the wounds that many practitioners in the West confront. This style seems particularly well suited to lay students, who play a predominant role in Western schools of Buddhism. Buddhist philosophy has been adapted through the language of Western psychotherapy by many contemporary teachers and authors of Buddhism, such as Sangharakshita, Lama Surya Das, and Soygal Rinpoche, to name just a few.

Other strategic mechanisms in the third stage of adaptation available to Buddhism in the West include marketing, consumerism, and electronic media. The Snow Lion newsletter, for instance, sells Buddhist items such as an inflatable meditation cushion (zafu). Under the caption "Liberate your senses!" is a description of Khatsa—a threesome of Tibetan hot sauce, barbecue marinade, and salsa. The newsletter also advertises a peace mandala computer screen saver and a peace mandala jigsaw puzzle. Adaptation through consumerism and marketing can also be seen in the North American fascination with exotic practices such as tantra. The Snow Lion book catalogue offers a variety of texts written specifically with North Americans in mind including tantric manuals, biographies of yogis, and books on the ancient wisdom of dream yoga, Tibetan arts of love, and the secrets of immortality. Endorsements for the books from scholars of Buddhism such as José Cabezon and Jeffrey Hopkins are found throughout. The electronic and printed media in secular society has meant that, as Said has argued about modern Orientalism in general, information on Buddhism in the West is forced into more and more standardized molds and cultural stereotypes (Said 1994, 26). The marketing of familiar Buddhist stereotypes and images is the predictable result of using the known and familiar to understand the unknown and unfamiliar.

Buddhists in the West are using the avenues available in a secular Western democratic and capitalist society—e.g., Western psychotherapy, consumerism, the media, and Christianity—to adapt the tradition from its foreign contexts. As a result, these avenues tend to color how Buddhism is depicted in the West. But the adaptation of Buddhism is also having a profound influence on its host: the rising number of convert Buddhists, the proliferation of Buddhist centers and residential communities, the popularization of Buddhist terms and concepts, the increased demand for courses on Buddhism at colleges and universities, the high profile of celebrity Buddhists (e.g., Richard Gere, Steven Segal, Harrison Ford, Leonard Cohen, the Beastie Boys), the box-office success of Hollywood movies based on Buddhist themes such as *Little Buddha* and *Kundun,* and the growth of best-selling books and magazines on Buddhism (e.g., *Tricycle, Shambhala Sun,* and *Buddhadharma).* Moreover, in Europe, Buddhism was named as the "trend religion 2000" (Baumann 2002, 85). These developments illustrate Buddhism's abilities to adapt to newer environments and to tap into the needs of Western societies. No doubt, this skillfulness often reflects and elaborates on structures already embedded in the amalgam forms of Western Buddhism. That is to say, commercialized Buddhism is an essentialized Buddhism, illustrated by such things as the Cadbury, IBM, and Jeep commercials that use images of sagacious monks to sell their wares, or Zen-inspired spa and skin care products. Unfortunately, this sort of representation only reifies Buddhism once again and fortifies the early Orientalist structures already embedded in its hybrid form.

The Reorientation and Innovation Stage

This final stage of the adaptation process of transplantation involves the assertion of the foreign religious tradition's distinctive identity. In theory, the ambiguities that may have arisen in the third stage of adaptation are examined and eliminated. This critical stage brings about a reorientation in the foreign religious tradition's self-identity within the host culture and defines its teachings and practices with more precision. This is the stage in which innovative self-development occurs and the stage that will likely continue to shape Buddhism in the West. Buddhism has grown immensely in the West since it first arrived, and several discourses have played an important role in the final stage of reorientation and innovation. One can only speculate about some of the more noteworthy innovations that are continuing to reorient Buddhism in the West and some that may emerge in the future.

Feminism

One of the most significant innovations in modern Buddhism is the encounter between Buddhism and Western feminism. Women in Western Buddhist communities are working for greater recognition of their equal status with men. In recent years, this topic has gained momentum, as illustrated by scholarly works such as Diana Y. Paul's *Women in Buddhism: Images of the Feminine in Mahayana Buddhism* (1979), Rita Gross's *Buddhism after Patriarchy: A Feminist History, Analysis, and Reconstruction of Buddhism* (1993), Miranda Shaw's *Passionate Enlightenment: Women in Tantric Buddhism* (1994), and Tessa Bartholomeusz's *Women under the Bo Tree: Buddhist Nuns in Sri Lanka* (1994), to name just a few. Anne C. Klein's *Meeting the Great Bliss Queen: Buddhists, Feminists, and the Art of the Self* (1995) has been particularly useful in this regard, because it also provides a corrective to Western feminism, especially in her dialogical discussion of the categories of identity, subjectivity, and self. To date, most feminist scholarship has focused on historical and textual portrayals of women in various schools of Asian Buddhism.

The contributions of women practitioners in, for example, Karma Lekshe Tsomo's *Sakyadhita: Daughters of the Buddha* (1988), *Buddhism through American Women's Eyes* (1995), and *Buddhist Women and Social Justice: Ideals, Challenges, and Achievements* (2004) offer valuable documentation of the specific needs and accomplishments of female Buddhists in the West. According to feminist practitioners within Buddhism, critical examination of androcentric hegemony and gender equity in Buddhist Dharma and Sangha is necessary. Feminism continues to raise practical concerns with regard to issues such as women's ordination, male authority and power, and the status of women in lay-identified communities in the West. This critique is also having an impact on international Buddhist communities. Since Buddhism in the West is almost exclusively a lay tradition, with leadership often provided by women, the innovative contributions of feminism are essential to counteract the traditional positions of power typically held by male (monastic and lay) teachers. The overall goal for many advocates is a feminist reconstruction of Buddhism that secures equal status for women not only in the West, but also in the international Sangha.

Ecology

Furthermore, the urgency of the global environmental crisis has made an impact on Western Buddhists and is already proving to be another innovation in Buddhist self-identification in the West. This impetus is evident in Ian Harris's (1991) term "eco-Buddhism," which for him describes a movement that is promoting the view of Buddhism as intrinsically environmentalist—a view that Harris himself does not hold. Others, however, such as Stephanie Kaza (1993, 2002), Joanna Macy (1991), Jeremy Hayward (1990), the Dalai Lama (Gyatso, 1990, 1992), and Williams and Tucker (1997) seek to identify and promote a congruence between Buddhist and environmental ethics. The doctrine of pratityasamutpada (dependent origination) provides a fundamental theoretical foundation for the environmental movement, linking it, for example, with general ideas about interdependent biological systems in life sciences. While this East/West theoretical fusion may be a sign of innovation in Western Buddhism, it ultimately may not be supportable in Buddhist scriptures (see Ian Harris 1991). Nonetheless, it seems likely that the synthesis of ancient Buddhist doctrine and environmental ethics is another major force that will shape and reorient Buddhism in its Western contexts.

Socially Engaged Buddhism

Engaged Buddhism represents another especially vital movement in the innovation stage of Buddhism in the West, especially in the United States. In many ways, the current wave of social engagement radically undermines prevailing nineteenth-century European images of Buddhism as nihilistic, world negating, and pessimistic. Furthermore, socially engaged Buddhist movements address a variety of contemporary international human rights issues that extend the notion of sila (morality, ethics) well beyond traditional and national boundaries.

Engaged Buddhism owes its visibility in the West to the activist and Zen master Thich Nhat Hanh, who laid out the principles of social engagement in 1965 when, inspired by the Mahayana teachings of direct realization, skillful means, nonduality, universal Buddha-nature, and the bodhisattva ideal, he founded the Tiep Hien Order (the Order of Interbeing). His movement employed tactics such as fasting, placing family altars in the streets of Saigon in front of armored tanks, shaving one's head, and self-immolation to protest against political oppression in Vietnam and for the right to practice Buddhism (King 1996). What is significant about Hanh's presence is that he is equally prominent in Western and Vietnamese communities. Subsequent Engaged Buddhist organizations (e.g., the Buddhist Peace Fellowship (BPF) founded by Robert Aiken, Gary Snyder, and Joanna Macy) integrate a distinctly American, liberal Protestant spirit of social justice. Today BFP is affiliated with a network of international organizations and has more than 4,000 members worldwide. Among its many initiatives are national and international medical programs, refugee initiatives, prison advocacy and ministry outreach programs, and the promotion of nonviolence through various forms of weapons control (e.g., mines, nuclear weapons).

What is clearly innovative about socially engaged Buddhism in the West is the way it is presented. It is not viewed simply as an act of dana (charity) or seva (social service), but also as a path or practice embodying the living bodhisattva ideal. Other organizations such as Bernard Glassman's Zen Peacemaker Order (ZPO or Street Zen); Joan Halifax's Upaya; Jon Kabat-Zinn's Stress Reduction Clinic and his Center for Mindfulness in Medicine, Health Care, and Society at the University of Massachusetts Medical Center; the Angulimala Buddhist Prison Chaplaincy in the United Kingdom (see Parkum and Stultz 2002); and the Buddhist AIDS Project, which offers home care, educational material on HIV-AIDS, free spiritually based hospice sites, and a guest house for the dying, are prime examples of the modern Buddhist social justice movement that has taken root in the West. These organizations demonstrate not only practitioners' social engagement, but also the radical reorientation and maturation of transplanted Buddhist precepts and ideals.

German Zen Priest, Heinz-Jurgen Metzger. Meditation on the Tracks at Bernie Glassman Roshi's Peacemaker Fellowship Bearing Witness Retreat (near the Auschwitz concentration camp), 1996. (Peter Cunningham manan@wordwiseweb.com)

The Internet

One of the most rapid, expedient means to network and promote recent innovations in Western forms of Buddhism is the Internet. Gary Ray coined the word "cybersangha" in 1991 to describe the evolving online Buddhist community. Information technology infrastructure provides resources to extend and develop the Buddhist Sangha into a global community that encompasses virtual reality and cyberspace. Electronic mail and newsletters, chat rooms and discussion groups, subscriber lists, archives and databases, online journals (e.g., *Journal of Buddhist Ethics, Journal of Global Buddhism*), virtual libraries, links to Buddhist centers, publications, meditation supplies, resources for the study of Buddhism such as online courses, helpful Engaged Buddhism sites, and, more recently, virtual communities and cyber temples through portals such as DharmaNet International have proliferated at an astronomical pace and function to transmit Buddhism via the World Wide Web (Hayes 1999; Prebish 1999). What is particularly significant about this innovation is that it is not distinctly Western in its orientation, making it an effective and distinctly modern electronic vehicle, or e-yana, for the transmission of Buddhist information globally among Asian communities as well.

Buddhist Teachers

Perhaps the most significant reorientation in Western Buddhism today is the presence of a new generation of Buddhist teachers. Emma Layman predicted years ago that the growth of Buddhism in America would depend primarily on three criteria: making meditation accessible to Americans leading secular lifestyles, translating Buddhist resources into English, and overcoming the latent and manifest forms of Orientalism in Western Buddhism (Layman 1976). Most of these recommendations are being realized. Layman also stressed the need for Western leaders in the principal schools of Buddhism (i.e., Zen, Tibetan, and Theravada). It seems only feasible that the future of Buddhism in the West depends largely on its ability to produce strong and sagacious teachers who are capable of guiding the Sangha. Whether or not Buddhism reaches a large number of Christians, Jews, and Muslims in the West can, at best, only be speculation. Rather, what seems to be of more immediate concern is the cultivation and recognition of dedicated and eminent teachers, especially teachers indigenous to the West. The longevity of Buddhism in the West may also depend in large measure on the development of male and female monastics. This step runs counter to a predominantly lay-centered Sangha, but it has been key to Buddhism's success in other Asian countries, and it is likely essential to its longevity in the West as well.

The significant growth among Buddhist communities in North America and Europe is largely the result of effective Buddhist teachers leading the efforts to transplant Buddhism in the West. In the United Kingdom, Urgyen Sangharakshita (born in 1925 in South London as Dennis Lingwood) has been referred to as the founding father of Western Buddhism. Sangharakshita was ordained in the Theravada, Tibetan Vajrayana, and Chinese Chan Buddhist traditions. He played a key role in the Ambedkar movement in India and currently resides in the United Kingdom. In 1967, Sangharakshita started Friends of the Western Buddhist Order (FWBO), also called Trailokya Bauddha Mahasangha Gana (TBMSG), in India. In 1968 he founded the Western Buddhist Order (WBO). Today FWBO and WBO have centers in nearly twenty countries worldwide. His life and his teachings combine traditional Buddhist practice (such as the thirty-seven bodhipaksadharmas or Wings to Awakening—the Four Foundations of Mindfulness, Four Right Exertions, Four Bases of Attainment, Five Strengths, Five Faculties, Seven Factors of Awakening, and the Eightfold Path) alongside more experimental, innovative, and visionary ideas. His institution upholds the ideals of democratization in the Sangha, Buddhist ecumenism, and the integration of psychology and meditation as a means to wholeness and higher evolution. Another comparable figure is Tenzin Palmo (born in East London as Dianne Perry) of Dongyu Gatsal Ling Nunnery in India. She is the first Western nun to complete a traditional twelve-year retreat in the Himalayas. Palmo is now raising money to build a nunnery and establish a lineage of yoginis, or female meditators, in the Kargyu tradition of Tibetan Buddhism.

Meanwhile, in Canada, Namgyal Rinpoche (born in 1931 in Toronto as George Dawson) founded the first Dharma center in Canada in 1965 in Kinmount, Ontario. He was first ordained as Ananda Bodhi in the Burmese forest tradition under Sayadaw U Thila Wanta, was later recognized by the Dalai Lama and the Sixteenth Karmapa as an enlightened being, and was enthroned as Namgyal Rinpoche in the Kargyu tradition. Considered a master of Mahamudra practice, Namgyal Rinpoche taught what could be called a synthetic or universalist approach to Buddha Dharma at centers he founded in Guatemala, England, Ireland, France, Scotland, Germany, Switzerland, New Zealand, Australia, and the United States. He died in Switzerland in 2002, leaving the Dharma Center of Canada (along with his other groups) without a principal teacher. This situation is instructive, as many centers in the West will face the challenge of handling succession issues. Consequently, the need to develop strategies for continuity among teachers in the Western lineages is essential. Also, Pema Chodron (born in 1936 in New York as Deirdre Blomfield-Brown) is resident teacher/abbess of Shambhala/Gampo Abbey Monastery in Cape Breton, Nova Scotia. A disciple of the controversial Tibetan teacher Chogyam Trungpa, Pema Chodron was ordained in the Kargyu lineage by the Sixteenth Karmapa and took full bhikshuni ordination in the Chinese lineage of Buddhism in 1981. She runs the first Tibetan monastery for Westerners.

There are several noteworthy teachers in the United States as well. Lama Surya Das (born in 1950 in New York as Jeffrey Miller) traveled extensively in India, Nepal, and Japan. He studied Zen, vipassana with S. N. Goenka, and Tibetan Buddhism with the esteemed Kalu Rinpoche, Lama Thubten Yeshe, and Nyoshul Khenpo Rinpoche. In 1991, he started the Dzogchen Foundation in Cambridge, Massachusetts, and he has written several influential best-selling books including *Awakening the Buddha Within: Eight Steps to Enlightenment* (1997). Surya Das is aware that during its long history, Buddhism has had to reinvent itself in each of its new homelands, and now Western Buddhists face this immense challenge. Because of this, Surya Das has identified various trends that he hopes will ensure this crucial stage of innovative self-development. For example, he emphasizes a nonhierarchical and nonsectarian lay Sangha, the continued integration of psychological inquiry and social engagement, meditation practice rather than ritual, a rational approach to the teachings, and gender equity (Surya Das 1997, 383–386). Other prominent teachers and Buddhist masters born in the United States include Philip Kapleau, Jack Kornfield, Bernard Glassman, Richard Baker, and Robert Aiken, who have written influential books on Buddhism for Western audiences.

Scholarship

Another area of innovation serving to develop and refine Buddhist ideas and practices in the West can be seen in the area of scholarly research. The growth and development of Buddhist studies as an academic field is crucial to meet the educational needs of Western Buddhists, many of whom have little acquaintance with the religion. To this end, Prebish writes,

> In the absence of the traditional "scholar-monks" so prevalent in Asia, it may well be that the "scholar-practitioners" of today's American Buddhism will fulfill the role of "quasi-monastics," or at least treasure-troves of Buddhist literacy and information, functioning as guides through whom one's understanding of the Dharma may be sharpened. (Prebish 1999, 208)

Prebish calls attention to the need within the western Buddhist community to provide a "high level of Buddhist literacy" among its practitioners (Prebish 1999, 207). However, this also raises a much-debated issue in the field of religious studies regarding the role of the insider (i.e., theology) vis-à-vis the outsider (i.e., the social scientific study of religion) in teaching courses about religion within the context of publicly funded secular universities (Wiebe 2000). Ambiguities and tensions inevitably rise when academic scholars begin serving as religious counselors and teachers.

In addition to the field of Buddhist studies, critical and consequential work is being done in the area of postcolonial and subaltern studies by renowned scholars such as Gayatri Spivak, Homi Bhabha, and Ashish Nandy, to name only three. Their insights into the perverse and bewildering nature of colonial domination in the eighteenth and nineteenth centuries provide a powerful critique of the entrenched structures of Orientalist ideology in countries such as India and Sri Lanka. The far-ranging effects of postcolonialism on Buddhist studies can already be seen in two works by Donald Lopez. Lopez's *Curators of the Buddha: The Study of Buddhism under Colonialism* (1995) attempts to uncover the legacy of Orientalism in Western Buddhology, and his *Prisoners of Shangri-La: Tibetan Buddhism and the West* (1998) charts the idiosyncratic development of Tibetan Buddhism in North America. By investigating the Orientalized forms of Buddhism in Western scholarship, the latent and inherited notions of an Orientalized Buddhist practice can be deconstructed and revised.

Also, the relatively new field of cognitive theory is starting to have a considerable impact on Buddhism. And, at the same time, Buddhism is having an impact on research in cognitive science. Cognitive studies in religion attempt to explain the nature of religious experience from the perspective of the neural or cognitive function of the human mind/brain. Generally speaking, researchers hypothesize that religion is related to our human physiology. As such, cognitive theories introduce us to the possibility of the "naturalness" (i.e., phys-icality) of religious ideas (Boyer 1994) and to claims of universality based on "pan-human" properties of the mind/brain. In this new scientific paradigm, we are introduced to the ideas of engagement and embodiment based on a funda-mental presupposition of interdependence—a concept central to all schools of Buddha Dharma. Careful studies of the architecture of the brain have recently opened the way for a deeper understanding of human consciousness and the possibility of explaining what goes on in higher stages of Buddhist meditation. This area of research is still in its infancy and could have a significant impact on our future understanding of Buddhism and Buddhist studies in the West (see, for example, Payne 2002, Wallace 2002, Rosch 2002, Goldberg [forthcom-ing]).

In sum, although the accounts provided here demonstrate the extent to which both Asian immigrant and non-Asian converts to Buddhism have adapted to the modern West, it is worth remembering, as Prebish and Bau-mann (2002) observe, that most (if not all) encounters between Buddhism and foreign cultures in Asia took centuries before indigenous forms of Buddhism developed in new lands. In China it took many centuries for Pure Land, T'ien-t'ai, and Chan Buddhism to evolve and become established. In Japan, nearly 500 years passed before indigenous forms of Japanese Buddhism appeared. So too, Western forms of Buddhism have yet to mature, develop, and prosper (Pre-bish and Baumann 2002, 3–4).

Conclusion

Edward Said (1994) has shown that one major purpose of Orientalism is to make the Orient knowable. However, a living cultural reality such as Buddhism continually challenges and contradicts what can be known through Orientalist frameworks, since it continually changes and defies the essentialist reification of its textual forms. Living Buddhism has proven this time and again in its transplantation throughout Asia and, more recently, the West. What is clearly evident in the history and development of Buddhism as a world religion is that its mechanisms and strategies for adaptation and transplantation have proved fairly successful. Living Buddhism disrupts the reified image of the religion in Orientalist thought and, it seems, is well equipped to deal with the marginaliza-tion, projections, abstractions, mystifications, false dualisms, essentialism, and so forth that characterize the West's need to create a knowable, stable subject. The rejection of a stable, unchanging subject in Buddhist thought would then appear most appropriate for reinforcing the idea that the entire Buddhist tra-dition is likewise subject to change and adaptation.

References

Ambedkar, Bhimrao Ramji. 1957. *The Buddha and His Dhamma.* Bombay: People's Education Society.

———. 1989. Annihilation of Caste. In *Dr. Babasaheb Ambedkar Writings and Speeches.* Vol. 1, 23–99. Bombay: Education Department, Government of Maharashtra.

Bartholomeusz, Tessa. 1994. *Women under the Bo Tree: Buddhist Nuns in Sri Lanka.* Cambridge, UK: Cambridge University Press.

Batchelor, Stephen. 1994. *The Awakening of the West: The Encounter of Buddhism and Western Culture.* London: Aquarian.

Baumann, Martin. 1994. The Transplantation of Buddhism to Germany: Processive Modes and Strategies of Adaptation. *Method and Theory in the Study of Religion* 6(1): 35–61.

———. 1996. Methodological Smugness and the Transplantation of Symbolic Systems: A Reply to Eva K. Neumaier-Dargyay. *Method and Theory in the Study of Religion* 8(4): 367–372.

———. 1997. Cultural Contact and Valuation: Early German Buddhists and the Creation of a "Buddhism in Protestant Shape." *Numen* 44(3): 270–295.

———. 2001. Global Buddhism: Developmental Periods, Regional Histories, and a New Analytical Perspective. *Journal of Global Buddhism* 2: 1–43.

———. 2002. Buddhism in Europe: Past, Present, Prospects. In *Westward Dharma: Buddhism beyond Asia,* ed. Charles S. Prebish and Martin Baumann, 85–105. Berkeley: University of California Press.

Boisvert, Mathieu. 2005. Buddhists in Canada: Their Unrecognized Religion. In *Religion and Ethnicity in Canada,* eds. Paul Bramadat and David Seljak, 89–110. Toronto: Pearson.

Boyer, Pascal. 1994. *The Naturalness of Religious Ideas: A Cognitive Theory of Religion.* Berkeley: University of California Press.

Carus, Paul. 1973. *Gospel of the Buddha.* 1894, 1915. Reprint. LaSalle, IL: Open Court Publishing.

Doyle, Tara. 2003. "Liberate the Mahabodhi Temple!" Socially Engaged Buddhism, Dalit-Style. In *Buddhism in the Modern World: Adaptations of an Ancient Tradition,* eds. Steven Heine and Charles S. Prebish, 249–280. New York: Oxford University Press.

Fields, Rick. 1981. *How the Swans Came to the Lake: A Narrative History of Buddhism in America.* Boulder, CO: Shambhala.

Goldberg, Ellen. 2005. Cognitive Theory and Yoga. *Zygon* 40(3):613–629.

Gombrich, Richard, and Gananath Obeyesekere. 1988. *Buddhism Transformed: Religious Change in Sri Lanka.* Princeton, NJ: Princeton University Press.

Gross, Rita M. 1993. *Buddhism after Patriarchy: A Feminist History, Analysis, and Reconstruction of Buddhism.* Albany: State University of New York.

Gyatso, Tenzin. 1990. *A Policy of Kindness.* Ithaca, NY: Snow Lion.

———. 1992. A Tibetan Buddhist Perspective on Spirit in Nature. In *Spirit and Nature: Why the Environment Is a Religious Issue,* ed. Steven C. Rockefeller and John C. Elder, 109–125. Boston: Beacon Press.

Harris, Ian. 1991. How Environmentalist Is Buddhism? *Religion* 21(2): 101–114.

Hayes, Richard P. 1999. The Internet as Window onto American Buddhism. In *American Buddhism: Methods and Findings in Recent Scholarship*, ed. Duncan Ryuken Williams and Christopher S. Queen, 168–180. Surrey, UK: Curzon Press.

Hayward, Jeremy. 1990. Ecology and the Experience of Sacredness. In *Dharma and Gaia*, ed. Allan Hunt Badiner, 64–74. Berkeley, CA: Parallax Press.

Hori, Victor. 1994. Sweet and Sour Buddhism. *Triangle* (Fall): 48–52.

Hallisey, Charles. 1995. Roads Taken and Not Taken in the Study of Theravada Buddhism. In *Curators of the Buddha: The Study of Buddhism under Colonialism*, ed. Donald S. Lopez Jr., 31–61. Chicago: University of Chicago Press.

Jong, J. W. de. 1998. *A Brief History of Buddhist Studies in Europe and America*. Tokyo: Kosei Publishing.

Kaza, Stephanie. 1993. Acting with Compassion: Buddhism, Feminism, and the Environmental Crisis. In *Ecofeminism and the Sacred*, ed. Carol J. Adams, 50–69. New York: Continuum.

———. 2002. To Save All Beings: Buddhist Environmental Activism. In *Engaged Buddhism in the West*, ed. Christopher S. Queen, 159–182. Boston: Wisdom Books.

Klein, Anne C. 1995. *Meeting the Great Bliss Queen: Buddhists, Feminists, and the Art of the Self*. Boston: Beacon Press.

King, Sallie B. 1996. Thich Nhat Hanh and the Unified Buddhist Church: Nondualism in Action. In *Engaged Buddhism: Buddhist Liberation Movements in Asia*, eds. Christopher S. Queen and Sallie B. King, 321–354. Albany: State University of New York Press.

Layman, Emma. 1976. *Buddhism in America*. Chicago: University of Chicago Press.

Lopez, Donald S. Jr. 1994. New Age Orientalism: The Case of Tibet. *Tricycle: The Buddhist Review* 3: 16–20.

———, ed. 1995. *Curators of the Buddha: The Study of Buddhism under Colonialism*. Chicago: University of Chicago Press.

———. 1998. *Prisoners of Shangri-La: Tibetan Buddhism and the West*. Chicago: Chicago University Pres.

Macy, Joanna. 1991. *Mutual Causality in Buddhism and General Systems Theory: The Dharma of Natural Systems*. Albany: State University of New York Press.

McLellan, Janet. 1999. *Many Petals of the Lotus: Five Asian Buddhist Communities in Toronto*. Toronto: University of Toronto Press.

McMahan, David L. 2002. Repackaging Zen for the West. In *Westward Dharma: Buddhism beyond Asia*, ed. Charles S. Prebish and Martin Baumann, 201–217. Berkeley: University of California Press.

Nattier, Jan. 1998. Who Is A Buddhist? Charting the Landscape of Buddhist America. In *The Faces of Buddhism in America*, ed. Charles S. Prebish and Kenneth K. Tanaka, 183–195. Berkeley: University of California Press.

Obeyesekere, Gananath. 1972. Religious Symbolism and Political Change in Ceylon. In *The Two Wheels of Dhamma: Essays on the Theravada Tradition in India and Ceylon*, ed. Bardwell L. Smith, 58–78. Chambersburg, PA: American Academy of Religion.

Parkum, Virginia Cohn, and J. Anthony Stultz. 2002. The Angulimala Lineage: Buddhist Prison Ministries. In *Engaged Buddhism in the West*, ed. Christopher S. Queen, 347–371. Boston: Beacon Press.

Paul, Diana Y. 1979. *Women in Buddhism: Images of the Feminine in Mahayana Tradition*. Berkeley: Asian Humanities Press.

Payne, Richard K. 2002. Cognitive Theories of Ritual and Buddhist Practice: An Examination of Ilkka Pyysiainen's Theory. *Pacific World: Journal of the Institute of Buddhist Studies*. 3(4): 75–90.

Prebish, Charles S. 1979. *American Buddhism*. North Scituate, MA: Duxbury Press.

———. 1999. *Luminous Passage: The Practice and Study of Buddhism in America*. Berkeley: University of California Press.

Prebish, Charles S., and Martin Baumann, eds. 2002. *Westward Dharma: Buddhism beyond Asia*. Berkeley: University of California Press.

Prothero, Stephen. 1996. *The White Buddhist: The Asian Odyssey of Henry Steel Olcott*. Bloomington: Indiana University Press.

Queen, Christopher S. 1996. Introduction: The Shapes and Sources of Engaged Buddhism. In *Engaged Buddhism: Buddhist Liberation Movements in Asia*, ed. Christopher S. Queen and Sallie B. King, 1–44. Albany: State University of New York Press.

Rosch, Eleanor. 2002. "How Do I Know Thee? Let Me Count the Ways": Meditation and Basic Cognitive Processes. *Pacific World: Journal of the Institute of Buddhist Studies*. 3(4): 33–54.

Said, Edward. 1994. *Orientalism*. 1978. Reprint. New York: Vintage.

Seager, Richard Hughes. 1999. *Buddhism in America*. New York: Columbia University Press.

Sharf, Robert H. 1995. The Zen of Japanese Nationalism. In *Curators of the Buddha: The Study of Buddhism under Colonialism*, ed. Donald S. Lopez Jr., 107–160. Chicago: University of Chicago Press.

Shaw, Miranda. 1994. *Passionate Enlightenment: Women in Tantric Buddhism*. Princeton, NJ: Princeton University Press.

Surya, Lama Das. 1997. *Awakening the Buddha Within: Eight Steps to Enlightenment*. New York: Broadway Books.

Tanaka, Kenneth K. 2002. Issues of Ethnicity in the Buddhist Churches of America. In *American Buddhism: Methods and Findings in Recent Scholarship*, ed. Duncan Ryuken Williams and Christopher S. Queen, 3–19. Surrey, UK: Curzon Press.

Thurman, Robert A. F. 1995. *Inside Tibetan Buddhism: Rituals and Symbols Revealed*. San Francisco: Harper Collins.

Trungpa, Chogyam. 1991. *Crazy Wisdom*. Boston: Shambhala.

Tsomo, Karma Lekshe, ed. 1988. *Sakyadhita: Daughters of the Buddha*. Ithaca, NY: Snow Lion.

———, ed. 1995. *Buddhism through American Women's Eyes*. Ithaca, NY: Snow Lion.

———. 2002. Buddhist Nuns: Changes and Challenges. In *Westward Dharma: Buddhism beyond Asia*, ed. Charles S. Prebish and Martin Baumann, 255–274. Berkeley: University of California Press.

————, ed. 2004. *Buddhist Women and Social Justice: Ideals, Challenges, and Achievements.* Albany: State University of New York Press.

Tweed, Thomas A. 1992. *The American Encounter with Buddhism 1844–1912: Victorian Culture and the Limits of Dissent.* Bloomington: Indiana University Press.

————. 2002. Who Is A Buddhist? Night-Stand Buddhists and Other Creatures. In *Westward Dharma: Buddhism beyond Asia,* ed. Charles S. Prebish and Martin Baumann, 17–33. Berkeley: University of California Press.

Wallace, Alan B. 2002. A Science of Consciousness: Buddhism (1), the Modern West (2). *Pacific World: Journal of the Institute of Buddhist Studies,* 3(4): 15–32.

Whitman, Walt. 1856. *Leaves of Grass.* Brooklyn, NY: Author.

Wiebe, Donald. 2000. *The Politics of Religious Studies.* New York: Palgrave.

Williams, Duncan Ryuken. 2002. Camp Dharma: Japanese-American Buddhist Identity and the Internment Experience of World War II. In *Westward Dharma: Buddhism beyond Asia,* ed. Charles S. Prebish and Martin Baumann, 178–190. Berkeley: University of California Press.

Williams, Duncan Ryuken, and Mary Evelyn Tucker, eds. 1997. *Buddhism and Ecology: The Interconnection of Dharma and Deed.* Cambridge, MA: Harvard University Press.

Chapter Eleven

Annotated Bibliography

Chapter One: The History of Buddhism in Retrospect

Buswell, Robert E. Jr., ed. *Encyclopedia of Buddhism.* **2 volumes. New York: Macmillan Reference, 2004.** A comprehensive and up-to-date treatment of many critical features in the history, literature, and practice of Buddhist traditions around the world. The entries, of varying lengths, are informative and written by a host of current scholars to be accessible for nonspecialists and useful for advanced researchers in the field.

Dumoulin, Heinrich, ed. *Buddhism in the Modern World.* **New York: Macmillan Publishing, 1976.** The English translation of a German work published in 1970 that surveys the contemporary status of Buddhism in several Asian countries as well as the West. Many chapters are fairly brief, but they still offer some important insights into observations of Buddhism in various lands in the 1960s.

Harvey, Peter. *An Introduction to Buddhism: Teachings, History and Practices.* **Cambridge, UK: Cambridge University Press, 1990.** A thematically arranged survey of the Buddhist religion written in a detailed yet readable manner. The author relies primarily on primary source materials to describe the variation in Buddhist thought and practice. Emphasis is given to ancient texts and traditions, although two chapters are devoted to modern developments.

Heine, Steven, and Charles S. Prebish. *Buddhism in the Modern World: Adaptations of an Ancient Tradition.* **Oxford, UK: Oxford University Press, 2003.** A recent collection of essays on selected modern developments in Buddhist traditions found in several different cultures. Eschewing attempts to present a comprehensive picture of modern forms of Buddhism around the world, this work instead offers detailed case studies that are intended to represent some of the ways that Buddhist traditions are adapted to reflect modern interests.

Lewis, Todd. Buddhism: Ways to Nirvana. In *World Religions Today,* **ed. John L. Esposito, Darrell J. Fasching, and Todd Lewis, 353–429. New York: Oxford University Press, 2002.** A lengthy chapter highlighting modern forms of Buddhism for an introductory survey text. The piece discusses many recent developments in the tradition in a succinct but detailed manner. The global diversity of Buddhism is the overarching theme.

Lopez, Donald S., Jr., ed. *A Modern Buddhist Bible: Essential Readings from East and West.* **Boston: Beacon Press, 2002.** A collection of original writings from influential Asian and Western authors of modern Buddhist works. The editor contributes a substantial introduction examining the development and key features of what is called "modern Buddhism."

Mitchell, Donald W. *Buddhism: Introducing the Buddhist Experience.* **New York: Oxford University Press, 2002.** A recent textbook that surveys the development of Buddhism both chronologically and geographically. Incorporating some important ideas from recent scholarship in the field, this text is informative and accessible to a wide range of readers. More emphasis is given to premodern eras and Mahayana traditions.

Robinson, Richard, Willard L. Johnson, and Thanissaro Bhikkhu. *The Buddhist Religion: A Historical Introduction.* **Fifth Edition. Belmont, CA: Wadsworth Publishing, 2003.** A classic textbook first written in 1970 and periodically revised with substantial additions since that time. This work is organized geographically to present a comprehensive historical overview of the spread of Buddhism across Asia and into the West. A detailed survey, though not as accessible as some.

Skilton, Andrew. *A Concise History of Buddhism.* **Birmingham, UK: Windhorse Publications, 1994.** A clearly organized historical survey that examines the development of Buddhism through the nineteenth century. The majority of the material in the text is drawn from doctrinal, sectarian, and literary developments in India. Short chapters on Buddhism in various countries are included, but there is little discussion of modern events.

Trainor, Kevin, ed. *Buddhism: The Illustrated Guide.* **Oxford, UK: Oxford University Press, 2001.** A recent work, organized thematically, that takes a comprehensive approach to the Buddhist tradition. Highlighted by full-color photos and reproductions of Buddhist art, the text contains brief sections that are written in an informed and clear manner. The scholarship herein is careful and up to date.

Chapter Two: Buddhism in Sri Lanka

Abeysekara, Ananda. *Colors of the Robe: Religion, Identity, and Difference.* **Columbia: University of South Carolina Press, 2002.** An innovative analysis of the contested definitions of Buddhist identity in modern Sri Lanka. Abeysekara's work examines several detailed case studies to illumine the various conceptions of Buddhism, nation, violence, and tradition that appear and clash in particular moments in Sri Lankan society. His work also contains criticism of earlier scholarship on Sri Lankan Buddhism.

Bartholomeusz, Tessa J. *Women under the Bo Tree: Buddhist Nuns in Sri Lanka.* **Cambridge, UK: Cambridge University Press, 1994.** One of the earliest and most complete studies of female renunciates in Sri Lanka. Although becoming slightly dated due to recent developments in this field, this book remains an essential work for understanding the modern origins for the reappearance of Buddhist nuns in Sri Lanka.

Bartholomeusz, Tessa J., and Chandra R. De Silva, eds. *Buddhist Fundamentalism and Minority Identities in Sri Lanka.* **Albany: State University of New York Press, 1998.** A collection of interdisciplinary essays written by scholars on various facets of ethnic identity and conflict in modern Sri Lanka. The essays consider Buddhist, Tamil, Muslim, Catholic, and Burgher communities as well as how the ethnic or religious "other" is constructed. The work fills important gaps in scholarship on Sri Lanka.

Bond, George D. *The Buddhist Revival in Sri Lanka: Religious Tradition, Reinterpretation and Response.* **Columbia: University of South Carolina Press, 1988.** An informed and comprehensive survey of modern developments in Sri Lankan Buddhism. Bond highlights the various revivalist efforts made by Sri Lankan Buddhists since 1956 to renew and strengthen Buddhism in the nation. He connects the rise of political monks, insight meditation, and Sarvodaya to the earlier revival of the religion undertaken by Protestant Buddhists.

Bond, George D. *Buddhism at Work: Community Development, Social Empowerment and the Sarvodaya Movement.* **Bloomfield, CT: Kumarian Press, 2004.** An informative and sympathetic study of the Sarvodaya movement in Sri Lanka. Bond's familiarity and long association with this group results in a comprehensive look at the current thought and activities of Sarvodaya. The book is well researched and accurately reflects current positions and approaches taken by Sarvodaya in the field.

De Silva, D. A. Premakumara. *Globalization and the Transformation of Planetary Rituals in Southern Sri Lanka.* **Colombo, Sri Lanka: International Centre for Ethnic Studies, 2000.** An ethnographic study of rituals performed for planetary deities among Sri Lankan Buddhists. This work considers the impact of globalization on Buddhism in Sri Lanka, detailing the resilience of traditional rituals through the adoption of new settings for their expression. De Silva notes that traditional bali rituals are being preserved in more personalized rituals as well as in nationalist displays of cultural heritage.

Gombrich, Richard, and Gananath Obeyesekere. *Buddhism Transformed: Religious Change in Sri Lanka.* **Princeton, NJ: Princeton University Press, 1988.** A voluminous study of contemporary Sri Lankan Buddhism by two renowned scholars. The work considers the formation of Protestant Buddhism under the influences of Christian missionaries and the rationalistic characteristics it adopted. It also examines cases of spirit religion and the ecstatic expressions of some recent urban cult groups. Although it is a landmark study, the work clings to a normative view of traditional Buddhism when identifying contemporary practices as either authentic or deviant.

Scott, David. *Formations of Ritual: Colonial and Anthropological Discourses on the Sinhala Yaktovil.* **Minneapolis: University of Minnesota Press, 1994.** Scott's work uses a field study of the Sinhala yaktovil ritual to examine what has been referred to as demonic exorcisms and anthropological scholarship on Buddhism in Sri Lanka. The book links recent scholarship on Sinhala rituals to enduring colonial forms of representing Sri Lankan culture.

Seneviratne, H. L. *The Work of Kings: The New Buddhism in Sri Lanka.* **Chicago: University of Chicago Press, 1999.** An important work examining the historical and sociological backdrop of contemporary Buddhist monasticism in Sri Lanka. Seneviratne's work, the most complete study of the rise of political monks, traces the development of the ideology behind monastic activism from Anagarika Dharmapala to the present. The book also functions as a sustained critique of contemporary trends found in the Sri Lankan Buddhist monkhood.

Tambiah, Stanley Jeyaraja. *Buddhism Betrayed?: Religion, Politics, and Violence in Sri Lanka.* **Chicago: University of Chicago Press, 1992.** An influential and controversial work written by an experienced anthropologist of Theravada Buddhism. Tambiah discusses the rise of political Buddhism and its ties to modern Sinhala nationalist movements. He links the modern refashioning of Sinhala Buddhism along political and ethnic lines to communal riots and other forms of violence in modern Sri Lanka. The work reflects a critique of Sri Lankan Buddhism compared with images of the religion drawn from ancient Pali texts.

Chapter Three: Buddhism in Burma

Aung San Suu Kyi. *Letters from Burma.* **London: Penguin Group, 1997.** This collection of letters, reminiscent of Martin Luther King's *Letter from a Birmingham Jail,* appeared initially as a series in a Japanese weekly paper. In each letter, the author focuses on a particular event, cultural custom, or critique of present practices. As a collection, it illustrates how Aung San Suu Kyi constructed her appeal to Burmese people and to Buddhists abroad.

Houtman, Gustaaf. *Mental Culture in the Burmese Political Crisis.* **Tokyo: Institute for the Study of Languages and Cultures of Asia and Africa, Tokyo University of Foreign Studies, 1999.** In this detailed study, Houtman describes the role that meditation plays in contemporary Burmese culture and politics. This work shows how Burmese practitioners of meditation construct an intrinsic connection between insight meditation and the prodemocracy movement.

Maung Maung, U. *From Sangha to Laity: Nationalist Movements of Burma 1920–1940.* **Columbia, MO: South Asia Books, 1980.** The monograph narrates the crisis of monastic authority and the eventual secularization of the nationalist movement in Burma. It is particularly informative concerning the inception and role of the Young Men's Buddhist Association in the early part of the twentieth century.

Mendelson, E. Michael. *Sangha and State in Burma, A Study of Monastic Sectarianism and Leadership,* **ed. J. P. Ferguson. Ithaca, NY: Cornell University Press, 1975.** This is an invaluable source for any student of Burmese Buddhism. Rich ethnographic accounts focus on Buddhist reforms in Burma since the nineteenth century. The first of three projected (but not yet published) monographs, it is based on ethnographic fieldwork done during the late 1950s. The focus is on the complex dynamics of state-Sangha relations during each period, supplemented by detailed accounts of specific historical conjunctions.

Myint-U Thant. *The Making of Modern Burma.* **Cambridge, UK: Cambridge University Press, 2001.** This historical study offers an insightful analysis into the effects of colonial rule on Burmese institutions and culture. The work is an invaluable narrative for understanding the later developments of the Burmese nation-state.

Sarkisyanz, Emanuel. *Buddhist Backgrounds of the Burmese Revolution.* **The Hague: Martinus Nijhoff, 1965.** In this book, Sarkisyanz focuses on the millennial aspects of Burmese Buddhist nationalism and its charismatic extensions. Particular attention is paid to the ways in which various Buddhist leaders have sought to integrate modern political ideologies into the Burmese cultural and religious landscapes.

Schober, Juliane. "Venerating the Buddha's Remains in Burma: From Solitary Practice to the Cultural Hegemony of Communities." *Journal of Burma Studies,* **vol. 6, 2001: 111–139.** This essay examines the veneration of relics in Burmese Buddhist practice. Beginning with meditation on the personal service the Buddha received from his devoted disciple Ananda, the discussion turns to the ways in which veneration of relics constitutes social communities.

Skidmore, Monique, ed. *Burma at the Turn of the Twenty-First Century.* **Honolulu: University of Hawai'i Press, 2005.** This collection of edited essays by scholars from a variety of disciplines presents the most recent scholarship on Burmese culture, politics, and society. Many of the studies are based on anthropological fieldwork and offer insights into recent developments in the country.

Smith, Donald E. *Religion and Politics in Burma.* **Princeton, NJ: Princeton University Press, 1965.** This classic study continues to distinguish itself as a reliable political analysis of the role Buddhism played in shaping the course of Burmese politics. It is a particularly valuable resource for understanding the events of the U Nu era in modern Burmese history.

Chapter Four: Buddhism in Thailand

Bizot, François. *Le bouddhisme des thais.* **Bangkok: Editions des Cahiers de France, 1993.** A good, basic (albeit short) introduction to mainstream Thai Buddhism. Bizot's particular focus is on modern practices, especially those in rural areas. He also questions the arbitrary divisions among magic, ritual, philosophy, canon, and commentary that seem to dominate studies of modern Buddhism in Thailand.

Brown, Sid. *The Journey of One Buddhist Nun: Even Against the Wind.* **Albany: State University of New York Press, 2001.** This biographical study tells the story of Wabi, a young poor woman who struggles to educate herself as a Buddhist nun. The work presents a unique perspective on contemporary issues related to gender in Thai Buddhism.

Hirsch, Philip, ed. *Seeing Forests for Trees: Environment and Environmentalism in Thailand.* **Chiang Mai, Thailand: Silkworm Books, 1997.** Presents seminal articles by James Taylor and Santita Ganjanapan regarding the ways in which Buddhist, Karen, and Leu religious beliefs, especially in northern and northeastern Thailand, have influenced environmental policy and have formed the backdrop for ecological protests. A good place to start for understanding the relationship in modern Thailand between religion and ecology.

Ishii, Yoneo. *Sangha, State, and Society: Thai Buddhism in History.* **Translated by Peter Hawkes. Honolulu: University of Hawai'i Press, 1986.** Still the most reliable study of the relationship between state/royal reforms and Buddhist administration and practice in contemporary Thailand. Although excluding a serious examination of regional Buddhist practices, it offers an excellent overview of elite, top-down changes. It serves as an excellent companion to Craig Reynolds' 1972 dissertation from Cornell University, "The Buddhist Monkhood in Nineteenth Century Thailand."

Kabilsingh, Chatsumarn. *Thai Women in Buddhism.* **Berkeley, CA: Parallax Press, 1991.** A wide-ranging series of commentaries on women and Buddhism in Thailand. Kabilsingh discusses the relationships between prostitution and nunhood, offers a feminist reading of several Buddhist texts, and presents her own vision of the future roles of women in religion in Thailand.

Sivaraksa, Sulak. *Global Healing: Essays and Interviews on Structural Violence, Social Development and Spiritual Transformation.* **Bangkok: Thai Inter-Religious Commission for Development, Sathirakoses-Nagapradipa Foundation; Distributed in USA by Parallax Press, Berkeley, CA, 1999.** The most comprehensive collection of writings of Thailand's most vocal Buddhist and social critic. Offers an in-depth explanation of Sulak's notion of "structural violence" and ways to incorporate Buddhist ethics into development work and democratic reform.

Swearer, Donald. *The Buddhist World of Southeast Asia.* **Albany: State University of New York Press, 1995.** Offers a novel perspective on the ways in which

Buddhist ritual, state reform, and local religious beliefs and practices are woven into ritual, art, and narrative in modern Southeast Asia (with a heavy emphasis on Thailand). The clearest and most sophisticated introduction to religion in Thailand.

Udomittipong, Pipob, ed. *Socially Engaged Buddhism for the New Millennium: Essays in Honor of the Ven. Phra Dhammapitaka (Bhikkhu P. A. Payutto) on his 60th Birthday Anniversary.* **Bangkok: Sathirakoses-Nagapradipa Foundation: Foundation for Children; Distributed in North America by Parallax Press, Berkeley, California, 1999.** A series of essays commenting on the growing trend in socially engaged Buddhism in Thailand. The contributors have been students and admirers of Thailand's most famous scholar monk, Phra P. A. Payutto.

Van Esterik, Penny. *Materializing Thailand.* **Oxford, UK: Berg, 2000.** A provocative approach to the diverse ways in which Buddhist and social ethics are manipulated and created in Thai society. Through a wide range of stories, Van Esterik tries to present the sophisticated and often stultifying ways in which gender is constructed in Thailand; however, she refrains from offering one totalizing concept of gender or Buddhism.

Yukio, Hayashi. *Practical Buddhism among the Thai-Lao: Religion in the Making of a Region.* **Kyoto, Japan: Kyoto University's Center for Southeast Asian Studies, 2003.** The most in-depth and sophisticated study of the relationships among nation building, regionalism, religion, and ethnicity. Traces the history of state/royal religious reform, communism, millenarianism, and ritual practice in northeast Thailand during the past century.

Chapter Five: Buddhism in Cambodia

Bizot, François. *Le figuier à cinq branches.* **Recherches sur le bouddhisme khmer. Paris: Ecole Française d'Extrême-Orient. 1976.** Inaugurating the series of publications that has established the existence and significance of a unique Cambodian Tantric Theravadin tradition, this volume's introduction explores the history of the esoteric tradition and its modern denigration. The bulk of the book consists in transliteration, translation, and commentary of an Abhidhamma meditation treatise involving mystic rebirth.

Bizot, François. "La grotte de la naissance." *Bulletin de l'Ecole Française d'Extrême-Orient 67:* **221–273 (Recherches sur le bouddhisme khmer 2). 1980.** Focused around meditation ritual performed in a cave complex in Cambodia's northwestern Battambang Province. The caves are shown to be conceived as the Earth Mother womb; through a series of ritual acts, participants are seen to be reborn on reemergence from the caves.

Bizot, François. *Le don de soi-même,* **Recherches sur le bouddhisme khmer 3. Paris: Ecole Française d'Extrême-Orient. 1981.** An in-depth study of the pansukul ritual in reformed and nonreformed milieux in Cambodia, Thailand, and Laos whereby monks are offered pansukul rags. With translations of associated Khmer texts, emphasis is given to the funerary aspects of the nonreformed tradition in which the pansukul cloth represents at once a shroud and a placenta.

Bizot, François. *Les traditions de la pabbajja en Asie du Sud-Est.* **Recherches sur le bouddhisme khmer 4. Göttingen: Vandenhoeck and Ruprecht. 1988.** Explores the origination of this esoteric tradition through detailed analysis of pabbajja ordination lineages in Southeast Asia. The volume contains two useful English-language texts: a preface by Heinz Bechert and an abstract.

Guthrie, Elizabeth. "A Study of the History and Cult of the Buddhist Earth Deity in Mainland Southeast Asia," PhD dissertation. University of Canterbury, New Zealand. 2004. (Available from the University of Canterbury, Christchurch, New Zealand Library.) A transnational, transhistorical, and interdisciplinary examination of the Earth Deity associated with the Buddha in Southeast Asian Theravadin traditions but conspicuously absent from the Pali Canon. Guthrie's comprehensive study considers art and biographical traditions along with performative texts and myths in Burma, Cambodia, Southern Vietnam, Central and Northern Thailand, Laos, and Sipsong Panna (Yunnan). The study is further informed by extensive ethnographic research on modern statues, political usage, and spirit possession in Cambodia and Thailand. Exploring the ambiguous relationship between the typically female Earth Deity and the Buddha whom she protects, the study bears on larger issues concerning gender and Buddhism.

Hansen, Anne. *How to Behave: Buddhism and Modernity in Colonial Cambodia, 1860–1930.* **Honolulu: University of Hawai'i Press. Forthcoming.** An original scholarly study of ethical concerns in Cambodian Buddhist modernist writings of the early twentieth century. Textual analyses are illuminated through close examination of the historical context, defined broadly, from the advent of the French Protectorate to the foundation of the Buddhist Institute, including consideration of Southeast Asian regional trends. Engaging with larger theoretical questions of the definition of "modernity" and drawing from an important body of primary source material never before used in scholarly publication, Hansen establishes the importance of Theravadin ethics in the imagination and expression of modernity among Cambodian reformist writers at this time.

Harris, Ian. *Cambodian Buddhism: History and Practice.* **Honolulu: University of Hawai'i Press. 2005.** A remarkable and unique reference work. The first two chapters consist in a meticulous, analytical compilation of virtually all available scholarly data on Cambodian Buddhism, from the earliest vestiges of Buddhism in the area to the advent of the modern era in the nineteenth century. Latter chapters, constituting the bulk of the book, compile available secondary material on the modern period and offer some original interpretation on particular themes, notably concerning the roles and uses of Buddhism in contemporary political affairs.

Huoth Tat. *Kalyanamitta rabas' khnum* **(My intimate friend). Phnom Penh: Buddhist Institute. 1993 (1970). Trans. in Penny Edwards, "Cambodia: The Cultivation of a Nation, 1860–1945." PhD dissertation. Monash University, Clayton, Victoria, Australia. 1999: 395–407.** This memoir was written by one of the monastic architects of Cambodia's Buddhist modernist movement during the colonial period and recounts the career of Chuon Nath, the movement's leader, who is venerated still today, across the country and regardless of sectarian affiliation, as the pillar of modern Cambodian Buddhism. Huoth Tat's personal account provides precious testimony to the motivations and workings of the emerging modernist cause and sheds light on the tensions developing within the Buddhist order at that time.

Marston, John, and Elizabeth Guthrie. *History, Buddhism and New Religious Movements in Cambodia.* **University of Hawai'i Press. 2004.** An important collection of specialist essays on a variety of questions concerning Cambodian religious thought and practice. Most chapters treat explicitly Buddhist phenomena; other purportedly non-Buddhist practices are inevitably situated in the context of relationships to Buddhism "proper." Essays cover a range of historical periods and disciplinary approaches, though emphasis is given to the modern period and ethnography. A general introduction, along with thoughtful editorial presentations of the different sections, highlight concerns common to all chapters regarding the close association between Cambodian religious practice and the conception of Cambodia as a social and political body.

Yang Sam. *Khmer Buddhism and Politics from 1954 to 1984.* **Newington, CT: Khmer Studies Institute. 1987.** A well-documented and personally engaged analysis of the intersection of Buddhism and politics from independence to the immediate aftermath of the Khmer Rouge period. This concise volume contains data unavailable elsewhere. Some commentary on earlier Buddhist history is, however, factually inaccurate.

Chapter Six: Buddhism in China and Taiwan

Chandler, Stuart. *Establishing a Pure Land on Earth: The Foguang Buddhist Perspective on Modernization and Globalization.* **Honolulu: University of Hawai'i Press, 2004.** This book analyzes how the Taiwan Buddhist group Foguangshan takes full advantage of contemporary modernizing and globalizing trends. The group's two central slogans, "Humanistic Buddhism" and "Establishing a Pure Land on Earth," are placed in historical context to reveal their role in shaping Foguangshan's attitudes toward capitalism, women's rights, and democracy, as well as toward traditional Chinese Buddhist concepts such as links of affinity (jieyuan) and resonance (ganying).

Jones, Charles Brewer. *Buddhism in Taiwan: Religion and the State, 1660-1990.* **Honolulu: University of Hawai'i Press, 1999.** Charles Brewer Jones is a leading authority on the practice of Buddhism in contemporary Taiwan. This book focuses especially on the role that the Buddhist Association of the Republic of China played in mediating relations between the Kuomindang and the island's Buddhists during the latter half of the twentieth century.

Laliberté, André. *The Politics of Buddhist Organizations in Taiwan, 1989–2003: Safeguard the Faith, Build a Pure Land, Help the Poor.* **New York: RoutledgeCurzon, 2004.** Laliberté's book gives ample attention to political and institutional matters, although his work also supplies general background about three of Taiwan's largest Buddhist groups: the Buddhist Association of the Republic of China, Ciji Gongde Hui, and Foguangshan. Laliberte shows how differing theological assumptions have significantly shaped the approach each group has taken toward political involvement: The Buddhist Association of the Republic of China relies primarily on lobbying the central government to advance its interests, Foguangshan takes the tack of remonstrance, and Ciji Gongde Hui eschews all political activity.

Luo, Zhufeng. *Religion under Socialism in China,* **trans. Donald E. MacInnis and Zheng Xi'an. Armonk, NY: M. E. Sharpe, 1991.** This book offers a translation of a series of essays on the official status of religion in post-Mao China that were written by a group of scholars from the Institute for Research on Religion at the Shanghai Academy of Social Sciences. Of special interest are the chapter on productive-labor projects in Buddhist Monasteries and the chapter concerning why some younger Chinese people become Buddhists.

MacInnis, Donald E. *Religion in China Today: Policy and Practice.* **Maryknoll, NY: Orbis Books, 1989.** MacInnis provides translations of governmental documents and transcriptions of interviews to lend insight into the status of various religions in the People's Republic of China from the end of the Cultural Revolution through the 1980s. Of particular interest is the opening segment of Part 2 (123–203), which deals with Buddhism on the local, provincial, and national levels.

Overmyer, Daniel L., and Richard Edmonds, eds. *Religion in China Today,* **China Quarterly Special Issues, New Series, No. 3. Cambridge, UK: Cambridge University Press, 2003.** This special issue of the *China Quarterly* provides a series of essays on the status of Christianity, Islam, Daoism, and Buddhism in China today. Raoul Birnbaum's piece, "Buddhist China at the Century's Turn," focuses on the current situation of Buddhist monasteries in the People's Republic of China. Paul R. Katz provides insight into the political and social status of Buddhism in the Republic of China in "Religion and the State in Postwar Taiwan."

Pittman, Don Alvin. *Toward a Modern Chinese Buddhism: Taixu's Reforms.* **Honolulu: University of Hawai'i Press, 2001.** Ven. Taixu was arguably the most influential master of Republican-era China. Pittman does a wonderful job of tracing Ven. Taixu's life, dreams, and accomplishments, including the direct and indirect influence he has had on later Buddhist leaders, including Vens. Shengyan, Xingyun, and Zhengyan.

Welch, Holmes. *The Practice of Chinese Buddhism 1900–1950.* **Cambridge, MA: Harvard University Press, 1967.** This work is the first of Welch's three volumes that provide the definitive treatment of Chinese Buddhism during the first seven decades of the twentieth century. This first volume gives an overview of the most influential monasteries and teachers during the Republican years.

Welch, Holmes. *The Buddhist Revival in China.* **Cambridge, MA: Harvard University Press, 1968.** In this second volume of his trilogy, Welch provides a history, analysis, and critique of the rhetoric of revival that was so prominent during the Republican years. He pays special attention to Ven. Taixu's understanding of the concept of revival in Chinese Buddhism.

Welch, Holmes. *Buddhism under Mao.* **Cambridge, MA: Harvard University Press, 1972.** As the final volume of Welch's trilogy, this book traces Buddhism's political travails over the two decades following the establishment of the People's Republic of China.

Chapter Seven: Buddhism in Korea

Buswell, Robert, Jr. *The Zen Monastic Experience: Buddhist Practice in Contemporary Korea.* **Princeton, NJ: Princeton University Press, 1993.** A detailed, first-hand account of how Zen was practiced in a contemporary Korean Buddhist monastery. The author treats the Zen tradition as a living system of practices and institutions, challenging the iconoclastic images of Zen. The chapters examine the daily life of monks, their meditation training, their relationship with the laity, operations of the monastery, and the hierarchy of monks.

Harris, Ian, ed. *Buddhism and Politics in Twentieth-Century Asia.* **London and New York: Pinter, 1999.** A collection of essays on the modern development of Buddhism in relationship to politics. The essays deal with the formation of Buddhist identity, the emergence of Buddhist nationalism, colonialism, modernity, and nation-states. It considers Marxism in the Buddhist countries of Myanmar, Cambodia, Sri Lanka, Japan, Korea, Laos, Thailand, Tibet, and Vietnam.

Hogarth, Hyun-key Kim. *Syncretism of Buddhism and Shamanism in Korea.* **Seoul: Jimoondang Publishing, 2002.** A detailed study of the influences on one another of Buddhism and local shamanism in Korea. The author gives particular attention to these exchanges in contemporary Korean society and offers descriptions of rituals and songs associated with Korean mudang, or shamans.

Kim, Kwangsik. *Kunhyondae Pulgyo ui chaechomyong.* **(New studies of modern Korean Buddhism). Seoul: Minjoksa, 2000.** Studies of Korean Buddhism during the colonial period and the Purification Movement. The work includes noteworthy chapters on the antireligious movement of the 1930s, decolonization after independence, and the investment of the Purification Movement.

Lancaster, Lewis, and Richard Payne, eds. *Religion and Society in Contemporary Korea.* **Berkeley: Institute of East Asian Studies, University of California, 1997.** A collection of essays on contemporary Korean religions, including shamanism, Confucianism, Buddhism, Christianity, and New Religions. There are important chapters dealing with contemporary Buddhism, including the Korean Buddhist response to modernity, Buddhist lay movements, and lay associations.

Shim, Jae-ryong, *Korean Buddhism: Tradition and Transformation.* **Seoul: Ji-moondang Publishing, 1999.** Chapters cover Korean Zen Buddhist traditions, Chinul, modern Buddhist issues (Buddhism, geomancy, and tourism; Buddhism and democracy), the sudden/gradual debate, and vernacular translations of Buddhist scriptures.

Tonguk taehak Songnim tongmun hoe, ed. *Han'guk Pulgyo Hyondae sa.* **(Modern history of Korean Buddhism). Seoul: Sigongsa, 1997.** Detailed account of Korean Buddhism after independence in 1945. The book begins with the Purification Movement and extensively examines contemporary Buddhist practices such as the development of propagation, translations and publications of Buddhist texts, the Sangha education and environment, and other Buddhist social movements.

Wells, Kenneth, ed. *South Korean's Minjung Movement: The Culture and Politics of Dissidence.* **Honolulu: University of Hawai'i Press, 1995.** A collection of essays on the Korean minjung movement. This book offers interdisciplinary perspectives on this important aspect of modern Korean history, including those of anthropology, history, literary criticism, religious studies, and sociology. The essays shed light on minjung in relationship to nationalism, socioeconomics, the Confucian tradition, shamanism, Christianity, popular culture, the farmers' movement, the reunification movement, and Korean literature.

Chapter Eight: Buddhism in Japan

Covell, Stephen G. *Japanese Temple Buddhism: Worldliness in a Religion of Renunciation.* **Honolulu: University of Hawai'i Press, 2005.** This book addresses the contemporary life and institutions of Japanese Temple Buddhism. The book combines ethnographic work with textual and historical research. Funerals and the commodification of practice, Buddhist welfare activities, the relationship between the temple and its lay members, clerical marriage, and law and tax issues are examined to broaden the manner in which Buddhism is approached in Japan.

Covell, Stephen G., and Mark Rowe, eds. Traditional Buddhism in Contemporary Japan. In *Japanese Journal of Religious Studies* **31:2. 2004.** This work opens new avenues to the study of Buddhism in contemporary Japan. The introduction outlines problem points in the study of Japanese Buddhism; articles include research on the lay-focused teachings of Temple Buddhism, popular writings on Buddhist teachings, robe sewing as contemporary Japanese Buddhist practice, Buddhist research institutes, religion and civil society in contemporary Japan, an overview of Buddhist nongovernmental organizations in Japan, and sectarian universities.

Hardacre, Helen. *Lay Buddhism in Contemporary Japan: Reiyukai Kyodan.* **Princeton, NJ: Princeton University Press, 1984.** This early work remains a solid introduction to modern Japanese lay Buddhism. Through ethnographic and historical research, Hardacre introduces various aspects of Reiyukai, a Buddhist lay movement based on the Lotus Sutra from which other major lay movements such as Rissho Kosekai developed. Hardacre introduces the organizational structure of Reiyukai, the movement's views on family and gender, and ritual practices for healing.

Jaffe, Richard. *Neither Monk nor Layman: Clerical Marriage in Modern Japanese Buddhism.* **Princeton, NJ: Princeton University Press, 2001.** Clerical marriage is one of the most critical issues in contemporary Japanese Buddhism. This work examines how clerical marriage became such a significant issue and in the process introduces the reader to the development of modern Japanese Buddhism. In addition to provide a rich history of the issue, Jaffe provides detailed insights into the life and teachings of numerous important Buddhist intellectuals.

Jaffe, Richard, and Michel Mohr, eds. *Meiji Zen. Special Issue of the Japanese Journal of Religious Studies* **25:1–2. 1998.** This volume adds to our knowledge of the development of modern Japanese Buddhism as described in Jaffe and Ketelaar's works. Included are papers on the following topics: teaching assemblies and lay societies; Meiji religious policy and clerical marriage; the contrasting lives of two Soto Zen monks, one who was executed for his alleged plot against the state and one who worked to support the state; politics in Meiji Zen; the Zen Master Toju Reiso; and the variety of Zen responses to the changes brought about in the modern period.

Ketelaar, James Edward. *Of Heretics and Martyrs in Meiji Japan: Buddhism and Its Persecution.* **Princeton, NJ: Princeton University Press, 1990.** This work delineates the manner in which Meiji period Buddhists sought to transform their religion from being persecuted to being a necessity for state and society. Ketelaar begins with an analysis of pre-Meiji views of proper Buddhism-state relations and then examines various critiques of Buddhism. Ketelaar argues that these critiques of Buddhism were part of a large re-signification process that occurred as state leaders strove to modernize Japan. In so doing, he provides important details on state-religion relationships during the earliest moments of Japan's modern period.

LaFleur, William R. *Liquid Life: Abortion and Buddhism in Japan.* **Princeton, NJ: Princeton University Press, 1992.** This book describes the history and development of the Buddhist practice of mizuko kuyo, a rite for fetuses that do not survive to term and children who die before coming of age. LaFleur aims his work at the ongoing debate over abortion in the United States. Helen Hardacre's *Marketing the Menacing Fetus in Japan* (Berkeley: University of California Press, 1997) offers a contrary view of the history of this ritual.

Reader, Ian, and George Tanabe. *Practically Religious: Worldly Benefits and the Common Religion of Japan.* **Honolulu: University of Hawai'i Press, 1998.** This book argues that Japanese religion can best be understood as being based on a common religion centered on worldly benefits. Worldly benefits, while usually understood as the focus of the new religions, are shown here to be of primary importance to traditional Buddhism and Shinto as well. The authors trace the textual development of worldly benefits within Buddhist sacred scriptures and offer examples of worldly benefits practices at temple and shrines throughout Japan.

Victoria, Brian A. *Zen at War.* **New York: Weatherhill, 1997.** Victoria sheds light on the darker side of modern Japanese Buddhism in this unremittingly critical history of Zen Buddhism and war. Numerous examples of the ideological and practical support given by Japanese Buddhists to the state are provided. This work furthers our knowledge of state-religion in issues in modern Japan.

Chapter Nine: Buddhism in Tibet and Nepal

Beyer, Stephan. *The Cult of Tara: Magic and Ritual in Tibet.* **Berkeley: University of California Press, 1973.** Based primarily on textual materials and oral commentaries received by the author, this is a fascinating, but at times rather dense and technical book. Beyer's work remains to this day the most in-depth and detailed examination of the mechanics of tantric ritual in Buddhism.

Gellner, David N. *Monk, Householder and Tantric Priest: Newar Buddhism and Its Hierarchy of Ritual.* **Cambridge, UK: Cambridge University Press, 1992.** Based on extensive anthropological fieldwork in the Kathmandu valley and complemented by textual materials, this is one of the most exhaustive accounts of Newar Buddhism, with a particular focus on the priestly caste and its rituals. This work remains one of the rare examples of a good ethnography of tantric Buddhism.

Goldstein, Melvyn C., and Matthew T. Kapstein, eds. *Buddhism in Contempo-*

rary Tibet: Religious Revival and Cultural Identity. **Berkeley: University of Califor-nia Press, 1998.** A pioneering collection of essays on contemporary religious developments in Tibetan areas within China by leading textual scholars and anthropologists in the field. The four ethnographic case studies are a diverse and interesting sample of situations varying in terms of regional setting, geographical and sociological context, and religious forms.

Holmberg, David H. *Order in Paradox: Myth, Ritual, and Exchange among Nepal's Tamang.* **Ithaca, NY: Cornell University Press, 1989.** An in-depth anthropological analysis of the complex religious field of the Tamang, a community in central Nepal speaking a Tibeto-Burman tongue, with a central focus on their Buddhist married lamas, the bombo shamans, and (to a lesser extent) the lambu sacrificial priests.

Huber, Toni. *The Cult of Pure Crystal Mountain: Popular Pilgrimage and Visionary Landscape in Southeast Tibet.* **New York: Oxford University Press, 1999.** Based on interviews with Tibetans who lived near Pure Crystal Mountain (one of the major sacred mountains in Tibet) or who participated in the pilgrimages around the mountain, as well as on textual sources, the result is one of the most interesting ethnographic (or ethnohistorical) studies of Tibetan religion. The study reveals the complex interrelations between elite and popular practices and conceptions.

Karmay, Samten G. *The Arrow and the Spindle: Studies in History, Myth, Rituals and Beliefs in Tibet.* **Kathmandu: Mandala Book Point, 1998.** A collection of essays (some of which were originally published in French) by a leading expert on Tibetan history, the Bon religion, and common Tibetan religious traditions. The approach is generally rather text-centered but is complemented in several cases by some ethnographic data.

Lewis, Todd T. *Popular Buddhist Texts from Nepal: Narratives and Rituals of Newar Buddhism.* **Translations in collaboration with Sabarba Man Tuladhar and Labh Ratna Tuladhar. Albany: State University of New York Press, 2000.** This work examines the development of a Buddhist ritual culture among the Newar community in the Kathmandu valley. The focus is on localized forms of Buddhist life, with special attention given to the convergence of ritual, economic, and political activities in the lives of Buddhist householders. A major theme is the pragmatic use of Buddhist texts in ritual spheres to meet worldly needs.

Mumford, Stan Royal. *Himalayan Dialogue: Tibetan Lamas and Gurung Shamans in Nepal.* **Madison: University of Wisconsin Press, 1990.** This study analyzes the relations between the religious spheres of Buddhist Tibetans and shamanist Gurungs living in neighboring villages in the Gyasumdo area of northern central Nepal. It draws heavily from Bakhtin's model of dialogism and temporal stages of modes of consciousness. It remains, however, a valuable source of ethnographic data on Tibetan rituals. The diversity of local Tibetan perceptions (not to mention the Gurung) is somewhat filtered out by an account that privileges the interpretations of the ethnographer's main informant, a Tibetan monk.

Samuel, Geoffrey. *Civilized Shamans: Buddhism in Tibetan Societies.* **Washington, DC: Smithsonian Institution Press, 1993.** This is the most recent book-length study of Tibetan religion. Written by an anthropologist who has read very extensively the available secondary sources, this book and its detailed index comprise a highly useful reference tool. It is theoretically ambitious and at times very insightful, although some of its assertions and terminology are strongly debatable. In particular, the shamanic terminology adopted by the author to refer to tantric elements in Tibetan religion is somewhat problematic.

Tucci, Giuseppe. *The Religions of Tibet,* **trans. Geoffrey Samuel. Berkeley: University of California Press, 1980.** Before Samuel's *Civilized Shamans,* this was the most up-to-date synthesis of Tibetan religion available, and despite some outdated passages, the book remains very useful. The author was primarily a highly erudite textual scholar, and several of his text-based analyses remain among the most useful sources available. At the same time, he was an explorer who had traveled extensively in Tibet, and he displays an ethnographic feel for his topic.

Chapter Ten: Buddhism in the West

Coleman, James William. *The New Buddhism: The Western Transformation of an Ancient Tradition.* **Oxford, UK: Oxford University Press, 2001.** Coleman's book incorporates a sociological approach to understanding the attraction and development of Buddhism in western societies. This book emphasizes the eclectic origins and politically liberal attitudes found in Western forms of Buddhism. Attention is also given to the contentious issues surrounding sexuality in Western Buddhist communities.

Klein, Anne C. *Meeting the Great Bliss Queen: Buddhists, Feminists, and the Art of the Self.* **Boston: Beacon Press, 1995.** A constructive and largely successful effort toward fostering a dialogical discussion between Tibetan Buddhism and western feminism. Klein offers a nuanced analysis of selfhood and subjectivity in the light of both intellectual traditions.

Lopez, Donald S., Jr., ed. *Curators of the Buddha: The Study of Buddhism under Colonialism.* **Chicago: University of Chicago Press, 1995.** A particularly useful collection of essays examining the colonial influence on Buddhism as a scholarly subject of inquiry in the West. The pioneer contributions of Jung, Suzuki, Tucci, and others are considered and subjected to critical analysis.

Prebish, Charles S., and Kenneth K. Tanaka, eds. *The Faces of Buddhism in America.* **Berkeley: University of California Press, 1998.** An excellent multi-authored collection of essays on Asian American schools of Buddhism. This pioneering work provides an excellent overview and useful bibliography for further inquiries into the subject.

Prebish, Charles S. *Luminous Passage: The Practice and Study of Buddhism in America.* **Berkeley: University of California Press, 1999.** One of the leading scholars of western Buddhism examines the varied development of Buddhist identities and communities in the United States. This work provides a useful, recent overview of the American Buddhist Sangha and includes an important discussion of the differences among imported, exported, and immigrant forms of Buddhism in the West.

Prebish, Charles S., and Martin Baumann, eds. *Westward Dharma: Buddhism beyond Asia.* **Berkeley: University of California Press, 2002.** A useful collection of essays by well-known scholars such as Thomas Tweed, B. Alan Wallace, and Christopher S. Queen. The chapters focus on history, global development, practices, and strategic patterns present in Western forms of Buddhism.

Seager, Richard Hughes. *Buddhism in America.* **New York: Columbia University Press, 1999.** Seager's book is a well-researched historical survey of the introduction and establishment of different schools of Buddhism in America. Particularly useful is the attention given to Asian immigrant views and practices. He also considers issues of gender, social activism, and relations among various Buddhist groups.

Tweed, Thomas A. *The American Encounter with Buddhism 1844–1912: Victorian Culture and the Limits of Dissent.* **Bloomington: Indiana University Press, 1992.** Tweed's book offers a lucid history of the transplantation of Buddhism to the West. The definitive scholarly study of this early period of Buddhism in America, the work focuses primarily on the encounter of Buddhism with Christianity in the nineteenth century.

Williams, Duncan Ryuken, and Christopher S. Queen. *American Buddhism: Methods and Findings in Recent Scholarship.* **Surrey, UK: Curzon, 1999.** This work offers a useful look at Asian American Buddhism, new Buddhists, modes of transmission, and the role of the scholar in Western Buddhism. The bibliography and the references to dissertations and theses on American Buddhism are particularly helpful.

Chapter Twelve

Glossary of Terms

abhayadana
The "gift of freedom from fear" is a form of Buddhist giving whereby an individual acts to spare a person or animal from death. This act is traditionally seen as highly meritorious.

Abhidharma/Abhidhamma
The third of three sections in a Buddhist Canon of scriptures chiefly concerned with psychological and philosophical matters related to meditation and the nature of existence.

Ambedkar, Bimrao
Indian nationalist leader who led thousands of low-caste Hindus to convert to Buddhism in an effort to escape caste discrimination in Indian society. This movement of Buddhist converts has survived its leader's death and continues to be a small but significant religious community.

Amitabha/Amida
The cosmic Buddha of Infinite Light and Life who is understood to be presiding over a heavenly paradise called *Sukhavati* or sometimes the Pure Land to the west. He remains a popular figure of devotion in East Asian Buddhist traditions.

anatta
A Pali term meaning "no self" or the absence of an eternal self or soul among all beings. A doctrinal stance that denies the existence of any permanent core to one's individuality, and thus it is directed toward diminishing egoism and attachment.

Ashoka/Asoka
The historical, legendary king of ancient India in the third century BCE.

Accounts of King Ashoka claim that he converted to Buddhism after expanding and consolidating his empire as a Wheel Turning (cakravartin) Monarch. He is alleged to have promoted Buddhism within his realm and beyond.

Atthakatha
The Pali term for commentarial texts written to explain and provide the contexts to words spoken by the Buddha in canonical scriptures.

Avalokiteshvara
The bodhisattva of compassion who is a focus of contemplation, prayers, and calls for help among Mahayana Buddhists. He was reconceived as a female figure in East Asia and renamed Kuan-yin in China and Kannon in Japan.

bhikkhu
The Pali term for an alms recipient or Buddhist monk who lives off the food and other material requisites donated by laypersons. These figures live a renunciatory lifestyle modeled after the Buddha and the disciplinary code he established.

bhikkhuni
Female renunciates or nuns in the Buddhist tradition who have undergone the formal higher ordination procedure and adhere to the additional disciplinary rules laid down by the Buddha.

bodhisattva/bodhisatta
Terms used to refer to beings who have made a vow and are on the path to becoming a Fully Awakened Buddha in the future. This notion is found in most Buddhist traditions and may connote a higher being to venerate, a figure in Buddhist narratives, or a condition to which contemporary practitioners may aspire.

Bon
A religious system native to Tibet that has developed alongside Buddhism and shares with it several common institutional and ritual characteristics, despite being generally viewed as a distinctive, and often a non-Buddhist, tradition.

Brahmanism
The term used to describe ritualistic Hindu systems marked by the performance of Vedic rituals by Brahmin priests. Brahmanism represented an important influence on and contrast from Buddhist traditions in South and Southeast Asia.

buddhacization
Attempts by Buddhist clergy or others to impose or enhance conformity to normative systems of Buddhist thought and practice.

cakkavatti/cakravartin
The Pali term for a world conqueror, usually used to designate a powerful king whose reign and influence are felt throughout the land.

Chan/Zen
The Chinese and Japanese names for the meditation school of Buddhism. Despite a varied and storied history, the various lineages that developed in East Asia emphasizing meditation as a practice for attaining Awakening, or enlightenment, are generally thought to comprise a more or less unified school.

Chogye
The celibate order of monks in Korea, possessing the largest numbers of monks and monastic properties in the country.

Ciji Gongde Hui
A Taiwanese form of Humanistic Buddhism. This group's name translates as the "Compassionate-Relief Merit Society." It is led by the nun Ven. Zhengyan and has a membership dominated by Buddhist laywomen.

clerical marriage
The term commonly used to refer to the sometimes controversial practice whereby Buddhist monks in Japan and Korea have elected to marry and start families while remaining in their robes and retaining their monastic identity.

cosmology
A system that defines to how the structure of the universe is mapped or more generally understood.

Dalai Lama
Title given to the reincarnated head of the Geluk monastic order in Tibetan Buddhism. The Fourteenth (and current) Dalai Lama lives in exile in India and serves as a prominent advocate for Buddhist modernism and cultural self-determination for the Tibetan people.

dana
The word that translates as "giving" or "gift," it signifies meritorious acts of donating gifts to the monastic community or needy recipients.

Dhammakaya

Buddhist movement founded in the mid-twentieth century in Thailand and noted especially for its method of meditation that focuses on the body of the Buddha.

dhammaraja

A term used in Theravada Buddhist contexts that refers to a righteous king or King of Dharma who governs his realm in accordance with Buddhist moral principles.

Dharma/Dhamma

Sanskrit and Pali terms referring to the teaching of the Buddha that is characteristically treasured and venerated by both monastic and lay Buddhists. Although the term possesses several technical meanings, it is used most often to mean the ultimate truth discovered and taught by a Fully Awakened Buddha.

dukkha

Frequently translated as suffering, this term signifies one of the existential truths discovered by the Buddha and affirms that a lack of contentment and satisfaction is a basic condition to all forms of life in the cycle of birth and death (samsara).

eco-Buddhism

Recently coined term referring to movements among Buddhists, predominantly in the West, to promote the convergence of Buddhist practice and environmental concerns.

Engaged Buddhism

A label used for modern forms of Buddhism, motivated in part as responses to Western critiques of the tradition as quietistic, that stress social action and the improvement of life for beings in this world.

Foguangshan

A modern Buddhist organization based in Taiwan that emphasizes the need to make Buddhism responsive to people's social and material needs in the present world. Led by Ven. Xingyun, it advocates a form of Humanistic Buddhism that seeks to bring about a Pure Land on earth and is practiced at affiliated temples around the world

forest monk

Term used to refer to monks who are reputed to be more especially disciplined and virtuous practitioners of the Buddha's Dharma than their urban and village counterparts.

gain

Burmese word used in place of *nikaya* to refer to a particular monastic sect or ordination lineage in the Buddhist Sangha.

Geluk

The Tibetan monastic order that derives from the reforms of Tsong Khapa in the early fifteenth century. Headed by the Dalai Lama, the Geluk order has been renowned for its commitment to monastic discipline and scholarship.

globalization

A sociological term used to refer to the contemporary condition of the world wherein an increase in economic, political, and cultural relations between citizens and governments of different countries has the effect of shrinking the distances between markets and cultures. In this context, Buddhist traditions may be spread farther abroad to new cultures, yet they must also contend with new challenges to their authority in defining truth and practice in local settings.

hegemony

A form of power through which one person or group achieves power over others through a combination of coercion and consent. This idea extends beyond the notion of a formal system of values and beliefs articulated in an ideology imposed from above to reflect a more complicated vision of reality that is constituted and reaffirmed in everyday practice, although still susceptible to challenge and transformation from below.

hoguk Pulgyo

A Korean term used to refer to the nationalistic Buddhism for the state that arose out of the decolonization period in Korea.

hoza

A modern form of Buddhist practice in Japan whereby groups of practitioners sit in circles to counsel one another on their problems and collectively look for guidance in Buddhist teachings.

humanism

A philosophy valuing the ability of human beings to understand and order their world without relying on a supernatural power for assistance.

Humanistic Buddhism

A phrase commonly used in Taiwan to refer to forms of Buddhism that emphasize this-worldly needs and interests of humans rather than their future destinies in the afterlife.

Jodo Shinsu

The True Pureland Sect of Buddhism established in Japan by the legendary monk, Shinran, in the thirteenth century. It has remained popular in modern Japan and was one of the first Buddhist sects to be established in North America.

Kagyu/Kargyu

A Tibetan monastic order founded out of the teaching lineage of Marpa, Milarepa, and Gampopa. It has typically maintained a strong orientation toward meditative and ritual practices.

kami

Gods or spiritual beings thought to be native to Japan and the focus of much Shinto religious practice. For much of Japanese history, Shinto kami have been worshipped alongside Buddhas in shrine-temple complexes and in people's homes.

lama

Term used in Tibetan Buddhist traditions, usually to refer to the religious master of an individual or an entire religious community, or more generically for any person with a high religious status, either in the monkhood or as a lay teacher.

lokiya

This Pali term for "worldly" is commonly used in Theravada countries to denote the domestic sphere of lay life and mundane concerns, in contrast to the supramundane sphere of existence, wherein the attainment of nirvana represents the chief aim or condition.

Lotus Sutra

A well-known, widely revered Mahayana Buddhist text originally composed in Sanskrit in India around the beginning of the third century CE. It includes distinctive teachings on the transcendent Buddha, the use of skillful means to teach the Dharma in different ways, and the goal of Buddhahood for all.

mae chee

The term used for female renunciates in Thailand who have not undergone the formal higher ordination, yet nevertheless adopt the first eight to ten monastic precepts, shave their heads, and wear white robes.

mahathera
An elder monk who has been ordained in the higher ordination ceremony for at least twenty years.

Mahavihara
An ancient Buddhist monastic lineage founded in Sri Lanka and responsible for the development of Pali canonical and commentarial texts on the Dharma. The monks in this lineage held fast to the Theravada tradition and rejected Mahayana influences.

Mahayana
The Great Vehicle school of Buddhism referring to one of the major divisions of the tradition that was spread and established in northern and eastern Asia. This school is known for its expansive canon of scriptures and its emphasis on the goal of Buddhahood for all.

mandala
A geometric two- or three-dimensional figure traditionally used for meditation practice in certain Buddhist traditions.

mantra
A Sanskrit term for a ritual formula, often either a verse or a syllable, recited to assist practitioners when invoking a deity or meditating.

mappo
The Japanese term used for the age of decline when the Buddha's Dharma is thought to be in a condition of degeneration and it becomes more difficult for people to attain liberation.

merit
The nearly universal idea among Buddhist traditions that moral deeds performed with the proper intention will generate a positive, fortunate result in accordance with the Buddhist theory of karma. The term "merit" is often used as a translation for various terms denoting the good results that may be experienced by the doer of good deeds in the future or transferred to benefit someone else.

metonym
A figure of speech wherein a part is used to refer to the whole. Thus, a word or

term used metonymically serves as a substitute for or a symbol of something else of which it is normally regarded as an aspect or part.

Metteya/Maitreya

A bodhisattva widely recognized in Theravada and Mahayana forms of Buddhism as the next Buddha to appear on earth. He has been a focal point for Buddhist devotion and occasionally millenarian movements in different cultures and communities throughout the Buddhist world.

minjung Pulgyo

The Korean concept of Buddhism for the masses, which carries socialist undertones, was constructed in contrast to the pejoratively labeled Bureaucratic Buddhism that was commonly denigrated for its official ties to the colonial Japanese government.

modernity

The period of time, variously defined and divided into stages, that generally refers to the intensive changes in society and thought experienced by people living in modern societies. Often contrasted with tradition, modernity is defined largely by the development of industrialization, capitalism, and nation-states and is characterized by the significant cultural changes resulting from their establishment.

Mount Meru

The name of a legendary mythical mountain traditionally held to lie at the center of the world-realm in ancient Buddhist cosmologies.

mo wiset

Thai term denoting charismatic holy men who regularly claim to possess supernatural powers and who occasionally led rebellions against the centralizing power of the Thai state.

Myanmar

The formal name for the state of Burma adopted by the military regime that seized control over the government in the 1980s.

nat

Term referring to Spirit Lords or deities worshipped by many Burmese Buddhists as part of a popular folk religious practice.

nembutsu
A Japanese term for the practice of chanting the name of Amida Buddha with the expectation that such efforts will lead to one's rebirth in that cosmic Buddha's heavenly realm.

nikaya
The Pali term that denotes a monastic lineage into which members of the Sangha typically organize themselves. It may also refer to a grouping of discourses (sutras) in the Buddhist Canon.

nirvana/nibbana
The ultimate goal of Buddhist teachings and practice that represents an immortal and unconditioned state free from pain, death, and suffering in general. It constitutes the liberation of an individual from the cycle of birth and death.

Nyingma
The name of a Tibetan order whose lineage is said to go back to the eighth-century Buddhist master Padmasambhava's first propagation of Buddhism in Tibet. This order has historically laid the strongest emphasis on meditative practice among Tibetan orders.

Orientalism
A system of thought and mode of scholarship popularized in the eighteenth and nineteenth centuries in conjunction with Western colonialism. Subject to critique by contemporary scholars, Orientalism nevertheless played a formative role in the founding of the study of Buddhism and emphasized the ancient, textual origins of the religion.

orthopraxy
A term referring to "correct practice" that usually connotes a strong commitment to the correct performance of a ritual or ritual practices.

Pali Canon
Also called the Tipitaka, it is the collection of Buddhist scriptures preserved in the Pali language and deemed authoritative by Theravada Buddhists in South and Southeast Asia.

patipatti
The Pali term that refers to activities surrounding religious practices such as meditation.

pariyatti
The term used to refer to scholarly activities connected with texts in Theravada Buddhism.

p'ogyo-so
Korean Buddhist temples devoted to propagating and popularizing Buddhism within the country.

poya
The word used in Sinhala for a Buddhist Full Moon Day that marks a time for special religious observances and celebrations.

prasat
A Khmer word referring to ancient funerary temples built especially during the Angkorian period of Cambodian history between the ninth and thirteenth centuries.

pratitya-samutpada
The Buddhist term for "dependent origination" found in early Buddhist texts and signifying the causal, interrelated nature of existence.

puja
Translated as "veneration" or "offering," this term encompasses devotional activities performed in honor of the Buddha, including giving flowers, incense, and other offerings at shrines.

Pure Land/Pureland
The name of an East Asian school of Buddhism that venerates Amida Buddha in the hope of being reborn in his heavenly paradise also known as the Pure Land.

reflexivity
A scholarly term that designates a mode of self-conscious awareness and an intentionality behind one's choices and actions. It is often contrasted with the idea of self-identity as being somehow given or fully formed.

renjian Fojiao/rensheng Fojiao
Chinese terms that have been used by some modern Chinese Buddhists to refer to a form of Buddhism oriented toward meeting present human needs and interests in this world.

Rissho Koseikai
A Buddhist lay movement founded in modern Japan by Niwano Nikkyo and emphasizing efforts to understand the Lotus Sutra and pattern one's life after this text.

rupakaya
The Buddhist term for the form or material body of the Buddha. It may also be broadly used to denote any object representing the physical presence of the Buddha.

Sangha
The assembly of monks and sometimes nuns viewed as one of the three jewels most worthy of veneration in Buddhism. This word refers to the entire body of Buddhist renunciates.

sasana
The Pali term used to denote the dispensation or the teachings and institutions founded by the Buddha. This word is roughly equivalent to the idea of Buddhism.

secularism
A mode of thought that seeks to ground political authority in the institutions of nation-states rather than religious texts and institutions. As a political doctrine, it upholds individual freedom and responsibility as something distinct from religious identities and precepts.

setya min
Burmese term referring to a universal monarch (cakravartin) who is modeled after King Ashoka in ancient India and displays limitless righteousness and sovereignty.

Shakyamuni
Another name for the historical Buddha Siddhartha Gautama. Translated as the "sage of the Shakya clan," the word is popularly used among East Asian Buddhist communities.

Shinto
The indigenous Japanese religion centered on the worship of local deities at shrines for this-worldly goals. Historically, Shinto was often practiced in combination with Buddhist forms by the Japanese.

shunyata

The Sanskrit term for "emptiness," *shunyata* signifies the lack of any essential or independent substance within all forms of life and matter. The idea of emptiness became elaborated on in Mahayana thought and became a key doctrinal concept in several Mahayana schools.

Shwegyin

A reform-minded monastic lineage founded in nineteenth-century Upper Burma characterized by its strict adherence to the Vinaya or Buddhist monastic code.

skandhas

The aggregates of conditioned existence that include physical form, feelings, perceptions, mental formations, and sensory consciousness.

Soka Gakkai

A modern Buddhist lay movement once connected with Japan's Nichiren Buddhist establishment but now forming an independent, worldwide organization stressing individual betterment and the creation of a peaceful, harmonious world.

soteriology

A term used to describe a system of ideas and practices related to the achievement of an ultimate religious goal such as liberation or salvation from the world.

srok

A Khmer word describing settled, cultured, or civilized space. This word is often used in contrast with *prei* (the forest) to form an opposition between civilization and wilderness in the Cambodian religious imagination.

stupa

The Sanskrit term that refers to a reliquary or monumental shrines that house bodily relics of a deceased Buddha or enlightened sage (arahant).

Sukhavati

The Land of Bliss or the Pure Land located in a heavenly region west of the world of humans. It is believed that the Buddha Amitabha presides over this realm, and those fortunate and faithful enough to be reborn there enjoy an existence free from any form of suffering and focused on the Dharma until liberation is attained.

syncretism
A hybrid mixture of related, nondiscrete forms of Buddhist and non-Buddhist traditions into a singular system of religious practice and symbols.

tantra
The word referring to an esoteric form of Buddhism that typically revolves around the use of ritual objects, the propitiation of deities, and the cultivation of innate bodily powers to realize Buddhahood. The term is also used to refer to the class of esoteric texts that describe these practices.

Tantrist
A practitioner of tantric Buddhism. The term has a specialized usage for non-monastic householders who act as religious specialists of tantric rituals in Tibetan communities.

Tendai
An ancient syncretic form of Japanese Buddhism based on the Chinese T'ien-t'ai school. Tendai Buddhism has traditionally stressed the idea of the universal Buddha-nature of all beings.

terma
Hidden treasures in the form of objects or teachings thought to have been purposely concealed by Padmasambhava or sometimes other great Buddhist teachers in Tibet for the later discovery and use by Buddhists.

Thammadut/Dhammaduta
Envoys of the Dharma, or monks charged with the task of spreading knowledge about the Buddha and his teachings to those who are unfamiliar with them.

Thammayut
Monastic sect founded in Thailand by King Mongkut and Prince Wachirayan in the mid-nineteenth century. Originally established to promote the Thai royalty's idea of pure, unadulterated Buddhist practice, this sect has evolved over time to symbolize a more independent tradition of forest asceticism.

Thathanabain
Title of the Supreme Patriarch of the Burmese Sangha, formerly appointed by the king.

theosophy
A modern, inclusive form of spirituality, heavily influenced by universalistic

interpretations of Buddhism and Hinduism. The Theosophical Society was founded in New York in the 1870s by Helena Blavatsky and Henry Steel Olcott as a movement with interests in spiritualism and mysticism, and it played an important role in supporting Buddhist and Hindu reform movements in Sri Lanka and India during the British colonial period.

Theravada
The Way of the Elders school of Buddhism referring to one of the major divisions of the tradition that was spread and established in South and Southeast Asia. This school is known for its more narrowly circumscribed canon of Pali scriptures and its emphasis on the goal of attaining liberation, or Awakening, through moral discipline and meditative practice as an arhat rather than a Buddha.

transplantation
A term that can be used to describe the process whereby a religious tradition such as Buddhism is imported and appropriated to fit into a new cultural context. This process may take several stages and many years before a religion is firmly established in its new environment.

Tripitaka/Tipitaka
The Sanskrit and Pali names for the Three Baskets of Buddhist scriptures attributed to the Buddha. Although there may be significant variation in texts included in a particular Buddhist school's canon of scriptures, the threefold method of categorizing texts as part of the Vinaya, Sutta/Sutra, or Abhidhamma/Abhidharma collection is consistent across Buddhist traditions.

trulku/tulku
Incarnate lamas who have chosen to be reborn again among sentient beings to bring about their well-being. Such figures typically have occupied leadership roles in the Tibetan Buddhist clergy.

upasampada
A term used by Theravada Buddhists to refer to the higher ordination ceremony held by a quorum of already ordained monks and/or nuns that confers the full status of a monk or nun on an individual who is at least twenty years of age.

upaya
A term meaning "skillful means," it refers to a method of instruction whereby enlightened beings employ whatever method is appropriate and at hand to impart an understanding of the Dharma.

Vajrayana
The Diamond Vehicle or Thunderbolt Vehicle, it is used to designate a distinctive school of Buddhism that expands on older Mahayana practices and texts by incorporating quicker, more powerful tantric practices to attain complete Buddhahood.

vamsa
A genre of historical narratives found in Theravada Buddhist schools that typically connect the life of the Buddha to the establishment of his religion in lands outside of India.

vernacularization
A term that may refer to the process whereby texts written in "classical," translocal languages are rewritten in the local literary dialects of spoken languages and are frequently changed in the process.

Vesak/Wesak
The Buddhist Full Moon Day in the spring that commemorates the date when the Buddha was born, attained his Awakening, or enlightenment, and passed away from the world of continuous rebirth.

Vinaya
The word for the Buddhist monastic code that outlines the appropriate disciplinary conduct for monks and nuns. It forms one of the three major divisions of Buddhist scriptures found in the Tripitaka.

Vipassana
A popular form of meditation in several modern Buddhist cultures. It emphasizes the development of insight through centering attention on one's own bodily processes.

wat
A term used in Cambodia and Thailand to refer to a Buddhist temple where monks reside and laypersons visit to participate in religious and sometimes cultural events.

Index

About the Editor

Stephen C. Berkwitz is an associate professor of religious studies at Missouri State University, Springfield, Missouri. He earned his PhD in religious studies at the University of California at Santa Barbara in 1999. His research is focused on the history, literature, and culture of Buddhism in Sri Lanka. He has published a book entitled *Buddhist History in the Vernacular: The Power of the Past in Late Medieval Sri Lanka* (2004) that examines the ethical and rhetorical features of Buddhist historical narratives composed in Sinhala. His current research interests include Sinhala poetry written during Portuguese colonialism and the discourse of contemporary Sinhala Buddhist nationalism.